CLOSE UP
1927–1933

CLOSE UP
1927–1933
Cinema and Modernism

EDITED BY
JAMES DONALD,
ANNE FRIEDBERG
AND LAURA MARCUS

Princeton University Press
Princeton, New Jersey

Published in the United States of America in 1998 by Princeton University Press, 41 William Street, Princeton, New Jersey 08540

Published in Great Britain in 1998 by Cassell, Wellington House, 125 Strand, London WC2R 0BB

ISBN   0-691-00462-5 (cloth)

          0-691-00463-3 (paperback)

Cover still: H.D. (Hilda Doolittle) in Kenneth Macpherson's *Wing Beat* (*Close Up*, Volume I, no. 1)

Typeset by Ben Cracknell Studios

Printed and bound in Great Britain by Martins the Printers Ltd., Berwick upon Tweed

http://pup.princeton.edu

          10 9 8 7 6 5 4 3 2 1
          10 9 8 7 6 5 4 3 2 1
          (Pbk.)

CONTENTS

PREFACE

The journal *Close Up*, edited by Kenneth Macpherson, the novelist Bryher and the poet H.D., was published between 1927 and 1933. It represented a major attempt by a group of literary intellectuals to assess, at a crucial moment of transition, the aesthetic possibilities opened up by cinema within, despite and against its commercial contexts. The importance of *Close Up* for histories of both modernism and cinema is being recognized more and more widely, and so an anthology which makes even a sample of its work more easily available is timely.

Our selection of material has been guided by a number of principles. First, we wanted to show the range of issues and concerns that dominated the journal during its six years of publication. Second, we have attempted to convey the lively and dynamic tone of the magazine, and to give an impression of the type of cinema it promoted. Third, we have included examples of the writing of all the regular contributors, with their various enthusiasms and phobias, although we have generally concentrated on material that is not easily accessible elsewhere. Fourth, however, there is an argument implicit in one quite deliberate imbalance. We have placed a special emphasis on the writings of H.D. and Dorothy Richardson. This is not only in recognition of their literary, and sometimes even poetic, qualities. We want to give their speculations on film and cinema wider currency primarily in order to pose the question whether *literary* modernism – and especially the modernism of women like Virginia Woolf as well as the *Close Up* contributors – should be seen in large part as a response to, and an appropriation of, the aesthetic possibilities opened up by *cinema*.

The book is organized in the following way. The first part offers a cross-section of articles, mostly by regular contributors. In a compressed way, it captures the flavour of the polemic in *Close Up* and indicates some of the things it stood for: its enthusiasm for 'the film for the film's sake', its hostility towards mainstream Hollywood and British films and its commitment to the 'Negro viewpoint' in cinema. The second part touches, all too briefly, on one of the key topics of debate in *Close Up*: the coming of the talkies, or as it was often seen, the decline and fall of the universal language promised by silent films. In this section Sergei Eisenstein makes a fleeting appearance as joint author of a statement on sound cinema with Pudovkin and Alexandrov.

Eisenstein's absence elsewhere needs some justification, as *Close Up* often figures in the history of film theory as the conduit through which his ideas about film were introduced into the West. Vladimir Petric, for example, in discussing the transmission of Soviet film theory to an American context, concludes:

> Not only did *Close Up* provide most Americans with an introduction to the many theories and issues of Soviet cinematic theory, it also provided many American film theorists with an audience for their essays and articles on Soviet filmmakers and their work.[1]

In the January 1929 issue of *Close Up*, the frontispiece displays a photograph of Eisenstein inscribed: 'To K. Macpherson – Editor of the Closest Up to what cinema should be.' This tribute marked the beginning of a relationship which was as much writer to editor as it was master to student. *Close Up* published nine translations of Eisenstein's writing between May 1929 and June 1933, in addition to a number of occasional pieces about him and his work.[2] Given the constraints of space, we have reluctantly decided that republishing Eisenstein's work must take a lower priority than retrieving less well-known writing. To get a true sense of both the range of writing in *Close Up* and the strength of its commitment to Eisenstein's ideas, our selection should be read in conjunction with the work to be found in *Film Form*, *The Film Sense* and Eisenstein's *Selected Writings*.[3]

The writings of H.D. and Dorothy Richardson are presented in the third and fourth parts of the book. The majority of H.D.'s contributions are included: her three-part article on 'The Cinema and the Classics', published between July and November 1927, and five other articles, although not the poem *Projector*, published in two parts in July and October 1927. This is available in her *Collected Poems*.[4] We have included all Richardson's 'Continuous Performance' columns. We believe that they offer an account of the novelty and modernity of the *experience* of cinema which is comparable in its scope to the pioneering essays being written by Siegfried Kracauer in the same period, and which also prefigures in intriguing and suggestive ways recent scholarship on cinema and modernity.[5]

The major piece in Part 5 is H.D.'s long essay on the film *Borderline* (1930), written and directed by Macpherson and featuring H.D. and Bryher as well as Paul and Eslanda Robeson among its cast. This was not published in *Close Up*, but as a separate pamphlet by Mercury Press. We have included it here not only as another example of H.D.'s critical writing but also because the film probably represented the ultimate expression of Macpherson's interest in cinema and because, as a result, the fate of the journal was intimately bound up with the critical response to the film.

Part 6 is devoted to *Close Up* articles on psychoanalysis and cinema. This work represented a significant and imaginative departure in exploring the fascination and possibilities of film. Part 7 illustrates how active *Close Up* was in attempting to create the institutions and conditions necessary for a vibrant and radical 'film culture' (to use a term from the 1970s). Far from being aloof, contributors like Bryher, Dorothy Richardson and Ralph Bond energetically promoted amateur forms of production and exhibition, and campaigned against the particularly hidebound censorship in the United Kingdom which prevented many of the films they valued most highly from being screened.

Our selection represents only a fraction of the work published in *Close Up*, and quite properly it reflects our tastes and priorities. We hope, however, that the collection will contribute to today's debates about the cultural, aesthetic and social consequences of the technological media in the first half of the twentieth century. It is intended less as an exercise in the archaeology of film theory than as an attempt to provide a relevant intellectual and historical context for those debates by showing how the issues were experienced, imagined and discussed at the time.

This book, perhaps a little like *Close Up*, is itself the outcome of a three-way editorial collaboration. When it emerged that Laura Marcus and James Donald in England and

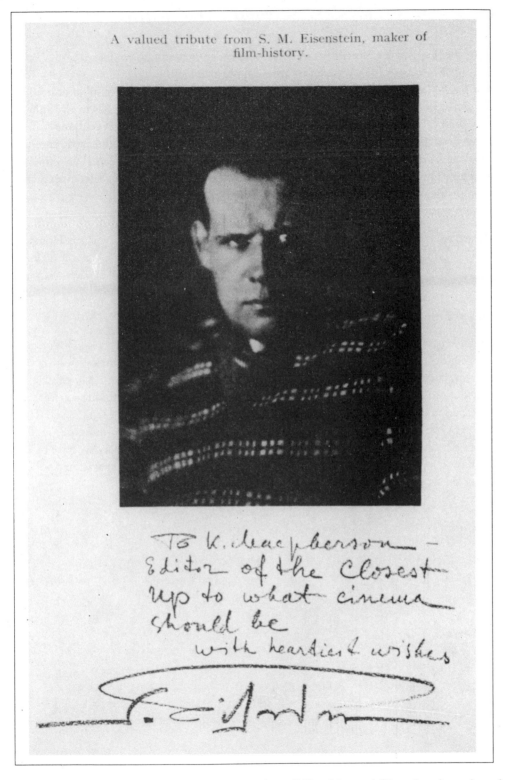

A valued tribute from S. M. Eisenstein, maker of film-history.

'A valued tribute from S.M. Eisenstein, maker of film-history.' Signed and captioned photograph of Eisenstein: 'To K. Macpherson – Editor of the Closest Up to what cinema should be/with heartiest wishes.' Frontispiece (Vol. IV, no. 1, January 1929).

Anne Friedberg in the United States were independently planning anthologies, the pooling of resources and ideas, mostly through the media of fax and e-mail, proved – for us at least – both pleasurable and productive. We would like to thank a number of friends and colleagues for their comments, suggestions and support, especially Kevin Brownlow, Ian Christie, Miriam Hansen, Laura Mulvey, Michael O'Pray and Jim Pines. Jane Greenwood at Cassell and Deborah Malmud at Princeton have been enthusiastic and (as far as can be reasonably expected) patient editors; we must also thank Sandra Margolies, our Cassell house editor. Above all, we should acknowledge the generous encouragement given to research in this field by H.D.'s daughter, Perdita Schaeffner.

We respectfully dedicate the book to her.

September 1997

James Donald
Anne Friedberg
Laura Marcus

Note on the treatment of texts

The production of *Close Up* is a great testament to the enthusiasm, energy and efficiency of its editors, Bryher in particular, although style and presentation at times appear idiosyncratic to the late-twentieth-century eye. We have reproduced original spelling and punctuation, despite inconsistencies, but have corrected obvious typographical errors. Punctuation has been left as it stands, unless it makes sentences difficult to read and interpret. We have added modern or more familiar spellings of well-known figures in square brackets (e.g. 'Pudowkin [Pudovkin]'). The only consistent changes we have made are in design points, such as the removing of extraneous spaces around marks, and we have used single quotation marks for ease of reading.

INTRODUCTION

Reading *Close Up*, 1927–1933

Anne Friedberg

A new form of film-writing

> The close up is the soul of the cinema … the close up limits and directs attention. As an emotional indicator, it overwhelms me. I have neither the right nor the ability to be distracted. It speaks the present imperative of the verb to understand.[1]

> The close up has not only widened our vision of life, it has also deepened it.[2]

> With the close up, space expands; with slow motion, movement is extended. The enlargement of a snapshot does not simply render more precise what in any case was visible, though unclear; it reveals entirely new structural formations of the subject. … The camera introduces us to unconscious optics as does psychoanalysis to unconscious impulses.[3]

> If … an article does not slide into being simply a synopsis, it can reflect the stimulated thoughts of a spectator under the immediate impression of the work. … This is an examination of the film itself in close-up: through a prism of firm analysis the article 'breaks down' the film into its parts, resolves its element, to study the whole just as a new model of construction is studied by engineers and specialists in their own field of technique.
> This must be the view of the film from the standpoint of a professional journal.
> There must be an appraisal of the film from the positions of both 'long shot' and 'medium shot' – but firstly it must be an examination 'in close-up' – a close-up view of all its component links.[4]

'Close up' was a technical term for magnification through a lens, but also – more metaphorically – it meant close analysis, scrutiny, an 'optic'. To many, the close-up played a critical role in a wholly new visual rhetoric. To the French film-maker and theorist Jean Epstein, the close-up was an essential component of *photogénie* – it limited and directed attention, indicated emotion, magnified aesthetic import. To the Hungarian scenarist and director Béla Balázs, the close-up produced revelations of a new emotional and dramatic magnitude in showing the 'microphysiognomy' of the human face.[5] To the German cultural critic Walter Benjamin, the close-up supplied a new visual order, rendering

Cover wrapper (Vol. I, no. 4, October 1927).

'entirely new structural formations of the subject'.[6] Soviet film-maker and theorist Sergei Eisenstein appropriated the film technique of the close-up and deployed it as a model for a certain kind of writing about film through 'a prism of firm analysis'.[7] The close-up provided a particularly modern optic, a newly revelatory epistemology. As the title for a film journal, *Close Up* implied the conflation of technical specificity with philosophical endeavour.

From the beginning of its publication, the writers for *Close Up* were determined to transform the cultural topography of the cinema and its future. To do so, they were invested in the power of writing *about* film, enlisting it as a discursive midwife to aid in the development of the cinema's potential. Certainly, as Christian Metz would later point out, the writer about cinema – the critic, the historian, the theoretician – is inextricably bound by the same desires and intentions that move film-makers and film spectators alike: 'to maintain a good object relation with as many films as possible, and at any rate with the cinema as such'.[8] In these terms, Metz warned, writing about the cinema is always in danger of having the discourse *about* its object swallowed up by the discourse *of* its object. Popular film criticism, academic film histories and – perhaps especially – the philosophical tracts of film theory may each have very separate audiences and agendas, but they all function – Metz argued – to imitate or prolong the cinema's imaginary effects. *Close Up* writers reversed this discursive formula. Instead of using writing to extend the cinema's effect, they advocated a cinema that mirrored the aesthetics and production of their own written discourse: discourse *about* the object, artfully designed, psychologically astute, independently financed, free from commercial constraints. *Close Up* writers hoped that writing which contested the commercial illusionism of the 'Hollywood code'[9] would create a cinema whose imaginary effects they could determine *a priori*.

Close Up first appeared in July 1927: a handsomely printed, plainly bound journal in a distinctive pumpkin-coloured wrapper. The first covers were minimal: the words CLOSE UP were bannered simply across the top, the month and year discreetly placed in the lower left, the price in the lower right. Each issue was wrapped in a three-inch white paper band with more descriptive text: 'CLOSE UP, an English review, is the first to approach films from the angles of art, experiment and possibility.' The wrapper was changed monthly to announce the key mottoes of the journal:

— 'WE WANT BETTER FILMS!!!'

— 'The Official Guide To Better Movies! – With illustrations from the best films – TECHNICAL. FRIENDLY. INFORMATIVE.'

— 'The Only Magazine Devoted to Films As An Art – Interesting and Exclusive Illustrations – THEORY AND ANALYSIS – NO GOSSIP.'

Close Up became the model for a certain type of writing about film – writing that was theoretically astute, politically incisive, critical of films that were simply 'entertainment'. For six and a half years, *Close Up* maintained a forum for a broad variety of ideas about the cinema; it never advocated a single direction of development, but rather posed alternatives to existing modes of production, consumption and film style.

In retrospect, the body of writing in *Close Up* appears as its own form of 'literary montage' – a serial project with the random architecture of juxtaposition, an exhibit of documents which offer the contemporary reader an extensive tour of the ardent debates about cinema as it emerged as an aesthetic form.[10] The arguments contained in the pages of *Close Up* demonstrate, above all, that writing about cinema played a significant role in the struggle to maintain alternatives to, and to resist solidification of, a too-rigidly fixed institution. As the 1929 advertisement shown on page 24 attests, the editors of *Close Up* resisted the ephemeral qualities of the cinema itself and provided instead a written fixative, a textual archive of the cinema at a critical age:

> Bound volumes of *Close Up* are collectors' books, and should be in the possession of all followers of the cinema. With much that is exclusive and unobtainable elsewhere, they will be undoubtedly of the greatest value as
>
> REFERENCE BOOKS FOR THE FUTURE
>
> as well as for the present. The theory and analysis constitutes the most valuable documentation of cinematographic development that has yet been made.[11]

'Reference books for the future'

Yet the texts published in *Close Up* have eluded the historian's need to easily classify, ground and identify them; to locate their importance as anything more than a secondary source. Because the writing in *Close Up* crosses many borders – between literary prose and theoretical writing, between avant-garde manifesto and journalistic *feuilleton*, between film production and literary modernism – it effectively overruns the canonical boundaries of disciplinary republics. Perhaps this very *débordement* explains why *Close Up* has not been more widely understood as a significant site of discourse about the cinema.[12]

The writing in *Close Up* inhabited the same cultural moment as other texts that have had a more indelible influence on contemporary film histories and theories. The theoretical writing of Soviet film-makers, the speculations on film and photography by practitioners of the German *kulturkritik* and later the writings of French film critics and theorists have dominated the major accounts of cinema's first fifty years.[13] The years of *Close Up*'s publication – 1927–33 – define its own period as a 'critical age', situated symmetrically on the brink of two decades; at the threshold, as well, between silent cinema and the sound film. *Close Up* commenced publication in 1927, the year that Siegfried Kracauer wrote the essays 'The Mass Ornament' and 'Photography' and that Walter Benjamin began his project on the Paris Arcades.[14] It ended in 1933 as the Weimar Republic was on the wane, a month before Hitler came to power. An examination of the texts in *Close Up* illustrates the uncertainty about cinema's future at a moment when, as Annette Michelson has suggested, alternatives were posed as a 'spectrum, rather than a polarity of possibilities'.[15]

Since the mid-1980s, as the writing of film history has taken a more Foucauldian bent, scholars have begun to examine writing *about* cinema as a primary source – discursive documents that impart their own form of historical knowledge.[16] *Close Up* provides an exemplary archaeological site for the aesthetic, economic, ideological and technological questions posed to a cinema struggling to form itself. In its pages, the theoretical writings of Sergei Eisenstein were translated into English for the first time, the psychoanalysts

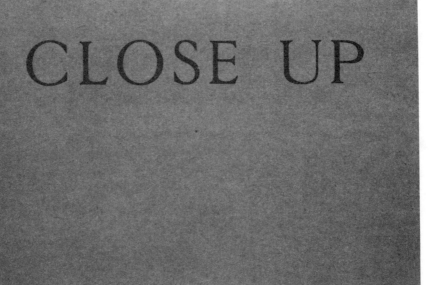

Cover wrapper, 'We Want Better Films' (Vol. I, no. 5, November 1927).

CLOSE UP

THE OFFICIAL GUIDE TO BETTER MOVIES!

With illustrations from the best films

TECHNICAL.   **FRIENDLY.**   **INFORMATIVE.**

1 shilling / or 1 mark / or 5 francs / or 35 cents.

Vol. II - No 3.   MARCH 1928

Cover wrapper, 'The Official Guide to Better Movies' (Vol. II, no. 3, March 1928).

Hanns Sachs and Barbara Low debated the unconscious effects of cinematic spectatorship, and a strong contingent of female literary modernists – H.D., Dorothy Richardson, Gertrude Stein, Marianne Moore – began to write on cinema. The journal also contained a range of speculations about film technology; promoted the alternative distribution and exhibition networks of *ciné-clubs* and film societies; addressed the problems and potentials of a British cinema; campaigned against film censorship; championed Soviet film-making and film theory; had a persistent critique of racism in the cinema; and continually assessed the state of film theory and criticism. Many of the critical and theoretical questions which troubled the contributors to *Close Up* between 1927 and 1933 returned, as if to haunt film writers and theorists, in the 1970s and 1980s. In this regard, it is striking that the debates in *Close Up* were not strategically excavated; interest in alternative exhibition and distribution, political questions about representation, concerns about the economic domination of first-world national cinemas, theorizations of the role of the spectator, psychoanalytic theories of the cinematic apparatus and debates about censorship dominated the agenda of 'contemporary' film theory. 'The archaeology of film theory' – the recovery of film theory's own history – was not a priority for film theorists of the 1970s and 1980s and would have to await the efforts of theoretically bent film historians.[17]

The writing in *Close Up* demonstrates how the cinema – grasped for its potentials, feared for its foreclosures – transformed the very fabric of psychic, gendered and racialized experience, and explored – against cinema's commercial domination – the radical possibilities of film as a new medium of aesthetic expression. Introducing the texts from *Close Up* now, in the late 1990s, prompts a reconsideration of a pivotal period in this century's cultural history, of the existing accounts of film history and theory and of the cinema's relation to literary and artistic modernism.

Until now, *Close Up* has predominantly been used as source material for histories of national cinemas. Jay Leyda relied on *Close Up* as primary source material in his *Kino: A History of the Russian and Soviet Film*, as did Siegfried Kracauer in *From Caligari to Hitler*.[18] Rachel Low, in her *History of British Film 1918–1929*, describes *Close Up* in more detail than any other standard film history. She assesses its historical contribution as 'very great despite its small circulation … the *Close Up* writers addressed the magazine and a few books to each other and a small circle of film initiates'.[19] While Low identified many of the *Close Up* writers, she did not acknowledge the contribution of the poet H.D. – a writer of key importance to the journal.[20] Yet Low uses H.D.'s prose in uncredited quotations throughout the book to generalize about the style of writing in the magazine: 'the characteristic style was affected, fashionable writing in an elliptical and casual manner'.[21]

In 1980, Don Macpherson's collection, *Traditions of Independence: British Cinema in the Thirties*, productively challenged the dominant histories of the period by pointedly attacking the emphasis placed on the role of John Grierson and the GPO film unit, and reclaiming a 'forgotten tradition' in British independent film production.[22] In his essay for the volume, Deke Dusinberre describes the importance of *Close Up* as the 'focal point for avant-garde film activity in Britain'.[23] *Traditions of Independence* was intended as a historiographically rigorous counter-history, but it also inadvertently produced its own historical counter-myth. The ardent anti-censorship campaign evident in *Close Up* before

CLOSE UP

THE ONLY MAGAZINE DEVOTED TO FILMS AS AN ART

Interesting and Exclusive Illustrations

THEORY AND ANALYSIS   NO GOSSIP

1 shilling or 5 francs (French) or 1 mark (German)
35 cents   1 franc (Swiss)   1½ shillings (Austrian)

Vol. III   No. 4   **OCTOBER 1928**

Cover wrapper, 'The Only Magazine Devoted to Films as an Art' (Vol. III, no. 4, October 1928).

the 1930s – one of the journal's key battles with British film culture – was effectively elided.[24] The editors of *Close Up* were on the Council of the Federation of Workers' Film Societies (FOWFS), and they argued the cause of Soviet cinema as well as the German social realists Pabst and Metzner. *Close Up* was involved in challenging the dominant prejudices of the film industry, but it did so in terms not directly political or ideological. Rather, it typified a vanguard modernism less directly allied with political action than with experimentation in aesthetic form.

Close Up and the 'borderline' subject: all over the map

In the spring of 1927, the collective enterprise known as 'POOL' was 'announced' in advertisements placed in select literary and film magazines:

POOL

is announced.

It has projects. It will mean, concerning books, new hope.

It has projects. It will mean, concerning cinematography, new beginning.

New always. Distinguished, and with a clear course.

BOOKS   FILMS

... encouragement.

CLOSE UP, a monthly magazine to begin battle for film art. Beginning July. The first periodical to approach films from any angle but the commonplace. To encourage experimental workers, and amateurs. Will keep in touch with every country, and watch everything. Contributions on Japanese, Negro viewpoints and problems, etc. Some of the most interesting personages of the day will write.[25]

With manifesto-like declarations, POOL began as a publisher of books, a producer of films and the publisher of a monthly magazine *Close Up*. The metaphor implicit in the name expressed a combination of a 'pool' of resources and 'pool' as a surface for reflection.[26] Although the actual members of POOL were not officially listed on any of their publications, *Close Up* referred to Kenneth Macpherson as its 'Editor' and Bryher as 'Assistant Editor'. Bryher and Macpherson were unknown to the readers they courted. *Close Up* was launched to give them a voice.[27] The poet H.D. was a less visible – yet essential – accomplice. Indeed 'pool' may have seemed a suitable metaphor for the fluid and yet quite complicated relationships that existed between H.D., Bryher and Macpherson.[28]

POOL books and *Close Up* were pursued with similar intensity. Between 1927 and 1929, POOL published eight handsomely produced books: two novels by Macpherson, one memoir by Bryher, one memoir by her younger brother and four film-related books.[29] But by 1929, it became apparent that *Close Up* was the more important POOL publication.

The journal's appearance resembled that of the literary masterpieces of the decade: hand-set smallish books with plain paper covers. It began as a 'little magazine' in both size (5½ inch by 7¾ inch) and circulation. Five hundred copies of each issue were printed, selling at 1 shilling, 5 francs, 25 cents – twice the printing cost. *Close Up* was printed in France because of the favourable exchange; copies were sent direct to bookshops in Paris, Berlin, London, Geneva, New York and Los Angeles.[30]

In the tradition of other 'little' literary magazines of the period (*The Dial, Broom, transition*, etc.), *Close Up* aspired to an internationalism – it was not pronouncedly English, Swiss, German or French. Edited primarily from offices in Territet, Switzerland, with correspondents in Moscow, Berlin, Paris, Geneva, London, New York and Los Angeles, the journal would play an important role in a growing community without borders – the internationally disperse group of patriots dedicated to developing the potentials of the film as an art. The editorial address – 'Riant Chateau – Territet – Switzerland' – revealed little about its source.[31] As the first English-language journal devoted entirely to the 'art of the film', *Close Up* aspired to do for English-language film writing and for the dissemination of film theory what the silent cinema did for the spectator: transcend the boundaries of language and of nation. The writing in *Close Up* created a mobile discursive forum, a diffused salon.

Although *Close Up* was addressed to an international audience, it was published in English, providing news of alternatives to the cinemas of English-speaking countries – Britain and the United States.[32] The journal represented the established geography of modernism in an almost electoral manner, covering as it did the cinematic 'beat' in the cities of Paris, Berlin, London, Moscow, Geneva and New York. And even though the location of *Close Up* correspondents in European capital cities gave the impression that the magazine was first-world oriented, the journal devoted special issues to Russian, Japanese and 'Aframerican' cinema, and articles about Indian, Spanish, Argentinian and other cinemas were actively encouraged.

Close Up did not need to include advertising, nor did it need to sell copies. Bryher's constant financial support gave the journal a solid economic base and left its editors free from the constraints of commercial publication. But the true material base of *Close Up* was a fortune made in the empire of British international commerce. Bryher – whose family money made the whole project possible – concealed her identity as heiress to the Ellerman shipping fortune.[33] Her chosen *nom de plume*, Bryher – after one of the Scilly Isles off Cornwall – disguised both her gender and her class. In fact, to hyperbolize, the material base for much of literary modernism was in the shipping and travel fortunes amassed by two British financiers, and dispensed through their daughters – Nancy Cunard (whose Hours Press published Samuel Beckett, Laura Riding, Richard Aldington, Louis Aragon and others) and Winifred Ellerman (whose family money went via Robert McAlmon to support his Contact Editions, publishers of Gertrude Stein, H.D., Mina Loy and Hemingway, and to direct stipends for Joyce and Dorothy Richardson).

For Bryher and for H.D. – who also chose a genderless pseudonym – itinerant lifestyles permitted a freedom from class, from family, from pressures toward a heterosexual norm. It was her marriage to Robert McAlmon in 1921 that first allowed Bryher to escape her parents' protective demands. While her mother and father were alive, Bryher chose to live outside of London in Paris, Berlin or Switzerland. Her second marriage, to Kenneth

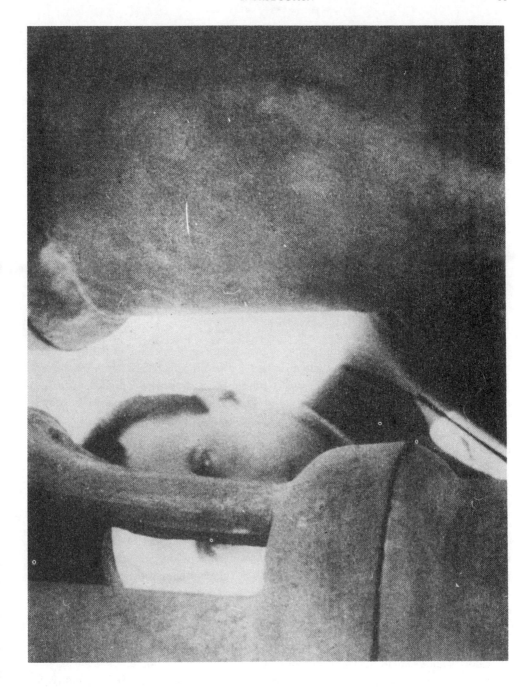

Kenneth Macpherson in Oswell Blakeston's film *I Do Love to Be Beside the Seaside* (1927).

Macpherson, was another 'marriage of convenience'. Bryher adapted her lesbian attachments to the conventions of the day, conducting marriage in such a way that she avoided its conventional connubial demands. Both of her marriages were possible only because the partners travelled constantly and were rarely in the same place.

It is tempting to speculate that bisexuality, travel, the efforts to escape class and gender designations parallel the stridency that *Close Up* maintained about being a *trans*national journal and about advocating a *trans*national cinema, blurring all borders. The urge to avoid bindings of class, nation and sexuality created countless diasporas, experiences of displacement, exile and chronic travel. One author lamented the dispersal of British literary energies in the 1920s and 1930s with the question 'Is there no one writing at all in England?'[34] The editorial threesome of *Close Up* – Kenneth Macpherson, Winifred Bryher and the poet H.D. – travelled widely and frequently enough to conduct pilgrimages, not to cities but to screens.[35] The imagined international reader of *Close Up* was a psychically slippery subject, constructed at the borderlines – geographic, social, sexual and national.

French precedents, British base

Close Up's antecedents were as much the modernist literary magazines of the period as they were the French journals dedicated to the cinema.[36] In this regard, the French weekly *Le Film* (founded by Henri Diamant-Berger in 1914) formed a precedent for a new discourse about 'the film' aimed at an intellectual and literary readership. In May 1917, Diamant-Berger hired Colette to write a series of articles on the cinema.[37] Louis Delluc followed in this direction when he took over the editorship in June 1917. By the time he left *Le Film* in 1919, Delluc had solicited articles from actors, scriptwriters and directors and had published Aragon and Apollinaire.[38] By the late 1920s, the French had established a tradition of literary respect for the cinema – the writings of Blaise Cendrars, Colette, Louis Delluc and Jean Epstein helped to develop this legacy.[39] 'Film culture' in France was developed with the discursive support of a plenitude of film journals and it was also closely allied with the *ciné-club* movement.[40] The French *cinéaste*, in addition to having the advantage of reading about films in journals that championed the cinema as an art form, could also view films in venues which afforded alternatives to commercial cinemas and could see films repeatedly or out of the sequence determined by commercial release.

Considering the French precedents, *Close Up*'s starting date of 1927 seems to imply that its writers were relative latecomers to the cinema. Journals like *Le Film* and *Cinéa* were notable pioneers in the campaign for cinema as an art form, and others such as *Cinéa-Ciné pour Tous* and *Gazette des Septième Arts* contained articles which were directly theoretical; yet *Close Up* remains distinct from its French predecessors because of its strong distaste for the Hollywood film. The French journals, while containing articles by Delluc, Epstein and Dulac that explored the essential qualities of the cinematic, also revered Chaplin, De Mille, Sennett and others. By contrast, *Close Up* writers were uniformly unimpressed by Hollywood and turned instead towards the work of the Germans and the Soviets, where they found more promising indications of the cinema's aesthetic potential.

Close Up was initially edited from Switzerland, but bore consistent evidence of a British base. In the words of American critic Harry Alan Potamkin, *Close Up* was an 'English project ... continually stern with England, the one constantly critical voice'.[41] *Close Up* provided a forum for English-language writers to engage with the cinema without the demand for an allegiance to American popular culture or to upholding the British film.

Certainly, the contributors to the journal saw their task as improving the state of British film criticism. As one *Close Up* writer, Hugh Castle, wrote in July 1929:

> Criticism in itself, is, of course, a strange word in England. Read the Sunday newspapers, the film features of which are usually written by enterprising residents of the outer suburbs, with mentalities to match their environment. Read their verdict and ponder them carefully. Then invert the result and stay away from the picture.[42]

Or as Robert Herring wrote in *Close Up* in May of the same year:

> Compare most of our trade and fan papers with those of any other country. They are a very bad joke. And where is our *Photociné*? And what English paper has written such a sane account of a film as did *Cahiers D'Art* of *The Way of All Flesh*?[43]

The British trade press mostly reviewed films at trade shows which were scheduled once every six months. This meant that by the time a film opened, the public – if it had read the review – probably did not remember it. British film criticism, even as a consumer guide, had an extremely indirect relation to film-viewing.

By the time *Close Up* commenced publication, the London Film Society – launched in October 1925 – had completed its second season and had already brought its share of international cinema to Britain.[44] Almost as if in direct reaction, the *London Mercury*, an established organ of literary modernism, began to review films in November 1925.

The *London Mercury* framed its approach to writing about film in relation to the deplorable state of journalistic criticism:

> Most of the newspaper comment on the cinema at present is either mere news-announcement or contemptibly undiscriminating judgment of all and sundry films – with an occasional breakout into a demand for protection of British films or, on the contrary, into a denunciation of the paltry efforts of British filmmakers. Of course, the criticism of the movies offers certain difficulties not present in relation to the other arts. *There are no criteria, or practically none, established by masterpieces of the past, and if there were the critic would have great difficulty familiarizing himself with them; there is no British Museum or National Gallery for classic films.*[45]
> [emphasis added]

Taking up the challenge to pioneer a new English-language critical discourse about this fledgling art form, *Close Up*'s initial agenda was to bring the English literary world to the cinema. Announcements were made about forthcoming articles from Osbert Sitwell, André Gide, Havelock Ellis, Dorothy Richardson and H.D.[46] Articles were solicited from Virginia Woolf and Gertrude Stein.[47] The letter that Macpherson wrote to Gertrude Stein reveals his intentions for the journal to encourage a select group of modernist writers to engage with the cinema:[48]

Riant Chateau
June 24, 1927

Dear Miss Stein,

I am sending you under separate cover a copy of my latest book *Poolreflection*, and
the first issue of *Close Up*, a monthly magazine to deal with films from the artistic,
psychological and educational points of view. I hope you will enjoy both of these
but especially *Close Up* which I am editing and which I believe will be welcomed by
the greatly increasing numbers of people who are coming to regard films as a
medium for the possible expression of art in its most modern and experimental
aspects.

I consider you have done more toward the advancement of thought in art than
almost any other writer. Apart from which, one derives a real and stimulating
pleasure from your writing. I really want to ask now if perhaps sometime you would
send a poem or article for *Close Up* in which this development of experimental art
is concerned. You will see that H.D. has written a charming poem *Projector*, which
has this bearing upon form in the films. *The most modern tendency seems so linked up
in this way and the kind of thing you write is so exactly the kind of thing that could be
translated to the screen that anything you might send would be deeply appreciated.*
[emphasis added]

Our terms are two guineas for a poem or short article, three guineas up to three
thousand words, our limit. The intent is to form a kind of debating ground for
distinguished minds, in contemporary thought and art, and to go on from there.

With compliments and best wishes,

Kenneth Macpherson

Stein responded by sending two prose pieces, 'Mrs Emerson', which appeared in the
August 1927 issue, and 'Three Sitting Here', which was published in the October 1927
issue. Although neither of the pieces directly addressed the cinema, 'Mrs Emerson' may
suggest an indirect reference:

> I cannot see I cannot see I cannot see. I cannot see.
> I cannot see besides always.
> I have not selected my pronunciation. I have not selected my pronunciation.
> *I repeat I will not play with windows. In the new houses there are not windows for
> ventilation or any other use. They say that that is their use. They say that kindly amazing
> lights they say that kindly amazing lights* and they say no that is not the use of a word,
> they say that unkindly certain lights, anyhow when I am pronounced that certain
> cheerful shapes are fainter, they say that they have pronounced exceptionally. ...
> *All the chances of intermediate investigation are so argued that the recent disturbances
> fit the first change in silent rugs. Silent rugs.* I thought that I would state that I knew

certainly that she was so seen that if her eyes were so placed no violently not verbally so placed. She is not agreeable. She is not so agreeable. I wish I could safely legitimize, and I will.[49] [emphasis added]

To interpret the above literally as about cinema would be forcing meanings on Stein's intentionally slippery polysemic play. Yet the 'new houses' without windows could easily be cinema theatres; the 'kindly amazing lights', the films; the 'recent disturbances fit the first change in silent rugs', the transition to sound.

Close Up gradually shed the need for external legitimization from the literary world, but in the first issues, its own insecurity about being 'The Only Magazine Devoted to Films as an Art' was quite evident. Yet even after the journal had a well-established critical foothold, there were still those who would dismiss the cinema as unworthy of serious intellectual attention in England. In the first issue of *Scrutiny*, the Leavisite journal which began in May 1932, William Hunter expressed his scepticism about intellectual interest in cinema, maintaining: 'No film yet produced can justify the serious critical approach demanded (for instance) by a good novel or poem.'[50] In a separate pamphlet, *Scrutiny of Cinema*, Hunter made a more direct attack on the style of film criticism found in *Close Up*:

> The customary tone of the more pretentious criticism of today (e.g. *Close Up*) is to speak of *Storm Over Asia* as if it were on the level of King Lear, of Eisenstein as a second Leonardo da Vinci, of Chaplin as 'that mighty genius of the film world' and so on.[51]

Hunter was, in his own form of scrutiny, waving a danger flag against too positive an approach to cinema. 'Even intelligent people surrender to the insidious appeal which cinema offers', he warned.[52] Despite *Scrutiny*'s doubts about *Close Up*'s discursive tone, Macpherson insisted: 'Films need to be carped at. Need an awfully firm hand. Need snobism. Need to be sneered at, that is to say, need standards of value ...'[53] This was, from its beginning, *Close Up*'s task.

'As Is'

The opening salvo of Kenneth Macpherson's first editorial 'As Is' performed a dramatic mid-millennial historical assessment of the status of the cinema at a 'critical age': 'Fifty odd years hasn't done so badly in getting an art into the world that fifty more will probably turn into THE art, but now, after somewhat magnificent growth, *one feels here is its critical age*'[54] [emphasis mine]. Macpherson's editorial presence was acutely visible for the first three years of the journal's publication: at the front of every monthly issue from July 1927 until December 1930, Macpherson wrote an editorial column on the state of cinema entitled 'As Is'.[55]

Macpherson's 'As Is' set the tenor for the journal – he advocated amateur production,[56] alternative exhibition,[57] demanded an active spectator,[58] criticized the British policy of censorship.[59] With rhetoric full of 'utter newness',[60] of experiment and progress, Macpherson's goal was to fulfil the medium's aesthetic potential: 'To get the medium developed so far as to be FIT for art.'[61] He viewed the cinema as a broad intellectual

FROM " WING BEAT "

A film of telepathy. The feeling of "something about to happen" pervades the whole, reaching a climax at the point from which this "still" is taken.

Kenneth Macpherson in *Wing Beat* (Vol. I, no. 1, July 1927).

FROM " WING BEAT "

A portrait of H. D. illustrating an incident from *Wing Beat*, a POOL film now in preparation. This is H. D.'s debut in films, and her many admirers will welcome the opportunity to see her. The same clear genius is in her acting that sets her so high among contemporary poets and authors. Works by H. D. appear in this issue.

H.D. in *Wing Beat* (Vol. I, no. 1, July 1927).

ON THE WAY
WING BEAT!

A POOL film. A study in thought.
The screen has had all these equivalents :

  the epic,
  the novel,
  the chronicle,
  the fantasy,
  the play.

But no free verse poem. WING BEAT
is the first. Telepathy and attraction, the
reaching out, the very edge of dimensions
in dimensions, the chemistry of actual
attraction, of *will* shivering and quivering
on a frail, too-high, too inaccessible brink.

WING BEAT shakes and trembles from
its first moment, wings beating, ploughing
wet clouds ; sky and space as it were, chains
and layers of interminable journey, wings
driven, tired but desperate. Of minds and
spirits, not of persons.

Advertisement for *Wing Beat* (Vol. I, no. 1, July 1927).

battleground with skirmishes between the heteroclite assortment of national cinemas.[62] As a critic and a theorist Macpherson's limitations were that he avoided – or was incapable of – incisively analysing a film's social or political statement. He was attuned, instead, to the formal properties of cinematic construction and psychological realism.

While Macpherson snidely dismissed 'English cinema' as oxymoronic ('It is quite useless to expect any art to indigenously flower there. … the Englishman can only be roused to enthusiasm on the football field.'[63]), he nonetheless hoped to transform it. 'There are men and women of intellect, power and conviction', wrote Macpherson in March 1929, 'who could build the English cinema to a position of triumph equal to the Russians.'[64] *Close Up* hoped to combine the climate of alternative production and exhibition established by the French *ciné-clubs* and *cinéastes* with the stylistic lessons of Soviet experimentation with montage and, from this fertile hybrid, to help revitalize the British cinema.

If *Close Up* was the discursive branch of this effort, POOL films was its practical extension. Between 1927 and 1930, POOL produced three short films (*Wing Beat, Foothills, Monkey's Moon*) and one feature (*Borderline*, 1930) (see Part 5). All were to be seen in alternative exhibition contexts, in repertory theatres or film societies. As the years wore on and the POOL film projects were not well received, Bryher and Macpherson became more stridently indignant about the British film sensibility. As Bryher wrote in 1930:

> there seems to have developed a dangerous tradition in England that the cinema 'must be simple'. And if this statement be investigated it will be found to mean 'the cinema must not think' … Eisenstein has probably one of the most complex minds in the world today and many sequences of his films (though they apparently deal with simple things) require the spectator to think and not merely see. … Unless intellect can dominate the cinema, let us put films away with mecannos [*sic*]and picture blocks.[65]

Bryher's most radical statement about the future of film production suggestively presages post-war 'New American Cinema' and London Co-Op film-makers. As she wrote in 1931:

> If the cinema is to survive it will be only through a few groups refusing to visit commercial kinos, and working out their ideas, as Kuleshov did, on paper. They will have to be more avant-garde than the French in 1927, more cut off from equipment than the Russians after the revolution. They will have to attack the formula and not tolerate it; they must learn to walk out from pictures that however technically perfect are based on false ideas. They will have to make scraps of film that every commercial producer would refuse and project them on kitchen walls before small groups determined to tear them to pieces.[66]

Neither the editors or writers for *Close Up* held to this agenda.

G.W. Pabst and *Close Up*

Before Bryher and Macpherson had read, published or understood Soviet film theory, the films of G.W. Pabst supplied something that struck them as the pinnacle of cinematic achievement: psychological realism. 'I came late to the cinema,' wrote Bryher in December 1927, 'and I came because of *Joyless Street*.'[67] Her critical enthusiasm was not based on

Pabst and his
cameraman Wagner:
'The joys of
cinematography. In
Montparnasse,
waiting for the sun'
(Vol. I, no. 6,
December 1927).

cinematic elements of editing, camera movement or even acting, but on the realism of character psychology. Of Pabst, she wrote: 'He sees psychologically and because of this, because in a flash he knows the sub-conscious impulse or hunger that prompted an apparently trivial action, his intense realism becomes, through its truth, poetry.'[68]

In June 1929, the French correspondent for *Close Up*, Jean Lenauer, wrote: 'G.W. Pabst once said to me – and rarely do I forget a word of what he says – that only the journalists can change the abominable state of affairs in the cinema world.'[69] From the many articles devoted to Pabst in *Close Up* and from the unpublished correspondence among its editor and writers, it seems that Pabst also invested heavily in the power of the magazine's 'journalists'.

Bryher and Macpherson first met Pabst in October 1927. Bryher describes the scene of their first meeting in a letter from Berlin:

> 'My car, the studios, my films, my thoughts are all at your disposal,' said the medium-sized FIDO. 'Ah how my friends and I have discussed CLOSE UP. It is so funny, so furchtbar funny you permit, that an Englishman should have written it. The thing we all desire, the paper that expresses our inmost psychological thoughts and an Englishman has done it. ... Ha ... ha ... you perceive, do you not, how furchtbar funny it is ... How funny that an Englishman should have started CLOSE UP. For English films!!!!!!!'[70]

They were totally charmed by him ('We are both in love with Pabst'[71]). In December 1927, Bryher published 'G.W. Pabst. A Survey' and Macpherson penned an article on *Jeanne Ney*. In November, Oswell Blakeston wrote an article on Pabst. In 1929, there were six articles about the director, including H.D.'s 'An Appreciation': 'G.W. Pabst was and is my first recognized master of the art.'

In the spring of 1928, Macpherson quotes a long letter from Pabst in his editorial. In desperation for a production company that would allow 'good films ... made without concession, without compromise', Pabst appeals for *Close Up*'s help:

> Certainly in Europe there are, shall we say, thirty million cinema-goers. Is it not feasible to take out of this thirty million only ten per cent? Three million, then, are of our opinion and our outlook in respect of good films. These three million are today without voice or shelter in the midst of the manufacturers and the remaining twenty seven million. They do not find good films, because whether born here or there, no star leads them to the good films, and they resign themselves, bury their love and their desire, and say at last, films cannot be any good. Films are merchandise and will never be the artistic expression of the world ... Would it not be a lifework for *Close Up* to give those who want good films the directors who are willing to make them, and the theatres which are willing to show them? Supposing a European company were founded for the creation and production of good films. Somehow the three millions must be reached. Let *Close Up* help in this, and let the three million join the membership of this band of fighters and be stockholders of the company. You pay ten marks per year which gives you the right to see ten films in the year. The Stock Company has now thirty million marks (one and a half million pounds). They fill the excellent cinemas which are specially built. All this costs twenty million marks in organization, losses, salaries, outlay, etc. Does it not

leave over every year ten million marks? Well then, every year, ten films by ten
directors are made at a cost of one million marks, which is quite a lot, and enough to
show the world what film art really is when freed from commercial limitations.
These films will be made without concession, without compromise. Must these
three millions therefore not be found, though it takes years of pain and battle, is
there not here a life task for *Close Up*? [72]

Pabst's internationalist-utopian proposal did not become the 'life task' of *Close Up*, but
the journal did endorse the principles that he appealed to, and as Lotte Eisner put it, they
'ardently championed' Pabst's work.[73] Throughout its publication, *Close Up* followed
Pabst's career in careful detail. At least sixteen articles were devoted to his film work and
issues were generously illustrated with high-quality enamel-stock stills from each Pabst
film as it was released. Some of the most reverent writing about Pabst in the pages of
Close Up was composed by the American Imagist-poet-turned-*cinéaste*, H.D.:

> He holds, as it were, the clue, must hold his position almost as the keystone to the
> vast aesthetic structure we call now unquestionably the Art of the Film. The
> Germans hold the key really, are the intermediaries between Russia and the outside
> world that still believes Red to be a symbol of murder and destruction.[74]

What struck H.D. most profoundly in Pabst's work – from the revelatory moment when
she and Bryher saw *Joyless Street* in a little Montreux cinema in 1925 – was Pabst's
direction of his women, from Garbo to Asta Nielsen to Louise Brooks.

If the *Close Up* writers were enthusiastic about Pabst, Pabst was equally enthusiastic
about the POOL films. In Berlin, in August 1928, Bryher and Macpherson screened
Foothills, the second short POOL film, a *kammerspiel* with H.D. and Robert Herring. In a
letter full of the playful banter that marks the correspondence between them,
Macpherson wrote to H.D., telling her of Pabst's ecstatic response to her screen presence:

> he [Pabst] loved the Kitten [H.D.] and said how STRONG is H.D., it is amazing,
> how strong, what power, how consistent. And what he really liked about the film was
> that you showed up the utter futility of the Hollywood tradition and that beauty was
> something quite different. And I am wondering if he still wants Louisa [Louise]
> Brooks for LULU or whether he is writing to the Kitten tonight to book her!! ...
> He is going to come and make a film with us in Territet, he and me together.[75]

The collaborative project between Macpherson and Pabst never did materialize, but as the
letters between Bryher, Macpherson and H.D. from 1928 to 1932 indicate, there were
moments when it seemed quite certain.[76] Bryher's letters from Berlin, always full of gossip
about the Langs, the Metzners and Elisabeth Bergner, also included details about Pabst. On
3 May 1931, just after Pabst had seen *Borderline* in Berlin, Bryher wrote to Macpherson:

> Pabst says did you get the wire he sent you? They won't risk *Borderline* at the
> Kamera but P is angry as he says he wanted all his cameramen and electricians to
> see it. He is so impressed himself with the camerawork. And lighting. He says it is
> the only real avant-garde film. Pabst told me that he would like to have you work for
> him if he ever did an English version of [*The Threepenny Opera*] ...[77]

The letter also proposed a number of film projects suggested by Erno Metzner, to be produced independently by Macpherson. Bryher continues: 'I think this is certainly the way to work if you want to continue in films as Pabst says you should.'

Surely these letters might overstate Pabst's enthusiasm, but the daydream of collaboration continued. In June 1932, Bryher writes from Berlin:

> Pabst by terms of the new regime if enforced in July can never make another film in Germany. He has been awarded the *Legion d'Honneur* and hopes to get a permit to work in France. Metzner also must leave and hopes to go to Paris. It is much more serious than even I ever thought, but I must not write of politics, I fear. I think there is a chance for the English film, if only we could get people working in England.[78]

When Pabst left for Paris in June 1932 and Sachs for Boston, Bryher returned to Territet. In August, she wrote a series of letters to Macpherson that expressed an increasing sense of ultimatum about his film projects: 'If you would like to make a film I feel that commercially early autumn is the moment to do it. BUT I cannot push prod or pull you through a film you only half want to make'.[79]

Close Up concluded its journalistic coverage of Pabst's career with the hope that he would succeed in Hollywood in 1933 where Eisenstein had not: 'Pabst's presence in America [is] so much more hopeful than Eisenstein's. We have always liked the German film worker, and there has seldom, if ever, been any suspicion of him. I think this will follow in the case of Pabst.'[80] Pabst and Eisenstein were the two heroic – if theoretically incommensurate – figures the *Close Up* writers thrust into their critical limelight. Eisenstein's ambitions for intellectual montage and Pabst's acumen for psychological realism were seen as separate – but critical – strategies to advancing the film as an art.

Theory/practice

While most of his editorials answer implied charges against the cinema, Macpherson was fearful of an overly prescriptive theoretical practice. Despite the fact that the journal was first promoted as providing 'theory and analysis', Macpherson became more and more dubious of 'film theory':

> Sometimes we feel that writing about it all is like trying to tie a collar on it. It would certainly be so if we said the cinema is this, cinema is that. The fact is what we are really trying to do is open the gate and let it out over the hills with the rolling cloud that critics will call composed or well constructed.[81]

> The more one dabbles in theory, the more mythical, evanescent and intangible does theory become. Not in the sense of unattainable divinity, but in the sense of sheer invalidity. Theory made too precise can only impoverish. ... Theory. Theory. There is the theory that builds theory. And the theory that explodes theory. Remember, *your* theory is more valid, more valuable to you than any you can borrow. Remember, action came first, theory afterwards.[82]

> One of the reasons why I do not like 'film theory' text-book acquired, text-book practised, text-book formulated, is that film theory cannot be learned that way.[83]

Advertisement for bound volumes of *Close Up* (Vol. V, no. 1, July 1929).

Midway in *Close Up*'s tenure, Macpherson seemed to have lost faith in the power of writing about film to change the course of the medium's development. While Macpherson's editorial writing was uninterrupted and perhaps buoyed by his work on the POOL film projects, his editorial energies began to wane after 1930. When his feature film, *Borderline*, was completed and screened it met with an aggressively hostile critical response.[84] In the November 1930 issue, Macpherson made a strident attempt to defend *Borderline* and answer the complaints about the film's 'obscurity' and 'chaotic' structure. In many ways, *Borderline* became a critical turning point for the journal. *Close Up*'s switch to a quarterly format at the beginning of 1931 – while explained in terms of the changing demands placed on its editors by the transition to sound – may have also been due to Macpherson's own exasperation and disappointment with a cinema world that did not appreciate his film work.

In his second to last 'As Is' (September 1931), Macpherson wrote an excited review of Helmar Lerski's book of photographs, *Köpfe des Alltags*. In the same issue, he published two of his own 'photo-montages'.[85] Macpherson's interest in the cinema was seemingly displaced by an enthusiasm for *Neue Sachlichkeit* photography; perhaps his excitement about still photography increased at precisely the moment when the sound cinema appeared inevitable and the restraints of film censorship seemed the most pronounced.[86] After 1931, Macpherson's 'As Is' appeared with less consistency. With the change to quarterly format, Oswell Blakeston – a staple contributor – was appointed as a second 'Assistant Editor'.[87] Macpherson never formally announced his retirement from editorial duties – he was still listed as editor for all fifty-four issues of the journal – but his investment in the magazine clearly diminished and, by 1933, he did not publish a single article in its pages.

Bryher's role, compared to that of the more mercurial personalities of Macpherson and H.D., was central and sustaining. Bryher performed most of the day-to-day editorial duties of the magazine: she stayed in contact with the correspondents, co-ordinated the articles, dealt with the mechanics of printing. While many of Bryher's first articles for the journal addressed practical issues for readers – what film books and magazines should be read, what kind of equipment amateur film-makers should use, how to start a film club, what films were appropriate for children[88] – she also wrote analytic accounts of the films of Pabst and of the Soviets. Her 1929 book, *Film Problems of Soviet Russia*, described films by Kuleshov, Eisenstein, Pudovkin, Room, Ermler and Preobrazhenskaia – films that could not be seen in England.[89] Bryher continued her editorial duties and writing up to December 1933, when the journal ceased publication. It was probably a combination of Bryher's growing outrage over political events in Germany (explicitly expressed in her June 1933 article, 'What Shall You Do in the War?') and the complex personal effects of the death of her father in July 1933 that made her abandon the project.[90]

The end of *Close Up*

Close Up was issued regularly every month for forty-two issues until, in January 1931, the journal changed its size and was issued as a quarterly. The despairing tone of Macpherson's December 1930 'As Is' gives some indication of how the transition to sound transformed the 'world situation' and forced the journal to reduce its frequency of publication:

With the establishment of the talking film, the world situation with regard to films was completely altered. Whereas, during the period of silent films, world distribution was fluid, now films are becoming more and more tied up within national limits. Circulation has to an enormous extent come to an end.[91]

In January 1931, *Close Up* placed a quarter-page advertisement in the third issue of the American journal *Experimental Cinema*, providing a further explanation of its switch to quarterly format:

Only by issuing *Close Up* as a quarterly are the editors enabled to cope with these developments intrinsically and fundamentally. As films – through speech – are becoming more and more national, in proportion the function of an international journal such as *Close Up* is complicated. … Each number will contain concentrated study, either of films of different countries, or of developments in technique with the theoretical deductions applicable to them. Thus each number will be also a record of permanent value in film history.[92]

These editorial pronouncements provide the clearest sense of the difficulties the *Close Up* editors saw for the future of the art form they had so passionately championed. When the journal ceased publication in December 1933, there was no clear statement explaining its end. The three editorial energies had dispersed: Macpherson was travelling with Norman Douglas; Bryher was studying to become an analyst; H.D. had begun her famous analysis with Freud.[93] In addition to the diminished frequency of publication, the last ten issues of *Close Up* demonstrate a lessening of intensity: each issue was thinner with less text and more photographs. As the promise of silent cinema as an *Esperanto* evaporated, the journal switched to a more predominantly visual format, as if to compensate for the loss. 'It will be very much enlarged,' announced Macpherson, 'printed on art-paper throughout, and much more fully illustrated, with subtitles in three languages.'[94] The journal that had so heavily invested in the transformative power of writing about the cinema had changed its strategy, relying instead on the power of images to argue its case. In 1933, when *Close Up* abandoned its forum, it was not left unattended – a number of subsequent English-language film journals took its place. In the United States, *Experimental Cinema* and *Cinema* began in 1930.[95] In England, *Cinema Quarterly* and *Sight and Sound* were first published in 1932, *Film* began in the spring of 1933 and became *Film Art* in 1934.[96] But *Close Up* had set the agenda, determined its priorities, had pioneered a new discursive forum about the cinema.

Macpherson's opening salvo in his first editorial 'As Is' ('Fifty odd years hasn't done so badly in getting an art into the world that fifty more will probably turn into THE art …') seems to echo ominously in the current context, seventy years later. One feels again that 'here is its critical age', not because the cinema needs guidance through another awkward adolescence but because its obituaries are already being written. As images become digital and are no longer photographically based, as screen formats get smaller and more portable rather than projection-based, as interactivity transforms 'spectators' into 'users', new technologies change almost everything about the cinema. As the age of the cinema comes to its end, the texts from *Close Up* remain, as the 1929 POOL brochure promised: 'undoubtedly of the greatest value as REFERENCE BOOKS FOR THE FUTURE. …'

PART 1

Enthusiasms and Execrations

INTRODUCTION

James Donald

For readers whose understanding of literary and film theory – or Theory as it is known to initiates – was shaped by the influence of journals like *Tel Quel* and *Screen* from the late 1960s to the early 1980s, the claim of *Close Up* to provide 'theory and analysis' of cinema may seem a bit odd. Here you will find no developed metapsychology of film spectatorship, no sustained political-aesthetic critique of the institution of art, no pressing of film art into the cause of progressive politics, nor even any real attempt at a taxonomy of the film styles endorsed by the magazine. What is most striking about these polemical writings from the 1920s and 1930s is their engaging mixture of exasperation and enthusiasm.

Against the mainstream

The exasperation is expressed – forcefully, frequently and in many ways quite conventionally – in critical condemnations of the banality of mainstream entertainment cinema. The tone is evident in Kenneth Macpherson's first 'As Is', or in Oswell Blakeston's 'British Solecisms'. It is the disdain they show, especially towards English cinema, that has led to a degree of suspicion regarding *Close Up* among British film historians, who sniff cultural elitism in the commitment to internationalism and a modernist aesthetic.[1]

It is true that *Close Up* tended to see art in terms of an autonomous aesthetic sphere, and the aesthetic potential of film as something to be sought in what is specific to the medium, or, perhaps more accurately, what is specific to the *experience* of the medium. Certainly, the magazine wanted a cinema quite distinct from the theatrical and literary traditions which were becoming increasingly dominant in entertainment films – especially with the arrival of the talkies. As Bryher's slightly breathless interview with Anita Loos suggests, however, *Close Up* was not wholly anti-populist, nor unwaveringly antagonistic towards what Hollywood *might* be. But enthusiasm for limited aspects of Hollywood (the comedy of Chaplin, Keaton or Stepin Fetchit, aspects of Griffith's narrational style, the epic Western) was grossly outweighed by a pervasive hostility towards its mediocrity. 'Hollywood can produce kitsch magnificently but cannot produce art,' pronounces Bryher in her two-part article 'The Hollywood Code' (September and December 1931). To substantiate her indictment of Hollywood values and its 'code' of film-making, and perhaps to some extent in reaction to Eisenstein's experiences in Hollywood in 1930, Bryher fantasizes how Hollywood might have made *The Battleship Potemkin*:

Maggots certainly would not have been permitted. Instead we should have opened with a sailors' bar, with plenty of females in sex-appeal promoting dresses, and a cheerful song. The doctor would be little changed, but he would have had sinister designs upon the heroine who would of course, have survived the perils of the underworld because of her love for an old father-mother-grandparent or a young brother-sister-orphan-child at choice, helped by the patent-enamel body paint into which American stars are dipped.

The leader of the mutineers would watch the doctor's advances, laugh, remember in a cut-back his old mother, knock the doctor out, pat the girl out of his way and sit down and drink. The doctor not being in uniform, would leave muttering, in sinister camera dissolves. Through the Odessa mists, the mutineer and the girl would discover love at first sight, to be broken apart at the first kiss clutch, by the memory of the sailor's waiting comrades. The heroine, jealous, would wander to the steps. Then, Hollywood is wealthy in ideas as well as cameras, there are at least three directions open to the story. Simple love, the sailor is accused falsely by the doctor, is about to be shot, but is rescued as the sheet drops, by a comrade or the girl; romantic drama, the sailor is an officer disguised as a mutineer in order to discover some treacherous plot to overwhelm the ship; or a play of gangster life, the ship is loaded with alcohol, and the doctor and the mutineer are leaders of two separate bootlegging establishments. But the end of all the stories must be the same: a triumphal bridal procession down the Odessa steps, Cossacks in front with bayonets decorated with orange blossom, sailors behind, the folk songs of the world, and on the edges, children with doves.[2]

If *Close Up* was against the formulistic kitsch of Hollywood and the British industry, what was it for?

The film for the film's sake

Most obviously, it was committed to the idea of a cinematic avant-garde. But even such a simple claim will have nuances for the reader in the 1990s which may skew a reading of *Close Up* on its own terms. Since the 1970s, the field of debate about avant-garde cinema has been largely defined by the terms laid down by Peter Wollen in his article 'The Two Avant Gardes', first published in *Studio International* in 1975. There he claimed that the two avant-gardes of the contemporary period – broadly, the formalist experimentation of people like Peter Gidal, Klaus Wyborny and the Co-Op movement versus the politically engaged cinema of Godard and Straub-Huillet – were prefigured by analogous movements in the 1920s. On the one hand, writes Wollen,

> films were being made by Léger-Murphy, Picabia-Clair, Eggeling, Richter, Man Ray, Moholy-Nagy, and others ... that were attempts to extend the scope of painting, to move outside the confines of the canvas, to introduce the dimension of time, to use light directly as well as colour, and so on.[3]

Although it is important to remember that Wollen was writing in a magazine primarily concerned with painting and the visual arts, his idea of exploring the specific nature and aesthetic possibilities of film as a medium was certainly close to the heart of *Close Up*. Macpherson, Bryher and their colleagues had not yet given up hope that film art could be achieved in the context of commercial cinema: witness their enthusiasm for Pabst's work at Ufa, Harry A. Potamkin's defence of directors like Abel Gance and Jean Epstein, working on the margins of the French industry, and H.D.'s articles on Conrad Veidt and *Joyless Street*. *Close Up* also publicized the cinematic experiments of established artists – Man Ray's *Emak Bakia*, for example. It documented not only the work of the French Surrealists but also the lesser-known and more diffuse activities of independents like the Belgians Charles Dekeukeleire and Gussy Lauwson. Enthusiasm for the idea of 'cine-poems' led the magazine to champion major individual figures working outside the cinema industry. The Swede Viking Eggeling, the Germans Hans Richter and Walter Ruttman and the English-based New Zealander Len Lye were all devoted at this time to creating the abstract or 'absolute' film. *Close Up* was committed to the establishment of an independent production and distribution sector, distinct from the mainstream of commercial cinema,[4] and they enthusiastically reported the setting up of avant-garde production groups like Cavalcanti's 'Neo-films' in Paris and Herman Weinberg and Robert van Rosen's 'Excentric Films' in New York.[5]

All this varied work pushed at the edges of the medium. Before the talkies, there did exist, however marginally, a dynamic and fractious sphere of production and exhibition in which the ontology of cinema could be investigated and expanded. *Close Up* existed in part to provide a forum for the critical debate about this kind of film. But, according to Wollen at least, this was not the only type of avant-garde film being produced. In his article, he identified this alternative tradition as those film-makers whose aim was to expand and exploit the analytic or epistemological power of cinema: 'On the other hand, there were the Russian directors, whose films were clearly avant-garde, but in a different sense: Eisenstein's *Strike*, Dovzhenko's *Zvenigora*, Vertov's *Man with the Movie Camera*.'[6]

Wollen's polemical opposition reflects the dominant avant-garde aesthetic of the 1970s. Perhaps it was always too stark. It is easy enough to carve up the variations and oppositions between different strands of avant-garde film-making in the 1920s in other ways: the search for specificity through abstraction versus the more figurative and lyrical work of the French modernists; those same modernists versus the Surrealists who denounced Germain Dulac's filming of Artaud's script for *The Sea-shell and the Clergyman*; the attempt to capture the commercial industry for art versus the creation of purist enclaves; and so forth. Nevertheless, Wollen's two traditions do provide a useful context for reading *Close Up*.

The range and diversity of the journal's enthusiasms give a sense of dynamic possibilities for a cinema which had not yet congealed into the constraining categories of film history (and niche marketing): entertainment cinema, art cinema, avant-garde cinema. But Wollen's meditations on what constitutes an avant-garde make it possible to discern the dominant critical tendency in *Close Up*. This is perhaps, paradoxically, most clear in Macpherson's introductions to Eisenstein's article 'The Fourth Dimension in the Kino' in March 1930. There, it is not the power of montage to decompose familiar perceptions of the world, to create a new and more analytical way of seeing and understanding, nor the possible exploitation of the pedagogy of cinema for political ends that Macpherson is concerned with – as, say, Walter Benjamin might have been. Macpherson is exclusively concerned with the implications of Eisenstein's 'new art of tone-film' for a phenomenology of skilled spectatorship. Bearing in mind his slogan in his first editorial – 'The film for the film's sake' – one might almost say that this is Eisenstein reread through Pater. Macpherson quotes at length from Hanns Sachs's article 'Film Psychology'.[7] His own conclusion focuses on the aesthetic possibilities of the overtones created for the spectator through montage:

> 'See' is inaccurate. 'Hear' is inaccurate. 'See and hear' is inaccurate. *Sense*, says Eisenstein, is the clue to overtone or fourth dimension. I sense – vividly, faintly, overwhelmingly, not at all. I sense must mean I re-organise, I *resound*. To see means little, means nothing, unless it is a process of absorption and creation. You need only walk round a picture gallery to know this, or to go to the opera, and realise the moment when you react no more to what you are seeing or what you are hearing, though, while you remain there, you will continue to see or to hear. With this saturation point, comes the cessation of creative energy that makes appreciation and assimilation. 'I sense' (I resound) is, therefore the paramount consideration and *subject to almost no restriction*. Psychic-physiological experience, conscious and unconscious, active and passive, symbolic and 'realistic', is a source of infinite supply, and authentic on almost any plane of organised, scientific selection. The new overtone montage will avoid saturation. It will stimulate and provoke, thwart and incite, until response is absolute.[8] [italics original]

The same concern with the power of the cinematic image to transform the objects it represents and to create a unique aesthetic experience for the film spectator can be found in Robert Herring's account of 'magic' in cinema. Its source, whether conscious or not, is identified in Harry A. Potamkin's discussion of French cinema when he refers in passing, and slightly dismissively, to the term *photogénie*. This was developed by the impressionist, or modernist, film-makers working in France in the 1920s, and has generally been abandoned as irredeemably bound up with a confused and anti-theoretical mysticism. In 1981, however, in *Afterimage*, a journal that in its own way reworked *Close Up*'s commitment to radical formal experimentation in film, Paul Willemen offered a limited defence of the term:

> As the 'law of the cinema', [*photogénie*] clearly sets in place a viewer's aesthetic. The defining characteristic of cinema is said to be something that pertains to the relationship between viewer and image, a momentary flash of recognition or a moment when the look at ... something suddenly flares up with a particularly affective, emotional intensity. The founding aspect of cinematic quality, instead of its specificity, is located, not in the recognition of an artistic sensibility or intentionality 'behind' the screen, as it were, but in the particular relationship supported or constituted by the spectatorial look, between projected image and viewer. As such *photogénie* is a term mobilised to demarcate one set of viewers – those able to 'see' – from others. In this context it functions like a mark of

distinction, differentiating those who are qualified to talk of cinema from those who are not. By extension this distinction will then serve to single out those who, by virtue of their sensitivity to *photogénie*, are qualified to make cinema and so install them in a position of cultural power over those who merely manufacture cinema, however professionally.[9]

Willemen sees in *photogénie* both a groping towards, and at the same time a refusal of, the theory of spectatorship eventually articulated in the 1960s by Christian Metz in 'The Imaginary Signifier'.[10] Willemen defends the notion on the ground that, however wilfully misguided it may have been, it at least took the unconscious dimension of cinema spectatorship seriously. Its proponents did not attempt to domesticate the unconscious through a set of procedures as the Surrealists did: for example, in their strategies for rendering the unconscious representable through such techniques as automatic writing. In *Close Up*, it is possible to see both the claim to skilled spectatorship and also the disavowal of its more disturbing connotations.

If the version of discriminating and inspired spectatorship implied by *photogénie* was indeed at the core of *Close Up*'s modernist aesthetic of cinema, that in itself may explain why its project quite quickly became unsustainable. But it is also important to note the external factors which undermined the ideal cinema Macpherson, Bryher and their colleagues envisaged. The economic and industrial conditions which made it possible to produce experimental films disappeared with the coming of sound. The rise of fascism in Germany, and of Stalinism and socialist realism in the Soviet Union, also brought into much sharper focus the choice between aesthetic radicalism and political commitment for avant-garde film-makers.

One key moment indicates that, even though *Close Up*'s catholic eclecticism may have just about been viable in 1927, the opposition between two avant-gardes projected backwards by Peter Wollen had become a reality by the turn of the decade. The event was the first International Congress of Independent Cinematography held at La Sarraz, Zurich, in September 1929.[11] Its topic was 'The Art of Cinema, Its Social and Aesthetic Purposes'. Although the organizers hoped that the Congress would lead to the creation of an international film-making co-operative, the delegates declared 'as an absolute principle, the difference in practice and spirit between the independent cinema and the commercial cinema'. 'Art cinema' thus began to emerge as a constrained and marginalized category separate from the mainstream commercial industry. The second, and final, meeting of the Congress in Brussels in 1930 went further in writing an obituary for the sort of 'film for film's sake' to which *Close Up* was committed. It recognized that 'the Avant Garde as a purely aesthetic movement had passed its climax and was on the way to concentrating on the social and political film, mainly in documentary form'.[12] The first movement 'expired', according to Hans Richter, because political tensions 'made poetry no longer suitable'. Artists working in film increasingly decided to adopt a more practical commitment to social action: 'Our age demands the documented fact.' Whether Richter envisaged as part of this new cinematic era the silencing of Vertov and the exile and recantation of Eisenstein in the Soviet Union, Leni Riefenstahl's staged song-and-dance paeans to Nazism, or the social democratic vision of John Grierson in Britain, is of course unlikely. But the compartmentalization of cinematic modes evident by 1930 suggests that the aesthetic moment of *Close Up* was probably over before the magazine ceased publication.[12]

The 'Negro viewpoint' [JD/LM]

Despite their passion for the specificity of film and for the experience of watching film, the contributors to *Close Up* were neither ignorant of, nor uninterested in, the social power of cinema. One striking instance of this, particularly in the early years, was a concern with the question of race, which led to the special issue on 'the negro' and cinema in August 1929. Macpherson's editorial on the topic remains shocking: at moments penetrating in its perceptiveness, but trapped within a racialized discourse characteristic of the time.

'Effort at universal cinema', runs Macpherson's opening salvo, 'has well shown that the only approach to it is strictly racial cinema.' By that he does not mean racist cinema. That he is genuinely and profoundly opposed to:

> Confronted with an instability (his own) which he calls a Race Problem, the white man is always going to portray the negro as he likes to see him, no matter how benevolently. Benevolence, indeed, is the danger. Apart from being the most tricky and unkind form of human selfishness, it is often more than humbug and always less than seeing, and does to sugar coat much that is not, so to speak, edible.[13]

What is Macpherson's alternative? In a prescient reading, he sees a hint of a different cinema in a subversive edge to the comic actor Stepin Fetchit, often denounced in later years as no more than a stereotype. But that disturbance is identified in terms which reiterate the way that 'blackness' was being celebrated by many white avant-garde artists. It is found in a certain physicality, a certain naturalness, and ultimately that primitiveness necessary for a modernist aesthetic's challenge to the suffocating reality of bourgeois life and the banal conventions of middlebrow art:

> watch [Stepin Fetchit] move and you will see what we mean. There is more than promise in the jungle, lissom lankness that slams down something unanswerable in front of what we let go past as beauty. This splendour of being is one good key to open a good many doors, all the way to our goal simply. … Fetchit waves loose racial hands and they, like life, touch everything that the world contains. They are startling with what nobody meant to put into them, but which is all too there – histories, sagas, dynasties, Keatsian edges off things make a voiceless trouble back of the eye and the recording mind. Only afterwards you are really beset by them. They are not Fetchit's hands, they are the big step we have not yet taken. First of all these so utterly not incantationish gestures are unselfconsciousness, perfectly inherited greatness of race and of race mind. It only begins there. We can scrap every trained toe waggle of a ballerina for the very least of these movements. Making this greatness articulate for the cinema is the fascinating pioneer work of somebody.[14]

The special issue on 'Negro Film' appeared as Kenneth Macpherson worked on the photoplay for *Borderline*, the POOL film which is discussed in Part 5. Long overlooked, the film is now more widely available for exhibition and has inspired significant critical interest, not least in the question of its racial representations and dynamics. Thomas Cripps, in *Slow Fade to Black*, argues that in *Borderline* black imagery becomes virtuous and white evil – 'black purity stands against European decadence' – though he also suggests that the object lesson of the film was that 'what passed for racial liberalism was often no more than a worship of presumed primitiveness'.[15] In this context, one could point to the ways in which the neurotic white man and woman – Thorne (Gavin Arthur) and Astrid (H.D.) – remain the film's centres of consciousness. H.D. plays the 'civilized' white woman whose psychological excess could be understood as a 'dark continent' which slides into association with the 'primitive', the racial other. But the film does create a space for the black or, in the terms of H.D.'s *Borderline* pamphlet, 'mulatto' woman, where a white woman/black man parallelism would exclude her. *Borderline* creates a complex set of interrelationships, crossing the 'borderline' of black/white.

Borderline was made in the context of a modernist culture which was beginning to recognize the contribution of black writers and artists to the cultures of modernity. The Harlem Renaissance was a movement of black political figures, writers, painters, film-makers and musicians in the New York of the 1920s, of which Paul Robeson was a part. Robeson's participation in *Borderline* was a significant coup for the POOL group – he was, by 1930, a celebrated stage actor and performer, and had appeared in one previous film: Oscar Micheaux's *Body and Soul* (1924). In bringing Robeson into the film, and in producing a special issue of *Close Up* on 'Negro Cinema' with contributions from black critics and cultural commentators (including a brief letter from Walter White, writer and Assistant Secretary of the National Association for the Advancement of Colored People), the POOL group could be seen as placing themselves within that interracial cultural dynamic which constituted an alliance between AfroAmerican and European modernisms, as in Nancy Cunard's *Negro* anthology. Yet this account is in turn complicated by demands, supported by *Close Up* contributors, for a 'pure' black cinema. As Robert Herring wrote: 'there should be Negro films made by and about them. Not black films passing for white, and not, please, white passing for black. We want no van Vechtens [Carl van Vechten, white author of *Nigger Heaven* (1926)] of the films.'[16]

Responses to black cinema in *Close Up* were also framed and bounded by the journal's placing in the years of the arrival of sound. Dorothy Richardson, conflating her arguments against the coming of speech in films with her responses to black cinema, found 'the noble acceptable twin of the silent film'[17] in the non-verbal aspects of (Negro) sound film – singing and the 'lush chorus of Negro-laughter' – but described the speech as 'annihilating'. Kenneth Macpherson implicitly aligned silence, film art and white/European cinema on one side of a divide and sound cinema with black culture on the other: 'Talking films took films from us but they have given us a glimpse of [the negro].'[18] *Close Up*'s understanding of black film is thus inextricably, and problematically, linked to the aesthetics and politics of the transition from silent to sound cinema.

In 1931, it was Macpherson who wrote on cinema for that monument to the modernist celebration of the Harlem Renaissance, Nancy Cunard's massive anthology *Negro*. Reflecting on his earlier editorial, he makes the following comment in 'A Negro Film Union – Why Not?':

> In this instance I had seen, perhaps I should say I had been haunted by, a sense of *virility or solidarity of being* which was at once discernible as imperatively Negroid.
>
> And the mind bounced down a long corridor of deduction, rather like an old tennis-ball, making swift if somewhat intangible links of recognition and discovery through old jungle civilisations to the present centralisation of progress in New York's Harlem. It was an odd sensation, fugitive enough but exciting; like a new hope, discerned but not yet described.[19] [italics original]

What Macpherson now envisaged was nothing less than a 'confederated Negro Socialist Cinema':

> Clearly, what would be necessary in the first place would be an Inter-State Academy of Cinema, run on exactly the same principles as the State School of Cinema in Moscow. Here teachers and pupils would work in vibrant, conscious *rapport*, with the exact ethics of social renewal. From this core the ideology and methodology of a truly forensic race polity would be discerned.
>
> How to start such an organisation, apart from instantly perceptible difficulties, remains a leading question, and, in the beginning, Negro students probably would have to study under the few really great – men like Eisenstein, Pudovkin – or, preferably, sit down together, as did the Russians at the beginning with Kuleshov, and work out their own specific formulae on paper, or if obtainable, on film.
>
> In this way would develop the quintessential Negro Cinema, saturated with the unique recognisable and inimitable characteristics of its creators – for apart from what is 'lithe and opulent', as I have called it, and apart from power grown and sustained darkly, inherent in root stock, and apart from the gift which Robert Herring ironically called 'freedom', here historically, socially, humanly, is the deep heart's core of drama.[20]

The notion of a racial cinema as the precondition for an effective universal cinema, however disturbing and perverse it may now seem, was a central tenet of *Close Up*'s modernism. Seen in this light, for example, despair at the mediocrity of British films may indicate less aesthetic snobbery than something like a cultural eugenics.

This often disavowed strand of modernism is evident in the first of the two contributions from the special issue we reprint here. The article by the American Marxist critic Harry A. Potamkin makes an interesting comparison with his defence of French cinema, for that too works with the idea that a native national intelligence should be the catalyst for a distinctively national film style. In contrast, the article by Geraldyn Dismond ('well-known American Negro writer') argues a less essentialist case about film representation, about cinema institutions, and about their possible, limited social consequences.

Vol. I, no. 1   **July 1927**

Kenneth Macpherson

AS IS

Fifty odd years hasn't done so badly in getting an art into the world that fifty more will probably turn into THE art, but now, after somewhat magnificent growth, one feels here is its critical age. Its humble Pier Penny Peep Show beginning is still far too evident, and one sees that in a very short while the thing that people now go to see will have become tradition, and standard, as the past tense in literature, harmony in music, and representative conventions in painting. Public was right enough FOR public when it began by saying 'Films are trash'. They went on being trash, but more pompous trash, and the public took to them. It was all purely box office stunts. Art had nothing to do with it. That was all perfectly alright. I went myself solemnly at the age of nine and watched stockades being burned by Indians in one reel, and although I wasn't sold on what I had gone to look at, I got the mesmerism of the thing, and something quite apart from purely conscious felt, oh yes, this is right, this is apt. This belongs.

The thing was, first of all, to get the medium developed so far as to be FIT for art. Box office stunts meant that one film producer was competing with other film producers, and it was up to them to get in first on anything new, and watch out, and borrow or purloin ideas, to develop and outshine with.

They did this hand over fist for a number of years. And films WERE awful. But they had something to them all the same. Something more than relaxation or dope, or a blurring over of mind, I honestly feel that the people got in some dim way the fact that here was something growing under their eyes, a sense of life and expectancy. They knew better pictures had been painted than anything of their own century, better books written, better plays better acted, better music better composed. Outworn mediums perhaps? Well, the creative thing was still going strong, and here was its channel, of all mediums here was one with fewest limitations. They flocked to the cinemas, not because they particularly cared for somewhat atrocious domestic and wild west dramas, but because of something to do with the old 'will to power'. This was new, and refreshed. Then the novelty wore off, and things looked up a bit. Problems of lighting and photographic quality gave art a bit of a fillip. How bad, those over-lighted interiors and haloes round heroines! But it meant that ideas were struggling. We said thank God when Germany pulled a wry mouth at all of it and blacked out seven eighths of the arc lamps. And so we looked to Germany with expectant eyes. And again our tails wagged. So much of it was again trash, but there was what we called a quality. Morbid, some said. We said not a bit of it, REAL. And there were moments that made us gulp more or less because we felt that if that level could be sustained we would forget to breathe. But it was only a glimpse here and there. The Germanic thing was getting across though, curious details, watchfulness, harking on claustrophobia. We filed Germany for future reference and peeped at Vienna. Here again was tripe. Hollywood was better. Italy a shade worse. France tied up in knots on problems of continuity. While England trundled deplorably in wake, the only thing that could be said for it that it didn't seem to mind being a laughing stock. Then we began to hear from Russia. We had got very sick of Russian novels and Russian plays, and in spite of a recrudescence of Russian influence in art and decoration, there was prejudice. But Potemkin and Aelita put an end to that. Russia was getting its finger on something. And Germany had done Joyless Street, so back we bounced to the Germanic thing. Hollywood gave The Big Parade, Germany, Metropolis, England it seemed was still being comic, and did Mons, while Italy, having done Quo Vadis, churned out the unspeakably atrocious Last Days of Pompei. France had finally somewhat ponderously dished out Victor Hugo and Michel Strogoff, and some perfectly uninspired eighteenth century films more authentic but less suave than Hollywood attempts at the same thing. However it had evolved the best colour process and was hard at work with experimental stuff.

And all this is very roughly, where we have arrived; a fifty fifty pull of good and bad, the time has come to know what it is all about and where it is leading and what one is to expect. Perplexities, debates, arguments. Cinematography has stuck itself in front of the artist, and the artist wants to work his medium straight. His conflict is with the business manager. He also wants HIS medium straight. The thing one sees in consequence is compromise, and the beginning of a problem. As usual there are ways and means, which we will talk about later. I want first of all to cavil a bit in a general way and work in a bit of analysis and criticism.

All this big talk, for instance about an English film revival. It is no good pretending one has any feeling of hope about it. At best it may, IF anything does eventually come of it, as one rather doubts, achieve a sort of penny in the slot success for those who are venturesome enough to back it. And I don't want particularly to be hard on England. Simply as one see it, the sort of thing England is about to begin trying is the sort of thing Hollywood will have to be about to discard if the popularity of the cinema is to remain. England is going to start, not with any new angle, not with any experiment, to go on trundling in wake, not deplorably perhaps, one hopes efficiently, but with a complete acceptance of the film convention as is. The truth is that the average attitude of England and the English to art is so wholly nonchalant and clownish that it is quite useless to expect any art to indigenously flower there. Isolated instances may here and there crop up, but REALLY the Englishman can only be roused to enthusiasm on the football field. A cup final will evoke tens of thousands of whooping maniacs. One doesn't mind that, but in the face of it one does ask WHY attempt art? The preference between the two is so undisputable. One can see that the English revival will be exactly along old lines. They are going to imitate. And unhappily the English thing has neither the *weltgeist* quality of the German nor the exactness of the American, both of which are fundamentally national. I haven't found out quite what the English quality is, but having seen all its principal films I hesitate to try to name it.

After all, what CAN you expect? England cannot even turn out a pepful magazine. Take any weekly, and you get the sort of thing I mean, that hugely sterile flimflam decorously and expensively printed on best quality art paper, and an attitude of really awfully indecent arrogance, especially toward anything new or progressive or intelligent.

None the less, England IS going ahead on this revival, and that its sole purpose is the revival of the film INDUSTRY, and not film ART, is no sin at all, because really good art IS commercial, and the mob has a curious nose for what is good – that is, what is *real*. We know that an announcement 'British Film' outside a movie theatre will chill the hardiest away from its door, and what a pity. Why?

After all, here is England with certain excellent, not to say unsurpassed qualifications for commercial adroitness, in some of its phases, admirable achievement. Turn to films and you get muck. The reason is clear. Where England is efficient you will find there SPECIALISTS. A hard technical training, and long experience back of it. I don't say you won't find specialists in the film industry, at least one expects to now in the face of things, but I do happen to know that any specialists there may have been have probably been living on the dole while the butcher and baker and candlestick maker solemnly were taking matters into their own hands, and making sort of town hall tableaux in a local church bazaar, borrowing sometimes London's worst and ugliest actor to draw the crowd.

And, oh hell, haven't you heard of that wretched alms-begging attitude, 'Poor little England, how can it be expected to stand up to America where there is so much money.' What rot. One hundred pounds will make a film as noble as anything you can wish to see. Money is no excuse. Nothing is any excuse for trying to put over rotten work on the public. The public isn't a pack of fools. Narrow and illiterate very often, but there are distinct limits beyond which one cannot descend, just as there are distinct limits beyond which one cannot AScend if one is out to grab its attention. You cannot trick and cheat your way into its favour. That is what the various butchers, bakers, etc would not learn, and what one feels, more in sorrow than in anger, the industry as a whole has yet to learn before it has a dog's chance. Actually, as things are, no new country can expect to build up an industry on old lines. Mediocrity has been so utterly perfected in Hollywood – mediocrity even flashed across, now and then, with greatness – that it is rather silly to butt in there. Germany has its quality, so has France, Russia might have too, only the Soviet administration has clapped a dog-collar on its chances and tagged it 'Slave to Soviet approval'. The point is HAS England a quality? I am rather afraid the English thing is barren, mind and super-mind and the dimensions (the only things which make for greatness) being so taboo. Oh, it's a mess. And yet one so sincerely wished them well, but there just doesn't seem anything to say. Making their films compulsory would be alright if they had something to show for them, but unless they scour and ransack and snap right up in every branch, it will mean only a needless loss for theatres that after all, are usually sufficiently discerning to choose what they feel will bring in money. Anyhow, va bene.

* * *

Laurels go to Germany. I like the German system quite frequently. I like the women it finds, usually to pass on to an inglorious fame at Hollywood, Greta Garbo, snow and ice and lovely clarity in Joyless Street, Camilla Horn, of Faust, white and terribly young, one felt in spite of everything, quite beyond the medaeval savagery piled with Germanic care of detail upon her, somehow by her loveliness, immune from it. Then Brigette [Brigitte] Helm of Metropolis, again so slender and young, so DIFFERENT. And what a tour de force her ecstatic robot life! And then back to Nju. The mothlike swiftness and slumberous slowness of Elisabeth Bergner. It is this, the finding out of new young people, someone different that gives freshness here. The anti-foreign movement in Hollywood may stop or at any rate considerably check this migration, which was so very good for art, keeping things moving all the time, new talent, new modes, new ways.

Do you remember GREED? Here Von Stroheim carried the German mind to America with the result no American could bear to look at it. Often banal, always dreary, it was so much more than a play, it was life, an amazing quality of realism. And what cynicism. Those dreadful beds with brass knobs, trams seen through upstair windows rattling this way and that over crossings, a common street, always some grimy, daily human thing going on outside, carts, a funeral procession, mean little interiors with cheap curtains across cheap doors, lives pecking and picking like hungry sparrows, awfully aware of turmoil and cross purposes. Repressed unhappy people, awful families doing what awful families do, bank holiday picnics in the suburbs, ceremonial visits, too many ill trained children yowling and quarrelling and being slapped. Hurdy gurdy music. One recognised everything, everything was as everything is. And it was epic, and failed dismally. Then von Stroheim with the same grand cynicism tossed down the Merry Widow in all its clammy eyewash. And of course it was the grand success it deserved to be. I mean because it was the snub of the artist reserving his pearls from swine.

Another of the films that impressed me most was Nju. Here Jannings was not only possible but downright good. It is true in Variété and Faust and Nero he made one ill, but here he was the artist, padding humbly, married. An uncouth person out of an office, simple and bovine and very much in love. A dreadful shilling-shocker story. The young wife falls for the slick young man. Things are found out, there is a grand scene (how grand!) and she leaves. The slick young man turns her down. She jumps into the river. The husband is seen following in wake of feet that too obviously mince! The slick young man is seen standing about in the empty room where the wife had sheltered. An old woman sweeps the floors, ignoring him, sweeps round where he is standing. Presently he goes quite simply out. The old woman turns, goes on sweeping. That is all. But except for some wretched and unnecessary moments where the usual child is lugged in as the usual mediator, and hugged in the usual way by the usual bereaved father, there was a marvellous power to the story. Veidt as the lover, oddly sinister, doing hardly anything. The young wife, very aware, currents beating in the air. Something in the way they stood in rooms, measuring one another, the suggestion of interplay of wills, of muffled nuances. A sense of fatality all the time, Nju should not have made that chilly plunge. She should have been left, perhaps walking in a wet street with leaves, facing her problem. It would have given more intensity to the moment when Veidt stood in the empty room. It is always so much more poignant that things are going on, than that they have ended. In many ways, perhaps this is the best film that has yet been done. It was chronicle not fiction. The child, as I have said, was a mistake, the only stunted note of pathos. For the rest, the story was told without blur or sentimentality, no deliberate pulling at heart strings, one was left to watch, one saw each pitiful side of the question as one does.

* * *

But films like this are rare. Nju might not please the English. I saw it in Vienna this spring, four years old, and had to visit the theatre twice before there was a seat.

Too rare.

It is just possible that D. W. Griffith and myself are talking the same language when we both say the hope of the cinema lies with the amateur. I don't imagine we are. Griffith is frightfully right in some things, but quite undistinguished. Occasionally a transcendental effect, very well done, but no sort of offering to sheer mind. Griffith, however, has been quoted in connection with amateur movie competitions in a very excellent movie paper, but one not dealing with uplift! So we can more or less discount it, since amateurs with an eye to competition in that paper will again do sub-Hollywood stuff, and the best imitation gets the prize.

Besides, it is always a bad incentive, this business of prizes. Since it sells cameras, it brings a different appreciation of sheer photographic effects, it brings one up against totally unforeseen difficulties of technique, and sets the ball of individual effort rolling, but it means in the long run the ruling out of the best. Again it is the competent commonplace that will set the pace.

It has to be the film for the film's sake.

* * *

I want to arrange that people making films, and experimenting in all sorts of ways shall be able to see what others are doing in the same way. Which means public showing, in Paris and London, one hopes. But it is not possible quite yet to arrange this, not until the rapport is established and people coming forward with films and suggestions. A great deal depends upon this rapport, or support. I hope that people enthusiastic over the idea will write, because it seems to me, the thing to do would be to form some sort of society, with definite plans about performances at fixed dates, each chosen film to go the rounds in Paris, London, Berlin, New York, Vienna. This will take time, but one does hope to begin, not too far ahead, with something of the sort. I am going to chew it over during the month, and next month write more fully, as now space is limited. Somehow something must be done to give films their due.

* * *

The first two numbers of Close Up will deal with the film problem as a whole. After that we propose in each issue to deal with special conditions in Europe and the States with numbers on the Negro attitude and problem and on the Far East in their relation to the cinema.

Vol. I, no. 2   **August 1927**

~~~~~~

Oswell Blakeston

BRITISH SOLECISMS

Written by a member of one of the leading British Film Studios, this article contains some inside facts which cannot be disputed. There is no malicious feeling. All who desire good British films must know the kind of thing they are up against as it is only by such knowledge that any success either artistically or commercially can be brought about. (Ed.)

Everyone is talking of a revival of British films.

The phrase is hardly felicitous. Where in the history of British pictures are to be found films with the aesthetic merits of 'Caligari'; 'Warning Shadows'; or 'The Last Laugh'? Rather should we speak of the birth of British films, but that would be too obviously a confession of weakness. If there is genius in a country it is bound to come out, to make itself felt in some way or other. Remember that England was supplying films to America before the war and then realize what a stigma it would be for us, after all these years, to speak of the birth of British films. So we point at dreadful scarecrows of the past and gibber of the revival of British films.

Of course film technique changes. When the Film Society decided to revive Lubitsch's 'Marriage Circle' in London the Committee did not get an opportunity to run the film through till a few hours before the actual performance. They were appalled! What they had thought subtle and witty a few years ago was now slow and heavy. They did their best to remedy the evil by projecting the film much faster than is usual but even then it sadly lacked its pristine brilliance.

Yet making all allowances for old British films not one of them can really be singled out as good. 'The very best British film ever made' recently reached the cutting room prior to revival. It got no further!

The disagreeable fact must be faced that Britain lacks film tradition. What then? Surely if there are no Robinsons, Murneaus [Murnaus], or Lupu Picks, there are at least men who are efficient, men who know their jobs? Surely England can acquire the slick polish that America spreads like treacle over her sentimental bread and butter plots?

Alas not even that!

A film was recently made in England on which the company, who were sponsoring it, had determined to spare no reasonable expense. An enormous set (that is enormous for conservative and timid Britishers) was erected on a big open field. It rained for weeks before the production. The field became sodden and transport almost impossible. The plasterers were held up, the carpenters found it impossible to continue work. Then on the very day that the publicity man had seen fit to give to the paper a glowing panegyric on the wonders of this particular set, and the suitability of the English climate in spite of persistent calumnious statements (oh irony of everything!) a hurricane blew. The ground was rotten, the supports could not hold, and the most important and substantial building collapsed. It was little short of a miracle that no men were killed, for the building was surmounted by massive plaster work. By the time the set was finished overhead expenses had mounted alarmingly. As the producer and some of the artists were under contract the company had been particularly anxious not to keep them idle. So a great deal of the money, instead of going into the production, had been dissipated in overtime for the labourers; who could not, however willing, have given of their best for such tiring long hours. A little foresight and the work might have been started earlier; certainly the same money could have kept the contract artists out of work for months. But now for the climax.

When the shooting began it was found that the pictures were flat. The set had been built the wrong way round! When the sun was in the best position for shooting it was behind the houses! That was not all. The street had been made particularly wide to fit the requirements of the scenario. The producer found that the ordinary crowds, that he had been accustomed to handle with great effect, were lost in the large street. Hundreds more extras were needed. No one had thought of that!

Neither had anyone foreseen that effect of the English climate – and how well they ought to realize that problem by now – in another recent film, this was a story of the orient. What an orient it was! After days of waiting for the sun to shine in tiny intervals some shots were taken by a producer boldened by ennui. The 'rushes' revealed an orient without the languorous atmosphere usually associated with the East, an orient of wildly swinging lanterns and billowing curtains!

While on the subject I might mention, for the benefit of those who have never had to 'stand-by' on a set all day waiting for a ray of reluctant sunshine, how impossibly handicapped England is by her climate. In Hollywood they say that they have twenty-five rainy days in the year! One producer, whom I know, circumvented the English climate in a most delightful manner. He was nine days behind schedule and in danger of the frowns of the powers that be. One night he took the script and blue pencil home with him and cut out half the scenario. The next day he arrived with a beaming face. He was up to schedule! Another example of British methods!

Most British producing companies are in a state of chaos. There is no organization, no centralization, no efficiency. In the art department it is sometimes impossible to obtain such simple materials as crayon or blue paper. The worst example of this policy of meddle and hope that I have met was during the construction of a street scene. The carpenters had been instructed to use as little wood as possible, but they found it necessary to order a small extra quantity. The clerk of works was immediately summoned to the head office. He explained the position and pointed out that the set was to be the principal one in the picture and therefore justified a little additional attention.

After a lot of humming and hawing one of the directors said 'Well, we are not quite sure if we can use this set in the picture.' They had only just started to write the scenario! There may be a lot to be said against the water tight scenarios of Hollywood but ...

Perhaps you cannot blame the companies entirely for the complete lack of initiative in their programmes. They have grown to distrust their producers, and seeing the number of 'duds' gathered in the British industry you cannot be surprised. Our leading

British producer confided in me, in a weak moment, that he directed his pictures with his tongue in his cheek. Another of the star directors might do something big if only he could be persuaded that there are other shots besides close ups. I have seen disconsolate actresses sit on a stool for hours on end while he secured hundreds of feet of 'close up'. The most typical English director I can think of is famed for his work. He has a complicated system of whistles by which he manoeuvres his supers.

I once asked him, 'Don't you ever get muddled with this intricate code of yours?'

'Not a bit old boy', was the answer, 'you see I know that something has to happen each time I blow the whistle, and the boys know that something has to happen. Neither of us knows quite what is to happen and that gives an effect of spontaneity don't you know.'

Much in the same strain was the statement of an art director who told me that he made his models in the hope that they would come out all right. A leap in the dark. If they didn't … he shrugged his shoulders.

There is one word that sums up British production. Haphazard!

'But this is all very well,' you say, 'but what of the fresh blood, what of the youth of the industry?'

To begin with the people now in pictures over here try to keep it a close circle. Each is trying to get his relations in, and oh what a web of petty jealousies!

In this fight money and influence are the determining factors, brains and education dead weights against you. To be branded a high brow is fatal.

I was talking to a youth who had just secured, through influence, a much sought after job on the floor.

'Are you keen on this work?' I enquired.

'Oh! no,' he said, 'you see my father tried to get me into a bank for two years but as I couldn't matriculate I drifted into this. There was nothing else to do without matriculation.'

The English directors of tomorrow!

Vol. I, no. 2   August 1927

〜〜〜〜〜〜〜〜〜〜〜〜〜〜〜〜〜〜〜〜〜〜〜〜〜〜〜〜

Man Ray

EMAK BAKIA

A series of fragments, a cinepoem with a certain optical sequence make up a whole that still remains a fragment. Just as one can much better appreciate the abstract beauty in a fragment of a classic work than in its entirety so this film tries to indicate the essentials in contemporary cinematography. It is not an 'abstract' film nor a story-teller; its reasons for being are its inventions of light-forms and movements, while the more objective parts interrupt the monotony of abstract inventions or serve as

Man Ray's *Emak Bakia* (Vol. I, no. 2, August 1927).

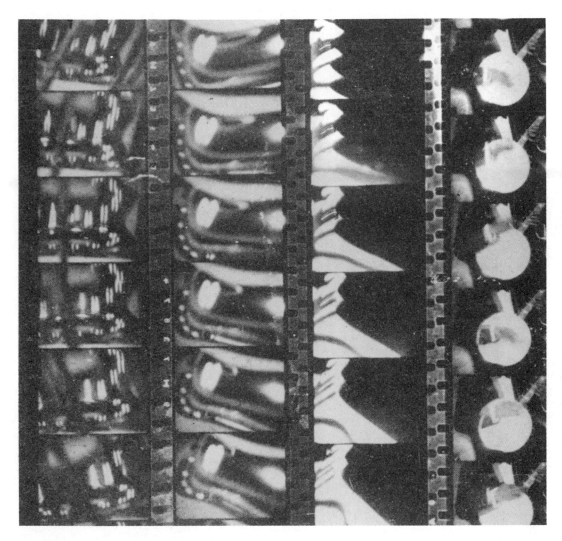

Emak Bakia (*ibid.*).

Emak Bakia (*ibid.*).

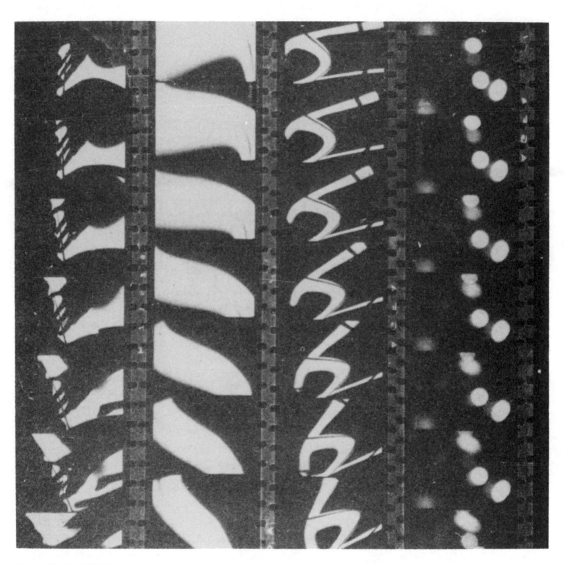

Emak Bakia (*ibid.*).

punctuation. Anyone who can sit through an hour's projection of a film in which sixty per cent of the action passes in and out of doorways and in inaudible conversations, is asked to give twenty minutes of attention to a more or less logical sequence of ideas without any pretension of revolutionizing the film industry. To those who would still question 'the reason for this extravagance' one can simply reply by translating the title *Emak Bakia*, an old Basque expression which means 'don't bother me'.

Vol. II, no. 4   April 1928

Bryher

AN INTERVIEW:
ANITA LOOS

Many telephone calls, many explanations, an appointment. We felt guilty as we waited in the hall (the London correspondent of *Close Up* and myself) knowing well enough how much we should resent ourselves having our few moments of privacy disturbed at an hour when work for the day should be over. But one does for the cinema what one will not do for one's self so we held firmly to our need of seeing Miss Loos if only for a few moments, partly because we wanted first hand information as to modern conditions in Hollywood and partly because Miss Loos being on the governing board of the Film Arts Guild, we hoped she might tell us about its programme and the trend of progress of the little cinema movement in the States. We wanted to meet Miss Loos herself but having very firm ideas on the subject of an author's right to be private, we should not have ventured to insist upon an interview for merely selfish reasons.

The hall of an hotel always suggests some casual sequence in a movie. Boys passed with trays; people chatted in a half dozen different languages. Outside the light was turning from dusk grey to deep blue. It was raining and cold gusts of wind broke into the room every time the door opened. London and Hollywood seemed very widely separated. I remember the ceaseless shooting of movie scenes under stiff palms and children playing, only one path off, too accustomed to seeing cameras to be interested in them any more. And this 'mixed' to the projection room at Neubabelsburg and the lash of surprise when the two lovers in *Jeanne Ney* walked through the rain toward each other. Cinematography taking not a step but a whole aeroplane flight with a single film. And now London and waiting. 'Miss Loos, you know, was one of the movie pioneers.'

We tried to sort our questions out into as concise a form as possible. And as we argued for the necessity of this or that, Miss Loos came suddenly upon us.

Forgetting all text books on 'how to begin an interview' we both began if rather too quickly, with much eagerness.

'Won't you tell us, Miss Loos, something of the present condition of the cinema in Hollywood?'

'You cannot do anything in Hollywood now for if it costs five thousand dollars an hour to make a picture, no single person is going to take that responsibility.'

Five thousand dollars is one thousand pounds. But how can expenses have been run up so tremendously?

'You see they have forced expenses up until nobody can go on. Vast studios exist and often fifty thousand feet of film are taken as a sort of rehearsal. They will photograph enough to make three full length pictures and then say "why, now we'll begin shooting." And that cannot go on. It is not real experiment. It is just chaos, lack of definite plan and wastage. THERE IS ONLY ONE HOPE FOR THE MOVIES AS AN ART AND THAT IS THE SMALL UNIT LEASING A CORNER OF A STUDIO AND MAKING INDIVIDUAL PICTURES. Pictures that are properly planned before they are begun. But Hollywood as it is at present can do nothing else but flop.'

'Are there many small companies working now in America?'

'The hope there is in the quickies. The American meaning of the word is, as it would indicate, a film rushed through in a few days by an independent company. Now one quickie called the BLOOD SHIP has been remarkably successful because it was a marvellous melodrama. It was made independently. But there is one thing that all my experience with the cinema has taught me and that is, that *you cannot keep a good picture down*. Not in the long run though it may have to wait for recognition. But until Americans follow the continental method of renting out studio space and making individual pictures we cannot expect to achieve much progress. But this is coming. It has on a small scale begun already.'

'And are you interested in the cinema experiments of Europe, Miss Loos?'

'The picture I have enjoyed most of recent months has been SHOOTING STARS. But they would not have that in Hollywood because the leading woman is not beautiful. But it is a fine and interesting picture.'

The telephone rang. We realised that we must not over stay our time. (Is anything worse than landing in a foreign country and being asked to give concise statements on questions that require profound study?) Between more calls we asked some necessary questions on the little cinema movement in the States and then as it was almost seven, rose to go.

One had the impression all the time of great vitality and wide interest and one wanted to ask a thousand questions ... not strictly cinematographic. About New York, American literature, America's attitude to Europe. But these must wait for some other, less hurried opportunity. 'May I tell *Close Up* readers, Miss Loos, that you feel the future is with the small film, made experimentally and individually?'

'You may certainly say that as far as my personal opinion is concerned the only hope for the movies as an art is in the small individual company.'

Taking into consideration the fact that Miss Loos has had a long and varied association with cinematography from its early beginnings, having, in her own words, 'grown up with the movies', her opinion cannot but be encouraging to all workers for the art of films, whose efforts, so far, have tended completely toward the line of advancement indicated by Miss Loos. In addition to this, since, doubtless, most *Close Up* readers have a clear conception of how pictures should be made, or, more likely still, a picture in mind which they have never dared to think might ever be made because of the present fabled costs of production, they will certainly find this final sentence full of promise of achievement.

Vol. IV, no. 4   April 1929

~~~~~~

Robert Herring

A NEW CINEMA, MAGIC AND THE AVANT GARDE

We cannot approach to a new cinema unless we understand what is at the bottom of cinema; I try to think that must be a platitude, but I look round and I am forced to believe it isn't, forced by what I see going on and by the bright plans for going on in a just as old and only slightly different way. So let it stand.

By 'new' I do not mean something wild and exotic and altogether inapplicable, but a cinema that is the result of our realising what cinema is, or even of our trying to realise it (that would be something). Such a cinema will be far enough away from all that we have now, all that we put up with, to merit the term New Cinema. There hasn't been much cinema yet, although men have been so busy making films for so long, and there never will be unless the magic of it is realised, just as much as how to use a camera (which isn't) and all the other facts. Magic is a fact itself, one of the hardest. Anything that is real is magical; magic is the name for the thing that is larger than the thing itself, and this larger thing is what makes it real. Another platitude.

I am not going to be called cranky and queer and generally unreliable because I mention magic as part of the rock bottom of cinema. It's not a question of inexpert blah and experimental enthusiasm. Aren't films just too wonderful and look what you can do in them: I do not think it is very useful of M. Auriol to suggest 'Let us conserve the world that exists on the screen as a heaven to which one might perhaps attain – as late as possible, however so as not to risk losing it'. Shots do not matter very much and gay reasoning about states of consciousness, my own as much as anyone else's, is to be distrusted, by myself as much as anyone else. That is all right, as far as it goes, but can't we really, good heavens, get any further? I think of Pyrenee motorists burbling in the lower Basque villages about mountains while their radiator cools down. Interval–chat. All right, perhaps, harmless, why not, still we know all about that. Get on.

But we can't get on unless we keep a firm hold on magic. As that is our foundation, it comes to keeping our feet on the ground. It is surprising that many prefer a tight–rope. The more matter-of-fact you are, the more poetic can you really be. The best gramophones are made by technicians. The third platitude is that the magic of the movies belongs to our age entirely. Part of a larger magic which finds expression in all sorts of other ways in our daily life. Entirely a modern magic, which has been used a long time, but has not till lately been consciously felt and known for what it is. No one needs proof that there is a spell to the cinema, for why else did they go in the old days into halls that just managed to bear up their load of stucco outside because they were almost solid blocks of darkness and disinfectant inside? Why else did we sit in draughts watching stories performed in gales and photographed apparently in rain flicker dizzily and uncertainly before our eyes? It was because something was being satisfied that had not been satisfied before, either because it had not been done or because it had not been done well. It was not due to the novelty, it could not have been, because that wore off and no adequately startling improvements took its place. The films flickered less, the photography grew better and the one projector broke down less regularly. But the actual entertainment offered was very little better and even now if you discount the trappings of plush, velvet and mighty organ, the same kind of solemn insanity and 'sex-charged commonness' is eagerly swallowed ten times for every once that something really worth while is gingerly nibbled at. You cannot claim novelty, you can no longer claim cheapness and you cannot wholeheartedly instance the pictures themselves. Magic remains.

This is what makes sometimes quite intelligent people delight, secretly, in stories they know to be rotten, untrue and the work of pathologicals. And now that they no longer need delight secretly, excuses are offered for this under the name of criticism, but the thing remains the same. It isn't the stories they accept. Get that. It isn't the stories, not the people in them (though occasionally they think so) but it's the way they move among rugs and rooms and now and again not nearly often enough, do real things in real places. Anything that is real, in however small a degree, is magical, in an equivalent degree, and behind even the worst photoplays there is the reality of light and of movement, and so there is a little magic everywhere where you see a cinema. These people respond to the spell. They are not drugged by light, as is so often said. That's wrong. Only half-way. They are stimulated by it and able automatically to discount incident and player without noticing it, and accept instead without knowing it the drama of movement and pattern. Images, if you like, in which it doesn't matter essentially whether it's a woman or a chair there. It's the space they occupy, the light they make manifest by being there. That's what is got. It's abstract.

I mean, fourth platitude, experimental films *aren't* very experimental. They give us just what we give ourselves, nine times out of ten, from any factory-made film. We don't know it, perhaps, because there is so much in the way of our realising it; the well-known dallying with the stage, the talk about good acting, the publicity, the personal contact and the kind of thing which calls *The Mastersingers*, *Love's Awakening* and describes it as a 'Bachelor's bid for a beautiful bride'. That is why the magic must be admitted and understood as any other machine is understood, and worked, and then we shall know where we are, which will be a good thing. It would give us a cinema so different from the dolled-up strumpet (with the usual good heart) that passes under that name, that it would in effect be a New Cinema.

The drama of movement, the fact that light is of all things what we need most and respond to most; they meet in the cinema. But the drama of movement detached, as it

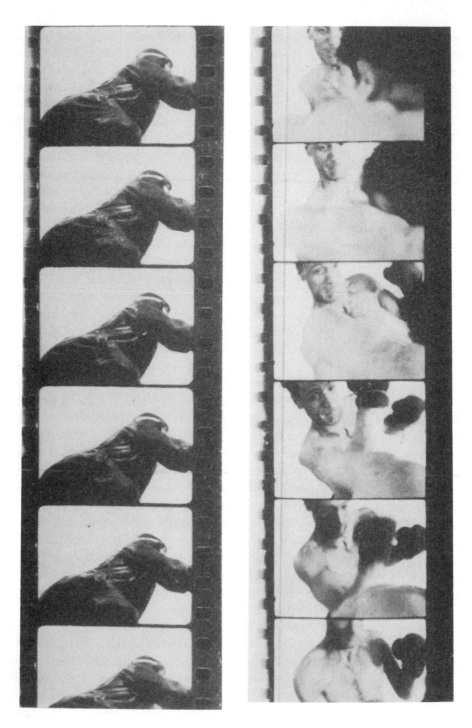

(*Left*) Charles Dekeukeleire's *Impatience* (Vol. V, no. 4, October 1929).
(*Right*) Charles Dekeukeleire's *Combat de Boxe*.

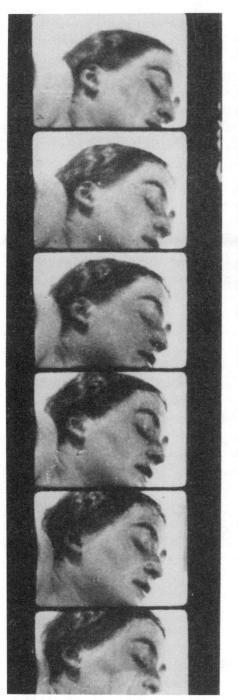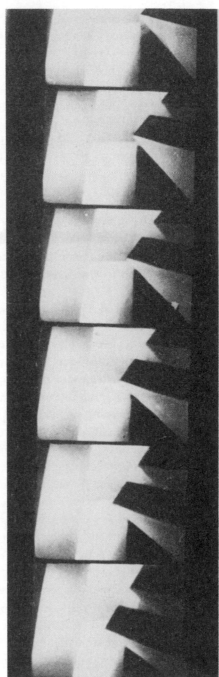

Impatience (Vol. V, no. 4, October 1929).

has to be nine times out of ten, is as nothing to what it might be if it was set going by some decent drama. I don't mean a studio story. Don't care about he loves and she loves so why can't they love. Mean the drama of all around us and what we fit into. Activity. Ordinary business. The most excitingly real dramatic thing I have seen in a movie lately was a few feet in a news-gazette which showed the policemen putting a stop to that bother in a Welsh colliery when the men attacked four blacklegs who were all that answered to the demand for two thousand men to work the mine. There was no 'Are you ready, Miss Glee? One of your eyelids wants a touch, I think'. There was instead the cinema getting right down to behindness of it; the lamp with one touch rubbing away the verdigris and showing the natural jewel. Not a Burma gem.

* * *

Of course you can never get over going to the movies and though that is a different kind of magic, you might look at what happens, to see what it means. Incidentally since this is a variation on a theme of forgotten platitudes, that is the only way to achieve meaning, looking at what does happen, not sighing and making heavens for what doesn't.

There is the screen, and you know the projector is at the back of you. Overhead is the beam of light which links the two. Look up. See it spread out. It is wider and thinner. Its fingers twitch, they spread in blessing or they convulse in terror. They tap you lightly or they drag you in. Magic fingers writing on the wall, and able to become at will (a qualified statement of course, for at whose will?) a sword or an acetylene drill, a plume or waterfall. But most of all they are an Aaron's rod flowering on the wall opposite, black glass and crystal flowers (just the kind of remark that does not help). Only now and again the rod becomes a snake, and whose films are those we know. One strand of the beam widens, a whiter finger detaches itself, goes off over the screen, while the others wait, continue, keep the thing going, confident that it will return. The finger is a cowboy's hat. It went off when he took his hat off and flung it on a table. Or it may be Menjou's shirt front. The smaller ones are hands in gesture and a handkerchief. Now feet are running up steps, the strands move faster, the feet are in a room, only a few strands now busy with them, while the others are demanded by the whole person, to whom the feet belong. You see how it is. These people who saunter so haughtily, who fight for their ends with such abandon, who hail taxis and dismiss servants with one imperious gesture, they are all slaves of that lamp in the projector. They are not really real, really. And if you have met them in the flesh, in studios, you know they are not real there either. They need the lamp to bring them to life and their life is one of movement and light which is not determined by them.

You need not be a chamber to be haunted, nor need you own the Roxy to let loose the spirit of cinema on yourself. You can hire or buy or get on the easy system, a projector. You then have, on the occasions on which it works, people walking on your own opposite wall. By moving your fingers before the beam, you interrupt them; by walking before it your body absorbs them. You hold them, you can let them go. When the projector stops, they stop. Their life is suspended, and can be begun again at any point. They are always potentially there, ready to be let out, all kinds of people doing the most fascinating things, saying how do you do and putting on a garden hat and rescuing each other and sweeping floors and kissing when they feel like it and the maker of the film lets them ... and as of course, popular taste, as reflected in the box office, demands. They are at your command, all the actions of life. At the moment they can only live again on the opposite wall, but that is not inevitable. If this magic is realised, it works hand in hand with the hard facts of how to get them by your camera, what to do, how to, what films are. What cinema is.

* * *

Supposing you know it. You have studied it. You are earnest and honest, though heaven forbid you should think you are and know it. But you have something to make and if you can't make it you will be pent-up and miserable and of course a public danger. What are you? What is your work? Avant-garde? No. You have made a bit towards the new, the real Cinema, but your's is not what avant-garde is, now. That's the pity. They stand out against commercialism, but the New Cinema won't come from them. I watch the avant-garde and I can't see where it's avant-ness lies. Cinema's more than tricks and the raising of *natures-mortes* to Lazarus life. More than the expression of an egg whisk and two toast racks, even if the racks and the whisk aren't really that or those. You can find the superficials of avant-gardisme in any commercially-sound Hollywood production. In the opening of *The Last Warning* and in the middle of *Manhattan Cocktail*. You find all there is to it and the something more (which is magic) in *Mother* and *Secrets of Nature* (Russian and British), and that something more is the thing that's cinema. I don't see what the avant-garde is in front of. If you are busy marching forward, an die Brücke, you are not so conscious of those others you are better than that the word 'avant' implies. You are simply aware of the enormous distance you are from your goal. Let's experiment, let's not rust in a rut, but let's not side-step out of development.

Even of its kind it doesn't seem to me to have done what its name implies. There ought to be a film of the life of a slot machine; that is something. What we get is the life of a twopenny-tube ticket, which is precisely the same as a passage of selected prose I read at school about the adventures of an ingot. There ought to be a mass-film of typists. The nearest we get isn't even avant, but naïve *Crowd*. There ought to be a film of a modern population living in a city unsuited to them and trying to make it a modern city. There ought to be this final thing I am suggesting. First, all the Woolworth curios should be thrown out and anyone who thinks he is en avant must measure himself by this, because the avant people of the cinema are the technicians, just as the real modernity of architecture is due to engineers and not to architects. Cinema among other things is architecture in time.

Now. We know sound waves can be caught on wax. The human voice recorded. Up till now, it has only been possible to reproduce it. That is very thrilling of course, that the noise made by a person some time ago can be let out again later, it is doing things with time. But it remains reproduction. You can't get voice pure, but reproduced voice. But suppose there is a machine which really lets the living voice itself out into the room. That is not so odd. Voice originally comes from one kind of mechanism, it can be caught by another (for recording is in advance of reproduction), then suppose it can be let out again just as purely as from its first source. That is not so very wild. But it is avant enough, and it gets somewhere. Up till now gramophones have only given us the likeness of a voice. Soon they will give us the actual thing. That means a voice is held over from time. Telescopes and other machines bridge space; it is not impossible to bridge time. We have films of things with people moving in incidents already past. Light waves those are, it could be done with sound waves, for sound can be transformed into light. Now, we have been able to detach and keep a person's voice. That is, the vibrations he makes when he does certain things with his mouth, tongue, breath, etc. Could not the avant people, the real ones, do the same with the visual image? Can we not see people as we shall soon hear them? At present there is the screen and gramophone. But the gramophone will soon cease to insist itself any more than the person's presence detracts from the voice. If the voice can leave this machine, as I know it can, and be itself, why should not the visual image leave the screen, why should we not do without screens? They are giving stereoscopy to the images, giving them depth and solidity. They will be able to be brought into the room, as the voice is. It is after all, absurd to be tied down to a screen. There was a time when one was tied down to a canvas on which only static things could be represented. Before that, man could keep nothing of himself. Little by little that has been changed.

First what he did can survive, now what he is. First the work of his hands, work of brain, the effects of his hands and brain. But all still and mute. Then his voice could be kept, and his image could be kept. Moving. Now they will have to be detached, and instead of him contenting himself with making dolls and statues and music he could only hear as it was being played, he will have these images in which sound and sight meet, detached so to speak from their owners. Man making man, of a kind. Isn't this more logical than men of steel? These won't be let loose. They'll be created just as tunes and films are created and composed. A man's voice only records what he or the song demands. It is not all for him, and he is not all of it. It is the bit taken up and used; what side of them is brought out varies with different directors. Each brings out the aspect he wants. The people don't have much to do with it. Their image is what is wanted, and it is detached in the form and relation to other images that are wanted. These move on the screen. So far they have no solidity, but they will have. They used to have no voice, but [now] they have. So far, it is reproduced voice, but soon it will be voice. There is logically – and of course that is not the only way so there is 'but there is logically' – no reason why he should not ultimately create himself in motion and speech, moving in the patterns of his creation, just as he made the best he could when he made dolls like himself, etc. and *only* doing that. Things queerer, if one had been in at the beginning, have happened, and in any case this is the kind of tack the avants ought to be on, instead of triple-exposing their washing to the moon.

* * *

It would be thrilling to draw the rest of one's life out as the grandson of one's great-grandson's son, to see what is happening, but that is not yet possible. We can at least make things interesting for them and let them get on instead of having to disentangle, by ceasing to be so silly about the cinema. We really might discover what it is, and that would be quite a good piece of work. It would do so much more good than being so damned serious, to consider just one or two plain facts, and think on them. It really is time we had a bit more cinema. A bit less quackery, a bit more appreciation of magic which is not cameratricks in black and white.

Vol. V, no. 1   July 1929

Harry A. Potamkin

THE FRENCH CINEMA

Jean Lenauer, writing in the May *Close Up*, has said some true things which, because they are not qualified, are dangerous. To say, for instance, that to him the French have no sense of the cinema is no light charge, and, one may counter with one of two remarks: this is a prejudice and not a critical judgement, or the question, a sense of what cinema? For M. Lenauer, like his young French colleagues, is all for the American cinema. It is true that he charges the French directors with apeing the American successes, but from every indication his cinema-mind has been formed by the U.S.A movie. He is in this a European and particularly a Frenchman, although his nativity is Viennese. Like the young Frenchmen, he claims the movie as his and only his, and to have been born before the film or with it – as in my own case – is to be put beyond the pale. The young Frenchman delights in saying the French are without a cinema-sense. Lenauer has in the May *Close Up* only repeated M. Auriol in transition No. 15, M. Charensol in La Revue Federaliste of November, 1927, and the first utterer of this condemnation, the late Louis Delluc. There are a host of others. In truth, the young Frenchman is developing a defeatist mind, and Lenauer is throwing on his little pressure.

One of the slogans of the French counter-French critic is the denial of youth in the French cinema world. Everyone I have met has complained of this, and Cavalcanti was glad to have even an inane actress in *Captain Fracasse* because she was young. Youth! Youth! It is a perennial cry. And what does it here signify? What does Youth claim in this instance? That the cinema belongs to it. And how does it substantiate its claim? By repeating the attitudes of the Frenchmen who first began to swear fidelity to the film. Auriol utters Soupault's adorations of the American action–film. And everyone of them echoes Canudo. Except that, typical of youth of all ages, these youngest Frenchmen are rebelling against the old cinema – of France. The Revolt of Youth? Nonsense. The Rebellion of Youth! Impatience and arrogance mostly. There is little development here in France of that salutary skepticism among intelligent young men which included in its scrutinies Youth. For Youth is not a fact, it is a symbol and that symbol has no reference to the date of one's birth. It is true that art and youth are related, but it is not the youth of which Lenauer talks, but youth which means fervor. Will Lenauer say that the older Frenchmen whom he condemns are all without fervor? And am I, are we, to deny sincerity and depth of devotion to the film to all those who do not love the

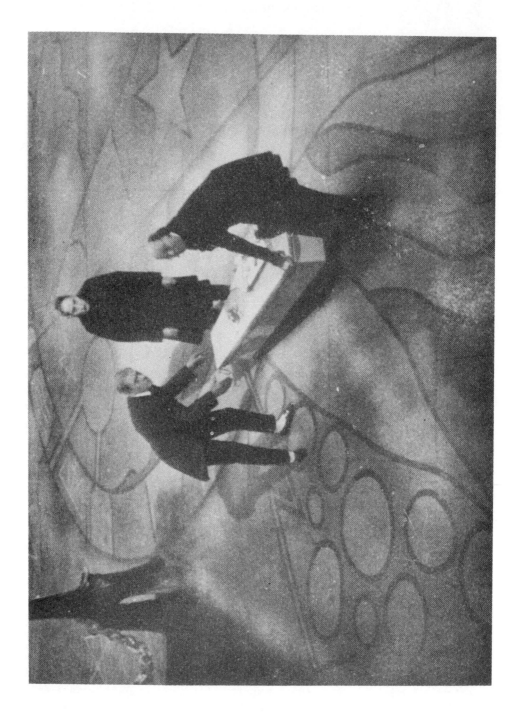

Jean Epstein's *The
Fall of the House of
Usher* (Vol. V, no. 3,
September 1929).

*The Fall of the House
of Usher (ibid.).*

film in the way Lenauer says he loves it? And just how does he love it? Is it a sign of love
to condemn all who challenge the beloved? That is chivalry in the wrong category. And
just when did Lenauer begin to love the film? Of course these questions are not for
M. Lenauer himself.[1] Nor do I ask for an answer. These questions contain certain
implications:

    I.   The cinema was not born with the motion picture. It has its origins in the first
experiences of mankind, and its sources are all the manifestations of life.

    II.   To care for the film only may be a good way to a career but it is certainly no
assurance that the film will be enriched. Creation in one art, or activity in one
profession, does not, even in this age of specialization, bar one from another art or
another profession.

    The cult of youth has produced some interested conditions in the French cinema.
There is no differentiation here between the amateur and the professional. And this is
bad for the amateur, the beginner. The group of young men which included Auriol
and Lenauer will agree that what I say about the inflation of the amateur is true, but
they will not agree that they are contributing to the very condition they mock. If there
is snobbism in France, and there is, they are strengthening it by their attitude, and one
of them is youth. Any number of youngsters (some of older age) put out a film deriving
rudimentarily from *Rien que les Heures* (without full awareness of the principle) or
Berlin and enter the ranks of the *metteurs en scene*, with the footnote: forgive the
transgressions, they are young and they had no money. To produce a film without
money always excites the professional (or better commercial) world, but it should mean
nothing to the beginner – that's just how he should begin, and moreover, why should
his first work be made public? In America we distinguish between the amateur and the
professional, and that is the amateur's salvation. It is a part of the discipline of any
artist to 'be rejected' or to be ignored – that he may learn how really insignificant his
infant labors are. If youth is not favoured in the large French companies, its favor in the
specialized halls is certainly less creditable.

    If the young Frenchmen really cares about the French film, he will not heed the cry
of defeat (which is really a self-inflation) but will examine the French film to learn the
French idiom, which must be his. That the American film, by its very remoteness from
his own physical experience, enchants him is not enough reason for him to mistake that
enchantment for the complete and sole experience of cinema. If he really loves the film,
he will not show it by talk upon the influence of the movie on customs, such as gum-
chewing, to which he is an addict, or physical gestures after James Murray or George
Bancroft. Nor will he show it by damning the French girl for Joan Crawford or Louise
Brooks. Nor by an ignorance of the past of the American film, which he so much idolizes.
Nor by limiting motion to antic, action, speed. Nor by finding Victor MacLaglen a great
artist, whereas that lucky Irishman has a constant (hence non-artistic) personality no
matter what the film. Nor by denying the meritorious Catherine Hessling because she
casually recalls Mae Murray. He will stop chattering and go to work. He will discipline
himself and question his enthusiasms, or at least examine them to know where to put
them. AND HE WILL STUDY THE FRENCH INTELLIGENCE IN ITS
EXPRESSION IN THE FRENCH FILM, whether he likes its makers or not. His
head is now stuffed with American idioms, but he will need to be re-born an American

before he will make an integral film of them. The Frenchman remains a provincial all his life.

To remain a provincial is no limitation to an artist. The Frenchman's Frenchness has been one of the chief reasons for his cultural and aesthetic survival amid influences that should have long destroyed or reduced him. He creates within his own boundaries. Nowhere is this condition more apprehendable than in the cinema. The French mind shows itself constantly in the success and the failure.

The French mind is, first, a pictorial mind. The French cinematist is pictorial-minded. He is not in the least, as is the American, action-minded. This is as noticeable in the old serial thrillers, whose idiom is action, as in the absolute films of the avant-garde. Nor is the pictorial mind counter-cinema. Nothing is counter-cinema. *And no people are incapable of making films.* The task is to use the mind where it can legitimately function. It cannot function in police films: do not attempt police films. It functions in documentaries, films of restricted areas, films psychological and metaphysical, etc.: set it to work in these milieus. The pictorial mind can be set to work badly or well. It is daily perceived in the 'grand' French films where it is resultant in a tedious, over-adorned spectacle like *Koenigsmark*. The pictorial mind does not lend itself very easily to 'big' films. Action alone makes these supportable. That is one reason why the French cannot compete commercially with America. But the cinema is not justified by commerce, no more than Balzac's right to exist is determined by the public taste for Dekobra.

The pictorial mind succeeds best when it functions independently within limited areas. Germaine Dulac does a fascinating film in *The Sea-Shell and the Clergyman* and a charming film in *Mme. Beudet*, but when she turns to do a 'large-scale' film she puts out the sentimental 'poesie' of *The Folly of the Valiant*. 'Poesie' is the pictorial mind forced to extend itself out of its non-literary milieu. Gance is full of 'poesie'. He belongs to the France of Rodin, and with Poirier, to the France of Lamartine and Hugo without their vision. The best instance of the pictorial mind rightly applied is Jean Epstein. He insists upon the image, lingers over it, penetrates it. What does it matter that *Finis Terrae* is slow? What does it mean that it does not satisfy those who wanted the subject treated *physically* instead of *psychically*? Epstein has shown how the physical material may be rendered psychical by persisting in the examination of the physical image. The pictorial mind here transcends itself.

It is in keeping with the pictorial mind that the French has made so much of the term 'photogenic,' that Germaine Dulac indefatigably urges the *film visuel* as against the *film anti-visuel*. It is right that Man Ray should have found his centre in Paris, and that the best short, non-narrative films should come from France: *The Octopus* of Jean Painleve as well as that early nature study, *The Germination of Plants*, *The Zone* of Georges Lacombe, *La P'tite Lily* of Cavalcanti ...

This leads to a second deduction, the source of the French film is in the traditional *atelier* of French art. It is true, in the main, that the film dependent upon collective labors has a hard row in France (but, from another point of view, does it have such a good time in America?).[2] This is not irremediable. My deduction is not, however, made from negative conditions but conditions which are organic and positive. All that I have said before leads to the deduction, and the most interesting films are those made from the *atelier*, single-artist viewpoint. This does not infer that the French film must rest in the *atelier*, as the pictorial mind does not infer that the French film must remain in the framed set. Not in the least. The instances of *Finis Terrae, En Rade, Two Timid Souls* are sufficient to gainsay such inferences. Yet these films are films with their sources in the *atelier*-mind and the pictorial-mind. With Epstein the *atelier* becomes the study, for speculation and metaphysics. *En Rade* is the pictorial mind providing an enveloping environment. *Two Timid Souls* is evidence of the pictorial mind creating comic rhetoric of the picture. Comedy in America is action. The gag in *Two Timid Souls* is a pictorial gag, in Harold Lloyd it is the antic gag. Chaplin makes very little of the picture.

The *atelier*-source does not (the word 'source' is the explanation) limit the French film to the laboratory where Jean Lenauer confines it, although the experimental film will always be a French contribution. Nor does it restrict the film to its absolute forms. It means simply that the film companies must recognize the *mind* of the French artist and work according to it. The Société Générale des Films promised to be just that sort of corporation, allowing the director, and not the fiscal policy, to set the pace. At present the Société Générale seems to be biding its time amid the confusion caused by the talking picture. But its single-film policy is the accurate one for the French cinema. For that cinema, because of the characteristics detectable in it (which I have considered above) will not be a world's popular cinema, and no *contingement* can make it that. In fact, the French have not, in their entertainment, the gift of the popular, whether in the revue, the vaudeville show or the motion picture.

The French need to be vigilant against two related faults: sentimentality and refinement. The French sentimentality is not moral sentimentality, as in the case of the English and the American, but aesthetic sentimentality.[3] It is present in almost every French film, but where it is held within the boundaries of each instance it aids rather than oppresses the film. It is sensitivity in *The Sea-Shell and the Clergyman* of Germaine Dulac, and in her *Cinegraphic Study upon an Arabesque*; it is sensitivity bordering on collapse in *En Rade*; it is sensitivity avoiding collapse by larger references in Epstein; it is a diffusive and soft sentimentality in Poirier and Gance. Leon Poirier has made beautiful documents in *The Black Journey* and the second part of *Exotic Loves* where the image is the end, but in *Verdun* and *Jocelyn*, where the image refers to its sources in national and literary experience, he offends with his superfluous stresses of sentiment, and that is sentimentality, or one form of it. Gance continually associates his image with some 'poetic' phrase: Violin and the lily, Napoleon and the eagle (in *Napoleon*), 'the rose of the rail' (in *The Wheel*). And both enjoy the sur-impressed symbol: The Spirit of France. I have said Gance was Hugo without Hugo's vision. That makes him the counterpart in cinema of Eugene Sue. The French 'big' film is eighteenth-century romanticism. In that it is very much the France of to-day. Eighteenth- and nineteenth-century romanticism.

Of this ilk is the recently sponsored humanitarianism of the French film. Another sentimentalism. For an inclusive humanitarianism is not in keeping with the French temperament of non-projection and dispassion. Therefore it is frequently false, particularly when uttered by those who find in the slogan profit. M. Tedesco hails the 'new humanitarianism' of the American film, finding that sympathy in films like *The*

Crowd, *Lonesome*, *Underworld*, *A Girl in Every Port*, etc. I shall not here go into any examination of the American films. But to discover one's human experience at this level of cinema content, indicates that the discovery is hardly profound. This acceptance of American 'human interest' films as human experience accords with the frequent French declaration that the movie is not an art. This is the Frenchman's justification of his affections. The whole matter of art is resolved in the levels of experience. The level at which the matter of life is experienced, determines the category of art or non-art.

The dispassion of the French keeps them, on the whole, more rational towards the love-life than other peoples. Therefore the Frenchman who declared against the need for Freud was not so much in error as Lenauer implies. But this dispassion does make it difficult for the French to project themselves into the loves of a less indifferent, more passionate people. But to say that they never project themselves into such lives is to forget that the French have been the most persistent admirers of the Swedish film, the only fully realized passionate pictures. Here I think French critical rationality recognizes the level of tragic experience at which the Swedes have conceived their films. I do not like the way in which *Sunrise* was received by the French multitudes, but I must admit that the level at which it was conceived, sustained though it was throughout the enfoldment of the narrative, was a level at which it might just as easily have been rejected. For the material may have attained to the tragic, in the German conception it reached only pathos, and pathos is not far from sentimentality, emotional sentimentality. (I say all this despite my admiration of the film and its director.) The French reject emotional sentimentality, but they accept decorative sentimentality.

There have been a few French instances of *approximative* tragedy in the cinema, and those few instances indicate a milieu which the French have not nearly begun to exploit. I refer at this moment to the domestic tragedy, which provides immediate activity for all the French qualities of provincialism, limited locale, pictorial-minded. The film that first comes to my mind is *Poil de Carotte* of Julien Duvivier (with continuity, I am advised, by Jacques Feyder). The film was poignant and convincing and in every particular French. *Therese Raquin* belongs to the French acceptation, despite the pronounced German qualities of the exterior lighting and the acting of the two male players. (Feydor, a Belgian, is assimilative.) The French, if they but knew, would do the domestic film. Dulac gave us *Mme. Beudet*, sensitive in its irony carried pictorially. Nine years ago Albert Dieudonné made *Une Vie sans Joie* (called *Backbiters* in England) and had he ceased where the tale demanded, he would have presented to a sympathetic audience a tragic idyll. Instead he continued the film into the episode of the runaway tramway, where it looked very much like a take-off of an old French tinted film of a locomotive's dash. Jean Benoit-Lévy and Marie Epstein have recently produced *Peau de Pêche*. It is a melange of many themes expressed in the images and the captions. But amid this melange one detects certain promises: in the images of both the city and the country, in the characterization of the chum of Peach-Skin, and in one episode which should have been the film. The little stream which is the sustenance of the neighbourhood runs dry. The peasants have assembled to hear the radio of one of their neighbors. While they listen a cry comes from one of the lads: 'The river is back!' An old man says: 'Of what importance is the world to us now? We have a river back.' A monumental theme expressed in the area of a small village in the provinces. A theme that obscures the entire film. A theme that indicates a possible point toward which the French film can strive. It is a theme for Jean Epstein.

Jean Epstein is an artist the rest of the French directors might study with profit. He is, although, I believe, a Jew, born in Poland, French in his virtues and his faults. His faults are almost always rendered virtuous by an all-inclusive mind which is not far removed from French sentimentalism, but which, by nobler intention and speculation, becomes mysticism. Epstein deals with inferences, the inferences of the penetrated image. His film, *Finis Terrae* is, I think, of highest significance to France. I can indicate some errors, like the shifting of the point of view from the boys and their mothers to the doctor, but they do not contradict the contribution. The film is entirely pictorial-minded. It takes the natives as it finds them and builds the image of their stolid movements. I detect in this, not the snobbery Lenauer finds, but relevant intelligence. However, I do not intend speaking upon Epstein here. I reserve that for a paper wholly upon him. I wish only to indicate that here is one source for the French cinema.

And what will the French film take from *Joan of Arc*? Its perfection does not mean that it does not contain the germ of propagation. It too is built of the image. True it was done by a Scandinavian. But it was done with French material and its method offers an opportunity for the French intelligence. Another source – and this is one out of the boundaries of France – is the Swedish film of the days of Sjöstrom and Stiller. The American film, whose 'technique' so infatuates the French mind, is not a source for that mind.

Sources: that is the first investigation every artist should make. I have dwelt upon the systemic sources for the French cinema. But, since the cinema, no more than any other art, is isolated, it will find its sources, not only in itself, nor the mind immediately referring to it, but also in the other aesthetic articulations. Dreyer went to the medieval French miniature for a source to embolden the imagery, and hence the drama, of *Joan*. The French theatre is full of sources of identical mind with the French cinema mind: take Gaston Baty's production of Molière's The Imaginary Invalid. The pictorial mind dominates. The French *cineaste* must cease his absolutes of non-accord between the theatre and the cinema. He must look into all his experience and expressions to discover himself. He must believe he can create cinema, if he is faithful to his own intelligence, intuition and experience.

NOTES

1. I am not, it is self-evident, directing my words against M. Lenauer. I am thinking of all the lovers of the cinema who cry their love aloud. I know too many parallel instances in America to be convinced too readily by the declaration: 'I love the cinema.' The American enthusiasts of 1923 – and now – were superior to the film only a few years before their discovery of it as 'art'. Their interest came only as a consequence of popular enthusiasm, and an urge to be of the time. But no critical affection is worth anything unless it has grown from the visceral pleasures of childhood. Are the young Frenchmen, and young Europeans, experiencing a belated childhood? (I dwell upon the American phenomenon in an article, French Opinion and the American Movie, appearing in Du Cinema.)

2. The collective difficulty in France is mainly the natural indifference of the French working man, and the financial closeness of the producer. As for the major collectivity between the artists, I think, on the whole, a better *esprit* exists in France than in America. And as for the intrusion of the mercantilists into the enterprise of the author, what grosser instance than that of Hollywood?

3. A signal instance of refinement applied wrongly is Renoir's *The Little Match-Girl*, where the operetta-Russian Ballet (which is really French in its mincingness) decorative sense was exercised upon a Danish folk-theme. Decorative refinement is one of the main obstacles to the creation of a French cinema comedy.

Vol. V, no. 2   August 1929

Harry A. Potamkin

THE AFRAMERICAN CINEMA

The negro is not new to the American film. The late Bert Williams appeared in a film before the war. But this did not get very considerable circulation due to Southern antagonism. It was the film of the Johnson–Jeffries fight that thrust the negro out of films and created the interstate commerce edict against fight films. Sigmund Lubin produced all-negro comedies in Philadelphia before the war. The negroes themselves have been producing pictures on the New Jersey lots, deserted by the white firms that migrated to California. These companies have starred actors like Paul Robeson and Charles Gilpin in white melodramas like *Ten Nights in a Barroom*. White impersonations of negroes have been very frequent, either in farces or in the perennial *Uncle Tom's Cabin*. Negro children have in the last years been appearing in such slapstick films as Hal Roach perpetrates with his tedious and unconvincing Gang. The treatment of Farina is typical of the theatrical (variety and film) acceptation of the negro as clown, clodhopper or scarecrow, an acceptation which is also social. No objections have been raised by the solid South to Farina's mistreatment by white children (to me a constantly offensive falsehood and unpardonable treachery of the director), nor to Tom Wilson's nigger-clowning.

The present vogue for negro films was inevitable. The film trails behind literature and stage for subject-matter. There has been a negro vogue since the spirituals were given their just place in popular attention. Many negro mediocrities have ridden to glory on this fad. Many white dabblers have attained fame by its exploitation. The new negro was suddenly born with it. Cullen and Hughes were crowned poets, but Jean Toomer, a great artist among the negroes, has not yet been publicly acclaimed. He first appeared before the hullabaloo was begun. The theatre took the negro up. First Gilpin and eventually came *Porgy*. Now the film. Sound has made the negro the 'big thing' of the film-moment.

Of course, the first negro film in the revival had to be *Uncle Tom's Cabin*. I praise in it the gaiety of the first part and the friendly, unsupercilious treatment of the negro and the general goodwill of the actors. I condemn in it the perpetuation of the clap-trap sentimentality. This is not the day to take Harriet Beecher Stowe too seriously. *Uncle Tom's Cabin* should have been produced as folk-composition, or better not at all. It is not important as matter or film. Sound is bringing the negro in with a sort of Eastman Johnson-Stephen Foster-Kentucky Jubilee genre, or with the Octavus Roy Cohen-Hugh Wiley crowd satisfiers, where the negro is still the nigger-clown, shrewd sometimes and butt always. And Vidor's *Hallelujah* with a good-looking yaller girl. As for me, I shall be assured of the white man's sincerity when he gives me a blue nigger. I want one as rich as the negroes in Poirier's documents of Africa. I am not interested primarily in verbal humor, in clowning nor in sociology. I want cinema and I want cinema at its source. To be at its source, cinema must get at the source of its content.

The negro is plastically interesting only when the makers of the films know thoroughly the treatment of the negro structure in the African plastic, when they know of the treatment of his movements in the ritual dances, like the dance of the circumcision, the Ganza. In Ingram's *The Garden of Allah* the only good moment was the facial dance of the negro performer.

The cinema, through its workers, has been content to remain ignorant. It might have saved itself a great deal of trouble and many failures and much time had he studied the experience of the other arts. Well, what can the negro cinema learn from The White Man's Negro and The Black Man's Negro in art, in literature, in theatre?

Graphic art: The Greek and Roman sculptors of black boys were defeated because they did not study the structure of the faces. In modern art, there is Georg Kolbe's fine *Kneeling Negro*. There are Annette Rosenshine's heads of Robeson and Florence Mills – elastic, lusty miniatures. And there is the vapid, external, gilded negro by Jesper in the Musée du Congo, Tervueren, Belgium. Compare. If you want to see how a principle can be transferred and reconverted, see what the late Raymond Duchamp-Villon learned from African sculpture. Relaxation among angles. Study Modigliani for transference to another medium. In painting examine Jules Pascin's painting of a mulatto girl and Pierre Bonnard's more stolid negro. But always the source: the sculpture of the Congo, the Ivory Coast, the Gold Coast, the bronzes of Benin, the friezes of Dahomy. Observe their relation to the actual African body, coiffure, etc., to the dance. What do you deduce?

Literature: In America I know of but one white man's novel that has recognized the negro as a human esthetic problem – which he must be to the artist - and not either a bald bit of sociology or something to display. I refer to Waldo Frank's *Holiday*. This eloquent though monotoned book is not a bare or ornamental statement of the inter-race. Its concern is not with the culmination of the tragedy in the lynching, but with the relationships involved. The horror and the sacrifice of the lynching are certainly unavoidable, but greater and above these are the relationships, and the denial of the beauty of these relationships by the final mob act. This is the one book I know of that has recognized the entirety as ultimately human relationship, which determines the aesthetic unity. There is not in this book the ethnographical–archaeological–sociological preoccupation that obscures the major motif in the other books. This is a novel, it is art, it is distillation, condensation, purity. Shands, Stribling, Peterkin, Van Vechten all strive to reveal their intimacy with the details of life and vocabulary of the strange folk they present. Shand's *Black and White* and Stribling's *Birthright* do free the central motif from a number of these interferences, leaving a clearer path to the culmination. But the motif should determine the book, which it does not in either case. Peterkin wishes to be genuine (but to be genuine is not to be unselective) and sympathetic and impartial. This makes her work a less questionable enterprise than Van Vechten's *Nigger Heaven*, the conscience of which must be severely doubted. *Black April* is better than *Green Thursday*. The former obscures the relevant data with data on folk-idiosyncrasies. It is the artist's business to evaluate the relevant data that he may be better able to know its potentialities, and not to record every detail contributing to the formation of that material. *Green Thursday* indicated no sense of the potential materials, their convertibility and relevant form. They were dark waters poured into

Director King
Vidor on the set of
Hallelujah (Vol.IV,
no. 4, April 1929).

Stepin Fetchit as
'High Pockets' in
John M. Stahl's *In
Old Kentucky*
(MGM) (Vol. V, no.
2, August 1929).

Hamlin Garland jugs or Mary Wilkins-Freeman ewers, taking the form and conveyance of the receptacles.

Theatre: the film may find instructive analogies and sources in three plays: *Earth* by Em Jo Basshe, *Porgy* by the Heywards and *The Emperor Jones* by Eugene O'Neill. *Earth* is an instance of a play with a concept in its theme, but no recognition of that concept perceptible in the language or human-arrangement of the play. The theme was meant to articulate the struggle with the negro between paganism and Christianity. Instead it is a struggle of personalities we witness. The theme indicates what the negro film promises in the way of experience, when the philosophic cinematist will be present. *Porgy* is more immediate indication. It lacks all concept. It lacks significant intention. It lacks a valuable narrative. Its tale is that of Culbertson's *Goat Alley* and the old white melodrama – the wicked man, the lured girl, happy dust, the cripple, sacrifice, vengeance. But its virtue is folk, always a good source. It has caught the folk in its rhythm and whatever idea the play possesses is in this rhythm. This 'rhythm as idea' makes of it a better play than Torrence's *Granny Maumee*, in spite of the latter's effort to convince us of folk authenticity. The tragedy of *Porgy* is no more important than the tragedy of *Goat Alley*. It is rendered more poignant simply because it has taken place in a folk-structure to whose rhythm the individual participants contribute. That is why the character of the crab-vendor, suggested by one of the actors and inserted into the completed play, does not obtrude. It is of the total folk-structure and easily finds its place in it. In the Theatre Guild production the play failed as a rhythmic unit, leaving us to enjoy, not the entity, but the details. This may be due somewhat to breaks in the authors' construction. The authors and the director failed to sustain the rhythmic counterplay between Crown's sacrilege and the Negroes' religion in the hurricane scene. This was a play meant to be produced not mimetically but choreographically, and moreover – as folk – to be stylized. It laid too much stress on a bad story, the songs were not intervalled with precision, and – most serious of faults – the diction was stereotype. This last, of course, has nothing to do with the production, it is the authors' weakness. The authors confess they did not take advantage of the original Gullah dialect because it would be incomprehensible to an audience not familiar with it. Should Synge have avoided the Gaelic on the same score? Synge exploited, and converted the difficult speech, suiting it to the language of his audience, which was his language-medium, and attained thereby a tremendous eloquence. Any author, intuitively gifted and philologically and rhythmically aware, could go to the documents and records of a Gonzales, a Bennett or a Reed Smith and re-create a diction at once original, relevant, convincing – and comprehensible. Yet Peterkin and the Heywards, operating in the very environment of the dialect, could do nothing with it but run away from it. These immediately foregoing words are full of meaning to the negro film with speech.

Coming to the negro talkie, we can find no more complete entrance than by way of *The Emperor Jones*. In itself *The Emperor Jones* is not particularly negro. One may question the thesis of atavism which runs through it, as one may easily deny the too patient psychology. But it is excellent theatre, a theatre of concurrent and joining devices. It is, in fact, better cinema than theatre, for its movement is uninterrupted. The uninterrupted movement can be borne only by the film and screen, for the necessity of changing the sets obliges an interruption in the theatre. There is a central motive of the escaping Jones. The theatre has not the capabilities to reveal the textural effects necessary to the drama, such as the increasing sheen of sweat on the bare body. Here is your 'photogenic' opportunity! The theatre can never equal the cinema in the effect of the gradual oncoming dark, also a dramatic progression in the play. The ominous and frightful shadows, the spectres of the boy shot at craps, the phantom galley – the cinema has long been well-prepared for these. And now the sounds. The play is dependent on the concurrences and reinforcements of sounds. The sounds are part of the drama. The drumbeats, the bullet-shots, the clatter of the dice, the moan of the slaves, and the recurring voice of Jones, his prayer – what a composition these offer for a sound-sight-speech film! This is the ideal scenario for the film of sound and speech. Here silence enters as a part of the speech-sound pattern, and becomes more important than ever it was in the silent film! Here one can construct counterpoint and coincidence, for there is here paralleling of sound and sight and their alternation. There is intervaling, a most important detail in the synchronized structure. But all this does not end *The Emperor Jones*. It must be negro! How? We can switch back to my earlier words: 'The negro is plastically interesting when he is most negroid. ...' The negroes must be selected for their plastic, negroid structures. Jones should not be mulatto or napoleonic, however psychologic requirements demand it. He should be black so that the sweat may glisten the more and the skin be apprehended more keenly. He should be woolly, tall, broad-nosed and deep-voiced. The moaning should be drawn from a source in the vocal experience of the negro, the medicine doctor's dance from a source in the choreographic experience. But beware! We do not want ethnography, this is no document. I am not asking for the insertions of *Storm over Asia*: I am asking for a tightly interwoven pattern. The sources are only sources. Folk, race are not complete in themselves. Dialect is not an aesthetic end. I am not asking for the duplications such as Langston Hughes writes. We shall have enough of these and they will be nothing but records, and records lacking even intelligent selection and commentary. What I have said in my remarks upon the negro in art and literature will indicate what the ideal negro-film must not be and must be. The documentary film is ethnographic. The documentary film is a source, but even in a document one cannot place everything and there must be concessions to the form. In the constructed film of the negro, the art-film let us say, the problem will always be, not the negro in society, but the negro in film. The problem will not be that of Edward Sheldon's *The Nigger*, filmed years ago with William Farnum (Fox Film *The Governor*). This sort of play in reality omits the negro, just as *A Doll's House* actually gave us no woman but a thesis. We are, I hope, far away now from films about 'the black peril' – although *The Birth of a Nation* is still with us and 'the yellow peril' is a constant offering. The problem of intermarriage and inter-race is not likely to be honestly dealt with on the American screen for a long time, but I do not complain of that – the problem play has generally been dull drama, it would be even duller cinema. When the cinematists have shown that they have intelligently examined the negro as subject-matter, that they know a great deal about him and his experiences, then the problem film of the negro can be attempted, for the problem will be comprised then, and only then, in a complete experience of a people. It is indeed reassuring that literature in dealing with the negro has become more sympathetic. The sympathy, however, has not extended as yet to the formal material, the convertible raw stuff – it is humanitarian, and that is good. But in

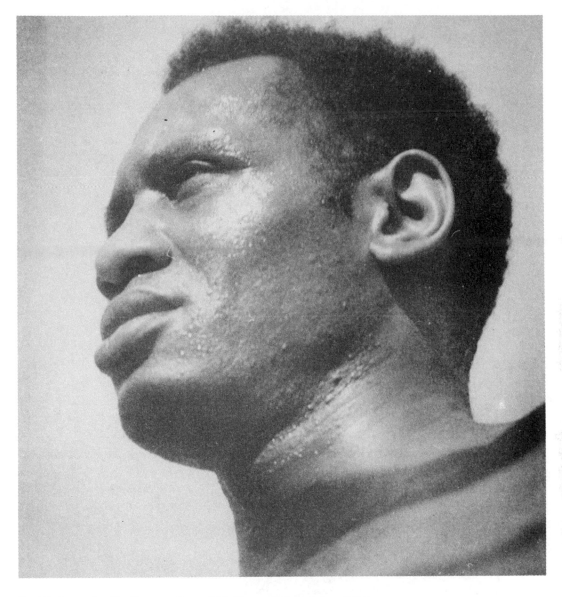

Paul Robeson in *The Emperor Jones* (Vol. X, no. 3, September 1933).

the humanitarian sentiment one still detects considerable patronage, indulgence, condescension and an attitude hardly judicious, that of the examiner of an oddity. In the documentary films of Burbidge and the Cobham journey, the captions are frequently supercilious, and in a document of a polar trip, a bit of non-documentation is perpetrated for humour: a negro hand runs off scared upon seeing a polar-bear, safely bound, hauled upon the deck. These caucasian evidences will persist a long time and wherever they will persist, there will be no proper attitude towards the negro as subject-matter.

Then is the hope in negro films turned by negroes? That would be a hope, if the American negro had given evidence of caring for and understanding his own experience

CLOSE UP

Editor : K. MACPHERSON
Assistant Editor : BRYHER
Published by POOL

RIANT CHATEAU · TERRITET · SWITZERLAND
LONDON OFFICE: 24 DEVONSHIRE ST., W.C.1

Contents :

Paris Correspondents :   { MARK ALLEGRET
                            { JEAN LENAUER
London Correspondent :   ROBERT HERRING
Hollywood Correspondent : CLIFFORD HOWARD
Berlin Correspondent :   A. KRASZNA-KRAUSZ
Geneva Correspondent :   F. CHEVALLEY
Moscow Correspondent :   P. ATTASHEVA

Subscription Rates :

ENGLAND . . 14 shillings per year
FRANCE . . 70 francs per year
GERMANY . . 14 marks per year
AMERICA . . 3 dollars and 50 cents per year
SWITZERLAND . 14 francs per year

Contents page for special issue on the 'Negro in Film' (Vol. V, no. 2, August 1929).

sufficiently to create works of art in the other mediums. But the American negro as graphic artist has shown very little awareness of this experience; as writer he is imitative, respectable, blunt, ulterior and when he pretends to follow negro materials, he does little more than duplicate them. Of course there are exceptions. The exceptions, I believe, will eventually create the rule. But that rule will be created only by artists who are strong enough to resist the vogue which would inflate them. We are now entering into a vogue of the negro film. Perhaps when that is over, the true, profound, realized negro film will be produced, and perhaps negroes will produce them.

It will have been observed that my preoccupation has been constantly with relationships. I have been preoccupied with relationships only because they are constantly present. The relationship between the African dances and the sophisticated Charleston and The Black Bottom is unavoidable, the relationship between native negro song and jazz is evident. We are always what we were: that is perhaps a platitude but it is also an important truth for the negro film. It suggests a synthetic film, a composite film, in which the audience's experience of a girl by Tanganyika becomes the audience's experience of an idolized Josephine Baker. Folk, race dominates the world. There is a theme. And the movie with its devices for simultaneous and composite filming offers the opportunity. Someone might similarly make an incisive film deriving the hooded Ku Klux Klan from the leopard-skin-hooded vendetta of the black Aniotas of Africa. In that way lies penitence for *The Clansman* which became *The Birth of a Nation*.

Vol. V, no. 2   **August 1929**

Geraldyn Dismond

(well-known American Negro writer)

THE NEGRO ACTOR AND THE AMERICAN MOVIES

The Negro actor and the part he has played in the development of the American movie is one of the most interesting phases of what is now one of America's greatest industries. Because no true picture of American life can be drawn without the Negro, his advent into the movies was inevitable; but also because of the prejudices which have hampered and retarded him since his coming to America, his debut was delayed. To be perfectly frank, the Negro entered the movies through a back door, labelled 'servants' entrance'. However, beggars cannot be choosers, and it is to his credit that he accepted the parts assigned to him, made good and opened the door for bigger things.

In order to better appreciate the attitude of the white producer toward Negro talent, we must keep in mind the change in the social status of the group. To put it briefly, at the time of the Civil War, the northern white man considered the Negro a black angel without wings, about whom he must busy himself in spirit and deed. On the other hand, the southern white man detested Negroes in general and liked his particular blacks. After the Negro had been given his freedom, there soon arose the feeling that he was an economic and social menace and we find him depicted everywhere as a rapist. Then the white dilettante, exhausted with trying to find new thrills, stumbled over the Negro and exclaimed, 'See what we have overlooked! These beloved vagabonds! Our own Negroes, right here at home!' And voila!—Black became the fad.

These types of thinking have influenced the development of the Negro as part of the moving picture game. Within the remembrance of all of us and still in some pictures and stage productions, we find whites blacked up for indifferent imitations of their dark brothers. But more and more is the practice falling into disrepute. The old cry that Negroes with ability cannot be found has not held water. In fact, it has been conclusively proven that under the proper director, the Negro turns out some of the best acting on the American screen and stage. A people of many emotions with an inherent sense of humour, and a love for play, they do not find it difficult to express themselves in action, or to bring to that expression the genuineness and enjoyment they feel. Nevertheless, excuse after excuse has been made to keep the Negro off the silver sheet and it was the servants of white stars, who as individuals, first got the breaks.

For example, Oscar Smith, who came to the Paramount Studios nine years ago as the personal servant of Wallace Reid, and at present owns the bootblack stand at the studio, has worked in two hundred pictures and has recently received a contract exclusively for Paramount talking pictures. Stepin Fetchit, who is billed as the star in the William Fox all-talkie *Hearts in Dixie* was the porter on the Fox lots. Carolyn Snowden, who played opposite Fetchit in *In Old Kentucky* was also a lady's maid for a prominent star. And so it went. Another point is also true. They worked in the early days in character. By that I mean, often the star's maid went on as her maid, provided she could be made to look homely and black enough. And all Negroes, perhaps with one or two exceptions, were cast as menials and as comedy characters.

As for the exceptions, they were for the most part African chiefs and the members of their tribes. One, however, I do recall from my first experiences with movies. He is Noble Johnson of whom practically nothing is heard now in connection with Negroes. The last time I saw him, he was playing the part of a Mexican bandit, and rumour has it that he owns considerable stock in the company for which he works and is used for all parts calling for a swarthy skin. The other two unusual individuals are Sunshine Sammy and Farina, the two juvenile favourites of the Hal Roach – Our Gang Comedies.

Negroes in any great numbers were first used for atmosphere – for mobs, levee and plantation, native African jungle and popular black belt cabaret scenes. Griffith's *The Birth of a Nation*, which, by the way, employed the old rape idea, and for that reason was so distasteful to Negroes, is an excellent example of the Negro as atmosphere. *West of Zanzibar*, a popular Lon Chaney film, and the *Stanley in Africa* pictures used large groups of Negroes for the jungle scenes.

The next move on the part of the producers was evident. Isolated Negro characters and Negroes as atmosphere were combined for the Universal feature production, *Uncle Tom's Cabin*, with James B. Lowe as Uncle Tom. Not all Negro parts, however, even in this picture, were assigned to Negroes. Topsy, Liza, her husband and baby were played by whites, but up to the introduction of the 'Talkies', *Uncle Tom's Cabin* was the outstanding accomplishment of the Negro in the movie world.

It is significant that with the coming of talkies, the first all–Negro feature pictures were attempted by the big companies. White America has always made much of the fact that all Negroes can sing and dance. Moreover, it is supposed to get particular pleasure out of the Negro's dialect, his queer colloquialisms, and his quaint humour. The movie of yesterday, to be sure, let him dance, but his greatest charm was lost by silence. With the talkie, the Negro is at his best. Now he can be heard in song and speech. And no one who has seen the William Fox *Hearts in Dixie*, featuring Stepin Fetchit, Clarence Muse and Eugene Jackson, or Al Christie's *Melancholy Dame*, an Octavius Roy Cohen all-talking comedy with Evelyn Preer, Eddie Thompson and Spencer Williams, will disagree with the fact that the Negro's voice can be a thing of beauty in spite of the mechanics of this new venture in the art of the movies.

Of these two Negro all-talkies which are now playing Broadway, *Hearts in Dixie* is by far the most pretentious. The story as such, is nil. Here indeed, we have the 'beloved vagabond'. It does embody the idea, however, that some Negros are not superstitious and are anxious to better themselves, and is a rather entertaining picture of plantation life; but it lacks substance. You were ever conscious of the fact that the producers were not interested in the plot, but rather in the talking and singing sequence. The ensemble singing and the voice of Clarence Muse were decided contributions and well worth the price of admission. *The Melancholy Dame*, a short comedy with little music or dancing, depends principally upon its comic dialogue which is given in the best Octavius Roy Cohen dialect, for its interest. Incidentally, Mr Cohen, himself, directed the picture.

Of course, it is generally believed that the Metro-Goldwyn-Mayer production, *Hallelujah*, will be the ace of the all–Negro talking pictures. King Vidor is directing. Daniel Haynes, formerly of *Show Boat*, has the principal role and is supported by Nina May McKenney of the Blackbirds of 1929; Victoria Spivey, a 'blues' recording artist; Fannie DeKnight, who played in *Lula Belle*; Langdon Grey, a non-professional, and 375 extras. There are forty singing sequences, including folk songs, spirituals, work songs and blues. Eva Jessye, a Negro, who has compiled a book of spirituals and trained the original 'Dixie Jubilee Choir', is directing the music. The story, which is devoid of propaganda, is that of a country boy who temporarily succumbs to the wiles of a woman, is beset with tragedy, and ultimately finds peace. It is a known fact that several studios are holding up all-Negro productions until the fate of *Hallelujah* has been pronounced.

In the meantime, *Show Boat*, a talkie using the present American *Show Boat* Company of both blacks and whites, has been made by Universal and had its première at Miami and Palm Beach, March 17th; Ethel Waters, greatest comedienne of her race, and Mamie Smith, blues singer of note, have been signed up by Warner Brothers for Vitaphone comedies; Sissle and Blake, internationally famous kings of syncopation, have been released by Warner Brothers; Christie Studio is preparing another Negro film; Eric Von Stroheim is working on the Negro sequence of *The Swamp*; and John Ford's *Strong Boy* is using a large number of Negroes.

Three by-products have resulted from this slow recognition of the Negro as movie material – Negro film corporations, Negro and white film corporations, and white corporations, all for the production of Negro pictures. They have the same motives, namely, to present Negro films about and for Negroes, showing them not as fools and servants, but as human beings with the same emotions, desires and weaknesses as other people's; and to share in the profits of this great industry. Of this group, perhaps the three best known companies are The Micheaux Pictures Company of New York City, an all-coloured concern whose latest releases are *The Wages of Sin* and *The Broken Violin*; The Colored Players Film Corporation of Philadelphia, a white concern which produced three favorites – *A Prince of His People*, *Ten Nights in a Barroom*, starring Charles Gilpin, and *Children of Fate*; and the Liberty Photoplays, Inc., of Boston, a mixed company, no picture of which I have seen. There is rumor of the formation in New York City of The Tono-Film, an all-Negro corporation, for exclusive Negro talking pictures and that its officers and directors will include Paul Robeson, Noble Sissle, Maceo Pinkard, Earl and Maurice Dancer, J.C. Johnson, F. E. Miller and Will Vodery, all of whom are known in America and abroad. So far, the pictures released by this group have been second rate in subject matter, direction and photography, but they do keep before the public the great possibilities of the Negro in movies.

In conclusion, it must be conceded by the most skeptical that the Negro has at last become an integral part of the Motion Picture Industry. And his benefits will be more than monetary. Because of the Negro movie, many a prejudiced white who would not accept a Negro unless as a servant, will be compelled to admit that at least he can be something else; many an indifferent white will be beguiled into a positive attitude of friendliness; many a Negro will have his race-consciousness and self-respect stimulated. In short, the Negro movie actor is a means of getting acquainted with Negroes and under proper direction and sympathetic treatment can easily become a potent factor in our great struggle for better race relations. And the talkie which is being despised in certain artistic circles is giving him the great opportunity to prove his right to a place on the screen.

PART 2

From Silence to Sound

'"One Talking Picture": A cynical study by Ralph Steiner, who made the film H_2O, from which *Close Up* readers may draw their own conclusions. Mr Steiner suggests it is a fairly good comment on movies, talking and otherwise' (Vol. VI, no. 2, February 1930).

INTRODUCTION

James Donald

Close Up began publication in July 1927. Within three months, on 6 October, *The Jazz Singer* opened in the United States. Is that the whole story: avant-garde experimentation destroyed by Hollywood talkies? The rapid increase in the cost of film production brought about by the talkies, and the massive investment needed to adapt cinemas for sound projection, led to a new economic regime in cinema. These new conditions entrenched yet more deeply Hollywood's domination of European markets, and played their part in constraining even further the production of a universal 'pure' film language and the creation of an internationalist film culture. So it is true that *Close Up*'s *raison d'être* was being undermined at the very moment the magazine came into being.

Of course, however, the story is much more complicated and more interesting than that. For a start, the issue was not *sound* as such. You would always have heard a musical accompaniment (whether a specially written score played by a full orchestra or an ill-prepared pianist trying to keep up), a lecturer commenting on the film and guiding audience reactions, a manager filling in while reels were changed, or simply the whir of the projector and the conversation and noisiness of other people. The objection was specifically to synchronized *speech*, and the increased reliance on the spoken word it implied. The emphasis on language, it was argued, would inevitably be bought at the expense of the inner speech that was supposedly invoked and conveyed by the art of silent montage. It would disrupt the integrity and coherence of film in the same way as intertitles and subtitles had done. And because synchronized speech would mean synchronized national language, talkies would destroy the universality of silent cinema, and so its internationalism.

The importance of *The Jazz Singer* itself is as much emblematic as historical. Although Sam Goldwyn's wife called its Los Angeles opening 'the most important event in cultural history since Martin Luther nailed his theses on the church door',[1] the film was less cataclysmic in disrupting Hollywood's aesthetic conventions than has often been supposed. Short films of musical numbers with synchronized sound were already a well-established feature of cinema programmes, and *The Jazz Singer* was more than anything an incorporation of that 'promo' mode into a full-length narrative. What came as a shock and a revelation were not Al Jolson's musical numbers, but the few passages of spoken dialogue. Even when Hollywood had grasped the potential of that change, the stylistic consequences were comparatively short-lived. Although the films of the transitional period show hesitations and uncertainties as synchronized speech was being integrated, David Bordwell concludes that 'Sound cinema was not a radical alternative to silent filmmaking; sound as sound,

as a material and as a set of technical procedures, was inserted into the already
constituted system of the classical Hollywood style.'[2]

Although technological and above all economic factors determined the nature and
speed of the switch to sound, the change did have far-reaching aesthetic and cultural
implications. *Close Up* remains important not least because it provided *the* forum for
a debate about those aspects of sound, one which initially became the focus for what
Ian Christie has called – perhaps too one-sidedly – a 'rearguard defence of the
aesthetics of silent art cinema'.[3] Here, the issue was less what sound would do to or
for Hollywood, than what it meant for the search for pure cinema. This became one
context in which Soviet film-makers, with their emphasis on montage rather than
theatrical narrative, were promoted by the magazines, as this comment from
Macpherson illustrates: 'We are able to safely feel that the future of pure cinema is
safe in [Soviet filmmakers'] hands, that the excrescent and reactionary strivings of
talking and talking colour films need not unduly disturb us.'[4] Here is Macpherson
again in July 1929, still aggressively hostile:

> The artists wait and wait. World sales, markets, exploitation, profits were
> hedging them in, closing them round, herding them, reducing and reducing
> their opportunity and scope, until, one by one, Sweden, Germany, France, went
> deeper and deeper to waste, leaving only Russia, firm in her beliefs but shaken
> financially and sounding the markets of the world for possible sales. The
> impregnable Eisenstein going and going to Hollywood. Pudovkin leading a role
> in a wholly callow and fatuous German film. Feelers ... indications ... premise.
> Quiet erosion everywhere. Then, like a monstrous tidal wave, the onrush of the
> talkie. Quiet erosion now a rapid crash and fall of land. Back ten, back fifteen
> years. Back to Sonny Boy and Mammie Mine and Don't Go Down the Mine,
> Daddie. Back to proscenium front. Back unashamedly to Little Dorrit and East
> Lynne. Back to a hundred thousand Dancing Daughters, back to the bootlegger
> and the thug. Back to Bella Donna and Mary Dugan. Back to Methusalah. Back,
> in short, to front![5]

All the attempts at articulating the specificity of film as medium seemed to
Macpherson to be threatened by the imposition of theatrical norms: 'rehash of
Somerset Maugham, of Frederick Lonsdale, of Michael Arlen, of theatre names we
had, not out of reason, expected to hear no more'.[5] This return to theatricality is also
identified as the great danger when in October 1928 *Close Up* published the famous
'Statement on sound' by Eisenstein, Pudovkin and Grigori Alexandrov, Eisenstein's
assistant on *Strike* and *Potemkin* and co-director and co-scenarist on *October* and *Old
and New*. The probable consequence of sound, the Soviet film-makers predict, will be
'an epoch of automatic utilisation for "high cultural dramas" and other photographic
performances of a theatrical nature'.[6] Again, it is not synchronized sound as such
which is seen as the problem, but what Ernest Betts in his contribution calls 'the
picture of synchronised speech'.[7]

In fact, Eisenstein, Pudovkin and Alexandrov acknowledged that the major problem
they really faced was the technical backwardness which prevented them from
exploring ways of incorporating sound as an element of montage (or 'mounting' as it

is translated here). Sound is a 'two-edged invention'. It probably *would* be used to subordinate film to theatricality, but it *could* be used to create 'new possibilities of developing and perfecting the mounting [montage]'. But to do that sound would have to be used in dialectical counterpoint to the image.

The statement, originally published in the Leningrad magazine *Zhizn'ikusstva* on 5 August 1928, had already provoked a furious row among Soviet film-makers. Pudovkin's cameraman Golovnya claimed that Pudovkin did not know much about synchronized sound when he signed the piece, and soon changed his ideas.[8] Writing in his own name in 1929, for example, Pudovkin continued to argue for a contrapuntal relationship between sound and image, but one that is less dialectical than associational.[9] Alexandrov at least remained committed to the theories articulated in the statement. He tried to put them into practice when he produced the first Russian-made sound film, *Romance sentimentale*, in France in 1930. The film ran the soundtrack backwards, used 'drawn sound' – that is, graphic figures such as letters, lines and profiles scratched onto the soundtrack of the film and then played back through the projector – and other techniques for manipulating sound, which he discussed with the *Close Up* contributor Harry A. Potamkin.[10] Eisenstein always denied any involvement in the production, but there is at least circumstantial – if hardly impractical – evidence that he played a central part. According to Luis Buñuel:

> Eisenstein's friends have tried to blame Alexandrov for the debâcle of the shoddy and dreadful production of *Romance Sentimentale*. But I saw Eisenstein making it with my own eyes, since he was shooting it on the stage next to me when I was making *L'Age d'or*.[11]

The point of the story is that Eisenstein – certainly the engineer in him – and Alexandrov were excited by the aesthetic possibilities opened up by sound. There was a debate and not just a line about sound in *Close Up*.

Some contributors, and especially the women among them, remained resistant. For Bryher, silent cinema was, or at least became in retrospect, 'the art that died'. (The 'gendering' of the debate about sound is discussed in the introduction to Richardson's work in Part 4.) Other contributors, Macpherson notable among them, soon began to be won over to the creative possibilities of contrapuntal sound for an enriched montage:

> People have not yet begun to speak, far less think, of sound in the same way as they think now and write in *Close Up* and elsewhere of vision. They must. The theory of sound and sound-vision is just as complicated, and in many ways similar. Sound must never be thought of alone. It must now be inseparably and forever sound-sight. The construction of sound-sight aesthetic must be taken in hand.[12]

In the editorial reprinted here, from which this programmatic quotation comes and which shows him at his most perceptive as a critic, Macpherson cites Alfred Hitchcock's *Blackmail* as an example of what could be achieved.[12] Enthusiasm has taken over from suspicion:

What a complicated, vast, never-ending science the investigation and
psychology of sound is going to present to us, and some of us already are
beginning to say that talkies are an art ... Till then, gee, honey, ah'm jes *crazy*
'bout yu, and I don't mind telling the world I miss the sound now in a silent
film, and *you'll* be with me.[13]

Vol. III, no. 4   **October 1928**

~~~~~~

S.M. Eisenstein, W.I. Pudowkin [Pudovkin]
and G.V. Alexandroff [Alexandrov]

THE SOUND FILM
A STATEMENT FROM U.S.S.R.

The cherished dream of a talking film is realised. The Americans have invented the technique of the talking film, and have brought it to the first stage of practical utilisation. Germany, too, is working strenuously in the same direction. All over the world people are talking of the dumb thing that has learnt to speak. We who are working in the U.S.S.R. are fully conscious that our technical resources are not such as to enable us in the near future to achieve a practical success in this direction. For the rest, we judge it not inopportune to enumerate a number of preliminary considerations of a theoretical nature, the more so that, judging from the information that has reached us, attempts are being made to put this new perfection of the cinematographic art to a mistaken use.

A misconception of the possibilities of this new technical discovery may not only hamper the work of developing and perfecting cinematography as an art, but also threatens to ruin its present actual achievements.

Contemporary cinematography, operating as it does by means of visual images, produces a powerful impression on the spectator, and has earned for itself a place in the front rank of the arts.

As we know, the fundamental (and only) means, by which cinematography has been able to attain such a high degree of effectiveness, is the *mounting* (or cutting).

The improvement of the mounting, as the principal means for producing an effect, was the undisputed axiom on which was based the development of cinematography all over the world.

The world-wide success of Soviet films was largely due to a number of mounting-devices, which they were the first to discover and develop.

1.   Therefore, for the further development of cinematography, the only important factors are those calculated to reinforce and develop these mounting-contrivances for producing an effect on the spectator.

Examining each new discovery from this point of view, it is easy to demonstrate the trivial significance of coloured and stereoscopic cinematography, as compared with the huge significance of *sound*.

2.   The sound film is a two-edged invention, and it is most probable that it will be utilised along the line of least resistance, that is to say, the line of satisfying *simple curiosity*.

In the first place, there will be the commercial exploitation of the most saleable goods, i.e. of *speaking films* – of those in which the record of the sound will coincide in the most exact and realistic manner with the movement on the screen, and will convey the 'illusion' of people speaking, of the sound of objects and so on.

This first period of sensations will not prejudice the development of the new art, but there will be a terrible second period, which will come with the fading of the first realisation of new practical possibilities, and in its place established an epoch of automatic utilisation for 'high cultural dramas' and other photographic performances of a theatrical nature.

Utilised in this way, sound will destroy the meaning of mounting.

For every addition of sound to portions of the mounting will intensify the portions as such and exaggerate their independent significance, and this will unquestionably be to the detriment of the mounting, which produces its effect not by pieces, but, above all, by the *conjunction* of pieces.

3. Only utilisation of sound in counterpoint relation to the piece of visual mounting affords new possibilities of developing and perfecting the mounting.

The first experiments with sound must be directed towards its pronounced non-coincidence with the visual images.

This method of attack only will produce the requisite sensation, which will lead in course of time to the creation of a new *orchestral counterpoint* of sight-images and sound-images.

4. The new technical discovery is not a chance factor in the history of the film, but a natural outlet for the advance guard of cinematographic culture, by which they may escape from a number of seemingly hopeless blind alleys.

The first blind alley is the film text, and the countless attempts to include it in the scenic composition as a piece of mounting (breaking up of the text into parts, increasing or decreasing the size of the type, etc.).

The second blind alley is the explanatory items, which overload the scenic composition and retard the tempo.

Every day the problems connected with theme and subject are becoming more and more complicated. Attempts to solve them by 'visual' scenic devices alone have the result either that the problems remain unsolved, or that the manager is seduced into employing over-fantastic scenic effects, which lead one to fear a reactionary decadence.

Sound, treated as a new element of the mounting (as an item independent of the visual image), will inevitably introduce a new and enormously effective means for expressing and solving the complex problems with which we have been troubled, owing to the impossibility of solving them by the aid of cinematography operating with visual images alone.

5. *The contrapuntal method* of constructing the talking film not only will not detract from the *international* character of cinematography, but will enhance its significance and its cultural power to a degree unexperienced hitherto.

Applying this method of construction, the film will not be confined within any national market, as is the case with the theatre dramas, and will be the case with the 'filmed' theatre dramas, but there will be an even greater possibility than before of circulating throughout the world those ideas capable of expression through the film, and the universal hiring of films will still be practicable.

Germaine Dulac's *Disque 957*: 'an experiment in visual music from a prelude by Chopin' (Vol. VI, no. 4, April 1930).

Disque 957 (ibid.).

Vol. IV, no. 4   April 1929

~~~~~~

Jean Lenauer

THE SOUND FILM:
SALVATION OF CINEMA

December 1928

I have erred, and I wish to confess. Not to a priest, for it's no priest's business. What then? I imagine I have erred like many others, and my confession may ease their remorse, and bring about conversion likewise.

When, a few months ago, people began to battle over the talking film, I was frankly hostile, and tried to combat it to the limit of my power.

The reasons for this are simple and quickly understood. I loved the silent film, and I foresaw a horrible deformation, a mere degradation, with the added words returning to the worst *theatre*. Naturally this I did *not* desire.

Analogy: The woman you love comes out one day wearing a new dress. Simply, at first, you are deceived, seeing a changed aspect of the adored and *known* image. It is only after a while that you perceive the new dress is becoming, and you love her in it as before. I will not insist on the fact that one can love the cinema as a woman, and even more deeply.

Eisenstein, Pudovkin, Alexandroff [Alexandrov], said recently in a manifesto: The new technical discovery (the sound film) is not a chance factor in the history of the film, but a natural outlet for the advance guard of cinematographic culture, by which they may escape from a number of seemingly hopeless blind alleys.

Yes, the cinema, the good cinema, is in a blind alley. And it is particularly moving that it is the Russian *cinéastes* who realise it; those who are still furthest off from it.

It is the perfection to which the cinema almost attains which presents the danger of stagnation, the tremendous danger of marking time.

I do not suggest this for the pleasure of being paradoxical, but solely through careful discernment. The perfection of an art is its death. A work of art alone is not enough, it becomes valuable only according to the promises it makes, by the possibilities of ultimate development. In this method of reasoning, the *Napoleon* of Abel Gance would be preferable to the *Joan of Arc* of Dreyer. The new and tentative methods of *Napoleon*, employed more reasonably, would perhaps be able to cause the creation of new things. But what remains to be done after and according to *Joan of Arc*?

There is still another thing. The present cinema is a cinema of actors. (As the directors tell themselves: an actor is only good through his director.) But American and Russian actors have arrived equally at a perfection of their art which, to my thinking, is not to be surpassed. See *Underworld (Les Nuits de Chicago)* and do not deny it. (Especially don't judge by the Paris version, where the film has been horribly mutilated through the imbecility of censorship.) We enjoy the actors' play more even for what it suggests than for what it shows.

And here, you will follow me.

The sound film will create a new form of acting. For, aided by words, the gestures will be more subdued, more strictly limited within absolute necessity.

I know that the first attempts will be for the most part misfires, but that is unimportant. The research which the new method of expression will necessitate, will bring just that renewal for which we are always greedy, and of which each art has constant need.

Don't you believe, for instance, that the gramophone has given birth to a new music, that the gramophone has given the essential creative impulse to contemporary musicians?

At first the faults will be grave, I am convinced. One has but to read the interview which Pirandello accorded to a German interviewer, in which he said that the sound film, which he now wants to use, should express cinegraphically only such parts of sound which cannot be rendered in words. It is clearly the opposite which he should have said.

I am confident all the same. There are, you know, the Americans. And they, don't let's doubt it, - though displeasing the retarded and obstinate detractors of American films – have the sense of the cinema. I would say nearly: they are born with the cinema, and know the cinema as the greatest artistic activity. Recently I saw *Broadway* by Messrs. Dunning and G. Abbot, playing at the Théâtre de la Madeleine. So, if they make plays for the theatre thus strongly 'cinema' – become theatre plays by hazard – one need not fear. With such innate comprehension of cinema and so strong an obsession of cinema, their mistakes cannot last for long.

It is perhaps going to be necessary to forget all that has yet been learnt. The hardy *routiniers* (directors, actors, scenarists and technicians) will be sufficiently confounded thereby. That is all the same to us. Those who cannot bring themselves to understand the *cinéma parlant* will disappear; we will not find ourselves any the worse off. We feel a renewal sufficient to yield magnificent and unquestionable joys. And all the crabbed and the peevish won't be able to stop us from attaining them. Nobody, not even a new Paul Souday will have the right to condemn the sound film for which we are waiting. Because they will not understand it any more than they have understood that which we have already, we will not be influenced by them.

The sound film will be as international as the silent one. It is again the three directors already cited who say ... there will be an even greater possibility than before of circulating throughout the world those ideas capable of expression through the film, and the universal hiring of films will still be practicable.

And you will see: they are right.

After that, I have perhaps the right to tell you that I have not yet seen a talking film.

Vol. IV, no. 4   April 1929

~~~~~~

Ernest Betts

WHY 'TALKIES' ARE UNSOUND

No doubt it is unfair to pre-judge in any set terms so vast a change to the moving picture as that suggested by the present talkie vogue. Talkies are in their infancy and their maturity cometh in questionable shape. Lovers of the silent film nevertheless feel outraged by all this babble. They feel strongly that an injustice has been done to them which may be perpetuated.

For the art of the film, like that of writing or song, begins with a conviction about something. Those who are convinced that the picture of synchronised speech is to be the film of the future are as likely to be wrong as those who hold the contrary view. The important thing is to be convinced, to root the thing deeply in heart and mind while it is fresh. Time will destroy or consolidate the contemporary view.

Of the soundness of the short subject talkie I do not think any doubt can be entertained. But the film business is not built up on its short subjects. They are the *hors d'œuvres*, the sweetmeats, to the main dish. We have seen some very brilliant talkies on these lines, notably the remarkable speech by Mr Bernard Shaw. And because of their novelty and the magnetism of the human voice such items will always have a place in our film programmes.

But that is very different from giving sanction to a general outburst of speech from our screens. On this point the battle rages. To have a running vocal commentary from the characters in a full-length film will utterly destroy its real eloquence, which lies in its silence. The moment a film actor speaks he is placing a limitation on his own medium, which is movement. If he is able to express himself in words, will he not diminish by so much verbal force all that he might accomplish by mime and gesture?

Similarly, all that the camera is able to record in action is lessened by the necessity for recording the voice, and we see this not only in the less interesting angles of photography, but in the slowing-up of the action. These are elementary considerations. Here are some more.

If we are going to cut across the main visual appeal of the film by an appeal to the ear also, we run the risk of killing a good effect with a doubtful one. Was it not Mr Arnold Bennett who said that nobody could help laughing if a cat walked across the stage in the middle of the 'knocking' scene in Macbeth? That would be a fatal division of interest and it is such a division we are contemplating when we fling words, however noble, however witty, into the middle of a moving picture.

If one's view were merely based on present technical deficiencies it could have very little justification, for the speaking film is a miraculous scientific achievement which is in the way of becoming mechanically perfect. Nor can one rightly oppose the talkie on the ground that silence in the cinema is golden and speech a nuisance. That is a matter of taste.

The real anti-talkie argument is that speech attacks the film's peculiar and individual function, which is to imitate life in flowing forms of light and shade to a rhythmic pattern. That may sound a piece of abstract nonsense, but it is not so when we see Chaplin or Emil Jannings or any other great pantomimic artist.

Put speech into films, and you will get speech plus film but you will not get a film.

Vol. V, no. 4   October 1929

Kenneth Macpherson

AS IS

Those who have mentioned *Blackmail* in *Close Up* have left much to say about it. We are not burning to make a written orderliness of its implications, but we are interested to do so, because it is a film of essentially an examinable nature, and of a nature that, once examined, is far and away the most significant determinant to unification of sound-sight deliberately and sustainedly that we have yet had. *Blackmail*, I want to establish, is the first sign of a comprehension of the relationship of techniques. I have seen most of the talking films. Without exception any power they may have had to hold us was fragmentary, accidental – purely and wholly accidental. Bouldery jumble without interrelation or any specific plan, without architecture and without mortar, the object of which must be considered to be served if it can get its story told.

Long before the word montage was ever heard, a film had served its purpose if it adequately illustrated its sub-titles. In those days it might have been likened to magazine illustrations. 'Overcome' said the subtitle 'with remorse, Felicitas determines to be revenged upon her betrayer, and that night …' In those days Felicitas would then have been shown on the usual tinted stock creeping exhibitionistically to the assassination. Mr Hitchcock, supposing that such a title were possible in these days, with a more modern technique would show a curtain billowing, fingers running mediumistically down the handle of a knife, then cut to Big Ben, and help his montage with a scream.

There now, wait here.

Montage. Mr Hitchcock is quite the first to have realised and profited by the fact that the talkies we all go to see are using a crassly naïve and retrospective manner which differs from the cinema's genesis only in that spoken dialogue now illustrates the picture-text instead of pictures illustrating written text. I think Mr Hitchcock began to see, and is probably working it out in his mind now, and will use it well in his next film, that sound is not an accessory to lollop clumsily beside a film leashed in a twin harness, but a direct spur and aid to simplification, to economy. Accoustical montage, in short. Take this instance from *Blackmail*, it is a good one. I said Mr Hitchcock would help his montage with a scream, which, in fact he did do. You remember Anny Ondra after the murder pacing the streets. You remember her obsession with the flung back, trailing hand of the murdered artist. At the end of her trudging, when she must have been, incidentally, very exhausted, the sight of a sleeping beggar with outflung, trailing hand, brings forth a scream. There is an immediate cut to the screaming face of the old woman who finds the artist's murdered body. This is neat and dramatic. It is important, because it is the exact use of sound in its right relation. Part of the building. It is suave and polished, but more important than any of these, it is intensely significant. I say it is part of building, and until sound and film are built in one, grafted, and growing together, not much is going to be done. The scream that was both the girl's scream and the concierge's scream banished a lot that we can well do without. Picture this silent. You could not very well leave Anny Ondra screaming there. The beggar would or would not wake. She would hurry on. This would probably have to be shown. At the point of her hurrying on there could be a cut to the bed curtain being pulled back and then the old woman's face screaming. That is to say, that at least there would have to be three additional un-dramatic shots needful to continuity, but causing a sagging of dramatic moment. Three at least. When you think of films you see, it is possible the script would have called for the old lady knocking, entering, pulling up the blind, going over to the bed, and so forth. Two shots and one sound did all this a hundred times better. There were the three shocks in sheer dramatic unity (in its Potamkin sense) piled in one. The effect could not but have been, as it was, ideal.

The far more obvious, though quaintly touching, bird song accompanying, in the best Pudovkin manner, contrapuntally the dazed, and in the circumstances, excusably meagre toilet of the heroine, should have its mention, as should, for just the same reason, the artist's words, 'I live right up there at the top' (or words to that effect) at which we look, as we would, not at his lips, but where he is directing our attention, namely up the stairs towards the top.

Here, by the way, although I did not like the *Seventh Heaven* mounting of the stairs, Hitchcock built very deftly his atmosphere of chilly squalor. The intentions of each and their knowledge of the implications had a power that reminded me of Pabst at his best but in slower tempo. The way in which slight contacts gave out under pressure of everything that makes contacts give out when you go to a new place for the first time, the augmenting distrust, were dwelt on carefully, with conscious, sustained slowness. The murder I did not like, but this is not relevant to the point I am making, that *Blackmail* appears to me to deserve our most serious attention, not as a story, not necessarily for its recording, which, by the way, a British Phototone product, was excellent, and very free from the bangs, roars and reverberations that sooner or later we shall have to accustom ourselves to if we can. *Blackmail* deserves our attention, as I have already said, because it has a conscious effort to bring technical thoughtfulness to bear on its own construction. The instance I have used of the scream I do suggest should be thought over as a clue. We just do not want sound as an accompaniment, and, if I may say so, neither do we want it solely as a counterpoint. We want it as part of the film, spliced on to it and inseparable. Not to slow the film, but to speed it. Let me proffer another hint from the Knife, knife, knife scene. 'Aren't you feeling yourself?' Anny Ondra's father asks her. A small screaming clang begins, which gets louder and louder and bursts like a shell. Meanwhile you are watching Anny Ondra's face, very drawn, half stupefied. Her father says 'another customer'. The clang-scream was the shop bell. Phobia has translated it thus to her, meaning psycho-analytically that through that door may come the police. The door bell has become unconsciously a thing of terror. This again is worth thinking of. You might call it cinematic sound. It is not sound only, it gives you a picture of a mental state, as well as having its rightful place in the narrative.

Both these instances are given as indicative of the way we must begin to think of sound if we are to do anything with it. I was touched and amazed to find it thus in a British film, far and away the best talkie we have seen. I had meant this to be an article of sound with *Blackmail* as something to evolve something else out of. Since I have considered it more objectively than that, let me add a word of praise for Joan Barry's ghosting for Miss Ondra's voice. The overlayer of 'refainment' on Cockney was superb. Donald Calthrop's more traditionally elocutional manner became good if you decided soon enough that there was a down-and-out actor, though no indication was given of the fact. The story condensed to a study in fear was excellent. If you preferred its more obvious, objective presentation it was a weak story, full of old clichés. After all, the heightened conduct and heightened impasse conventionally demanded of drama are not limitless, and to-day's innovation becomes to-morrow's cliché, and the day after to-morrow's joke. The story, however (and it's after all the crux of every argument on story value) was not beneath psychology. Everything was accountable, and it dealt largely with minds. The established statement that it's not the story but the way you handle it that matters can be accountable only after you have established several other conditions. The psychology possibility is one of the most important of them.

People have not yet begun to speak, far less to think, of sound in the same way as they think now and write in *Close Up* and elsewhere of vision. They must. The theory of sound and sound-vision is just as complicated, and in many ways similar. Sound must never be thought of alone. It must now be inseparably and forever sound-sight. The construction of sound-sight aesthetic must be taken in hand. An illusory amplification of reality is not achieved by adding odd effects haphazardly whether they be a third dimension, clairvoyance or every sound that the world contains. The silent film at its best has already shown that unquestioning credence can be tapped. In other words, any medium that can take you where it wants to and make you credulous is complete. If you are taken there is no further demand that can possibly be made of you. The film silent or forever sounding can be complete or not in the exact degree in which it is able to render you a participant, non-existent, obliterated and believing. If sound jangles you into self-consciousness, into any awareness, it is sound wrongly used, and the film would be better without it. Consider, after all, sound. Very few of the million noises surrounding us every second of our lives are received in the portentous, acutely self-aware manner in which they are thrust upon us in the cinemas. Sound[s] of motor cars, for example, react differently on different nervous systems. Here Hitchcock's method of the bell clang-scream is significant. Sound is more like this. And sound is not one isolated, reedy noise filling a whole auditorium. It can only be rendered symbolically always. The million sounds you hear have a special timbre, rhythm, sound-sight significance. What a complicated, vast, never-ending science the investigation and psychology of sound is going to present to us, and some of us already are beginning to say that talkies are an art. When you think, nobody has translated sound, except into music. It has remained an unclassified, unqualified, imminent and unresolvable substance over and around us, without symbolic form; without, let us say, the fierce lines of sculptured metal that somebody might submit as a shape for it – without any art form. And before we can use it as trimming or sewing thread even, we must set it an area, find terms for it and text books, know what sound is and what it does and what we do with it. And that will need a science more than medical, therapeutical, psycho-analytical, mechanical or philosophic. Till then, gee, honey, ah'm jes *crazy* 'bout yu, and I don't mind telling the world I miss the sound now in a silent film and *you'll* be with me.

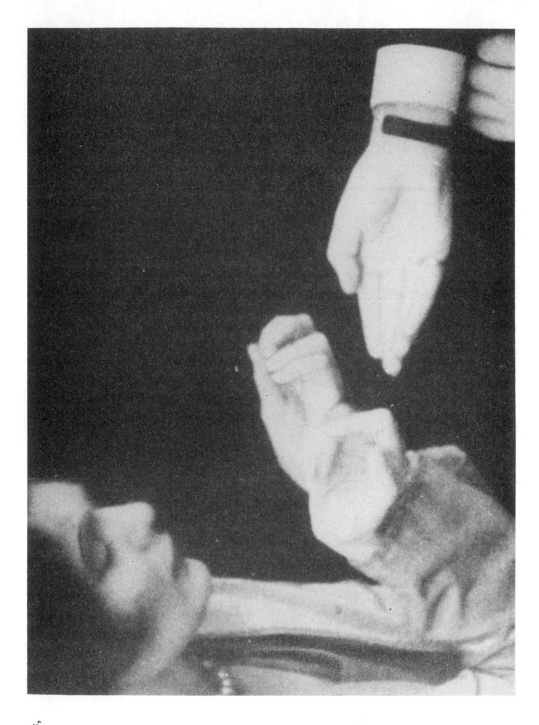

H. D. in *Foothills*,
directed by
Kenneth
Macpherson
(Vol. V, no. 1,
July 1929).

PART 3

The Contribution of H.D.

INTRODUCTION

Laura Marcus

I am now intensely interested [in film]... In fact am doing a little critical work for a new very clever movie magazine, supposed to get hold of things, from a more or less 'artistic' angle but not the highbrow attitude ... It is to be called, CLOSE-UP, a splendid title I think ... I feel [film] is the living art, the thing that WILL count but that is in danger now from comnerical [*sic*] and popular sources.[1]

The film is the art of dream portrayal and perhaps when we say that we have achieved the definition, the synthesis toward which we have been striving.[2]

The eleven articles the poet and novelist H.D. wrote for *Close Up* appeared in the journal's first two years; she made no written contribution after the December 1929 issue, apart from her pamphlet on the film *Borderline*, which was published separately, and anonymously, by the Mercury Press in 1930. Her first three film articles appeared under the title 'The Cinema and the Classics'. They are investigations and celebrations of film art as a new classicism, of a 'beauty' wholly submerged by Hollywood film, but revealed in the new German and Russian cinema (of Pabst, Kuleshov, Eisenstein) which is the topic of a number of H.D.'s subsequent *Close Up* articles. 'The problem of England and the beauty of England (psychically) is never that of the Scandinavians, and technically at least it should learn and study *not* from America but in and through the Germanic and Russian mediums,' wrote H.D. in her article 'Russian Films'.[3] Pabst's *Joyless Street*, which she had seen in 1925, was her cinematic touchstone, and Greta Garbo her image of a beauty destroyed when Garbo left Europe for America.

A number of the tenets expressed in the 'Cinema and the Classics' pieces echo the 'imagist' aesthetics with which H.D.'s early poetry is associated – spareness, directness, 'restraint' – as well as the 'Hellenism' which was a central aspect of her poetics throughout her long writing career.[4] 'True modernity approaches more and more to classic standards,' she writes in 'Restraint':

> The 'classic' as realism could be better portrayed by the simplest of expedients. A pointed trireme prow nosing side ways into empty space, the edge of a quay, blocks of solid masonry, squares and geometric design would simplify at the same time emphasize the pure *classic* note. ... Beauty restrained and chaste, with the over-weaving of semi-phosphorescent light, in a few tense moments showed that the screen can rise to the ecstatic level of the poetic and religious ideals of pure Sophoclean formula.[5]

The interplay between an aesthetics of formal restraint and one of emotional, spiritual or 'psychic' transcendence, between holding back and going beyond, runs throughout H.D.'s film writings. In her review of Kuleshov's *Expiation* she explores the idea that the film goes 'too far': 'The spirit goes as far as the spirit can go and then it goes a little further'; 'The Russian takes the human spirit ... *further* than it can go.'[6] Film can reveal, H.D. suggests, a reality as yet unrepresented in other media. She is admiring but critical of Dreyer's *Joan of Arc*, whose brutal realism is an excess which offers no visionary truth: 'Jeanne d'Arc takes us so incredibly far that having taken us so far, we are left wondering why didn't this exquisite and superb piece of screen dramatisation take us further?'[7] Dreyer's film, in H.D.'s account, victimizes not only Joan but the spectator: 'We are numb and beaten.'[8]

The experience and the locations of film-viewing are central to H.D.'s film criticism, and, as in Dorothy Richardson's 'Continuous Performance' articles, spectacle and spectatorship are intertwined. H.D.'s account of *Expiation*, for example, opens not with the film itself but in the streets of Lausanne outside the film theatre. She deferred, she writes, entry into the theatre and the film narrative in order to prolong the experience of her own movement and vision as a form of film-making:

> I so poignantly wanted to re-visualize those squares of doors and shutters and another and another bit of detail that of necessity was lost at first that I did illogically (I was already late) climb back. A boy ran obligingly across with a baker's flat tray-basket and someone else urged a cat to climb off the topmost row of a row of something that looked like the Concord grape baskets we used to have in Philadelphia. I ran up and down the scale, so to speak, of visual emotion, of memory, of visual sensation making that street and every one of its little graduations a sort of intellectual accordion from which to draw tunes, the sort of things one tries to put down sometimes (but never quite succeeds in doing) after a particularly poignant dream.[9]

'Real life' thus takes on a highly cinematic and filmed quality: the images (cat, boy, basket) are indeed central to the street-scenes in *Borderline*. Finally entering the cinema, 'when *Sühne (Expiation)* was about one third over', H.D. as film-viewer suggests that her preview (the act of imaginatively filming, of producing as film, the 'gay little street') was a necessary precondition for understanding the meanings of *Expiation* and the badlands in which it is set. There is thus both a striking contrast (the determined and determinate contrast by means of which 'montage' is composed) and a significant continuity between what is 'inside' and 'outside' the film. Narrating the film as she saw it – not from beginning to end, but from middle to middle – H.D. blurs the borderlines between film and vision. As she has her central character and autobiographical persona say in 'The Usual Star' (written in 1928; one of a group of short stories written during her period of involvement with film and with Macpherson): ' "We have made this thing, as people make screen vision. We have projected London".'[10] 'Life and the film must not be separated', she writes in 'Russian Films', 'people and things must pass across the screen naturally like shadows of trees on grass or passing reflections in a crowded city window'.[11]

Given H.D.'s emphasis on 'vision' (spiritual and artistic) as cinema, it is not surprising that she became for a time so centrally involved with film-making, both in front of and behind the camera. She acted in Macpherson's *Foothills*, *Wing Beat* and *Borderline*, and her somewhat negative portrayal of Louise Brooks in 'An appreciation [of Pabst]' may have owed something to the fact that she had at one point envisaged the part of Lulu as her own. She must also have acquired significant technical expertise in film-making; according to her (unpublished) 'Autobiographical Notes', she and Bryher undertook the cutting and editing of *Borderline* because Macpherson was unwell. Yet it is also unsurprising that she used cinematography to 'go beyond' films into visionary consciousness.

H.D. became increasingly fascinated by the cinematic apparatus – particularly the projector. 'I myself have learned to use the small projector', she wrote in the late 1920s, 'and spend literally hours alone here in my apartment, making the mountains and village streets and my own acquaintances reel past me in light and light and light. ... All the light within light fascinates me.'[12] Many of her writings on cinema are celebrations of light: 'Light speaks, is pliant, is malleable. Light is our friend our god. Let us be worthy of it.'[13] Her *Projector* poems – first published in *Close Up* – are invocations to Apollo, upon whom she bestows the godhead of cinema:[14] in the *Borderline* pamphlet she writes that 'Art and life walk hand in hand ... take hands, twine in sisterly embrace before their one God, here electrically incarnated, LIGHT.'[15] Nineteenth-century concepts of electrical energies, vitalism (here a belief in the capacity of electricity to restore exhausted energies), light and the power of light thus re-emerge in modernist consciousness and its celebration of optical technologies born of light.

Although H.D.'s approach to the cinematic is in many ways idiosyncratic, to be understood as an aspect of her broader concerns with language and symbol, psychoanalysis, mysticism and spiritualism, classicism and the celebration of women's beauty and power, her perspectives on film and her contributions to *Close Up* were nonetheless central to its project.[16] In H.D.'s film-writing, indeed, a number of different strands of the journal's concerns are intertwined. She conjoins Macpherson's avant-gardism and aestheticism, for example, with Bryher's concerns with film as education, the democratization of minority culture and the evils of censorship, particularly as applied in Britain to Soviet cinema. H.D.'s articles on Russian cinema, in particular, should be read alongside Bryher's neglected study *Film Problems of Soviet Russia* (1929); for both writers, representations of women in Soviet films are central.[17]

H.D.'s film-writing contains echoes of both Surrealism and Futurism, in their respective emphases on film as the art of dream-portrayal and, as in H.D.'s *Borderline* pamphlet, on the nexus of man and machine: 'Kenneth Macpherson, at work, is a hard-boiled mechanic, as if he himself were all camera, bone and sinew and steel-glint of rapacious grey eyes.'[18] H.D.'s analogies in the pamphlet between gun and camera, gunner and film-maker, artistic avant-garde and military advance guard further recall Dziga Vertov's description of the film-maker's 'armed-eye', and his equations of film-making and warfare.[19] In H.D.'s hands, the analogies become profoundly ambiguous, given her horror of war and of masculine militarism (she was haunted by the experience of World War I throughout her life). They serve, nonetheless, to represent the risks taken by the experimental film-maker, by contrast with the conservative and conventional 'snipers' in the traditional arts, and to conceptualize film as a 'no-man's land', which is also (and here we find the concept of film as a 'universal language', discussed more fully below) 'an everyman's land'.

H.D. also shared Robert Herring's fascination with the cinema as magic. In his 'A New Cinema, Magic and the Avant Garde', Herring speaks of the 'magical ... reality of light and of movement', of 'the fact that light is of all things what we need most and respond to most', and of the 'magic' of the cinematic apparatus:

> There is the screen, and you know the projector is at the back of you. Overhead is the beam of light which links the two. Look up. See it spread out. It is wider and thinner. Its fingers twitch, they spread in blessing or they convulse in terror. They tap you lightly or they drag you in. Magic fingers writing on the wall, and able to become at will ... a sword or a acetylene drill, a plume or waterfall. But most of all they are an Aaron's rod flowering on the wall opposite, black glass and crystal flowers ... Only now and again the rod becomes a snake, and whose films are those we know. ...
>
> You need not be a chamber to be haunted, nor need you own the Roxy to let loose the spirit of cinema on yourself. You can hire or buy or get on the easy system, a projector. You then have, on the occasions on which it works, people walking on your own opposite wall. By moving your fingers before the beam, you interrupt them; by walking before it, your body absorbs them. You hold them, you can let them go.[20]

Herring's models of the destruction of the 'aura' (the distance between spectator and spectacle) and of the blurring of a body/world division as the spectator inserts him or herself into the spectacle are characteristic of modernized vision and its altered perceptions of subject/object relationships. ('The film, by setting the landscape in motion and keeping us still, allows it to walk through us,' wrote Dorothy Richardson.[21]) His article imagines a future for cinema, an 'avant-garde', in which images would be rendered visible without the mediation of the screen, bodies and beings becoming solid projections of themselves. There is 'no reason', Herring writes, 'why [man] should not ultimately create himself in motion and speech, moving in the patterns of his creation'.

Herring's images in this article, his 'hieroglyphs' (rod, snake, flower), strikingly anticipate those of H.D.'s epic poem *Trilogy*.[22] More broadly, his vision of humanity (re)creating itself in a form of virtual reality is echoed in H.D.'s claim, in her article '*Turksib*', that in the great films – *Joyless Street*, *Jeanne Ney*, *Mother* – 'people moved, acted, suffered, we might also say for the first time, not parodies of people, at best ghosts, but spirits'. She writes (echoing Eisenstein, discussed below) of *Turksib*: '"Thought," one wanted to shout aloud, "is here for the first time adequately projected," ... These are not images made artificially but thought itself, seen for the first time, in actual progression. These images are not projected after they have been manufactured.'[23] For H.D., as for Herring, the power of cinema came increasingly to reside in the absence, or the fantasy of the absence, of technological mediation. It is a fantasy usefully understood, and grounded, through Walter Benjamin's account of the paradoxical aesthetic of cinema in 'The work of art in the age of mechanical reproduction' (1936):

> for contemporary man the representation of reality by the film is incomparably more significant than that of the painter, since it offers, precisely because of the thoroughgoing permeation of reality with mechanical equipment, an aspect of reality which is free of equipment. And that is what one is entitled to ask from a work of art.[24]

Herring's concepts of projection and of cinema as a 'writing on the wall' (recalling Lumière's name for cinema – 'cinématographe' – 'writing in movement') are central to H.D.'s project of 'cinematobiography'.[25] In *Tribute to Freud*, one of the accounts H.D. wrote of her 1933/4 analysis with Freud in Vienna, she represents her memories and dreams as moments of vision which are also moments in a history of pre-cinema and cinema: Aristotelian 'after-images'; an Archimedean construction of a burning-lens, as she recalls her brother using their astronomer father's magnifying glass to make fire – 'Under the glass, on the paper, a dark spot appeared; almost instantaneously the newspaper burst into flames.'[26] Most strikingly, there is the 'writing on the wall', her 'visionary' experience in Corfu in the early 1920s, which Freud apparently saw as the 'most dangerous symptom' and H.D. viewed as her most significant life-experience. She recounts, frame by frame, the inscription of hieroglyphs, images projected onto a wall in light not shadow. The first are like magic-lantern slides, the later images resemble the earliest films.[27] (I discuss the significance of H.D.'s 'hieroglyphics' below.) In a further memoir, *The Gift*, an account of her childhood, earliest memories appear as daguerreotypes, recent ones as films in colour.[28] As in Dorothy Richardson's *Pilgrimage*, autobiography is intertwined with a history of optics, the past is recalled by means of the *technologies* of memory, and, as Dianne Chisholm notes, child development is represented as technological advance.[29]

For H.D., as for Bryher, cinema and psychoanalysis were closely identified projects, historically and conceptually, their connection cemented in the cinema of Pabst, whose *Secrets of a Soul* was supervised by the psychoanalysts Dr Hanns Sachs (who became Bryher's analyst and wrote three short articles for *Close Up*) and Dr Karl Abraham. In the spring of 1933, as *Close Up* entered its final year and Bryher began to commit her considerable energies and financial resources to helping the enemies and the victims of fascism, H.D. left for Vienna and for psychoanalysis with Freud, bearing the recommendation of Hanns Sachs.

Although H.D. does not refer to her work on and in film in the (published) accounts she wrote of her analysis, the poetics and the politics of cinema and psychoanalysis become, at times, indistinguishable. It is probable that Bryher and H.D. saw the sessions with Freud as a way of continuing the work of film, finding in dream and symbolic interpretation an equivalent to, and extension of, the 'language' of the silent cinema, which they invested with both individual and 'universal' significance. Although the demise of *Close Up* almost certainly came about as a result of Macpherson's withdrawal of interest in film, combined with the changing political situation in Europe (Hitler became Chancellor in 1933) and the death of Bryher's father at this time, Bryher represented it in her memoir as a direct result of 'the collapse of the silent film'. The period between the late 1920s and early 1930s was, Bryher writes:

> the golden age of what I call 'the art that died' because sound ruined its development. I have written already that we had to get away from the nineteenth century if we were to survive. The film was new, it had no earlier associations and it offered occasionally, in an episode or a single shot, some framework for our dreams. We felt we could state our convictions honourably in the twentieth-century form of art and it appealed to the popular internationalism of those so few years because 'the silents' offered a single language across Europe.[30]

H.D.'s film-writings are less taken up with the issue of the transition to sound than, for example, those of Dorothy Richardson; her *Close Up* contributions ceased at the point at which the sound debate became central to the journal. A number of her discussions suggest that cinema's promise was for her that of a 'universal culture' (shared by, in her terms, 'the leaven and the lump') and that this was to an extent independent of the silent/sound divide. In the third of her 'Cinema and the Classics' articles, however, she focuses on the 'movietone', contrasting it (for the most part unfavourably) with the 'masks' of silent cinema which, like those of Greek drama, conceal, for H.D., a mystery and a vision destroyed by the 'mechanical', overtly automated technologies of 'movietone' sound.[31] Her film aesthetics and her model of vision are predicated on symbol, gesture, 'hieroglyph', 'the things we can't say or paint', as she writes in 'The Student of Prague'.[32] Her model of cinematic 'language' is closer to, in Freud's terms, 'thing-presentation' than 'word-presentation', with the work of writing-about-film acting as a form of translation from one to the other.[33] Her film-writing tends to provide not retrospective judgement on a film, but a performative running commentary on the processes of spectating which becomes a form of 'inner speech', acting as a screen onto which the film images can be projected.[34]

The contrast between H.D.'s narrative rendering of 'inner speech' and 'social speech' is highlighted in her account of her emergence from the realms of the 'pure' dream-language of the film she has been watching into that of the debased, Babel-languages (English and American English being represented as effete and philistine respectively) of her fellow-spectators:

> A small voice, a wee voice that has something in common with all these voices yet differs intrinsically from all these voices, will whisper there within me, 'You see I was right. You see it will come. In spite of "Gee" and "Doug Fairbanks" and "we must have something cheerful", it must come soon; a universal language, a universal art open alike to the pleb and the initiate.[35]

H.D.'s and Bryher's accounts of the 'universal language' of film are also closely echoed in H.D.'s writings on psychoanalysis, and, more specifically, in her gloss on Freudian dream-interpretation in *Tribute to Freud*:

The picture-writing, the hieroglyph of the dream, was the common property of the whole race; in the dream, man, as at the beginning of time, spoke a universal language, and man, meeting in the universal understanding of the unconscious or the subconscious, would forgo barriers of time and space, and man, understanding man, would save mankind.[36]

In *Tribute to Freud*, H.D. refers to the universal language of the dream as a hieroglyph. Her lifelong fascination with hieroglyphics was further stimulated by the writings of both Freud and Eisenstein, a conjuncture of poetics, politics, psychoanalysis (particularly Freud's theories of symbolization and of the 'dream-work') and film aesthetics which is central to subsequent developments in film theory. These areas are themselves conjoined by a 'modernist' fascination with the varying relations and interactions between different entities, temporalities, images and concepts, and the exploration of an art and a politics (both left and right) of juxtaposition, palimpsestic superimposition, simultaneity, collision, dialectic.

While Ezra Pound (with whom H.D. was for a time closely linked)[37] pursued, in Peter Nicholls's words, 'the spectre of the truly modern by the circuitous route of early Japanese theatre' ,[38] Eisenstein found in Japanese hieroglyphs 'the acme of *montage thinking*'. The combination of two hieroglyphs

> corresponds to a *concept*. From separate hieroglyphs has been fused – the ideogram. By the combination of two 'depictables' is achieved the representation of something that is graphically undepictable. ... It is exactly what we do in cinema, combining shots that are *depictive*, single in meaning, neutral in content – into *intellectual* contexts and series.[39]

Eisenstein's account of 'intellectual montage' as thought made visible was clearly a crucial influence on H.D.'s film-writings and on her concept of 'thought projection' more generally. His model of the ideogram, and of the film frame as a 'multiple-meaning *ideogram*' in his 'The Fourth Dimension of the Kino', further recalls Freud's accounts of the workings of picture-language in the dream, of the 'rebus' composed of multiple scripts and image-systems.[40] And for H.D., as Chisholm notes, the fourth dimension of the cinematograph becomes the 'living hieroglyph of the unconscious, which some "shock" of memory can re-present and decode'.[41] In *Tribute to Freud* H.D. locates the 'fourth dimension' in the fourth 'wall' of Freud's room (the wall with the double doors leading to the room beyond): 'The room beyond may appear very dark or there may be broken light and shadow.'[42]

The broader context for H.D.'s conceptualizations of film is, undoubtedly, the concept and dream of a 'universal language' which began to flourish in the seventeenth century, was revived in the latter part of the nineteenth century, and subsequently became closely linked with the image of (silent) film as a form of hieroglyphics, a thinking in pictures rather than words. Fuelled by the discoveries and translations of Egyptologists, most notably of the Rosetta stone, in the early to mid-nineteenth century (and reawakened by the opening of Tutankhamun's tomb in 1922),[43] a model of hieroglyphic language had taken root in North American literary culture, most influentially, as John T. Irwin has shown of the nineteenth century, in the work of the 'transcendentalists' Emerson and Thoreau, and in Poe, Hawthorne, Melville and Whitman.[44]

The dream of recapturing a prelapsarian, universal, pictographic language fed directly into early film aesthetics. Its chief North American exponent was the poet and critic Vachel Lindsay, author of the first book of film theory, *The Art of the Moving Picture*, published in 1915.[45] Here, as in his subsequent writings on cinema, *The Progress and Poetry of the Movies*, and in his poetry, Lindsay spelled out his vision of modern America (with its advertisements, billboards, newspaper photographs, sign-writings) as 'a hieroglyphic civilization far nearer to Egypt than to England'.[46] In *The Art of the Moving Picture*, in which he painstakingly analyses a set of Egyptian hieroglyphs, their Roman letter equivalents and their equivalents in 'the moving-picture alphabet',[47] Lindsay writes:

> Because ten million people daily enter into the cave, something akin to Egyptian wizardry, certain national rituals, will be born. By studying the matter of being an Egyptian priest for a little while, the author-producer may learn in the end how best to express and satisfy the spirit hungers that are peculiarly American. It is sometimes out of the oldest dream that the youngest vision is born.[48]

The expatriate, European-identified, anti-Hollywood, avant-garde H.D.'s models of 'universal culture' may seem remote from Lindsay's concerns with 'our America of Tomorrow', just as her habitual emphasis on hieroglyphic language as a coded, secret knowledge is apparently at odds with a model of hieroglyphics as, in Nick Browne's words, 'a mode of reading that bypasses critical judgement'.[49] There are, nonetheless, interesting links between these two poets and writers on film, not least their Swedenborgian perceptions of the power of 'light' and of the world as a 'grammar of hieroglyphs'.[50] The issue is less, however, the echoes of Lindsay's film-writing in H.D.'s. It is rather their shared, as well as disparate, relationships to the complex representations of film culture and language in the early twentieth century, and to the national, racial, democratic and commercial ideologies which these articulated – which could be gathered under, in Miriam Hansen's phrase, the 'ambiguous celebration of film as a new universal language, as a historically unique chance to "repair the ruins of Babel"'.[51]

In her brilliant reading of D.W. Griffith's *Intolerance* (a film which represents history, culture and 'race' through writing-systems, inscriptions, Babel-languages, 'writings on the wall'), in the context of early cinema and the public sphere, Hansen states: 'If *Intolerance* is proposing to recover a unity of popular and high art, it does so not by replacing writing with a superior language of visual presence, but by retrieving the common roots of both film and literature in the hieroglyphic tradition.'[52] This also works well as a way into H.D.'s conceptual strategies. It allows us to move beyond the opposition H.D. offers in *Tribute to Freud* – the (non-)choice between 'the writing on the wall' she saw in Corfu as 'symptom or inspiration'[53] – and to understand her focus on inscriptions and hieroglyphs as a form of cultural theorizing, whose roots may well lie in the Transcendentalist tradition of 'American hieroglyphs' and its understanding of hieroglyphics as both esoteric script and populist communication.

Yet the 'writing on the wall' is also an understanding that the writing was indeed on the wall in Europe between the wars. In *Tribute to Freud*, H.D. powerfully represents the rise of fascism in the Vienna of the early 1930s by means of its iconography and inscriptions. First there were 'occasional coquettish, confetti-like showers from the air, gilded paper swastikas and narrow strips of printed paper like the ones we pulled out of our Christmas bon-bons'. Then there were swastikas on the Berggasse (the street on which Freud's apartment was located), 'as if they had been chalked on the pavement especially for my benefit' and seemingly leading to Freud's door: 'I did not look any further. No one brushed these swastikas out. It is not so easy to scrub death-head chalkmarks from a pavement.'[54]

As she wrote in *Tribute to Freud*, H.D. was impelled towards analysis by the traumas of World War I and fear of the war to come. Throughout her writings on film we find not only claims for the new art of the cinema as a 'universal' art and the dream of a mass audience for minority or avant-garde culture, but an insistence on the role of film in bridging national differences or, at least, in allowing for a clear, undistorted perception of the terms of such differences. Her film-writings indicate the depth and strength of the political as well as the aesthetic aspirations for cinema between the wars:

> For the world of the film to-day (there is no getting away from it) is no longer the world of the film, it is *the* world. It is only those who are indifferent to the world itself and its fate, who can afford to be indifferent to the fate of the film industry and the fate of the film art. ... There has never been, perhaps since the days of the Italian Renaissance, so great a 'stirring' in the mind and soul of the world consciousness.[55]

Vol. I, no. 1   **July 1927**

THE CINEMA AND
THE CLASSICS

I

BEAUTY

I suppose we might begin rhetorically by asking, what is the cinema, what are the classics? For I don't in my heart believe one out of ten of us highbrow intellectuals, Golders Greenites, Chautauqua lecturers, knows the least little bit about either. Classics. Cinema. The word cinema (or movies) would bring to nine out of ten of us a memory of crowds and crowds and saccharine music and longdrawn out embraces and the artificially enhanced thud-offs of galloping bronchoes. What would be our word-reaction to Classics? What to Cinema? Take Cinema to begin with, (cinema = movies), boredom, tedium, suffocation, pink lemonade, saw-dust even: old reactions connected with cheap circuses, crowds and crowds and crowds and illiteracy and more crowds and breathless suffocation and (if 'we' the editorial 'us' is an American) peanut shells and grit and perhaps a sudden collapse of jerry-built scaffoldings. Danger somewhere anyhow. Danger to the physical safety, danger to the moral safety, a shivering away as when 'politics' or 'graft' is mentioned, a great thing that must be accepted (like the pre-cinema days circus) with abashed guilt, sneaked to at least intellectually. The cinema or the movies is to the vast horde of the fair-to-middling intellectuals, a Juggernaught crushing out mind and perception in one vast orgy of the senses.

So much for the cinema. (Our 'classic' word-reaction will come along in due course.) I speak here, when I would appear ironical, of the fair-to-middling intellectual, not of the fortunately vast-increasing, valiant, little army of the advance guard or the franc-tireur of the arts, in whose hands mercifully since the days of the stone-writers, the arts really rested. The little leaven. But the leaven, turning in the lump, sometimes takes it into its microscopic mind to wonder what the lump is about and why can't the lump, for its own good, for its own happiness, for its own (to use the word goodness in its Hellenic sense) *beauty*, be leavened just a little quicker? The leaven, regarding the lump, is sometimes curious as to the lump's point of view, for all the lump itself so grandiloquently ignores it, the microscopic leaven. And so with me or editorially 'us' at just this moment. Wedged securely in the lump (we won't class ourselves as sniffingly above it), we want to prod our little microbe way into its understanding. Thereby having the thrill of our lives, getting an immense kick out of trying to see what it is up to, what I am up against, what we all, franc-tireurs, have to deal with.

First as I say, amazing prejudice. The movies, the cinema, the pictures. Prejudice has sprouted, a rank weed, where the growth of wheat is thickest. In other words, films that blossom here in Europe (perhaps a frail, little, appreciated flower) are swiftly cut and grafted in America into a more sturdy, respectable rootstock. Take 'Vaudeville', for example, a film that I didn't particularly revel in, yet must appreciate, Zolaesque realism which succeeded admirably in its medium; was stripped (by this gigantic Cyclops, the American censor) of its one bloom. The stem is valuable, is transplanted, but the spirit, the flower so to speak of 'Vaudeville' (we called it here 'Variété'), the thing holding its created centre, its (as it happens) Zolaesque sincerity, is carefully abstracted. A reel or in some cases an artist or a producer, is carefully gelded before being given free run of the public. The lump heaving under its own lumpishness is perforce content, is perforce ignorant, is perforce so sated with mechanical efficiency, with whir and thud of various hypnotic appliances, that it doesn't know what it is missing. The lump doesn't know that it has been deprived of beauty, of the flower of some producer's wit and inspiration. The lump is hypnotized by the thud-thud of constant repetition until it begins to believe, like the African tribesman, that the thump-thump of its medicine man's formula is the only formula, that his medicine man is the only medicine man, that his god, his totem is (save for some neighbouring flat-faced almost similar effigies) the only totem. America accepts totems, not because the crowd wants totems, but because totems have so long been imposed on him, on it, on the race consciousness that it or him or the race consciousness is becoming hypnotized, is in danger of some race fixation; he or it or the race consciousness is so duped by mechanical efficiency and saccharine dramatic mediocrity that he or it doesn't in the least know, in fact would be incapable (if he did know) of saying what he does want.

He learns that there is a new European importation for instance of a 'star'; this importation being thudded into his senses for some months beforehand, his mind is made up for him; she is beautiful. We take that for granted. There I agree, the leaven and the lump are in this at one. The lump really wants beauty or this totem of beauty would not be set up by its astute leaders. Beauty. She is beautiful. This time 'she' is a northern girl, a 'nordic', another word they fall for. A Nordic beauty has been acclaimed and we all want to see her. I am grateful (it was my privilege) that I, for one, saw this grave, sweet creature before America claimed her. I saw her, as I see most of my pictures, more or less by accident. At least the divine Chance or classic Fortune that more or less guides all of us, led me one day to worship. I, like the Lump, am drawn by this slogan, 'Beauty', though this particular enchantress was not particularly head-lined on the provincial bill-boards. In fact, the whole cast was modestly set forth in small type along with the producer and I thought 'well it looks harmless anyhow' and it was raining and so in Montreux, Switzerland, I happened (as it happened) to see my first real revelation of the real art of the cinema.

I am led a little afield in trying to realize in retrospect the vast deflowering that took place in at least one rare artist. I dare say it is a common occurrence but in this particular case particularly devastating. I saw 'Joyless Street' ('Die Freudlose Gasse') in Montreux, some two or three years ago when it was first 'released' from Germany to take its tottering frail way across Europe towards Paris, where it was half-heartedly received, to London, where it was privately viewed by screen enthusiasts, only last winter, at one of those admirable Sunday afternoon performances of the London Film Society. In the meantime, I had seen Greta Garbo, deflowered, deracinated, devitalized, more than that, actively and acutely distorted by an odd unbelievable parody of life, of beauty, we were efficiently offered (was it at the Capitol about a year ago?) 'The Torrent'.

Greta Garbo in Montreux, Switzerland, trailing with frail, very young feet through perhaps the most astonishingly consistently lovely film I have ever seen ('Joyless Street') could not be, but by some fluke of evil magic, the same creature I saw, with sewed-in, black lashes, with waist-lined, svelte, obvious contours, with gowns and gowns, all of them almost (by some anachronism) trailing on the floor, with black-dyed wig, obscuring her own nordic nimbus, in the later a 'Torrent'. The Censor, this magnificent ogre, had seen fit to devitalize this Nordic flower, to graft upon the stem of a living, wild camellia (if we may be fanciful for a moment) the most blatant of obvious, crepe, tissue-paper orchids. A beauty, it is evident, from the Totem's stand-point, must be a vamp, an evil woman, and an evil woman, in spite of all or any observation to the contrary, must be black-eyed, must be dark even if it is a nordic ice-flower and Lya de Puttiesque. Beauty is what the Lump and the Leaven alike demand. So 'beauty, here it is,' says the Ogre. The Ogre knows that the world will not be sustained, will not exist without that classic, ancient Beauty. Beauty and Goodness, I must again reiterate, to the Greek, meant one thing. To Kalon, the beautiful, the good. Kalon, the mob must, in spite of its highbrow detractors, have. The Ogre knows enough to know that. But he paints the lily, offers a Nice-carnival, frilled, tissue-paper rose in place of a wild-briar.

Beauty was made to endure, in men, in flowers, in hearts, in spirits, in minds. That flame, in spite of the highbrow detractors, exists at the very centre, the very heart of the multitude. It is the business of the Ogre, the Censor, to offer it a serpent for an egg, a stone for bread. It is the duty of every sincere intellectual to work for the better understanding of the cinema, for the clearing of the ground, for the rescuing of this superb art, from its hide-bound convention. Perseus, in other words, and the chained Virgin. Saint George in other words, and the Totem dragon. Anyhow it is up to us, as quickly as we can, to rescue this captured Innocent (for the moment embodied in this Greta Garbo) taking frail and tortuous veils of light and shadow, wandering in photogenetic guise that Leonardo would have marvelled at and Tintoretto radiantly acclaimed. Greta Garbo, as I first saw her, gave me a clue, a new angle, and a new sense of elation. This is beauty, and this is a beautiful and young woman not exaggerated in any particular, stepping, frail yet secure across a wasted city. Post-war Vienna really wrung our hearts that time; the cheap, later clap-trap of starving stage Vienna had not yet blighted and blunted our sense of proportion and reality. Before our eyes, the city was unfolded, like some blighted flower, like some modernized epic of Troy town is down, like some mournful and pitiful Babylon is fallen, is fallen. The true note was struck, the first post-war touch of authentic pathos, not over-done, not over-exaggerated, a net of finely spun tragedy, pathos so fine and so intolerable that after all, we can't wonder that the flagrant, Parisian, commercial 'buyers' must disdain it. London could not (being governed also by a brother to our American Cyclops) allow this performance to be broadcast. War and war and war. Helen who ruined Troy seems to have taken shape, but this time it is Troy by some fantastic readjustment who is about to ruin Helen. Little Miss Garbo (I think of her as little; I believe from the columns of 'gossip' I read dished up in various Hollywood camera news productions that 'Greta Garbo is taller than John Gilbert', a thing they seem in some subtle way to have, among many other things, against her) brought into her performance of the professor's elder, little daughter in 'Joyless Street', something of a quality that I can't for the life of me label otherwise than classic. As long as beauty is classic, so long beauty on the screen, presented with candour and true acumen, must take its place with the greatest master-pieces of the renaissance and of antiquity.

For there is no getting over this astonishing and indubitable fact. Beauty as it has existed in pre-Periclean Athens, in the islands of the Cyclades, in the temple of Karnak, in the frescoes of Simone Martini and the etchings of Albrecht Dürer still does find expression, still does wander veiled as with dawn, still does wait for a renaissance to hail her. Miss Garbo is a symbol, was, I should say, a symbol as I saw her in 'Joyless Street'. She may again become some such glorified embodiment as flung itself in its youth and its strange, statuesque abandonment across the wretched divan of Madame whatever-was-her-name's evil house. Beauty, the youth and charm, by just a fluke, wasn't tarnished in that atmosphere. The odd thing was that this story of poverty and fervid business speculation and the lady of the world and her lovers and her pearls and the young financier and their meeting in this ill-flavoured establishment and the secret murder, wasn't commonplace, wasn't trivial, partook of the most ethereal overtones of subtlety. Tragedy rang like little bells, fairy bells almost. Tragedy didn't dare, those days, to stalk openly in its ornate purple. Not in Europe, not in London or Paris or Vienna. Murder and pearls and speculation seemed perilously a part of life in those days. Tragedy was a muse whose glory was for the moment over-shadowed with an almost mystical, hardly to be expressed quality that one might possibly define as pathos. Beauty and the warrior were at rest. For the rest of us in London and Paris and Vienna, there was something different, something too subtle to be called disintegration or dissociation, but a state in which the soul and body didn't seem on good terms. Hardly on speaking terms. So it is that this fine little Greta Garbo with her youth, her purity, her straight brows and her unqualified distinction found a role to fit her. She had, it is true, appeared, I am told, creditably in other films; it was my good fortune to meet her first in this 'Joyless Street' or, as it was billed in our lake Geneva small-town, 'La Petite Rue Sans Joie'. The theatre, I need hardly say, was half empty. The performance began with a street (will I ever forget it) and the sombre plodding limp of a one-legged, old ruffian. No appeal to pity, to beauty, the distinguished mind that conceived this opening said simply, this is it, this is us, no glory, no pathos, no glamour. Just a long, Freudian, tunnel-like, dark street. Nothing within sight, nothing to dream of or ponder on but … the butcher's shop with its attendant, terrible, waiting line of frenzied women.

Life is getting something to eat said the presenter of this 'Petite Rue Sans Joie'. Getting it somehow, anyhow. Beauty itself must come to me, says La Petite Rue Sans Joie and one after another through sheer boredom with starvation, the 'girls' of the neighbourhood, the banal, the merely pretty, the sometimes ambitious, and the sheerly slovenly are drawn within the portals of la Petite Rue. For in the little street there is a shop that rivals even the butcher's for gaiety and distraction. It is neatly disguised, yet thinly. Clothes are bought and sold by a certain suave Madame (the performance of this entrepreneuse whose name I have forgotten, was amazing) and the little bigger of the little daughters of the proud, utterly destitute, brilliant, youngish, middle-aged professor strolls from time to time discreetly to its portal. Madame who is so suave, so kind (will I ever forget the subtlety of her make up, that suggested shadow of a mustache across her sly upper lip) one day offers the little Mademoiselle a fur coat to wear home, she needn't pay for it yet, just wear it and keep warm, things are so hard, madame is so suave, so genuinely sympathetic. The little lady loses her job through the insidious gift. A fur coat. Everyone knows what that means in post-war Vienna. The Manager of the office is pleased, didn't know this wild-flower was a game one. He summons her, offers a rise in salary, the usual denouement, of course, she being she, can't possibly accept it. La Petite Rue Sans Joie seems perilously near to swallowing our Beauty. Helen walking scatheless among execrating warriors, the plague, distress, and famine is in this child's icy, mermaid-like integrity. Her purity shines like an enchanter's crown. We *know* nothing can happen to her, yet do we? Things happen, we ourselves have known them to happen ... one by one, our audience (already meagre) has risen, has blatantly stamped downstairs. I hear words, whispers, English. 'A thing like *this* ... filthy ... no one but a *foreigner* would dare present it.' La Petite Rue Sans Joie was a real, little street. It was a little war-street, a little, post-war street, therefore our little picture palace in our comparatively broad-minded Lake Geneva town, is empty. People won't, they dare not face reality.

And beauty, among other things, is reality, and beauty once in so many hundred years, raises a wan head, suddenly decides to avenge itself for all the slights that it has negligently accepted, sometimes through weariness, sometimes through sheer omnipotence, sometimes through cynicism or through boredom. Simonetta, the famous Medician Venus (though I don't care for her), one and one and one, all stand as witnesses that once in so often, beauty herself, Helen above Troy, rises triumphant and denounces the world for a season and then retires, spins a little web of illusion and shuffles off to forget men and their stale formulas of existence. Well beauty has been slurred over and laughed at and forgotten. But Helen of Troy didn't always stay at home with Menelaus. Beauty has been recognised and for that reason (as the world will not face reality and the ogre, the Censor, this Polyphemus knows well enough that beauty is a danger), Miss Garbo has been trained, and that with astonishing efficiency, to sway forward and backward in long skirts with pseudo-Lillian Gish affectation, to pose with a distinct, parrot-like flare for the Gloria Swansonesque. Her wigs, her eye-lashes have all but eclipsed our mermaid's straight stare, her odd, magic quality of almost clairvoyant intensity. She simpers. Something has been imposed, a blatant, tinsel and paper-flowers and paste-jewel exterior, yet it doesn't quite dominate this nordic ice-flower. Beauty brings a curse, a blessing, a responsibility. Is that why your Ogre, the Censor, is so intent on disguising it, on dishing it up as vamp charm, as stale, Nice-carnival beauty-as-we-get-it-in-a-beauty-contest? Greta Garbo remains Greta Garbo. Let us hope she takes it into her stupid, magic head to rise and rend those who have so defamed her. Anyhow for the present, let us be thankful that she, momentarily at least, touched the screen with her purity and glamour. The screen has been touched by beauty, and the screen, in spite of all the totems, must finally respond, Polyphemus of our latest day, to the mermaid enchantment.

Vol. I, no. 2   August 1927

THE CINEMA AND
THE CLASSICS

II

RESTRAINT

We need, I think, next more precision, more 'restraint' in the presentation of classic themes. Such films as *Quo Vadis* or *Theodora* are excellent in their milieu and since dealing with turbulent and late periods, they are of necessity, ornate, over-crowded, over-detailed and confused. However, even this is a moot point. *Helen of Troy* was excellent in particulars. But to present the 'classic' it is not necessary to build up paste board palaces, the whole of Troy, the entire over-whelming of a battle fleet. The 'classic' as realism could be better portrayed by the simplest of expedients. A pointed trireme prow nosing side ways into empty space, the edge of a quay, blocks of solid masonry, squares and geometric design would simplify at the same time emphasize the pure *classic* note. There is already a stamp, a tradition. A room, in a pseudo-classic film, as a rule, reaches on and on, through doors and door-ways. The *Last Days of Pompeii* was in this particular the most excruciating. A Greek interior should be simple, cold and chaste, with one blocked in door-way, not a vista of ten; with one single fountain jet, not an elaboration of Jean Bologniaesque detail. Again with the costume. We need simple beautiful line, bodies almost naked as in the German production *Force and Beauty*. This experiment failed, of course, grievously in parts as all really broad innovations are bound to do, but there was one short excerpt of life as it should be, German classic that became almost Greek classic. Young men swing through a door way, this time consistently weather worn (why must these 'classic' interiors all smell of varnish?) across (this was excellent) strewn earth and sand down to an open circus-like palestra. In the distance there were figures wrestling in pure vase-gesture, black-figure vase pre-fifth century gesture. The men swaying forward walked as soldiers not as ballet dancers. They did not mince. There was also one exquisite naked silhouette of a woman, the famous judgement of Paris tableau. The contour of this film Aphrodite was beautiful and the setting adequate, but again simplification would have rammed in the really exquisite and inspired creation. The 'classic' as seen on the screen suggests (with rare and inspired exceptions) a rather rowdy Chelsea arts ball rather than a pre-fifth or fifth century piece of sculpture or clean line drawing. We want to remove a lot of trash, wigs in particular, Nero's wig, the blond Mary Pickford curls of the blind Nydia in Pompeii, hair piled and curled and peaked and frizzed like old photographs of our 1880 great aunts. Sweep away the extraneous.

Now this is not so difficult as it might seem. According to preconceived cinema rote (cinema tradition is mercifully young enough to be modified, to be utterly re-inspired) a classic 'set' is built up, is constructed and before it, classic figures, even the most

successful, are apt to be blurred or cheapened. Expense has to be considered and this
is where the young innovator has his big chance. The true classic is not a thing of built
up walls, any more than the true Elizabethan gains by elaborate stage scenery and
pasteboard perspective. Streets and by-ways should be on one plane, we should be
somewhere, not all over the place. We should be *somewhere* with our minds, lines should
radiate as toward a centre not out and away from the central point of interest, whether
that central point is an altar, a shop, a street corner, a window or a person. We should
be somewhere, our getting on somewhere else will come in due course. The days of
paste-board Rialtos is, or should be, over in the art of the stage as well as in the more
subtle, though for the moment less traditionally evolved, art of the cinema. There is
where our hope lies. It isn't too late to get down to dots, to begin at the beginning, to,
if necessary, sweep away what has already been over-elaborated and lay fresh altar
blocks. As I say our least set should have its focus of simplicity, its as it were altar block,
should mean something. Should *be* somewhere. This 'somewhere' is easy to accomplish,
a blank drop scene, a room, such as we live in to-day, bare of accessories. A bare square
room is to-day what it was in Pompeii, what it more or less was in Athens, in Syracuse.
A garden remains a garden and a rosebush a rose-bush. Laurel trees still exist outside
suburbia and a classic laurel grove for instance is easy to represent; one branch, placed
against a soft back drop, or against a wall of any empty room, with suitable cross-effect
of shadow. The fascinating question of light alone could occupy one for ever; this edge
of a leaf and this edge of a leaf; the naturalistic and the sheer artificial must merge,
melt and meet. The pure classic does not depend for effect for instance, on a whole, a
part has always been important, chiselling and cutting, shaping and revising. A laurel
grove rises in one branch set against a plain room wall, and a figure without
exaggerated, uncouth drapery becomes Helen or Andromeda or Iphigeneia [Iphigenia]
more swiftly, more poignantly against just such a wall, obtainable by anyone, anywhere,
than in some enormous rococo and expensive 'set' built up by the 'classicists' of
Hollywood who spread Nero's banquet table with Venetian glass and put the
quattrocento Romola to sleep (or to dine) in a more or less eighteenth century milieu.
Not that I have any quarrel with any of the 'set' makers, with scene shifters or the
general miracle-workers of such elaborate and startling effects as, for instance, the
flight of the Children of Israel and the Pharaoh's chariots. Pharaoh's chariots, Pharaoh's
horses were excellent, but sand and horses and excellently trained circus-riders have
their place. I am concerned here chiefly with attempts at more subtle simple effects; they
so often fail for lack of some precise and definite clear intellect at the back of the whole,
one centralizing focus of thought cutting and pruning the too extraneous underbrush
of tangled detail. Someone should slash and cut. Ben Hur drove his chariot with
decorum and with fervour but ... when I would begin to criticize I am lost myself in
a tangle of exciting detail, am myself so startled and amazed by certain swiftness, certain
effects of inevitable precise mass movement (such as, in another instance, the crowd again
crossing sand in Babylonian *Intolerance*) that I lose my own clue, become sated and
lost and tired. Isn't that the danger? Satiety? Having become sated with the grandiose,
can't someone with exquisite taste and full professional share of technical ability light
our souls with enthusiasm over, as I have said, one laurel branch, one figure sitting
sideways, one gesture (not too frigid and not too stagily static) as for example toward

a waiting enemy? Iphigenia pleading for her life against one rough edge of built-up altar, with severe wall again, and possibly (to balance the edge of altar) the slim, updarting geometric line of half an Ionic (or, correct me, Doric?) pillar. Sand and rock and sea. These are the Greek equivalent for the Roman mass of soldiery, the Prætorian formations and the vast thronging of the colosseum. You and you and you can cause Odysseus with one broken oar to depict his woefulness. You can bring Callypso [Calypso] back with violet tufts, herself placed perhaps against one single heavy rock, a thread of violets perhaps in her tight bound hair. Don't above all, let hair stream in the wind as happened (perhaps not without a certain charm) in *Helen Of Troy*. Keep slightly natural, naturalistic but formalised. If the hair must hang, it must hang heavy, like gold threads in a Crivelli altar piece, like the carved Ionic maidens of the Acropolis Museum, like the Delphic Charioteer himself, should he unloose his head-band.

Or if madness is indicated, make it a psychic manifestation done with intricate but simple fade-outs or superimposed impressions. Here the camera has it over all other mediums. Success is obtainable in representation of psychic phenomena, can be obtained, has, in certain instances, been. The pseudo-classic madness of Victor Varconi in *The Last Days of Pompeii* was banality incarnate. But, turning from madness to vision, not only can we recall men and women of antiquity, but the gods themselves. Hermes, indicated in faint light, may step forward, outlined in semi-obscurity, or simply dazzling the whole picture in a blaze of splendour. Helios may stand simply and restrained with uplifted arm. And here again no suggestion, I beg you, of drapery. If he must stand sideways let him do so, but for heaven's sake don't deface the image of god with a dish-clout! Tear away hideousness from the human form, from the human mind and from the human spirit. A perfect medium has at last been granted us. Let us be worthy of it.

You and I have got to work. We have got to begin to care and to care and to care. Man has perfected a means of artistic expression, that, I assure you, would have made Phidias turn in his grave (if he had a grave) with envy. Light speaks, is pliant, is malleable. Light is our friend and our god. Let us be worthy of it. Do not let us defame light, use and waste brilliant possibilities, elaborate material, making light a slave and a commonplace mountebank. Light has bounced on broncos, has levelled shafts at iron Indians, has burst into barricades, and has minced in crinolines long enough for one generation.

Elaborate experiment – *that* was well enough – and waste and waste and waste must inevitably precede perfection of any medium. But don't let's put up with too much of it. Here is our medium, as I say here is the thing that the Elusinians would have been glad of; a subtle device for portraying of the miraculous. Miracles and godhead are *not* out of place, are not awkward on the screen. A wand may (and does) waft us to fabulous lands, and beauty can and must redeem us.

But it must be a chaste goddess that we worship and a young goddess, and perhaps a little a ridiculous goddess. We must expect to be laughed at, must expect detractors and defamers as Athene must expect them if she strolled full armed or without arms down the Tottenham Court Road. We don't want exaggeration certainly, but modernity in dress, in thought, true modernity approaches more and more to classic standards. How many perfectly exquisite studies can be made of youth, sans drapery, or even with slight modifications (if your youth happens to be a maiden) of its last party frock. A judicious arrangement of a simple headband, for example, may transform Mary Jones into an Isthmian Calliope or young Tom Smith into Thessalian Diomed.

This is partly what I mean by 'restraint', an artistic restraint that does not pre-visualise a Helen, an Andromeda, an Iphegenia, a Diomed, or a young Hercules as antiquated stage or ballet types done up in henna-ed wigs. Types approaching the most perfect of the pre-fifth century vase paintings and the most luminous of pre-Periclean sculpture are to be found, I am certain, among the unexploited. I have no quarrel with the professional as professional but with the professional in one art pretending to know everything about another art of whose very existence he is ignorant. Scholars should be brought in on this. Walls should arise if, for example, Troy-walls must arise, that are either exact in technical detail or else that are suggested merely, as I have earlier indicated by a few great stones. And so on. It is preconceived ideas that destroy all approach to real illumination. *What* do you know of beauty, of life, of reality should be the first questions that a manager or producer asks his scenic artist. Not what was your job in New York, Chicago, Brixton, or Hollywood. So with the costumier. Begin at the beginning. Don't begin in the muddled middle. Our classic ladies of the screen are so often reminiscent of the spirit that led the Bernhardts and the Duses of the period to appear in crinoline when playing Phædra. We want to do away with the crinolined Phædras of this latter day and get back to stark reality.

That is where the beauty of the human body as the human body should have some sort of innings, but will it? Simplicity, restraint, formalisation are all Greek attributes, Hellenic restraint and Hellenic naturalisation that never saw the human body frankly other than the body of its deity. God made man, we are taught from our earliest days, in his own image. Well, let's up then and teach our teachers, our great-aunts who heard us our catechism that we *do* believe in God and do believe in beauty. Get away from all this broncho-chest-muscle business. Why can't some girl or boy just walk on, in a fleecy peplum if you want but somehow just *be* the thing, do the thing with no exaggeration of sentiment such as we were treated to by Diotima in that nightmare (to me) *Heilegeberge (Wrath Of The Gods)*. Mountains are classic, the sea, sand, and the really charming grace and agility of Tom Jones when he leaps on a crowded City bus. Haven't you yourself noticed it? Untrained yet unsullied movement should merge with professional power and tact. The screen is the medium par excellence of movement – of trees, of water, of people, of bird wings. Flowers open by magic and magic spreads cloud forms, all in themselves 'classic'. Though, on the other hand, the most ornate back parlour crowded with gimcracks can represent 'restraint' if the mind presenting it has its own intense restrained unit of idea. Take *Greed* as an example of the classic mind at work upon ornate exaggeration of detail in a sordid modern tenement atmosphere.

Here is my point and my contradiction; the over elaborate tenement detail of *Greed* struck a far more classic note than those sentimental German slow-ups of Diotima doing bare-foot dancing on an uncomfortable slab of sea rock. The classic then, coming down to dots, is a point of view and 'restraint' is a classic virtue which means simply tact and intuition and a sense of the rightness and the fitness of things in their inter-relation. Diotima dancing on the mountains was so simply silly. With all its over elaborate detail, the dramatization of the impulse that led an illiterate, self-educated quack dentist to die in a desert with vultures hovering over his gold-laden, dying mule was Aescuylean. It is obvious that certain self conscious portraits of semi-naked studies must be fore-ordained banality. While perhaps some little unexpected effect of a bare arm lifted might bring back (as it does sometimes in a theatre) all of antiquity. We must work self-consciously and at the same time leave vast areas of mind and spirit free, open to idea, to illumination. I feel (though up to the present only in part successful) the only reality of this sort has come from Germany. The young men and the Paris tableau of the first instance in the *Force and Beauty* (Kraft und Schönheit) that I have mentioned and another 'throned Cytherian'; that proud simple figure curled this time on a great shell in the prologue of *Helen of Troy*. Could anything be more true, more real, more unsullied, more unstudied yet more exactly artificial, in the sense of art made reality? Aphrogeneia. She is there always in my mind as an example of what art can do, what can be done and what must be done. Beauty restrained and chaste, with the over-weaving of semi-phosphorescent light, in a few tense moments showed that the screen can rise to the ecstatic level of the poetic and religious ideals of pure Sophoclean formula.

Vol. I, no. 5   November 1927

THE CINEMA AND THE CLASSICS

III

THE MASK AND THE MOVIETONE

The problem arises (it has been dogging us for some time) is the good old-fashioned conventionalised cinema product a more vivid, a more vital, altogether in many ways a more inspiring production than his suave and sometimes over-subtlised offspring? Our hero with sombrero, our heroine with exactly set coiffure, each in himself, in herself a mask of himself or herself, one with sleek dutch-doll painted in black cap of piquante elf like mahogany coloured hair, another with radiant curls, so many dolls, are treasures – boy dolls in sombreros – are they to be discarded, are we going to be asked to discard them for another set of boxes, containing such intricate machinery, such suave sophistication of life that we wonder if we really want them? Do we want little ivory balls for instance, pretty as they are, fitting into ivory balls, and all the intricate paraphernalia of meccano or jigsaw puzzle to tax our little minds to breaking? Don't we really want what we know, what we see, what intellectually we can aptly 'play' with? Don't we? Or do we? I mean do we really want to give up curls and painted-in dutch-doll fringes, and beautifully outlined eyes and eyelashes and doll-stuffed bodies (doing for instance trapeze turns just likc real circus people) for something perhaps 'better'? Do we really want to discard our little stage sets and all the appliances that we have grown so used to for something more like 'real' life? Well, do we or don't we? Please answer me. I am at my wits' end. Do we or don't we want to scrap our old dolls? The problem reasserted itself with renewed force at a New Gallery demonstration of the Movietone.

Here we have our little people. Here comes our heroine. Truly it is not the heroine exactly of our most most vapid romances, of our most, most old box of dolls and paper-dolls but it is the sort of toy that we are used to, a doll, a better doll, a more highly specialised evolved creation but for all that a doll (Raquel Meller) steps forward. It bows, it smiles, it is guaranteed to perform tricks that will shame our nursery favourites *but do we want it?*

The doll in question, a Spanish doll this time, done up in Castillian [Castilian] embroidery, not over exaggerated with suitable *décor* of operatic street scene and so on, steps out smiles pathetically, tragically, or with requisite pathos, familiar gestures but somehow sensitized, really our old bag of tricks. And then wonder of wonders, the doll actually lifts its eyes, it breathes it speaks – it *speaks*. This is no mechanical voice off, it is the vision itself, the screen image actually singing with accuracy and acumen, with clear voice and beautiful intonation, singing and moving, moving and singing, voice accurately registering the slightest change of expression (Raquel Meller with her *Flor del Mar* and *La Tarde del Corpus*) each tiny fall and lift of note following raised eyebrow or curl of lip or dejection of drooping shoulder. Voice follows face, face follows voice, face and voice with all their subtle blending are accurately and mechanically welded. They are *welded* – that is the catch. The catch is that the excellent actress with all her beauty and her finished acting had a voice as beautifully finished as her screen image but it was (wasn't it?) *welded* to that image. Her voice and herself moving with so finished artistry were welded not (and this seemed some odd catastrophe) *wedded*. The projection of voice and the projection of image were each in itself perfect and ran together perfectly as one train on two rails but the rails somehow functioning in perfect mechanical unison, remained a separate – separate entities, fulfilling different mechanical requirements. It seemed to me, astonished as I was at both (beauty of face and mellow finish of song) that each in some diabolic fashion was bringing out, was under-stressing mechanical and artificial traits in the other. Each alone would have left us to our dreams. The two together proved too much. The screen image, a mask, a sort of doll or marionette was somehow mechanized and robbed of the thing behind the thing that has grown to matter so much to the picture adept. A doll, a sort of mask or marionette about which one could drape one's devotions, intellectually, almost visibly like the ardent Catholic with his image of madonna, became a sort of robot. Our old doll became replaced by a wonder-doll, singing, with musical insides, with strings that one may pull, with excellent wired joints. But can we whisper our devotion to this creature? Are we all beings of infinite and pitiful sentiment? I didn't really *like* my old screen image to be improved (I might almost say imposed) on. I didn't *like* my ghost-love to become so vibrantly incarnate. I didn't like to assert my intellect to cope with it any more than I should have liked Topsy (of the old days) suddenly to emerge with wired-in legs and arms and with sewed-on bonnet and really grown-up bead bag dangling (also sewed on) from one wrist. We want, don't we, our old treasures? Or do we want a lot of new toys, mechanical and utterly proficient?

O well, there it is. I know and see and admire. I do think it is wonderful to hear and see. 'Speaks for Itself' reads the slogan on the folder. But do we want our toy dog to 'speak for itself'? Do we really want our rag doll to stand up and utter? Don't we, like the pre-fifth peoples of Attica, of Crete, of the Cyclades treasure old superstitions (even the most advanced of us) and our early fantasies? Take away our crude upright pillar, take away our carved symbols of Demeter and our goat-herd chorus, said pre-fifth century Athenians and you rob us of our deity. Haven't we been just a little hurt and disappointed that our dolls have grown so perfect?

Well, that is for you to say and you to say and you to say. We each have an idea and a sentiment. We are all sentiment when it comes to discarding dolls for (it seems incredible) robots. Don't look so nice, and sing so nicely at the same time, I want to scream at Raquel Meller, for I seem to be about to be done out of something. *She* is doing everything. I want to help to add imagination to a mask, a half finished image, not have everything done for me. I can't *help* this show. I am completely out of it. This acting, singing, facial beauty is perfected. This screen projection is not a mask, it is a person, a personality. That is just it. Here is art, high art, but is it our *own* art? Isn't cinema art a matter (or hasn't it been) of inter-action? We have grown so used to our conventions, our intellectual censors have allowed us to acclaim such silly and sometimes vapid figures. You may fall in love said our censor with things so patently outside the intellectual scope of your realities. You may fall in love with gilt curls or a sailor doll or a brainless sombrero image. For these were masks, images of man, images of women, the feminine, the masculine, all undistressed, all tricked up with suitable accoutrements. Then we sank into light, into darkness, the cinema palace (we each have our favourite) became a sort of temple. We depended on light, on some sub-strata of warmth, some pulse or vibration, music on another plane too, also far enough removed from our real artistic consciousness to be treated as 'dope' rather than accepted in any way as spiritual or intellectual stimulus. We moved like moths in darkness, we were hypnotized by cross currents and interacting shades of light and darkness and maybe cigarette smoke. Our censors, intellectually off guard, permitted our minds to rest. We sank into this pulse and warmth and were recreated. The cinema has become to us what the church was to our ancestors. We sang, so to speak, hymns, we were redeemed by light literally. We were almost at one with Delphic or Elucinian candidates, watching symbols of things that matter, accepting yet knowing those symbols were divorced utterly from reality. The mask originally presented life but so crudely that it became a part of some super-normal or some sub-normal layer of consciousness. Into this layer of self, blurred over by hypnotic darkness or cross-beams of light, emotion and idea entered fresh as from the primitive beginning. Images, our dolls, our masks, our gods, Love and Hate and Man and Woman. All these attributes had their more or less crude, easily recognised individual complements. Man and Man and Man. Woman and more and more and more Woman. Bits of chiffon became radiantly significant, tiny simple and utterly trivial attributes meant so much. Or didn't they? I mean that is what the moving pictures have done to us sometimes. We are like pre-fifth Athenians waiting for our Aeschylus, our Sophocles, our Euripides. We are being told that the old gods won't do and we know they won't do really. We must have refinement and perfection and more intricate machinery. Now I know that this is quite right. I do know. I know and utterly appreciate for instance the immense possibilities of the Movietone in certain circumstances. If it were used properly there would be no more misunderstandings for instance (or there shouldn't be) of nations. I mean that five minutes of what I call 'bottled' America should do more for the average intelligent English mind than ten weeks on that continent. Look at 'Lindy'. Now we have all seen this charming gentleman, alighting, arising, swooping a little, crowded and pushed and pulled here and there and which way. But did we know 'our Lindy' till we saw him, till we heard him at the New Gallery Movietone performance? 'Colonel Lindberg's departure for Paris and reception in Washington' read the second number on our programme. The first bit ('departure for Paris') showed blatantly the flaws of the excellent Movietone. I mean the crowds came up in funny little squeaks and whistles and gasps. Someone whistling (I suppose at random) somewhere, cut across vital and exaggerated while more important factors of group surge and voice rhythm were blurred over utterly. The buzz and whirr of the plane wheels was excellent but we were not particularly impressed by that as we have been so long familiar with the same sort of thing adequately represented 'off' at the average cinema. The plane buzzed off dramatically but the slice 'departure for Paris' was really only the somewhat usual topical budget number somewhat more skilfully presented. But that 'reception in Washington' should teach statesmen better. I mean look and look and look at what I call 'bottled' America and look and look and look. Turn on that reel ten thousand times and then talk to me of international understanding. Does the average Englishman understand the average American (I say average) and vice versa? Can they? Do they? If you want to understand America, I feel like saying to Lord Birkenhead (who made an address, 5 on our excellent programme) go (or come) and look and look and look at this particular reel, 'and reception in Washington'. Nations should understand (but they won't, with the best of intentions, do) nations. It would make life so simple if we really wanted, really to understand anybody. Where would be our speeches and our receptions and our conferences and our gatherings? Half of life would be out of an occupation. If we could not sit up nights hating Englishmen or Frenchmen or Italians or Spaniards or American (or Americans) where, where would all our energy and our spirit flow to? I mean where would we get to? We would be, like pre-Periclean Athenians, I fear, really ready for an Art Age.

Art, art, ahrt and arrrt and AHRT age. Yes, we would be ready for an art age. Turn on a thousand times and go on turning bits of 'bottled' Germany, and 'bottled' America, kings and presidents and the reception by varied peoples of varied kings and generals and senators and presidents and we will understand each other. Nations are in turns of wrists, in intonations of voices and that is where the Movietone can do elaborate and intimate propaganda. Peace and love and understanding and education could be immensely aided by it. The Movietone outside the realm of pure sentiment, treated from a practical viewpoint is excellent in all particulars. Oh, how we could understand if only we wanted to understand, each other. Take the president's voice for instance. In it is an America (or should I say *the* America) that many of us, even through natives of its eastern sea-coast, never meet with. The words of President Coolidge cut across London mist and our Europeanized consciousness like dried brush crackling in a desert. Arid, provincial, pragmatic and plain it held singular vitality. I mean (speaking all too personally) Lord Birkenhead, standing in a garden before a hedge of oak trees (or it ought to have been, if it wasn't, oak trees) was really bottled 'England' just as the president with his arid talk of republicism and his 'man of the people' stunt was 'bottled' and then distilled America. The Germans, we are told, are delighted and rock with mirth at the screen aspect of the French president. Well, let us rock and scream and laugh at one another. Laughter precludes a sort of affectionate acceptance. Let us laugh but let it be in temples, in gatherings, the group consciousness is at the mercy of Screen and Movietone. Let us understand one another. Let the Movietone become a weapon in the hand of a Divinity.

UNDERSTANDING was the deity of Athens, Mind and Peace and Power and Understanding. Know thyself (we all know) says the deity of Delphi, who is Beauty and Inner Understanding (which is mantic) and more Beauty and Art in the abstract that we all hope for. This new invention seems an instrument of dual god-head. A miracle is literally unrolled before our eyes. We are too apt to take divinity for granted. Understanding, Athene with her olive wreath, another sort of understanding, Helios with his justice and his power of divination, are both eager for new neophytes. Here is an instrument of twin divinity. Tone and vision, sight and sound, eyes and ears, the gate ways to the mind are all appealed to. We are visionaries, we may become prophets. We are adepts, moving at will over foreign lands and waters, nothing is hidden from us. Apply the Movietone to questions of education and international politics and you will do away with revolutions. Well, there it all is in a nut-shell, 'bottled'. But are we ready for so suave simplification? Some of us will grow in outer and in inner vision with the help of this invention. Others will be left cold as they would be left inert before another Mons or Marathon. Yet it stands to reason that a new world *is* open, a new world of political understanding, of educational reform, or art (in its pure sense) even. Art, I repeat unparenthetically, may in its pure essence be wedded not merely welded to art. I felt frankly disappointed in Raquel Meller. By some ironic twist of psychic laws, it seems impossible to be luke-warm, to be 'almost good enough', Madame Meller does not lack power and personality. But some genial sub-strata of humour or humanity seemed wanting. Mechanical efficiency, technique carried to its logical conclusion do not make divinity. I felt however in Nina Tarasova and Miss Gertrude Lawrence (numbers 7 and 11 on our programme) a full-blooded vitality that nothing can diminish. Madame Tarasova registered sorrow and despair with almost oriental subtlety; though her gesture was obvious, her real artistry redeemed her curious appearance and her bulk, unwieldy as our now familiar *Chang* elephants only served by some ironic twist of circumstance to increase our appreciation. The grandeur of voice in this case seemed healing and dynamic. Madame Tarasova, magnified to the size of Big Ben almost, became as hugely interesting. One laughs, (or used to) at scientific projections, lizards like dinosaurs, beetles exaggerated out of recognition, gargantuan night-moths, flower petals that would enclose Cleopatra's Needle. We used to laugh hysterically at these things, but now take them for granted. So for the moment the spectacle of an operatic singer complete with voice strains our credulity. Voice and body beat and pulsed with what dynamic energy. We laughed of course. But as I say, didn't we used to laugh in somewhat the same fashion at the exaggerated antics of enormous ants and hornets? We are used to nature, expanded and ennobled past all recognition, now we must again readjust and learn to accept calmly, man magnified. Man magnified, magnified man, with his gestures, his humors, his least eccentricities stressed to the point of almost epic grandeur. Art to conceal art. Is there any more damaging revelation than art revealed? Art is cut open, dissected so to speak by this odd instrument. Movietone creates and recreates until we feel that nothing can remain hidden, no slightest flaw of movement or voice or personality undetected. It is odd how damaging this double revelation is to some otherwise (we should think) unassailable artistes, while others apparently not so fine, emerge unscathed and smiling. Gertrude Lawrence for instance endured this double ordeal with wit and subtlety. The screen Gertrude Lawrence, at first sight a slim mannequin, became animated with fluid inspiration. Her gesture and her speech, in this case completely *wedded*. The pure artist perhaps cannot be assailed, and certainly Madame Tarasova and Miss Lawrence stood this trying ordeal valiantly.

There it is. We stand by our own gods, like or dislike, there is no possible strict standardization to be arrived at. We cannot weigh and measure our affections, we cannot count and label our wavering emotions. I like this, you like that, X or Y or Z like something different. Personally, though I admit the brilliance of this performance, I was not totally won over by it. I think for a long time we have perhaps unconsciously, accepted, as I said earlier, the cinema palace as a sort of temple. So I say yes to anything having to do with reality and with national affairs and with education: then the Movietone is perfect. The outer vision, yes, should be projected, the outer sound, yes, should be amplified and made accessible. Everyone should have access to great music as easily as to books in libraries. This Movietone places people and things, catalogues them. It is excellent as a recorder, as a corrective of technical flaws, or as a means of indefinitely protracting artistic perfection. Art under this magnascope can be dissected and analysed. As an instrument of criticism, yes, as an instrument of international understanding, yes and yes and yes. As a purveyor of ideas and even ideals, yes. But somehow no. There is a great no somewhere. The Movietone has to do with the things outside the sacred precincts. There is something inside that the Movietone would eventually I think, destroy utterly, for many of us. That is the whole point really of the matter. Is our temple, our inner place of refuge, to be crowded out with gods like men, not masks, not images, that are so disguised, so conventionalized that they hold in some odd way possibility of some divine animation? If I see art projected too perfectly (as by Raquel Meller) don't I feel rather cheated of the possibility of something more divine behind the outer symbol of the something shown there? The mask in other words seems about to be ripped off showing us human features, the doll is about to step forward as a mere example of mechanical inventiveness. We cannot worship sheer mechanical perfection but we can love and in a way worship a thing (like Topsy with her rag arms) that is a symbol of something that might be something greater.

We feel fearful that our world may be taken from us, that half-world of lights and music and blurred perception into which, as I said earlier the being floats as a moth into summer darkness. Like a moth really we are paralysed before too much reality, too much glamour, too many cross currents of potentialities. There is too much really for the soul to cope with, and all these out-reaching odd soul-feelers, that you and I and

Tom Jones and the shop girl and the barber and the knife boy have sometimes felt threatened with odd maladies. We want healing in blur of half tones and hypnotic vibrant darkness. Too mechanical perfection would serve only I fear, to threaten that world of half light. We hesitate to relinquish our old ideals and treasures, fearing we may lose our touch with mystery by accepting this new (this sort of Euripidean sophistication) in place of the old goat-herd and his ribald painted chorus.

Vol. I, no. 3   September 1927

CONRAD VEIDT
THE STUDENT OF PRAGUE

A small room, a stuffy atmosphere; a provincial Swiss lake-side cinema; the usual shuffle and shuffle and the unaccustomed (to the urbane senses) rattle of paper bags. Crumbs. 'Mlle must not smoke here.' Of course I might have known that, I never smoke in these places, what made me this time? Something has been touched before I realise it, some hidden spring; there is something wrong with this film, with me, with the weather, with something. The music ought, it is evident, be making my heart spring but I don't like student songs and these Heidelbergish melodies especially leave me frigid. There's something wrong and I have seen those horses making that idiotic turn on the short grass at least eight times. What is it? I won't stay any longer. The music *ought* to be all right – my slightly readjusted ears make that slight concession. I wish I had stayed at home, or why didn't I go instead to that other little place, it's better ventilated, across the way. And so on. This storm that doesn't break. I have no reaction to anything ... O *that's* what the little man is after.

For I see now. There is a rhythm within the rhythm, there is a story within the story. The little man (it is curiously he whom I personally met before in Joyless Street, disguised now out of recognition) beckons at the top of a sandy hill. The little tree twists and bends and makes all the frantic gestures of the little tree at the cross-roads under which Faust conjured devils. That's it precisely. This has something behind it, in it, through it. That little man means much more than that. He isn't an absurd little obvious Punchinello. He is a symbol, an asterisk, an enigma. Spell the thing backwards, he seems to be saying, spell it right side to or back side to or front or behind and you'll see ... his little leer means something. The horses filing again, in obvious procession, mean something. They are going to spell something, make a mystic symbol across short grass, some double twist and knot and the world will go to bits ... something is going to happen.

I have forgotten the paper bags. The music *does* fit in. I have forgotten the lilt and rise and lilt and fall of the violin that doesn't in the least know that the piano is existing. That's it exactly. The piano and the violin live in separate elements, so this and this. The little obvious Italian Punchinello doesn't in the least mind being jeered at. He wants to be jeered at. He has opened doors to the uninitiate. *They* don't know that that umbrella tucked so ridiculously under his left arm-pit, means something. I know that it means something but I don't know what (outside the obviously obvious) it does mean. There is a world within a world, the little man gesticulates. The horses have all gone ... the music has come right.

Students sing under summer trees. Students have filed under summer trees and seated in a garden make obvious opera bouffe groups with beribboned guitars. Students sing in a garden ... grey eyes cut the opera bouffe to tatters. The student of Prague has entered.

His visage, his form, the very obvious and lean candour of him spell something different. He is and he isn't just this person sitting under a tree. The little man gesticulating at the top of a sandy hill has given one the clue to the thing. This is and isn't Conrad Veidt or this is and isn't Baldwin the famous fencer. His eyes cut the garden, the benches, the sun-light (falling obviously) to tatters. How did this man get here? Steel and fibre of some vanished lordlihood. Conrad Veidt has entered.

A gesture, a tilt of a chin, the downward sweep of a wide-rimmed student's cap and the world has altered. With the same obvious formality and the same obvious banality as the little Italian conjurer, the least hunch of shoulder of this famous artist has some hidden meaning. He is lean and wild. He is firm and sophisticated and worldly. He will break from his skin like a panther from a tight wicker box. He is tight in his personality and behind his personality his mind glints like his own steel. Conrad Veidt impersonating the famous Baldwin may not be the Conrad Veidt of *The Hands of Orlac*, or *Nju*. I have seen only this film. But I don't want to see another Conrad Veidt if it must abuse my mind of this one.

The story is obvious. The English literary critical papers accompany their 'still' of the famous mirror scene with some such explanatory blurb: this is the Doctor Jekyll and Mr Hyde of German legend. Doctor Jekyll and Mr Hyde, how apt, certainly. Doctor Jekyll however shuddered in horror at the sodden parody of himself that Hyde presented. This Jekyll and Hyde are alike elegant, alike poised, alike at home in the world of fact and in the supernatural. For by a magnificent trick of sustained camera magic we have Baldwin the famous fencer student selling his shadow, rather his brave reflection to the little obvious Italian magician of the first reel. The little Punchinello obtains it, by a trick; gold poured and poured Danae shower, upon the bare scrubbed table of the student's attic, 'for something in his room'. The student has lifted his magnificent blade ruefully and cynically has decided (as that is the only object worth a sou in the bare attic) to be done with it. It is not *that* blade that our friend Punchinello's after. He beckons with his obvious buffoon gesture toward the mirror. Baldwin regards (in its polished surface) the face of Baldwin. Tall, alert, with that panther grace, like some exquisite lean runner from an archaic Delphic frieze, Baldwin regards Baldwin. It is true there should be Baldwin upon Baldwin, Veidt upon Veidt, elegantly pursuing (across some marble entablature) Baldwin upon stripped Baldwin, Veidt upon naked Veidt. In that, the little Punchinello shows his aptitude for beauty. Such charm, such lean and astute physical intellectuality should be repeated. Gold, flowing from leather cornucopialike wallet has dripped (Danae shower) from the bare table and Baldwin has sold 'something' (not his fine blade) 'in this room' to this mysterious little person. The bargain has been made. Baldwin regards the purchase. With elegant lithe movement, with uncomparable agility, the reflection steps forward. Baldwin on the bare floor, quivers slightly, makes one of those perfect hieratic steps to one side. But the image doesn't answer him. The image, the 'purchase' has another master. The little ridiculous Punchinello with his repellant friendliness lures it forward. As the distant horses made turn and double eights across windy grass, directed by this obvious jester, so now this rare thing. The image of Baldwin strides steadily forward and following our magician, leaves the chamber empty.

There is of course a love story connected with all this. Punchinello has promised our hero a fortune or rather an heiress and that's what the horses were solemnly about. There were making circles and double eights and abracadabra-like turns on the short grass in order finally to spill the big-boned but somehow impressive heroine into (literally) the arms of our steely hero. The hero having so fallen to the charms of this impressive, beautifully modelled lady, must methinks have clothes for his wooing, peg-top trousers, all the paraphernalia that goes with the rather 1860-ish type of get-up. Arms, legs, cloth moulds those arms, legs that were somehow out of elbow for all their statuesque divinity in the simple student. The student (grey eyes tearing tapestries, satin and old lace this time) now is able to present the lady-of-the-manor with suitable 1860-ish baskets of heavy blossoms. (His small early discarded violet-cluster and that violet-seller is another story, a leit-motive [sic] that merges and melts subtly with this other noble matter.) The real lady of his affection is affianced (I believe is the word) to a gentleman in some sort of aldermanic or diplomatic-circles, knee breeches. This person flicking our hero across the cheek bones with the usual gauntlet, is summoned for the usual purposes at dawn or sunset. Anyhow as might have been expected, the hero having been forestalled by the father of his beloved, has promised in best Prague style only to prick his adversary. As again might have been expected, owing, we are led to imagine to the machinations of the Punchinello, the wheel of the carriage bearing our hero to the rendez vous is broken by the usual lonely cross-road and Baldwin, stumbling forward to keep his appointment, his honour so being called to question, is met dramatically by his one (in the world) possible rival. Face to face under a great tree, sweeping branches, mysterious yet naturalist décor. Hyde meets Jekyll. Or Jekyll meets Hyde. It's impossible to choose between them, though at this exact moment, sympathies are with the spectre. Perhaps that is because he wears the attributes of the student fencer in which Conrad Veidt first appeared, the student cap pulled so forcefully and drastically over those steely eyes and the beautiful leather boots. However time is short. We know what is bound to happen. The spectre in all the accoutrements of the gentleman duellist, strides forward leaving the *man* gasping at his predicament. He beholds in, as it were, ambush the inevitable dénouement.

There are gaspings, now direct disapprobation, cuttings, a gentleman, as the world knows does not break his parole d'honneur and all the paraphernalia. Jekyll (or Hyde) the *man* anyhow is dropped anyhow by the vast circle that has been entertained royally in his drawing rooms. His beloved can not meet him, the murderer of her betrothed. The Student of Prague, the famous fencer Baldwin is cut by fencing companies, societies. What you will. He is thrown into the arms of the common Alma Tademesque little violet seller. Things march from worse to still worse. This is what comes of selling one's shadow to a stranger. There is, as is obvious, the really clever stalking of the shadow and the merging and cross-currents of two images. We never lose sight of the identity of either; this too is a triumph. The spectre is the slim gaunt creature in the early student get-up, the man is the somewhat out at heels distrait discarded gentleman. The spectre grows in distinction, in power apparently. The man diminishes. The spectre remains the Student of Prague and Baldwin, his begetter, is hounded by this Frankenstein. Doors are no impediment. The spectre in triumph of film-photography glides discreetly through and into the most sacred milieu. Baldwin the man sinks into the scum of fetid cellars. The spectre and the little early mistress, the small, common, yet uncommonly pretty, violet-girl sink with him. Baldwin becomes violent, destructive. The spectre shares his evil end, gloats in it. Yet apart ... having some life outside humanity ... following, following, till we want to scream, 'strangle him get rid of him, one or the other, let this duality perish if Baldwin perish with it.'

Baldwin does so finally perish, having lured the shadow back into the frame of the mirror in the now deserted attic. He shoots the spectre only to find himself bleeding with the bullet wound. The bullet aimed so adroitly at the breast of the image in the mirror has, by some psychic affinity, entered his own heart. So dies Baldwin. Across our vision however there is something that will never die. It can't go. It lives among other things, in the haunting melody (the music finally did come right) of *du meine Herzen, du mein Ruhe*. Baldwin (before the final dénouement) has finally, in wind and storm (this might have been well pictured to the Erlkönig motif) broken into the garden and the manor of his mistress. We find her great-eyed and adequate, without charm but with some fine distinction in 1860-ish surroundings; great mirrors, heavy candelabra, the wide French windows and the sweeping of wind-blown branches. There is authentic swish and swirl of branches and has anything ever been more subtly dramatic than the entering of broken rose-petals and damp leaves with the opening of that wide door? Baldwin, the man become a shadow, stands before his Lady. We see in a moment, she is that. What she lacks in charm is supplied by the ardour of her lover. He is at her knees, at her feet. He will explain. He will and he will and he will. We know what is about to happen. He lures her to a mirror. It is not he but his missing shadow that has done this. She stares straight into nothingness. There is a dramatic pause, the ten seconds that might be ten minutes, the ten minutes that might be ten years and the lady is lying like some dramatic beautiful Niobe (fainting? Dead?) marble, sculptured on the floor. The beauty of that scene is one that must always remain, that must always come back, it seems now, with wind and wind-swept branches. The screen has purified and idealized, is a medium for purity and idealization. No one could remain unmoved before the sheer technical beauty of that interior. There are volumes of de Regnieresque subtleties on it. This on the screen. There is the intolerable beauty of the Erlkönig come (for all its apparent unrelation) true. There are the things we can't say or paint at the sight of windows half-closed in moonlight. There is the spirit of the garden, the spirit of the water, the lake, the sea, the wind, the ghost itself of all our lives come visually before us. (*Du meine Herzen, du mein Ruhe* sings the violin now and we can't for the life of us notice that it is out of key with the piano.) There is beauty and unfulfilment and the struggle of the spirit and the body and the spirit become body and the body become spirit and the constant strife between Lucifer and the angel Michael.

Michael stands before us and Lucifer. This time there is no mistaking. The spectre is an evil thing now, wishing to snatch, we see it, the living spark of divinity from the man become shadow. Baldwin has flung himself and his secret at the heart of his 'Frieden' his 'Ruhe'. *Du bist mein Grab*, we remember the song continues and we see now its application. He has betrayed the secret of the under-world to a mortal and the spectre, looking athletic and determined, has his hand on the bell rope. He will ring and the man knows that he must vanish. It is the man now who is completely at the will of the shadow.

Du meine Herzen, du mein Ruhe. Baldwin climbing back to his old poor surroundings knows that he is conquered. Baldwin the apparent man, that is. There is something indomitable left, symbolized by the little silver cross that his Lady has given him on that first dramatic meeting in the bare fields. He has saved her life (for all there was distorted magic in it) and the little cross was his reward. Tapestries, laden baskets, the minuet and ladies with lovely ankles, all that came, was swept aside by the pursuing shadow and lost simply. A vision is not so easily relinquished, says the tried soul. I have lost everything says Baldwin but not one thing. Raising himself on one elbow along the splintered glass, he realised that his death has brought him his fulfilment. More than his lady, more than his steel blade, *himself*. Baldwin, dying, clasps a broken edge of triangulated glass to his stained breast. Containing his image simply.

A tiny provincial lake-side cinema ... a small room, by luck I have got a front seat on the little balcony at the room's rear. Languages filter into my consciousness. French? German? I have been following the subtitles in these languages. A tired language, an effete language, not French, not German, is remarking, 'These Germans over-do things ... look at Faust now ... and this is just as morbid.' Another language resembling only in bare particulars that one (is it the same language?) is remarking, 'gee, why don't they have more live-stuff these days. Though they did advertise Doug Fairbanks last week.' Languages filter into me, languages and the music fanfaring away at some familiar sideshow rate and 'the show is over' is indicated by a sudden, crude blare of extravagant electricity. 'Say – you can see electricity's cheap here.' Languages ... languages ... dead languages, living languages. A small voice, a wee voice that has something in common with all these voices yet differs intrinsically from all these voices, will whisper there within me. 'You see I was right. You see it will come. In spite of "Gee" and "Doug Fairbanks" and "we must have something cheerful", it must come soon: a universal language, a universal art open alike to the pleb and the initiate.'

Vol. II, no. 5   May 1928

EXPIATION

I was precipitated suddenly, after the sinuous run along the edge of Lake Geneva, unto the cobbles of the formal irregularities of the Square of Saint Francis at Lausanne. Thence, informed that the car couldn't take the little steep down-drop of the street of Saint Francis, I was tumbled out dazed and exulted at the head of a sort of dimensional dream-tunnel. I was precipitated between so to speak, built-up and somewhat over-done little shops with windows and wares; oranges, boxes of leeks, lettuces on the pavement; bright green shutters. Dazed and re-vitalized by the run, I plunged down this little street somewhat reeling, making jig-jag to find just how those shadows cut just that block (and that block) into perfect design of cobbled square and square little doorway till I found myself at the entrance of a slice of a theatre, the Palace of Lausanne. I couldn't go in, must climb the little street again like a fanatic bob-sleigh runner in order again to run down. I so poignantly wanted to re-visualize those squares of doors and shutters and another and another bit of detail that of necessity was lost at first that I did illogically (I was already late) climb back. A boy rang obligingly across with a baker's flat tray-basket and someone else urged a cat to climb off the topmost row of a row of something that looked like the Concord grape-baskets we used to have in Philadelphia. I ran up and down the scale, so to speak of visual emotion, of memory, of visual sensation making that street and everyone of its little graduations a sort of intellectual accordion from which to draw tunes, the sort of things one tries to put down sometimes (but never quite succeeds in doing) after a particularly poignant dream. It was of course too the sudden flood of mid-March sunlight that was responsible for my heady intoxication and a bunch of somehow over-done (the whole street was preposterous) bundles of daubed-in spring flowers; yellow and blue make the grey and yellow of the street come back at one, back-fire again at one in its hectic over-done insistence on the raw reality of beauty.

Well, it was hardly fair that after climbing up the narrowest of cinema theatre stairs, I should find myself seated beside the 'others' who didn't have a breath left to gasp 'you're late you fool, you've been missing it' but one of them whispered like someone before the high altar explaining to a neophyte 'it's Russian – it's Alaska'.

Someone had apparently killed someone. I had arrived when *Sühne (Expiation)* was about one third over. Someone was heaving a weight of something and against an upright ledge of mud, the rain poured and soaked and ran and gorged runnels in the already over-soaked bit of bed earth. Bad lands, something wasted, wasteful, overdone and done with. Rain poured over a slab of earth and I felt all my preparation of the extravagantly contrasting out of doors gay little street, was almost an ironical intention, someone, something 'intended' that I should grasp this, that some mind should receive this series of uncanny and almost psychic sensations in order to transmute them elsewhere; in order to translate them. Rains soaked across a slab of mud, runnels bored and jabbed and pockmarked and gusseted it. There was never an earth that could be ever again so drab, so unproductive. 'It's Russian – it's Alaska.'

Apparently there had been death in this bad land, how could there be other? But death and all its drab significance rose in its starkness to some almost Elusinian note of purity. So abstract the land, so remote and symbolical the two figures of the living that dragged the two sacks or canvas sails that had been wrapped about the two long bodies of the slain, so heavy and dreary the rain, so slippery the mud, so terrible the lowering of the sky above the rain (which one sensed was there simply for the re-harrowing of these living figures) that the spirit as in the Aescuylean drama rose above it, shouted almost audibly with the elements, *the soul, the soul survives*. The soul was embodied in two figures, man and woman, if that long ungainly creature with the hair whipped about lean, gargoyle face was a woman or some intransient slip of fibrous girlhood. A girl, a child with incredibly thin legs, hurled herself on the ice and snow crusted bad earth, clung to it, like some wan and exquisite Perserphone [Persephone], crying to be buried, dragged in, taken back and back away from human consciousness, like those two others, above whom the man has already set those sort of crude identification boards that we have grown accustomed to in trenches. One realized instinctively that this was no 'grave', but some 'trench' holding victims, slain why and how one couldn't grasp till afterwards. But the intention of the story, greater than its mere plot, could not possibly be misread; death and death and death and bad lands and waste and the Aescuylean lowering of blank skies.

The two return to find the murderer half slipped out of his bonds, lying physically exhausted, practically frozen to death, beside the steps of the woodshed or cabin. They probe him back, lunge with him as they had lunged lately with those two bodies indoors. The half-dead is propped up against the log-wall, the girl guards him with a gun, the man busies himself with clearing up the remains of the interrupted dinner. Sympathy knows no dividing line, we feel alike for the dead under the mud, gone violently, in haste; the murdered, the criminal worse than dead, bound hand and foot; the slip of gargoyle of a girl who sits with gun propped across rigid almost cataleptic knees; the man himself, the one survivor of the 'company' with this care and responsibility toward this girl (his wife), the murderer (his former servant) and the elements. Rain soaks and pours and pours and soaks and the elements have these at their mercy. The ice breaks, the river rises, the hut is flooded and here in a heroic series of sequences we find the girl and the man wading about, knee-deep, in icy water while great chunks of rock-like edges of icebergs bump and grind against the frail sides of the little cabin. On and on and on. Till the Aescuylean bleak terror wears even itself out ... the tide subsides, the little house stands firm, one branch wavers outside against the grey flood and a bird from somewhere announces (as is customary) spring.

To say that spring comes is to put it mildly. The gestures of this woman are angular, bird-like, claw-like, skeleton-like and hideous. She has a way of standing against a sky line that makes a hieroglyph, that spells almost visibly some message of cryptic symbolism. Her gestures are magnificent. If this is Russian, then I am Russian. Beauty is too facile a word to discuss this; this woman is a sort of bleak young sorceress, vibrant, febrile, neurotic, as I say, almost cataleptic. She has one authentic mad scene: her mind breaks after hours of watching the prisoner with the gun placed edge-wise like some iron bar across numbed and frozen knees. She is skeleton-like and death-like. Her face when the bird sings outside the window can hardly be called beautiful.

Her teeth protrude, her cheek bones are hollow, her skull is picked, so to speak, of its meat by misery and waiting. Her mind is on the raw edge of breaking, her eyes roll in terror and madness and numbness of misery ... a bird sings. Her face can be termed beautiful in the same way that dawn can be termed beautiful rising across stench and fever of battle ... there is no word for such things. Her mind, her soul, her body, her spirit, her being, all vibrate, as I say, almost audibly. One is beyond personal discernment. This is psychic, compelling, in a way destructive. I could not see many of these Russian films if there are others like this. This is my first. It is as poignant an experience almost as my first 'real' German film, the exquisite and now world known and discussed *Joyless Street* of G. W. Pabst. Pabst, the Austrian is the greater constructive artist, the Russian (L. Keleschow [Kuleshov]) uses the screen almost as a psychic medium, art on the high almost un-natural level of the Aescuylean (I find I can only repeat) trilogies.

Is Art religion? Is religion art? This is where the point comes. But all discussions of Art, Religion and Life are febrile and old-fashioned really. All I can know is that I, personally, am attuned to certain vibration, that there comes a moment when I can 'witness' almost fanatically the 'truth'. I knew as regards the Germans that G. W. Pabst is an artist, an intellectual, a being, a giant of realism. Yet realism for all its devastating sincerity in *Joyless Street* maintains a sort of sanity, a meaning that applies to everybody. In other words it is a work of art as we are accustomed to understand the term in all its implication. This *Sühne (Expiation)* goes as one of our party said 'too far'. Perhaps it does do. Perhaps the human mind is not yet ready to receive the 'message' the Russian has to give us, though I personally must frankly acclaim this profoundly as moving and touching a drama as I have seen on the stage or screen.

But is that enough? I have said that it was my first Russian film and I have said that it is perhaps destructive. Beauty is that. This sort of raw picked beauty must of necessity destroy the wax and candy-box 'realism' of the so much so-called film art. It must destroy in fact so much that perhaps it does 'go' as one of our party said 'too far'.

How far *can* one 'go'? G. W. Pabst the realist, takes the human mind, the human spirit acting and re-acting against the elemental human terrors of famine and erotic-neurotic impulse, as far as it can go. The Russian takes the human spirit acting and re-acting against human sub-strata of animal instinct, *further* than it can go. The spirit goes as far as the spirit can go and then it goes a little further. That is the poignant realism of *Expiation*. Rain and flood have done their worst as the three, the girl, the threatened husband (who has just escaped death in the mad frenzy of the Irish servant) and the servant. About 'Jack' formidable black Aescuylean wings are forever beating, bearing toward some incohate expression of justice, brotherhood, manhood, human rightness due to every human spirit. The material gold that he had found on the (up to that moment) worthless property of his masters, the group of god diggers, headed by the Englishman Nelson and his wife Edith, is only a symbol. Fraternity, confraternity the old equation is here set out with a freshness that no mere republican American, no mere psuedo-republican Frenchman can appreciate. The old coinage has been debased of its spiritual value. The modern Russian says no, no

to the old but fresh coin, standardized and poignant, spiritual coinage, here it is ...
three men 'masters', one man 'servant' and one woman, a sort of winged sprite, an
angel and a sort of devil of remorseless justice. Fling then down in the mud, in the
ice, in the water, in the fire. Every element must be drawn upon, death,
decomposition, cold and heat, clouds and rain and rain *and* rain. Fling down your
stamped coinage and weight it beside unstamped gold. Jack digs out gold from a
furrow in the mud after the Russian and the German (the two other members of the
'company') have decided that they must pull up stakes, that the soil along the river is
unprofitable. Jack having been sent to make ready the luggage, pauses beside a sort of
wooden funnel-like trough: (since beginning this article I have been back to the little
Palace, Saint Francis Street, Lausanne to see *Sühne* for a second time). Jack in literally
pulling up stakes (a sort of wooden trough or runnel for conveying, one judges, water
to wash bed-silt) bungles on a little gleaming strata. He fills his mining basin with the
mud and water turning, turning this round basin in his hands, he is turning, turning
worlds; Jack is Atlas with a world of new discovery, new possibility, the new, so to
speak, Russia – the new so to speak spirit and ideal wherever and however it may be
found. Jack the Irishman, the servant, finds gold. There is one thing to do, faithful
servant, he rushed back to his 'masters' to find them in short time so overwhelmed
with the weight of their discovery that they forget, if ever they remotely realized,
that it is this Jack, this loutish and uncouth camp-servant who has put them on the
track of miraculous possession.

Jack one evening is a little late for dinner. The other four are in jovial spirits, spring
may come soon, it must do, they will take off in separate directions (England, Russia,
Germany) and forget the old trail of penury, of heart sickness and homesickness, in a
new blaze of civilization and of wealth. O won't we be gay, won't we be recklessly
happy, chants the Russian to his ikon, grunts the German to his muddy boots, as beside
the fire, they each think of the months of labour, of the profit of their isolation, and of
this lessening period of sheer physical discomfort. 'A-ee Jack' shouts the Russian as
the servant lumber in 'don't you wish you were in our shoes, don't you wish you had
just such a gold mine, just such possibility of power as we have?' The words are hardly
spoken. Jack raises his gun and fires. The Russian is neatly punctured in the back, the
German is instantly killed. The girl, the inhuman gargoyle of a woman seeing the
weapon aimed at her husband, springs, wild-cat at the servant. Jack and she struggle
until Nelson, half stunned for the moment leaps forward. Nelson pounds and beats
the murderer, blind, himself about to expiate murder with more murder. The girl in an
agony of neurotic almost epileptic strength drags off her husband. Now the story
continues (where I first began it) with the uncanny ice burial.

So watching Jack through the flood months, spring comes ... but how can we, how
can we hear this any longer? Twice Nelson has been about to fire on Jack, get him out
of the way as Jack himself suggests, bring the thing to an end somehow. Justice, human
justice, this odd gargoyle of a Pallas Athene, Edith, Nelson's wife, as often intercepts
him. That would be murder she insists, we must have justice. Justice, justice cried
Edith and again pity, pity. But justice is stronger than pity in Edith, she is a blighted
uncouth being, a tree riven by lightning for all that lightning has somehow entered her
odd spirit. Justice, justice she cries and after the pathos of the birthday incident, the

candles, the little cake, the exquisite lyrical 'confession' of Jack (I did this thing, because … well, because I wanted to be like the rest of you and I couldn't stand you making fun of me all the time and because I wanted to take presents to *my* people at home) none of them, they all confess severally can stand it any longer. Will you, says Edith, submit to our judgement in the name of … in the name of the Queen of England? Jack says yes. A sort of old-fashioned cheap colour print of the Queen of England is pinned up on the wall above the seat of justice. The Queen of England smiles above the heads of Edith and Nelson. The Queen of England smiles over and through it all as smug, as remote, as untouched, as relentless as a piece of pink frosting on a wedding cake. The image of the Queen of England, Victoria in her youth, is the sort of ikon justice that Edith had to re-invoke to aid her, to fill in her heart her angelic poignant pity. Tears stream down Edith's face but in the name of the Queen of England the court of high appeal decides that Jack is guilty. In all right and form, formal indictment, Jack accepts it. The Queen of England tacked on the log wall of the little cabin, smiles over Jack's head 'he shall hang by the neck till he dies'.

Reversing the process of the Elizabethan 'let mercy season justice' says Edith, beyond mercy is justice and she stalks out to fulfil the bidding of justice; Joan of Arc, all the women from Pallas Athene to Charlotte Corday that have personified some grave principle is in her fanatic gesture, in her set gargoyle posture, in her lean attenuated determination. Edith herself lunges with steel-like shoulder at the box upon which Jack is standing. Nelson must run to aid her, together they push the high box out from under Jack's boots. The boots are left swinging, struggling hardly at all, heavy pendant, swinging a pendulum stroke in the empty arctic air. Swing, swing, justice is greater than mercy cries Edith, her face twisted in an effort of unbelievably poignant acting. Edith is an angel who has lost faith in the angelic hierarchy.

Nelson drags her from the other side of the great tree, Nelson literally drags her back to the little cabin. Edith is a great locust, all legs, hardly any flesh, a sort of Flemish saint, a worn-down, sea-wind battered statue that has been rubbed raw by weather, hardly any personal significance in the figure; it certainly has gone too far. Beauty stalks, a skeleton, in Edith, in Edith rightness is robbed of all extenuating comfort. Rightness is pure undiluted suffering. Justice is sheer pain and pain and pain. Even her prayer book valiantly held against the storm clouds didn't help her. The little cross marked so forcefully on the dark surface of her prayer book is power against all evil. We know that the little cross will take Jack straight, like the dying thief, to eternity. But a voice somehow, somewhere seems to whisper, is it enough? Is religion of prayer book all so valiantly upheld, is Joan d'Arc determination toward nobility enough? Is Charlotte Corday justice enough or is smug Victorian beauty dressed in wide lace sleeves enough? Is anything enough anywhere? Here or in Alaska or in Saint Petersburg or in Mudville, South Dakota, is anything 'enough'? The Russian, in that, has the word after the last word. Too much is enough only for him, the word after the last word is spoken, the unreliability of everything, justice, injustice, beauty, ugliness. All, all, are as in the Aescuylean trilogy, subject to something greater than God even, that is Fate. Jack stalks back, standing in the rain smitten door-way to say the word beyond the last word.

The Russian, as I have said, takes the human mind and spirit *further* than it can go. 'It wasn't meant to be' says Jack, 'your rope was rotten, it broke.' He stalks in and scrapes up a handful of gold nuggets from the table. Then he disappears into the muddy blackness.

But before going, he flings his hangman's rope upon the table. 'Take it' he says 'they say a hangman's noose brings good luck.'

Vol. III, no. 1   July 1928

JOAN OF ARC

'The Passion and Death of a Saint' is a film that has caused me more unrest, more spiritual forebodings, more intellectual racking, more emotional torment than any I have yet seen. We are presented with Jeanne d'Arc in a series of pictures, portraits burnt on copper, bronze if you will, anyhow obviously no aura of quattrocento gold and gold dust and fleurs-de-lys in straight hieratic pattern, none of your fresco that makes the cell of Savonarola make the legend of Savonarola bearable even to this day. Jeanne d'Arc is done in hard clear line, remorseless, poignant, bronze stations of the cross, carved upon mediæval cathedral doors, bronze of that particular sort of mediæval fanaticism that says no and again no to any such weakening incense as Fra Angelico gold and lilies of heavenly comfort. Why did and why didn't this particular Jeanne d'Arc so touch us? Jeanne d'Arc takes us so incredibly far that having taken us so far, we are left wondering why didn't this exquisite and superb piece of screen dramatisation take us further? Carl Dreyer, a Dane, one of the most superb of the magnificently growing list of directors, is responsible for this odd two-edged sort of feeling. His film, for that, is unique in the annals of film art. The passion of the Jeanne is superbly, almost mediumistically portrayed by Mlle Falconetti. Heart and head are given over to inevitable surrender. Heart broke, head bowed. But another set of curious nerve-reactions were brought into play here. Why is it that my hands inevitably clench at the memory of those pictures, at the casual poster that I pass daily in this lake-side small town? Is it necessary to be put on guard? *Must* I be made to feel on the defence this way and why? Also why must my very hands feel that they are numb and raw and bleeding, clenched fists tightened, bleeding as if beating at those very impregnable mediæval church doors?

For being let into the very heart, the very secret of the matter, we are let out of ... something. I am shown Jeanne, she is indeed before me, the country child, the great lout of a hulking boy or girl, blubbering actually, great tears coursing down round sun-hardened, wind-hardened, oak-tree hardened face outline and outline of cheek hollow and the indomitable small chin. Jeanne is first represented to us, small as seen from above, the merest flash of sturdy boy figure, walking with chained ankles toward judges (too many) seated in slices above on ecclesiastical benches. Jeanne is seen as small, as intolerably sturdy and intolerably broken, the sort of inhuman showing up of Jeanne that from the first strikes some note of defiance in us. Now why should we be defiant? I think it is that we all have our Jeanne, each one of us in the secret great cavernous interior of the cathedral (if I may be fantastic) of the subconscious. Now another Jeanne strides in, an incomparable Jeanne, indubitably a more Jeanne-ish Jeanne than our Jeanne but it just isn't our Jeanne. Worse than that it is a better Jeanne, a much, much better, more authentic Jeanne than our Jeanne; scathing realism has gone one better than mere imaginative idealism. We know we are out-witted. This is a real, real, Jeanne (poor Jeanne) little mountain Newfoundland puppy, some staunch and true and incomparably loyal creature, something so much more wonderful than any greyhound outline or sleek wolf-hound is presented us, the very incarnation of loyalty and integrity ... dwarfed, below us, as if about to be tramped or kicked into a corner by giant soldier iron-heeled great boots. Marching boots, marching boots, the heavy hulk of leather and thong-like fastenings and cruel nails ... no hint of the wings on the heels of the legions that followed the lily-banner; the cry that sang toward Orleans is in no way ever so remotely indicated. We are allowed no comfort of mere beatific lilies, no hint of the memory of lover-comrade men's voices, the comrades that Jeanne must have loved loyally, the perfect staunch child friend, the hero, the small Spartan, the very Telisila upon the walls of that Argos, that is just it. This is *no* Telisila upon the walls of Argos, no Athene who for the moment has laid aside her helmet for other lesser matters than that of mere courage and fidelity. This is an Athene stripped of intellect, a Telisila robbed of poetry, it is a Jeanne d'Arc that not only pretends to be real, but that is real, a Jeanne that is going to rob us of our own Jeanne.

Is that the secret of this clenching of fists, this sort of spiritual antagonism I have to the shaved head, the stares, defiant bronze-statue, from the poster that I pass on my way to market? Is it another Jeanne in me (in each of us) that starts warily at the picture, the actual *portrait* of the mediæval girl warrior? The Jeanne d'Arc of Carl Dreyer is so perfect that we feel somehow cheated. This must be right. This must be right ... therefore by some odd equivocal twist of subconscious logic, *I* must be wrong. I am put in the wrong, therefore I clench my fists. Heaven is within you ... therefore I stand staring guiltily at bronze figures cut upon a church door, at friezes upon the under-gables of a cathedral that I must stare up at, see in slices as that incomparable Danish artist made me see Jeanne in her perhaps over-done series of odd sliced portraits (making particularly striking his studies of the judges and the accusers of Jeanne, as if seen by Jeanne her self from below) overwhelming bulk of ecclesiastical political accusation. I know in my mind that this is a great tour de force, perhaps one of the greatest. But I am left wary, a little defiant. Again why and why and why and just, just why? Why am I defiant before one of the most exquisite and consistent works of screen art and perfected craft that it has been our immeasurable privilege to witness?

One, I am defiant for this reason (and I have worked it out carefully and with agony: I and you and the baker's boy beside me and Mrs Captain Jones-Smith's second maid and our own old Nanna and somebody else's gardener and the honeymoon boy and girl and the old sporting colonel and the tennis teacher and the crocodile of young ladies from the second pension to the left as you turn to the right by the market road that branches off before the stall where the old lady sells gentians and single pinks and Alpenrosen each in their season (just now it is somewhat greenish valley-lilies) are in no need of such brutality. Not one of us, not one of us is in need of this stressing and stressing, this poignant draining of hearts, this clarion call to pity. A sort of bugle note rises and with it our own defiance. I am asked to join an army of incorruptibles to which long and long since, I and the baker's boy and the tennis champion in the striped red sash have given our allegiance. This great Dane Carl Dreyer takes too damn much for granted. Do I *have* to be cut into slices by this inevitable pan-movement of the camera, these suave lines to left, up, to the right, back, all rhythmical with the remorseless rhythm of a scimitar? Isn't this incomparable Dane Dreyer a very blue-beard, a Turk of an ogre for remorseless cruelty? Do we have to have the last twenty four hours' agony of Jeanne stressed and stressed and stressed, in just this way, not only by the camera but by every conceivable method of dramatic and scenic technique? Bare walls, the four scenes of the trial, the torture room, the cell and the outdoors about the pyre, are all calculated to drive in the pitiable truth like the very nails on the spread hands of the Christ. Do we need the Christ-nails driven in and pulled out and driven in and drawn out, while Jeanne already numb and dead, gazes dead and numb at accuser and fumbles in her dazed hypnotized manner towards some solution of her claustrophobia? I am shut in here, I want to get out. I want to get out. And instead of seeing in our minds the very ambrosial fields toward which that stricken soul is treading, foot by foot like the very agony toward skull-hill, we are left pinned like some senseless animal, impaled as she is impaled by agony. This is *not* good enough. There is some slur on the whole of human consciousness, it is necessary to stress and stress and stress the brute side of mystic agony this way. Somehow, something is wrong here. An incomparable art, an incomparable artist, an actress from whom any but praise were blasphemy ... and what happens?

I do not mind crying (though I do mind crying) when I see a puppy kicked into a corner but I do mind standing aside and watching and watching *and* watching and being able to do nothing. That is something of the antagonism I think that crept in, that is something of the something that made me feel I ought to go again, to be fair, to be *sure* what it was that upset me, perhaps cowardice on my own part, some deep sub-conscious strata or layer of phobia that I myself, so un-Jeanne-like, was unwilling to face openly. I said to myself next morning I will get this right; I am numb and raw, I myself watched Jeanne d'Arc being burnt alive at Rouen last night ... and I myself must go again ... ah, that is just it. We do not go and see a thing that is real, that is real beyond realism, AGAIN. I said I will go again but I did not go again. I did not and I don't think I failed any inner 'light', any focus of consciousness in so ceding to my own new lapse. I can NOT watch this thing impartially and it is the first film of the many that I have consistently followed that I have drawn away from. This is perhaps the last and greatest tribute to the sheer artistry and cunning of the method and the technique of Carl Dreyer. I pay him my greatest compliment. His is one film among all films, to be judged differently, to be approached differently, to be viewed as a masterpiece, one of the absolute masterpieces of screen craft. Technically, artistically, dramatically, this is a master piece. But, but, but, but, but ... there is a Jeanne sobbing before us, there is a small Jeanne about to be kicked by huge hob-nailed boots, there is a Jeanne whose sturdy child-wrist is being twisted by an ogre's paw because forsooth she wears a bit of old hard hammered unwieldy bulk of gold upon one finger, there is a numb hypnotized creature who stares with dog-like fidelity, toward the sly sophist who directs her by half-smile, by half-nod, by imperceptible lift of half an eye brow toward her defaming answers, there is a Jeanne or a Joan whose wide great grey eyes fill with round tears at the mention of her mother ('say your pater noster, you don't know your pater noster? you do? well who taught it to you?') there is a Jeanne or Joan or Johanna or Juana upon Jeanne or Jean or Johanna or Juana. They follow one another with precision, with click, with *monotony*. Isn't that a little just it? There is another side to all this, there is another series of valuations that can not perhaps be hinted at consistently in this particular presentation of this one kicked little puppy of a Jeanne or a Joan or a Johanna. Isn't it just that? Isn't the brute side of the flawless type, the Jeanne d'Arc of all peoples, of all nations, the world's Jeanne d'Arc (as the world's Christ) a little too defiantly stressed, a little too acutely projected? I know after the first half of the second reel all that. I know all, all that. Just that round child face lifted 'who taught you your pater noster?' gives me all, all that. I do not mean to say that there could have been any outside sort of beatific screen craft of heavenly vision. I don't mean that. But Jeanne kicked almost, so to speak, to death, still had her indomitable vision. I mean Jeanne d'Arc talked openly with angels and in this square on square of Danish protestant interior, this trial room, this torture room, this cell, there was no hint of angels. The angels were there all the time and if Jeanne had reached the spiritual development that we must believe this chosen comrade of the warrior Michael must have reached, the half-hypnotized numb dreary physical state she was in, would have its inevitable psychic recompense. The Jeanne d'Arc of the incomparable Dreyer it seems to me, was kicked towards the angels. There were not there, nor anywhere, hint of the angelic wing tip, of the winged sandals and the two-edged sword of Michael or of the distillation of maternal pity of their 'familiar' Margaret. Father, mother, the 'be thou perfect' perfected in Jeanne d'Arc as the boy of Nazareth, were in no way psychically manifest. Such psychic manifestation I need hardly say, need be in no way indicated by any outside innovation of cross lights or of superimposed shadows. It is something in something, something behind something. It is something one feels, that you feel, that the baker's boy, that the tennis champion, that the army colonel, that the crocodile of English and Dutch and mixed German-Swiss (come here to learn French) feels. We are numb and beaten. We won't go a second time. The voice behind me that says wistfully, taken unawares, 'I wish it was one of those good American light things' even has its place in critical consciousness. For all our preparation, we are unprepared. This Jeanne d'Arc is sprung on us and why should it be? There is a reason for most things. I think the reason is that it doesn't link up straight with human consciousness. There is a gap somewhere. We criticise many films, sometimes for crudity, sometimes for sheer vicious playing up to man's most febrile sentiment, sometimes for cruelty or insincerity. We criticise Jeanne d'Arc for none of these things.

The Jeanne d'Arc of the incomparable artist Carl Dreyer is in a class by itself. And that is the trouble with it. It shouldn't be.

Vol. III, no. 3 **September 1928**

RUSSIAN FILMS

The Editor of *Close Up* has asked me to write about Russian Films. I say, I want to write about Russian Films, and then I say but why should I? One does not sit down and write about the Book of Job or about Ruth in the corn, or about the harlot Rahab. The new great outstanding Russian films are in spirit Biblical films, they do not need to be written about. They are, and they stand, and will stand as long as the sheer material medium on which they are created will endure. No ... they will endure longer than that. The drive behind the Russian film at the moment is a religious drive. The ideas that have already been hammered in are as authentic and as great (if I may be forgiven an apparent exaggeration) as those carved in lightning on the rock of Sinai. For the Russian Film at the moment deals with hunger, with starvation, with murder, with oppression, with adultery, with incest, with infanticide, with childbirth, with the very throes of childbirth itself. Many of these films will be released in Germany. Certain others will be shown only to select audiences, specialists in political economy, psychology or psychiatry.

Well ... to be practical. Why should English people see these films, why should Americans? Let us be practical by all means. Why should the average every day hard working, straightforward Englishmen or the vibrant 'go and get 'em Americans' read the Bible. They shouldn't. If your life is full, if your road is straight, if your destiny is straightforward and you see the end, the goal of your life right in your own conscience, why you should be bothered with tales of murder and rape (for that is what the Old Testament consists of mainly) or with idealistic theories of friendship and brotherhood and poetic imaginative stories about sparrows and farthings and candlesticks and lamps and lilies, as set forth in the so-called gospels. Why should you disturb yourself with the ancient internecine history of the Old Testament, why would you unbalance yourself with the mystical doctrine of the New if your life is straight and your conscience is straight and your business is flourishing and your children are well and your cook is adequate. Why, why should people be tortured, be devitalized, be discouraged, be troubled? Why? I don't for one moment want to perturb anybody or force anything down throats that are not starving. The New Testament and the Old Testament are for people who are hungry, literally, spiritually hungry. So in a sense these Russian films. Many people will not want to see them, and why should they? To many people the Bible, even though they may treat it reverently, is a boring old volume and one utterly out of the general trend of living. But on the other hand, to the specialist in warfare, in politics, in political economy, in literature, in poetry, the bible is a never ending source of pure delight, of intellectual stimulus, of poetic charm. Those who must have the best in literature, in mystic doctrine, must eventually turn to the teachings of the minor prophets and the Prophet. So those who in no way sever life from art and religion from bread and butter or, if you prefer it, bread and red wine or white wine, these

Russian productions will offer a sustenance indeed like 'that shadow of a great rock', in the very 'weary land' of international dissension and internal discord.

For the world of the film to–day (there is no getting away from it) is no longer the world of the film, it is *the* world. It is only those who are indifferent to the world itself and its fate, who can afford to be indifferent to the fate of the film industry and the fate of the film art. The industry and the art are still divorced in most of the countries of Europe and the States of America. But no, not entirely divorced. There has never been, perhaps since the days of the Italian Renaissance, so great a 'stirring' in the mind and soul of the world consciousness. The 'stirring' shows itself in little things, in the great-little people, in the very great and in the people. I was told the other day by one of the most intelligent of the English producers (in fact, by the most vibrantly intelligent mind that I have encountered anywhere in the film world) that the fate of the producers hangs for the large part not on the West End London theatre-goers, but on the provinces, and that the small town provincial box offices are demanding more and more and MORE 'thick-ear stuff'. Well, where is this leading us? Concessions have been made to the public and (I heard the same complaint from one of the great German directors) the film art, the film industry is now in a state of psychic fixation. For the 'thick-ear' has set the standard, the slight concession has become a great concession and the demand of the box office is fast becoming a command.

Give me what I can sell. Right. You are right. Say to the box office you are right. They *are* right. Goods is goods, and if the people demand laudanum in bottles and raw spirits instead of the red wine and white wine of intellectual sustenance, by all means give them laudanum in bottles and raw, raw spirits. But do the people demand this? This is what I say, *do* they, *do* they? How do we know what the people want, have the people really a voice in all this matter? *The* people, I mean not just people. How do we know what the people want until the people have seen what they may or might want. The people do not know what film art is, so how can the people demand film art? The people sickened by the scent of laudanum, feeling numbness threaten stability and integrity say in many cases, *no* films. To the people, films stand in many, many instances for poison, for dope in its most pernicious essence, for aphrodisiacs that stupefy and drain the senses and cripple the desires. Because certain inferior bottles have held aphrodisiacs and raw spirits, and even more pernicious dopes, are all the flasks, and jars and bottles in the world to be damned and smashed equally? Is Egyptian porcelain that has held the heart of a Pharaoh and the wine goblets of Felenia and the crystals of Venice and the gold chalices of the Grail and the flask of Chianti, straw-bound flasks of the Tuscan foot-hills to be damned and smashed before the contents are even so much as sampled? The pity is that it is only the connoisseur and the specialists that have, at the moment, access to this thing we must now unreservedly term film ART. It is as much a duty of the educated classes and the connoisseur, the privileged classes in all countries, to see that the great art productions of each country are made generally accessible, as it was at one time the fiery mission of certain in office to translate the Bible. There is a great work, a great mission entrusted to the enlightened and privileged. And we dare not shirk responsibility.

The art is there. The achievement is assured. The great problem, in fact the only problem is the problem of presenting this art. I have had the privilege of talking with

Russians and Germans during the last month, with great minds of both these nations. The Germans (those, needless to say, of the great generous-beyond-pettiness variety) said 'we as a defeated nation feel more and more the power and greatness of England. England before the war was first in Europe. To-day England is first.' We spoke, possibly not as the average Englishman, not as the average American when we sought to meet that humility-in-greatness half way. Our answer was final, prophetic and unassailable. It was: 'you are *not* a defeated nation.' Germany with its future before it grubs down, down to the root of things, says 'we failed here, we failed there.' England says 'we have never failed, look at Trafalgar, we will never fail.' It is the worm in the wood that eats away the mast head, not the mighty tempest. England in its greatness preparing for the tempest, is in danger of neglecting (we must say it) the very root and fibre of its greatness.

For England whose great pride is rightly its sense of fair play in sport and politics and war is apt sometimes to play unfair to itself. Is not this fear of Russian films really a fear of itself? Why should the Labour parties rise and threaten the dignity and modesty of Buckingham Palace because they see the down-trodden and age-long degraded illiterate peasants of the great Russian steppes and sordid St Petersburg slums rising and storming the over-ornate Byzantine porches of the ex-Czar's cruelly remote and indifferent Winter Palace? There is no reason for the English working classes to rise and break and tear and rend. Would it not be a stimulus to the very pride of these salt-of-the-earth English working classes to see that these Russians were a different stock and root and yet behaved heroically? Heroism is without nationality and should be without prejudice. We should not think David was a Jew, Leonidas a Greek. These are epic characters, and as long as we are citizens or subjects of the world, the vibration set up by the heroism of a David or the beauty and restraint of a Leonidas belongs to us, to each one of us individually. We grow in pride, and self-respect and divinity when we see acts of heroism, of beauty, of unqualified valour. David's courage is my courage and Leonidas' death, my death. So in facing 'mother' with her red flag, I am 'mother', a mother to these people whose martyrdom is our martyrdom and whose crown is our crown.

We are no longer nations. We are or should be *a* nation. We all know everything about the so-called Great War, that A was base, that B was good, that C was heroic, that D lost some diplomatic papers, that E was really to blame, that it was all caused really by F shooting G. We know that. We have witnessed it, died for it. Well, then let us shuffle the cards, get down and back to values. Say I *am* my brother's keeper, and if A suffers, B suffers. If C has smallpox, no doubt D will catch it and hand it on to E, and maybe F even. In succouring C I am not being charitable (that is the joke of it), I am really being selfish. For if one suffers, eventually the other must, and if one nation to-day befouls its own integrity and strikes blindly at a lesser nation, the whole world, willy (as they say) nilly must be sooner or later dragged into the fray. Men must fight, it is true, just as women must have children. But don't let's fight if we must fight, blindly, let us *know* what it is all about, nations must understand each other, then if C is fighting D, there is much more fun to be got out of it altogether. We must know, know, KNOW. One of the most distinguished women of the political non-militant suffragette period said to me (in 1914) 'I have studied the problem from every angle, but I can dare not question our cause for going to war. If I questioned it for one moment, I should go mad.' I did not say to her then, 'well, go mad.' I would now. I would say. 'If you haven't the courage and decency to face the thing straight now and for all time you don't deserve your sanity, and I hope you lose it.' None of us in the light of later events dare slur over our mentality for the sake of any personal fear of intellectual or physical consequences. I do not for one moment doubt the justice of England's heroic move in '14. But I will say then as now there was even among the most enlightened a tendency to scrap blindly brain for sentiment.

Well … what is this anti-Russian feeling but a sentiment? What do you know of the revolution? What do you know of the Russians? Have you studied the Problem? Do you know how the 'workers' suffered? I do not mean that I in any way question the political justice, the rigid watchfulness of certain of the authorities here in England. The Great Strike and its dramatic denouement is still a matter of wonder and admiration among all political thinkers on the Continent. But the greatness of the Moscow art productions that it was my unique privilege to see last month in Berlin, puts the question of the Russian film (I speak naturally only of these real art productions) on a plane transcending politics. These films do not say to the British or the American workman, go and do likewise. They say look, we are your brothers, and this is how we suffered. The whole authoritative teaching of *Potemkin*, of *Mother*, of *The End of Saint Petersburg*, or *Ten Days That Shook the World*, are historical and almost religiously autochthonous character. There is no outward influence … no passing to and fro of foreign soldiers, in Russia for and about and through and with the Russians. It is putting Russia (real Russia) on the map, not handing out the saccharine opera bouffe stuff that Hollywood offers us, for instance, in Greta Garbo's Karenina, or in the yet unreleased Feodora of Pola Negri.

I do not say that Karenina and Feodora have no place in the scheme of things. They are both barley water, pink lemonade through a straw to quench naïf palates on a hot day at the fair. They are not wine red or white, they are not even poison or raw spirits, and that perhaps is one of their great dangers. They are pleasant, skilfully photographed, both of the actresses in these two cases are women of talent and undoubted personality. But Madame Baranowskaja standing before the onrushing feet of the great stallions of the Czarist's imperial bodyguard is in another category altogether. She is a figure of tradition, historical, mystical, Biblical.

The great horses rush forward. The crowds break before them. 'Mother' who has innocently given information concerning her own son (in this the unsuccessful pre-war abortive revolution) is left standing alone, clasping the discarded banner of her people … well that is all. The horses rush on across the iron bridge, and mother is left lying in the mud, clasping her riddled banner. Is this a 'red' flag in the sense of murder and outrage and insane threats of an illiterate gutter mob? That is what 'red' stands for to so many, many intelligent and educated people. The red flag of 'mother' as she lies, a peasant woman, trampled to unsightly death at the frigid command of an aristocratic cavalry officer, is as red as any Flanders poppy. It is only one of the most crass illiteracy who could face the beauty of 'mother' and remain untouched and unredeemed.

So with *Ten Days*, so again with *The End of Saint Petersburg*. The teaching is a teaching of brotherhood, of equality in its most sane and stable form. We are hungry.

You are not hungry. We are starving, and the baby in my arms is not yet quite dead. Well ... we know all that. But *do* we know all that? Do we really know until we have seen the Russian film as presented by the great Moscow art people, not the insane outpourings of an insane group-mind, nor the saccharine washed-out and sugared over productions of a commercially proficient colony, I do not mean, by that last diatribe, altogether against Hollywood. I mean yes and yes and yes, and no and no and no. Hollywood with reservations is all right (up to a point) for America, for up to a point *it is* America, slick, quick, superficial and stylish, and oh, so, so amusing. Yes, I love Laura La Plante with her slick little mannerisms, and no one could be a more enthusiastic 'fan' of little Patsy Ruth Miller than I am. Patsy Ruth Miller is an exquisitely finished artist. As is Rod la Rocque (to name one among many), Rod la Rocque with his charm and Buddy this and Buddy that who all have a place in my affections. Certain of the productions of the foreign directors in Hollywood leave nothing to be desired; but that is America, is Hollywood, and England has other problems. The problem of England and the beauty of England (psychically) is never that of the Scandinavians, and technically at least it should learn and study *not* from America, but in and through the Germanic and Russian mediums. Hollywood has put America on the film map, certainly Germany has its representatives of giant realism in the film world, and Russia has surpassed everybody. Now where is England?

Well, here is another problem, and to state my ideas and ideals for England is hardly writing about Russia. But then it *is* really writing about Russia, for your technical problems are much the same. The Russian has taught us, for instance, the fallacy of the 'star' as stars and the idiocy of the painted drip curtain, the elaborate and false studio interior, the beauty of shadow and rain and general natural effect that achieves depth and reality and the heights of impressionistic artistry through *naturalness*. I heard an English producer say the other day 'but what we need is stars, our people get stiff before a camera.' Russia has taught us that every man, every woman and every child is a 'star'. We are all 'stars'. There is not one of us who, under skilful directorship cannot create a character, provided it is a real character and an English character, and not a diluted and febrile imitation of Hollywood being English, or Russian or Fiji Island-ish. Hollywood is Hollywood, and it is slick and it is straight, and it is American. Give me your English people and I will give you an English film tradition that will make the Germans and the Russians and the Americans green with envy. Well ... perhaps not a little hyperbole, I grant you. But give us a chance anyhow. Let the people and the directors get together. The camera men and the stars. The camera man *is* the star and the star *is* the director. Or should be.

But give us the English people and we will give you the English film. We want films of the people for the people, and this ... and this ... and this ... BY the people. The great new Russian idea is not to make star personalities, but to let personalities make stars. God has made us, and we have made ourselves and each one of us is a 'star' in embryo. Life and the film must not be separated, people and things must pass across the screen naturally like shadows of trees on grass or passing reflections in a crowded city window. The Russian has taught us that life and art are in no way to be severed and that people to be actors must first and last be people. The great German who I quote constantly said to me 'the screen cannot lie'. But the screen in England has lied constantly and consistently about the English people, and in time foreign nations will cease to judge England by a past and vanished Trafalgar, and will expect nothing of a people who with such great wealth and with such rare and unique possibilities present so comparatively little on the screen that is really of political, sociological or artistic value. I do not mean (how could I) that all British films are rotten. One speaks naturally in extremes ... there is no time to discuss and too subtly differentiate. But I will say *for* the English films and *against* myself that one of the heads of the Moscow Art Film School said to me recently in Berlin 'I want to tell you one thing, and I want you to realize how sincerely I am speaking. I was impressed greatly with your *Dawn*. Your actress is magnificent, and your film altogether to be compared with the *best* of our Russian productions.' It will show you how weak I am in many matters, and how sometimes unreliable when I confess to you that I had to say to him, 'I have not seen it.'

Vol. IV, no. 3   March 1929

AN APPRECIATION

I was sitting in a warm corner of an exclusive Berlin restaurant just before Christmas. Our guest was late. One hardly expected him at all and had begun, as was agreed, before his arrival. I had not visited the sets of *Pandora*, but had been alive to each development and as keenly concerned as the most screen–struck school-girl over the various doings and *mots* and quaint sallies of the star, Miss Louise Brooks, who had been chosen finally after almost half a year's delay, for the somewhat problematical Lulu. 'What did Louise Brooks say to-day?'; ... 'O, she didn't say much. She was too busy complaining that the hen was a grandfather.' ... 'What hen?' ... 'Why, the lunch hen. She said it was a grandfather.' ... 'Did they get her another hen?' ... 'Certainly not. They didn't understand what she was saying. And besides, she had eaten it.' It was partly (not altogether) for this reason that our editor had an advantage over the rest of the company and learned much intimate matter about daily happenings that otherwise might have been reserved for more 'professional' converse. Perhaps, too, for this reason, I felt that I had a personal right to *Pandora*, that it personally was partly of my making, that I, too, had been introduced to the Sanctum and was on very familiar terms with the Olympians.

    Also the Christmas Pudding ... 'What happened to the pudding?' ... 'Well, the dresser insisted that it was in a flat dish. *I* said a basin, and they brought a jelly mould. Louise Brooks said that the Christmas pudding she had had in London was not flat, but round – basin shape. That she had liked it very much, and lived on it for a week when she was dancing at the Café de Paris. She told the dresser (who had dressed people in England) that she knew or ought to know the shape of a Christmas pudding.' ... 'What happened?' ... 'I drew one on the architect's table. Pabst said "That is what I want. Round. Is it not, Herr Macpherson, round?"'

All very solemn. Herr Pabst (one feels one should write it Maestro, or Cher-Maître) solemn, concerned, utterly 'wedded' to the least detail of his arrangement as to the last soul-shattering *dénouement*. The grain of mustard seed does not escape the eye of this almost mystically vigilant Austrian, neither does the spray of holly (and holly, Herr Macpherson?) – the immemorial symbol of some lost Druidic or Norse custom, still practised by the English-speaking races. The spray of holly became a symbol, invested with its mystery. 'WE' may be said to have assisted in the making of *Pandora*.

Mr Pabst arrived, very modest, utterly unassuming, almost 'not there'. But there he was, and we paid hardly any attention to his arrival, murmured something about 'you told us not to wait', went on eating, tried to get the waiter. The waiter arrived, people kept passing, coming, going ... Heinrich Mann, Olga Tschechowa sweeping through in search of a table, Lee Parry ... the nordic air from the opening door shot cold winter into our snug interior, that Berlin, magnetic-north winter that exhilarates, heals, inspires.

Mr Pabst said nothing. It was better to go on eating. He wanted nothing, yes; some soup, waving the waiter aside, must get rid of him somehow. Mr Pabst looked depressed. The rather wood-carved look of him, sitting with head hunched down, and shoulders hunched up, was somehow suggestive of depression. The soup arrived, he evidently did not want to talk. The soup was removed, he might have something, not much of anything. It arrived, some sort of 'hen', trusting it wasn't a grandfather. The hen was removed, black coffee ... Mr Pabst uttered. 'O, I am so unhappy.'

Unhappy? But why unhappy? Well, he was just unhappy. Did we mind if he didn't talk. Of course, there was no use, anyhow. No use of anything in Germany. What had Germany done, what had anyone done? What could anyone do? Everyone was against everything ... there was no use going on. He didn't want to smoke. Never smoked. He pushed back his coffee cup. Had Miss Brooks broken an ankle? Had the set in the London fog exploded by some process of self-combustion? Had spontaneous combustion of another sort blown up the whole of Staaken? What, anyhow, had happened? The Master uttered again. 'Now the French are doing things' ... 'Things? What things?'

The French, it appeared, had done a film called *Jeanne D'Arc*. Herr Pabst, it appeared, had just come from the early evening performance of *Jeanne D'Arc*, or *Johanna von Orleans*, at the Gloria Palast just round the corner. Well, was that it? *That* – it appeared to me – was 'nothing to write home about'. Mr Pabst thought otherwise. We were doomed, it seemed, to hear nothing now of *Pandora*. The French had done a film, and that film was *Jeanne D'Arc* and no ... he lifted a priestly and solemn hand, he would hear nothing, no, nothing whatever, against that film. That film was perfect, such technique, such originality, such grandeur, such 'prickle' (does that mean sparkle or merely stickle?), such strength, such beauty, yes, beauty ... 'They have been able to make the experiment. TWO years ... France is doing that now. And we are making ...' (he quoted two current popular successes). Something no one had done in Germany, could never do, how could we expect to do it in a world of quickies? It was not so much the film that had depressed him as the fact that France was able to make the experiment, and Germany was going where it was. How could anyone 'here in Germany' expect to do anything ever?

'Lulu'. Louise Brooks in G. W. Pabst's film *Pandora's Box* (Vol. IV, no. 4, April 1929).

Pandora's Box. 'A sinister impression of Gustav Diesel as Jack the Ripper' (*ibid.*).

Now, I have written about *Jeanne D'Arc* a little spitefully and a little unharmoniously. *Jeanne D'Arc* (see, if you must, some *Close Up* or other, some twelve months back) set me out of key. It positively bullied me as no film has yet done. I was forced to pity, pity, pity. My affections and credulity were hammered. I was kicked. I was throttled. I was laid upon a torture rack. Quite solemnly I was burned at the stake and lifting eyes to heaven I had forgiven my malefactors. Yes, the magnificent technique of Dreyer did that for me. But was I moved? Was I inspired or touched? *Jeanne D'Arc*, as represented by Dreyer, illustrated for me that famous Corinthians Thirteenth:—*And though I bestow all my goods to feed the poor and though I give my body to be burned* (etc., etc., etc.), *and have not love I am nothing.*

I gave every sentiment of which I am capable to that marvellous demonstration of Falconetti. But one. I reserved far off, and unassailable, a sentiment that is never called forth and never inspired and never made to blossom by technical ability, by sheer perfection of medium, by originality and by intellectualism, no matter how dynamic ... that sentiment is love simply. I did not *love* the Joan of Dreyer and the 'French', as Mr Pabst must call them. I love and always will love the most modest feminine creation of this Viennese cher-maître.

But how tell him all that? Here he is sitting over coffee, and yes, he has condescended to have just that half glass of white Rhine, it looks so gold, so he turns the stem of the wine glass meditatively. He is convinced for the moment in himself that he is nothing, he can say nothing for himself, and certainly he will say nothing for *Pandora*. Louisa (as he calls her) Brooks, yes, she has a hidden side, a strange quality. For himself there is nothing to be said. If the film is any good at all it is obvious it is going to be because Louisa Brooks has a strange quality ... 'There is another side to her.'

I must say that playing into his own hands, Mr Pabst has all unwittingly given the clue to that for which one searches. No amount of compelling clap-trap 'interview' journalese would draw just that fine phrase from him. We admit, and gladly, that the delightful elf-life spirit that remonstrated to a blandly puzzled Staaken waiter's '*was ist los?*' with the all-American '*Los?* It's not *los*, it's awful. It's a grand-father!' must have 'another side to her'. But who (I may at this moment be permitted forensically to ask) would ever discover, could ever have discovered that 'other side' but the perfectly preposterously modest director who sits facing us? 'Louisa' Brooks has another side to her. So, obviously, has Greta Garbo, Nielsen, the beautiful, more than beautiful Brigitte Helm, the calm-eyed Herthe van Walter, and the demure, delicious little Edith Jehanne.

All the women of Herr Pabst's creation, be it a simple super in a crowd scene or a waitress in a restaurant, have 'another side' to them.

At this point I bravely permitted myself to make a remark. '*Pandora* will be beautiful. Mr Macpherson says the highest, the highest things about it ... its atmosphere, its subtlety. He says the scene, for instance, of the Salvation Army in the foggy slum street is (I paused for the Gargantuan parallel) is "sheer Pabst".' I had found the right phrase, albeit the consultant on the court of last appeal for Christmas puddings had given it to me. 'This new film of G. W. Pabst is going to be (this is its highest glory) sheer Pabst.'

I write 'going to be', but last night the much-delayed *Pandora* was having its jubilant premiere at the Gloria Palast in Berlin. It is a grief to us that we could not be there, but in ourselves we are assured that no premiere of *Pandora* could ever affect us more than our first film, our introduction, we might say, to the whole of the possibility of screen art – *Joyless Street*, seen here in Montreux some five years ago. *Joyless Street* was my never-to-be-forgotten premiere to the whole art of the screen, and G. W. Pabst was and is my first recognised master of the art.

The place of the Russians is assured, this is no moment with which to deal with them. But G. W. Pabst, being a European, is, in a way, a more subtle figure or symbol. He is, as it were, the link between the old tradition, pure art ideas of the French, of the Viennese, of (in a word) Europe and the new America and Near East. He is, in that, in a more precarious psychological position. He holds, as it were, the clue, must hold his position almost as the keystone to the vast aesthetic structure we call now unquestionably the Art of the Film. The Germans hold the key really, are the intermediaries between Russia and the outside world that still believes Red to be a symbol of murder and destruction.

The new Russians, to digress, in their ideas of humanity, of equality, of the sheltering and housing of the poor and outcast, are, it is apparent, the only government not only in Europe, but in the world, who seem literally to have considered the teaching of that much misunderstood Jew of Nazareth at its face value. 'Feed the poor,' 'Sell all that you have and give it to the poor.' 'The last shall be first,' etc., etc. There has been, to my knowledge, no effort on the part of any government nor on the part of any organised body, 'house' or 'senate', to make the film a medium for promulgation of ideas other than intellectually sterile and of moron entertainment.

This is really as a purely aesthetic critical aside, has nothing to do with politics and 'politicians', of which I know nothing and of whom I know not one. It stands regrettably to reason, however, if in some weird Utopia one should be called upon to judge a country by its aesthetic film output, one would have to acclaim the Soviet first, the German Republic second. The film, one might have said, has nothing to do with countries, education or civic reform, and certainly has nothing to do with aesthetics. But the day of that sort of talk is over. The film *is* recognised and the people and the peoples of this world are being judged, openly condemned, condoned or contaminated by their film output. We know that. We don't have to go further into it. It also seems unnecessary to add anything to the already vast bulk of technical and aesthetic appreciation of the work of G. W. Pabst. However, I cannot help adding to it … as one cannot help looking at and appraising flowers in a garden.

For what are the creations of G. W. Pabst but growing, vivid and living beauty? They move and glow before him like sun-flowers to the sun. I have taken an almost diabolic delight in following the career of each of his stars. For no star, once G. W. Pabst had adequately placed her, seems to me to belong to any other. I know nothing of Greta Garbo personally, and it would be out of place to suggest that the curious disintegration of her screen personality has anything to do with her personally.

Let us put Miss Garbo out of it entirely and say that Greta Garbo, under Pabst, was (I quote an earlier article) a Nordic ice-flower. Under preceding and succeeding directors she was either an over-grown hoyden or a buffet Guinness-please-miss. The performance of Greta Garbo in that subtle masterpiece, *Anna Karenina* (*Love*), was inexplicably vulgar and incredibly dull. It was only by the greatest effort of will that one could visualise in that lifeless and dough-like visage a trace of the glamour, the chiselled purity, the dazzling, almost unearthly beauty that one recognised so acutely in the very-young figure of the half-starved aristocratic official's daughter in *Joyless Street*. Greta Garbo, in a little house dress, an apron and low slippers, sweeping the passage of the improvident home in *Joyless Street*, remained an aristocrat. Greta Garbo, as the wife of a Russian Court official and the mistress of a man of the world, diademed and in sweeping robes in the Palace of Karenin, was a house-maid at a carnival.

Perhaps the example of Greta Garbo is an exaggerated instance, and, I repeat, the young actress herself may have had little say in the hands of those who make her the devil in films where Gilbert is the flesh.

Take Brigitte Helm, who is always an artist. I have not seen all her films, but without question her performance of the blind girl in *Jeanne Ney* is one of her most striking – a feat that really lifted her above the realm of legitimate artists. She is almost an 'illegitimate' magician. 'Brigitte Helm did not look blind,' I heard repeated of her in Berlin, 'she *was* blind.'

Isn't that it? G. W. Pabst is almost a magician, his people are 'created, not made'? There is, indeed 'another side' to every one of his women, whether it be the impoverished little daughter of post-war Vienna or one of the extras in an orgy scene, each and every one is shown as a 'being', a creature of consummate life and power and vitality. G. W. Pabst brings out the vital and vivid forces in women as the sun in flowers. Brigitte Helm lifts a head like a proud Madonna lily. Her eyes in *Jeanne Ney* are the wide staring eyes of the blind, but in her blindness she is alive, aware, acute, clairvoyantly attuned to every sound, every movement, every shade of light and every shift of sun and shadow. Brigitte Helm did not look blind, she *was* blind. I was enthralled, to find in talking to Mr Pabst on my first meeting with him last summer, that I had myself gleaned the essence of her acting. I said 'I don't feel that Brigitte Helm is acting. I feel that she is in a trance. That she has the power to throw herself into a trance and to move and speak and live a life quite outside her own personal experience.' I thought my remark might meet with his disapproval or in some way seem over-drawn to him. But not at all. He was delighted. 'Ah,' he said, 'you see. You have it. Do you know in that scene when she walks with Jeanne Ney in the streets of Paris, she was almost killed.' … 'Almost killed?' … 'The actor driving the taxi was not a driver really, and had had to learn. He was not very sure of his steering. Brigitte Helm walked right in front of him. I had to run before the camera to save her. Do you know why? She was blind. She simply did not see it.' The force of vision of this acute director and the strength of spirit of Brigitte Helm had actually so transformed her. This miracle of acting had been achieved. She did not look blind, she *was* blind.

So, in a lesser degree, but in no less vivid manner, each and every creation of G. W. Pabst does not 'look' good or bad, happy or unhappy, wise or foolish, she 'is' for the time being what she typifies. G. W. Pabst, their creator, cannot realise how a thing 'created, not made', must forever take precedence to the most technically perfected image. I know that the image of the Maid or Orleans in the Dreyer conception is technically flawless. But to me (and not a few others) the *Jeanne D'Arc* is (I repeat it) *made*, the Image is carved and constructed.

Imagine Brigitte Helm in this role and directed by Pabst … we scarcely dare imagine such a thing. It were out of place to speak seriously of mediums and mediumistic

ALL

AMERICANS

in

FRANCE

SWITZERLAND

ENGLAND

are printing their books

AT THE SHOP

of the

MASTER PRINTER

MAURICE DARANTIERE

DIJON FRANCE

Advertisement for the 'master printer Maurice Darantière' (Vol. I, no. 3, September 1927).

trances ... but there are times when art so far transcends itself that we are forced into another set of symbols. The *Jeanne D'Arc* of Dreyer is art carried to its highest – wood-carving, if you will, bronze or even mediaeval silver, but it remains art as carvings on a cathedral. The life-like Image of a saint set at dusk in a cathedral causes us to cry 'magnificent', the opening of the violets in our garden touches us but causes no astonishment. We take it so for granted.

I have not taken part in the conversation that has been going on. I have not even been listening. (You will remember that we are seated in a warm corner of a Berlin restaurant just before Christmas.) There is some little stir and probably we must be going. I must say just one thing. 'Mr Pabst, I must ask you one thing' – he turned courteously from weightier matter – 'about, if you don't mind, *Joyless Street*.'

I had seen a still of a dead body, a very beautiful still of the figure of the mundane lady who, you will recall, is killed in the 'house' she went to with her lover. 'I wanted to know about that body of Madame —— ... I was wondering about it.' Mr Pabst did not wait for me to explain fully, he burst into a torrent of wailing and apology. 'O, a dead body ... a dead body ... there is no such thing as a dead body on the screen ...' One remembered an anecdote he had told, quietly and with no acumen, no hint of bitterness, of some half-dozen or more of his companions in their internment camp who, technically imprisoned and detained, had, after four hideous mutilated years of waiting, deliberately killed themselves *after the armistice*. 'The Valley of the Shadow of Death' has touched each one of us, perhaps none so poignantly as this vivid, sensitive Austrian artist, who, ignorant that war had even been declared, was seized with his companions on a returning New York passenger ship and, vibrating with his love of life and love of love and beauty, was buried dead-alive in that particular crowded barracks. Mr Pabst touched lightly enough on incidents of his companions who died there naturally (if such a word can ironically be used in this connection) during the period of war activity. He became hilarious and gay at the mention of the young French officers who (in the now credited stage and screen manner) made friends for the sake of whiling away tedium of forced inactivity and isolation. He makes more than a movie set of the young Americans who assisted the prisoners with the perilous underground tunnel from their dug-out, so that certain of their number could periodically 'escape' for an hour or two, to get warm and have a chat and, one hopes, some little snack of those then so justly famous tinned pork and beans in the friendly enemy quarters. All a game ... a somewhat grim and ironical performance (so he seems to intimate), but none to blame, not certainly that debonnaire French officer and that cluster of superficially humane Americans ... only his eyes went very strange and his face set when he spoke of his companions who saw fit to do away with themselves *after the armistice*.

We must leave that, we must leave dead bodies of heroes achieving no name on tablets set at a base of statues nor on gold-wreathed slabs set ornate and respectable above bank-presidents' mahogany roll-top desks. Our concern is not with politics or politicians, nor the housing of the poor nor the educating of the ignorant. Our concern is with screen art simply ... and with a particular still that did not match up with the cinema scene itself.

'I saw *Joyless Street* a second time. It was only last year. Then I did make a point of looking for the dead body and *did* see it. The first time I was so enchanted with light filtering through those shutters in that half-darkened room, I was so interested in the mass effect you got with the men's thick shoulders and blocked in shapes ... is it possible that in the earlier version the shots showing the dead woman on the floor were for some reason deleted?'

'Ah,' interrupted Mr Pabst delightedly, 'I did not *mean* you to see the body of the murdered woman on the floor.'

PART 4

Continuous Performance:
Dorothy Richardson

INTRODUCTION

Laura Marcus

> We are thrilled by the prospect of the Film paper [Close Up]. High time there
> was something of the sort. I can't however see myself contributing, with my
> penchant for Wild West Drama & simple sentiment. Now Alan [Richardson's
> husband, Alan Odle], has *Ideas*. However: I know I have some notes somewhere
> & will look them up. But I fancy they are simply about seeing movies, regardless
> of what is seen.[1]

> I'm trying to do some more stuff for Vanity Fair, get another Miriam written & a
> series of short articles for Close-Up, herewith. It is as you see rather a family
> affair for the moment. But several Big Bugs have promised articles: Havelock
> Ellis, Huxley, Lawrence ...[2]

Dorothy Richardson, despite initial reservations about her qualifications as a writer on
film, was enthusiastically involved in the project of *Close Up*, suggesting contributors
('You know Lawrence loathes films? *Foams* about them. I'm sure he'd foam for you.'[3])
and seeking subscribers among her friends and acquaintances, including the popular
novelist Hugh Walpole and the writer and cultural commentator H.G. Wells. Her
letters to Bryher record her enthusiastically 'talking Cinema': 'I'd only had one small
whisky and soda, but it occurred to me I'd better go before I began telling the waiters
[in the Cafe Royal] to send in articles.'[4] Moreover, the fact that her notes on cinema
were about 'seeing movies, regardless of what is seen' accounts for much of the
fascination of her writing on film. As she wrote in her final film article, the power of
film rests upon 'the continuous performance, going on behind all invitations to focus
upon this or that, of the film itself'.[5]

Richardson wrote more than twenty articles for *Close Up*, the majority of them for
her regular column 'Continuous Performance'. Occasionally she refers to specific
films. A number of her articles refer to film technique and exhibition; she wrote, for
example, about the use of slow motion, the function of film captions and of musical
accompaniment, and the spaces of the new film theatres. Her primary concern in
these pieces, as in all her writing on cinema, was with the ways audiences responded
to different aspects of cinematic representation, communication and viewing and with
the cinema-goer's changing, developing relationship to the new art of the film.[6] She
explored the conditions of cinema spectatorship in ways both practical (what shape
should a cinema auditorium be?) and phenomenological (how is the spectator
incorporated into the filmic spectacle?). Throughout her film column she also
focused on the meanings of cinema spectatorship for women and on cinema as a

woman's sphere. In one article, she recounts her visit to a picture palace in
North London:

> It was a Monday and therefore a new picture. But it was also washing day, and
> yet the scattered audience was composed almost entirely of mothers. Their
> children, apart from the infants accompanying them, were at school and their
> husbands were at work. ... Tired women, their faces sheened with toil, and small
> children, penned in semi-darkness and foul air on a sunny afternoon. There was
> almost no talk. Many of the women sat alone, figures of weariness at rest.
> Watching these I took comfort. At last the world of entertainment had provided
> for a few pence, tea thrown in, sanctuary for mothers, an escape from the
> everlasting qui vive into eternity on a Monday afternoon.[7]

Throughout 'Continuous Performance', Richardson maps the city through the
different sites of cinema spectatorship; cinema in the West End, cinema in the slums,
where it is presented as a far more effective, because impersonal, 'civilizing agent'
than the activities of philanthropists; cinema in the suburbs, where it becomes a haven
for women burdened by domesticity. Film offers the weary the opportunity of
contemplative distance and 'perfect rest'.[8]

In 'The Cinema in Arcady', she describes the effects of cinema in ways that
strongly echo Georg Simmel's account of the city in his essay 'The Metropolis and
Mental Life'.[9] Richardson writes:

> And whereas in the towns those who frequent the cinema may obtain together
> with its other gifts admission to a generalized social life, a thing unknown in slum
> and tenement, lodging-house and the smaller and poorer villadom, these people
> of village and hamlet, already socially educated and having always before their
> eyes the spectacle of life in the raw throughout its entire length, the assemblage
> of every kind of human felicity and tribulation, find in the cinema together with
> all else it has to offer them, their only escape from ceaseless association, their
> only solitude, the solitude that is said to be possible only in cities. They become
> for a while citizens of a world whose every face is that of a stranger.[10]

The cinema thus reverses the usual terms of *Gemeinschaft* and *Gesellschaft*,
community and anonymous social relations. (Richardson's rhetoric also links up with
general claims for the creation of 'world citizens' in the era of cinema.) Cinema in the
country creates the conditions of the city; in the city it gives access to forms of
community otherwise denied to urban dwellers.

In her creation of a film aesthetic, Richardson worked and reworked a number of
key terms: contemplation, distance, creative consciousness and collaboration between
spectator and spectacle, the stillness of the spectator, the movement of the filmic
world, unity, solitude, association, silence, vision, continuous performance. This last
term, significantly the title of her film column, has a number of associations. It refers
to a particular kind of film exhibition and viewing, an ongoing process of projection
and spectating, in marked contrast to the 'single performance' of the theatre. The
film's 'continuous performance' is also 'a continuous miracle of form in movement'.
The term suggests her interest in cinema in all its aspects and not merely in high-art

films, her concern with the cinematic as a way of seeing and as a total and totalizing experience, rather than with individual films as artefacts.

In many ways hers is a dissenting voice in the journal, at odds, in particular, with Kenneth Macpherson's aggressive avant-gardism. Richardson defends 'the movies', points to the relativity of aesthetic 'value' and argues against the critique, coming from both the cultural left and the right in this period, of popular cinema as a narcotic. Whereas the 'utopian' aspirations or dreams of many of the journal's other contributors were of attaining a mass audience for minority culture, Richardson more often conjures up a community of spectators becoming educated for modernity, 'Everyman [made] at home in a new world' by 'the movies': 'They are there in their millions, the front rowers, a vast audience born and made in the last few years, initiated, disciplined, and waiting;' 'The only anything and everything. And here we all are, as never before. What will it do with us?'[11]

By 1927 Dorothy Richardson was fifty-four and had established a reputation as a literary journalist and reviewer and as an 'experimental' novelist with a small but dedicated readership. Her life's work, in many senses of this term, was the thirteen-volume novel sequence *Pilgrimage*, a quest narrative and *Bildungsroman* whose first volume appeared in 1915.[12] *Pilgrimage* covers the period in Richardson's life between 1891 and 1912 through the consciousness of her autobiographical/fictional persona, Miriam Henderson. (Hence Richardson's reference to 'get[ting] another Miriam written' in the letter quoted above.) Richardson rejected the label 'stream-of-consciousness', applied to *Pilgrimage* from the outset, though the narrative is certainly marked by its immersion in its heroine's consciousness as it moves in and out of engagement with scenes, events and people. Space, movement, light and reflections are primary foci of attention; while the perceiving consciousness is centrally important, it is shown in a state of flux and process. It is striking that for both novel sequence and film column Richardson insisted upon overall titles – *Pilgrimage* and 'Continuous Performance' respectively – which would act as containers for series that were themselves open-ended and unbordered.

In her memoir, *The Heart to Artemis*, Bryher writes of the immense significance of *Pilgrimage* to her. *The Heart to Artemis* indeed opens with these words: 'When I was born in September, 1894, Dorothy Richardson's Miriam was a secretary.'[13] In 1916, after reading a copy of the second volume of *Pilgrimage*, *Backwater*, in which Miriam is unhappily employed as a governess and teacher, Bryher proclaimed to her schoolfellows, 'Somebody is writing about us':

> Perhaps great art is always the flower of some deeply felt rebellion. Then there was the excitement of her style, it was the first time that I realised that modern prose could be as exciting as poetry and as for continuous association, it was stereoscopic, a precursor of the cinema, moving from the window to a face, from a thought back to the room, all in one moment just as it happened in life. Dorothy Pilley [a schoolfriend] was just as enthusiastic as I was … and both of us knew the sudden exhilaration in spite of the pressure upon us, as we rode down a London street, like Miriam, on top of a bus.[…] I did not meet Dorothy

Richardson until 1923 but she was the Baedeker of all our early experiences and I have read and reread *Pilgrimage* throughout my life.[14]

Bryher, in fact, not only read but contributed to the production of *Pilgrimage*. The financial assistance she gave Richardson from the mid-1920s onwards helped buy her the time she needed to work on her fiction as well as on paid journalism and translations and, in the mid-1940s, she encouraged Richardson to write and publish the final, incomplete sections of the novel sequence, *March Moonlight*.[15]

In 1931, Bryher reviewed the tenth volume of *Pilgrimage*, *Dawn's Left Hand*, in *Close Up*:

> What a film her books could make. The real English film for which so many are waiting. ... *Dawn's Left Hand* begins (as perhaps films should) in a railway carriage. Miriam returns from a holiday in Switzerland: the London year goes by, apparently nothing happens, underneath the surface an epoch of life, of civilisation, changes. ... And in each page an aspect of London is created that like an image from a film, substitutes itself for memory, to revolve before the eyes as we read.[16]

Bryher's comments indicate the centrality of a 'cinematic' consciousness, as well as the relationship between city and cinema, in Richardson's work. Yet in a letter written to Bryher after the review had appeared, Richardson wrote: 'And what can I say about your review in C.U., emphasizing the aspect no one else has spotted.' She was referring, it seems safe to assume, to Bryher's comments on the cinematic dimensions of the novel.[17]

Like H.D., in her autobiographical writings, Richardson (as Carol Watts notes) suggests in *Pilgrimage* the importance of the optical devices of pre-cinema in shaping Miriam's consciousness and memories. In *Interim* (Volume 5), for example, Miriam recalls to her friends in ecstatic terms the optical games -- the kaleidoscope, the miniature theatre, the stereoscope – of her childhood: 'The kaleidoscope. Do you *remember* looking at the kaleidoscope? I used to cry about it sometimes at night; thinking of the patterns I had not seen. I thought there was a new pattern every time you shook it, for ever.'[18] In the next volume, *Deadlock*, the kaleidoscope as metaphor is used to represent the city as a series of shifting shapes and patterns:

> [Miriam] wandered about between Wimpole Street and St Pancras, holding in imagination wordless converse with a stranger whose whole experience had melted and vanished like her own, into the flow of light down the streets; into the unending joy of the way the angles of buildings cut themselves out against the sky, glorious if she paused to survey them; and almost unendurably wonderful, keeping her hurrying on pressing, through insufficient silent outcries, towards something, anything, even instant death, if only they could be expressed when they moved with her movement, a maze of shapes, flowing, tilting into each other, in endless patterns, sharp against the light; sharing her joy in the changing same same song of the London traffic; the bliss of post offices and railway stations, cabs going on and on towards unknown space;

omnibuses rumbling securely from point to point, always within the magic circle of London.[19]

Above all, *Pilgrimage* is a celebration of light. Consciousness is described primarily through shifting patterns of light and darkness, analogous to Richardson's descriptions of the 'essence' of cinema as 'light and shadow in movement'.[20] In the final volumes of the novel sequence, light and temporality become intertwined, with the future presented as a stream of light shining over the past and memory.[21] The linking of light and a cinematic consciousness is reinforced, as in H.D.'s work, by the imagery of projection. *Dawn's Left Hand* (which Richardson began writing in 1927, the first year of *Close Up*), opens with Miriam's return from Switzerland, where she found light at its most radiant, to London:

> The memories accumulated since she landed were like a transparent film through which clearly she saw all she had left behind; and felt the spirit of it waiting within her to project itself upon things just ahead, things waiting in this room as she came up the stairs.[22]

Consciousness becomes a screen (rather than a stream) on and through which the past and the future project their shapes and scenes.

In the early 1930s, responding to a question about art and consciousness and referring to the narrative modes of fiction, Dorothy Richardson wrote:

> The process may go forward in the form of a conducted tour, the author leading, visible and audible, all the time. Or the material to be contemplated may be thrown upon a screen, the author out of sight and hearing.[23]

The same theme is addressed in a 'Continuous Performance' article. Film, and particularly early film, provided, Richardson writes, 'an unlimited material upon which the imagination of the onlooker could get to work unhampered by the pressure of a controlling mind that is not his own mind'.[24] In her short story 'The Garden' (1924) (a sketch identified by Richardson's biographer Gloria Fromm as a central example of her cinematic writing) Richardson represented both childhood consciousness and the workings of memory: 'Pretty *pretty* flowers. Standing quite still, going on being how they were when no one was there.'[25]

The play with authorial absence and presence is closely echoed in Virginia Woolf's essay 'The Cinema' (1926), in which Woolf described the different 'reality' of screen images (referring to pre-World War I cinema): 'We behold them as they are when we are not there. We see life as it is when we have no part in it ... beauty will continue to be beautiful whether we behold it or not.'[26] In the 'Time Passes' section of *To the Lighthouse* (1926), Woolf attempted to produce an equivalent to the cinematic aesthetic of a future or potential cinema, not only by using visual images to express emotion and by animating objects into non-human life, but through a radical experiment in narration in which reality itself is presented as if in the absence of the perceiving subject. Through the production of fiction as film, these modernist writers sought to remove from the scene the omniscient author, identified with the closed and hegemonic worlds of nineteenth-century fiction. In so doing, they transcribe a ghostly realism, a spectral mimesis, which anticipates Christian Metz's characterization of the film image as signifying 'the presence of an absence'.

In principle, at least, Richardson maintained a conceptual distinction between fiction and film, though she repeatedly shifted the balance in favour of one or the other. She writes, in an article on 'Films for children', that 'the film, with its freedom from the restrictions of language, is more nearly universal than the book and can incorporate, for the benefit of the rest, the originality of each race unhampered by translation'.[27] In another *Close Up* article she argues strongly against what she takes to be H.G. Wells's view that 'literature, for so long prophesying unawares the fully developed film, [has] had its day', defending the sphere of the literary by drawing the film/literature distinction in the following terms: 'The film is a social art, a show, something for collective seeing ... Reading, all but reading aloud, is a solitary art ... The film is skyey apparition, white searchlight. The book remains the intimate, domestic friend, the golden lamp at the elbow.'[28] This last image is echoed in *Deadlock*, the sixth volume of *Pilgrimage*, in which Miriam comes to writing: 'Nothing would matter now that the paper-scattered lamplit circle was established in the centre of life.'[29] Richardon's representations of reading and writing are thus distinctly visual and cinematographic, crossing over the divide which they ostensibly serve to erect and reinforce. In a 'Continuous Performance' article on 'Captions', she in fact denies that word and image can be separated:

> The artist can no more eliminate the caption than he can eliminate himself. Art and literature, Siamese twins making their first curtsey to the public in a script that was a series of pictures, have never yet been separated. In its uttermost abstraction art is still a word about life and literature never ceases to be pictorial.[30]

Such representations are, for Richardson, predicated on the 'speaking silence' of the cinema. As Macpherson, Robert Herring, and other contributors to *Close Up* 'converted' to the merits of sound cinema, Richardson began to mourn the end of the silent era. From the outset, her column had investigated the terms of the cinema's silence. She was particularly absorbed by the question of 'musical accompaniment', and the film's 'continuous performance' is indeed made inseparable from accompanying music. She is hostile to 'the talkies' in large part because their multiple auralities – music, synch sound/speech, 'dead' silences – fragment the continuous stream provided by film music in silent cinema and its unifying aesthetic. The coming of sound brings: 'Apparatus rampant: the theatre, ourselves, the screen, the mechanisms, all fallen apart into competitive singleness.'[31]

While music 'enhances the faculty of vision',[32] speech entails 'the diminution of the faculty of seeing'.[33] 'Vocal sound', she writes, 'always a barrier to intimacy, is destructive of the balance between what is seen and the silently perceiving, co-operating onlooker';[34] 'the music is not an alien sound if it be as continuous as the performance and blending with it';[32] 'since the necessary stillness and concentration depend in part upon the undisturbed continuity of surrounding conditions, the musical accompaniment should be both continuous and flexible. By whatever means, the aim is to unify';[33] 'without music there is neither light nor colour ... the pictures moved silently by, lifeless and colourless, to the sound of intermittent talking and the continuous faint hiss and creak of the apparatus'.[34] Film music is thus represented as a suturing device, permitting, as Claudia Gorbman has noted, 'a deeper psychic investment in the grey, wordless, two-dimensional world of the silent film'[35] and evoking the paradox which Eisler and Adorno ascribed to film music and which Richardson makes the condition of (silent) film in general – its power to create a 'collective community' while simultaneously belonging 'primarily to the sphere of subjective inwardness'.[36]

If at times Richardson allows solitude and association or community to coexist, at others she polarizes them along the lines of the dichotomy between silent and sound film. The opposition silence/sound – which becomes an increasingly insistent aspect of Richardson's column as of *Close Up* in general – thus effects the construction of other polarities: seeing/hearing, literature/film, past/present and, most emphatically, feminine/masculine. Although Richardson's gendered aesthetic is one of the most striking aspects of her film-writing, the feminine/masculine divide should in this context be seen as in part a second-order construction (brought into being by the desire to represent the split between silence and sound) rather than as a founding opposition.

In her film column, as in *Pilgrimage*, Richardson began to gender silence as feminine, sound/speech as masculine and to portray women's film spectatorship as a negotiation of the terms of speech and silence. In one such article she writes that the woman on the screen shines from its surface:

> In silent, stellar radiance, for the speech that betrayeth is not demanded of her ... But it is not only upon the screen that this young woman has been released in full power. She is to be found also facing it, and by no means silent, in her tens of thousands ... [The only thing] to be said for the film that can be heard as well as seen is that it puts its audience in its place, reduces it to the condition of being neither seen nor heard.[37]

In her reworkings of Victorian injunctions for children's behaviour, Richardson points up the 'newness of this art', which 'has not yet established a code of manners', as well, perhaps, as the 'newness' of the 'new woman'. The woman who talks in the cinema destroys 'the possibility of which any film is so delightfully prodigal; the possibility of escape via incidentals into the world of meditation or of thought'. In so doing, however, Richardson argues, she exhibits the film audience's increasingly sophisticated response to early cinema; viewers no longer look in awed silence at anything and everything that is projected before them.

The woman who talks through the silent film also manifests a significant aesthetic response:

> she is innocently, directly, albeit unconsciously, upon the path that men have reached through long centuries of effort and of thought. She does not need, this type of woman clearly does not need, the illusions of art to come to the assistance of her own sense of existing. Instinctively she maintains a balance, the

thing perceived and herself perceiving. ... Not all the wiles of the most perfect art can shift her from the centre where she dwells.

Down through the centuries men and some women have pathetically contemplated art as a wonder outside themselves. It is only in recent years that man has known beauty to emanate from himself, to be his gift to what he sees. And the dreadful woman asserting herself in the presence of no matter what grandeurs unconsciously testifies that life goes on, art or no art, and that the onlooker is part of the spectacle.[38]

The modern woman, Richardson suggests, in her projects of self-realization, refuses the position of passive spectator; the cinema is the means whereby she inserts herself into the spectacle. Women find themselves, it is suggested, both in and in tension with the aesthetic of the silent cinema. The (female) spectator is neither absorbed by nor subsumed into the spectacle. We might compare this with Siegfried Kracauer's account of the cinema spectator as the self who 'relinquishes its power of control ... "In the theater I am always I", a perceptive French woman once told this writer, "but in the cinema I dissolve into all things and beings"'.[39]

If in the silent cinema the modern woman speaks, however, 'the feminine' is finally revealed in women's silence in the face of the coming of sound. In one of her last articles for *Close Up*, 'The Film Gone Male', Richardson suggests that silent film was essentially feminine, revealing 'something of the changeless being at the heart of all becoming ... In its insistence on contemplation it provided a pathway to reality. In becoming audible and particularly in becoming a medium of propaganda, it is doubtless fulfilling its destiny. But it is a masculine destiny. The destiny of planful becoming, rather than of purposeful being'.[40] Richardson returns to this idea of woman as Being, man as Becoming throughout her writing. It goes against the prevalent concept of the New Woman as an 'evolving' creature and is a central aspect of the suspicions Richardson expressed towards 'evolutionary' models of history and, more specifically, of women.

The epigraph Richardson used for her 'Continuous Performance' article on 'the woman, girl, who uses the C. as boudoir, trysting place, weepery' was '*Animal impudens*' and she was writing, she suggested to Bryher 'for & against her'.[41] The epigraph is intended to recall, mockingly, Juvenal's satire on women: Richardson's article is in part a satire on satires of women, just as many of her representations of 'types' of women are in fact satirical sketches of men's idealized and/or demonized versions of femininity. Although some of her pronouncements in her film writing, as in *Pilgrimage*, suggest an 'essentializing' view of masculinity and femininity, her definitions, gendered and otherwise, are radically unstable, veering between the historical and the mythic in the construction of 'woman'. Moreover, she replays, in 'Continuous Performance', arguments made in the 'non-cinematic' contexts of articles written in the early 1920s about women and art and women and 'the feminine',[42] inserting her views into the spectacle of the cinema and (for the most part implicitly) catching them up in the complex relationships between the 'retrogressive' images of the feminine projected onto the screen and the 'progressive' dimensions of the feminized public sphere of cinema spectatorship. Her writing, in the context of film as in other spheres, is highly encoded.

From 1929, when Richardson began to focus on the silent/sound transition (with an acute awareness of the 'either-or' reasoning forced upon aesthetic theorizing by the transition and divide), she began to write about silent film as 'memory'. Although resigned, she writes, to a 'filmless London' once 'speech-films' had taken over the cinemas:

> There was, there always, is, one grand compensation: we came fully into our heritage of silent films. 'The Film,' all the films we had seen, massed together in the manner of a single experience ... became for us treasure laid up. Done with in its character of current actuality, inevitably alloyed, and beginning its rich, cumulative life as memory. Again and again, in this strange 'memory' (which, however we may choose to define it, is, at the least, past, present and future powerfully combined) we should go to the pictures; we should revisit, each time with a difference, and, since we should bring to it increasing wealth of experience, each time more fully, certain films stored up within. But to the cinema we should go no more.[43]

Inscribing silent film as 'memory', she also begins to represent it in the mode of *Pilgrimage*, narrating, in her 'Continuous Performance' article 'A Tear for Lycidas', the city and/as cinema, the film spectator as flâneur:

> Wandering at large, we found ourselves unawares, not by chance, we refuse to say by chance, in a dim and dusty by-street: one of those elderly dignified streets that now await, a little wistfully, the inevitable re-building. Giving shelter meanwhile to the dismal eddyings and scuttlings of wind-blown refuse: grey dust, golden straw, scraps of trodden paper. Almost no traffic. Survival, in a neglected central backwater, of something of London's former quietude.
>
> Having, a moment before, shot breathlessly across the rapids of a main thoroughfare, we paused, took breath, looked about us and saw the incredible. A legend, not upon one of those small, dubious façades still holding their own against the fashion, but upon that of the converted Scala theatre: Silent Films. Continuous Performance. *Two Days. The Gold Rush.*[44]

The legend 'Continuous Performance' becomes one with Richardson's own running title, while its contiguity with 'Silent Films' marks the necessary relationship between the two phrases and their embodied concepts.

Richardson emphasizes that the attraction to silent film is not merely nostalgic. The Scala is a 'converted' theatre, showing silent films in, and in spite of, the full awareness of sound, just as the writer-wanderer's entry into the silent London by-street is preceded by the experience of 'the rapids of a main thoroughfare', and the cinema spectator watches silent film in possession of 'all we had read and heard and imaginatively experienced of the new dimensions'. The silent/sound divide can be crossed in both directions, and silent film, now viewed not 'innocently' but in the knowledge of sound, becomes a way of 'seeing again'.

Richardson, despite her consistent writing and theorizing against the coming of sound (or, more precisely, speech) could thus also be seen as a 'convert' of a kind. The aesthetic of the silent film becomes the gift of the transition to sound, brought into (new) being by what succeeds it. By implication, if the sound film is the film 'gone male', the implication may be not only that the film was once 'female', as Anne Friedberg has argued (and that silent film articulated a feminine aesthetic),[45] but that the coming of sound has (retrospectively) constructed, and bestowed, the space of the silent film as the space of women.

Throughout her column Richardson celebrates the cinema as a women's sphere, at times representing the picture palace as hospice, refuge and church, akin to the Quaker church and its embodied silences to which she was drawn throughout her adult life. Yet if the cinema is at one level a 'retreat', it also gives access to a new public sphere. In rural communities, she writes in 'The Cinema in Arcady', audiences are 'becoming world citizens', empowered to join in 'the world-wide conversations now increasingly upon us in which the cinema may play, amongst its numerous other rôles, so powerful a part'.[46] In her penultimate 'Continuous Performance' article, 'The Film Gone Male', she both mourns the loss of the 'old time films gracious silence' and reinserts it at, and as, the 'changeless heart' of the new, where it transmutes into female power, women's contributions to 'the world-wide conversations' now, and increasingly exigently, as the 1930s advance, taking place:

> The new film can, at need, assist Radio in turning the world into a vast council-chamber and do more than assist, for it is the freer partner. And multitudinous within that vast chamber as within none of the preceding councils of mankind, is the unconquerable, unchangeable eternal feminine. Influential.[47]

CLOSE UP

Vol. I, no. 1   July 1927

CONTINUOUS PERFORMANCE

... So I gave up going to the theatre. Yet I had seen one or two who possessed themselves upon the stage and much good acting, especially of character parts; but I have never been on my knees to character acting. The one or two I saw again and again, enduring for their sakes those others, many of them clever, all keyed up for their parts, all too high-pitched, taking their cues too soon. It was not that the pain of seeing them lose all our opportunities – their own and with them ours who were the audience – outweighed the joy of recreation at the hands of those others, makers and givers of life, but rather that on the whole the sense of guilt, of wasted performance for players and audience alike was too heavy to be borne. Waste and loss that could, it seemed to me, with ever so little control of the convulsionaries, be turned to gain.

Lured back by a series of German plays zestfully performed by a small and starless group, I found at once my persuasion confirmed that the English, whose very phlegm and composure is the other side of their self-consciousness and excitability, do not make actors. Watching for foreigners I saw a few French plays, saw Bernhardt and was more than ever ashamed of the remembered doings of the English castes. Not even the most wooden of those selected to surround and show up the French star could produce anything to equal the sense of shame and loss that at that time overshadowed for me all I saw on the English stage that was not musical comedy with its bright colour for the soul and its gay music for the blood. The dignity of the French art and the simplicity of the German restored my early unapprehensive enthusiasm for the theatre, even for the pillared enclosure, the draped boxes, the audience waiting in the dim light to take their part in the great game. I went to no more English plays. And for a long time there were no foreign ones to see. But photo-plays had begun, small palaces were defacing even the suburbs. My experience with the English stage inhibited my curiosity. The palaces were repulsive. Their being brought me an uneasiness that grew lively when at last I found myself within one of those whose plaster frontages and garish placards broke a row of shops in a strident, north London street. It was a Monday and therefore a new picture. But it was also washday, and yet the scattered audience was composed almost entirely of mothers. Their children, apart from the infants accompanying them, were at school and their husbands were at work. It was a new audience, born within the last few months. Tired women, their faces sheened with toil, and small children, penned in semi-darkness and foul air on a sunny afternoon. There was almost no talk. Many of the women sat alone, figures of weariness at rest. Watching these I took comfort. At last the world of entertainment had provided for a few pence, tea thrown in, a sanctuary for mothers, an escape from the everlasting qui vive into eternity on a Monday afternoon.

The first scene was a tide, frothing in over the small beach of a sandy cove, and for some time we were allowed to watch the coming and going of those foamy waves, to the sound of a slow waltz, without the disturbance of incident. Presently from the fisherman's hut emerged the fisherman's daughter, moss-haired. The rest of the scenes, all of which sparked continually, I have forgotten. But I do not forget the balm of that tide, and that simple music, nor the shining eyes and rested faces of those women. After many years, during which I saw many films, I went, to oblige a friend, once more to a theatre. It was to a drawing-room play, and the harsh bright light, revealing the audience, the over-emphasis of everything, the over-driven voices and movements of all but the few, seemed to me worse than ever. I realised that the source of the haunting guilt and loss was for me, that the players, in acting *at* instead of *with* the audience, were destroying the inner relationship between audience and players. Something of this kind, some essential failure to compel the co-operation of the creative consciousness of the audience.

Such co-operation cannot take place unless the audience is first stilled to forgetfulness of itself as an audience. This takes power. Not force or emphasis or noise, mental or physical. And the film, as intimate as thought, so long as it is free from the introduction of the alien element of sound, gives this co-operation its best chance. The accompanying music is not an alien sound. It assists the plunge into life that just any film can give, so much more fully than just any play, where the onlooker is perforce under the tyranny of the circumstances of the play without the chances of escape provided so lavishly by the moving scene. The music is not an alien sound if it be as continuous as the performance and blending with it. That is why, though a good orchestra can heighten and deepen effects, a piano played by one able to improvise connective tissue for this varying themes is preferable to most orchestral accompaniments. Music is essential. Without it the film is a moving photograph and the audience mere onlookers. Without music there is neither light nor colour, and the test of this is that one remembers musically accompanied films *in colour* and those unaccompanied as colourless.

The cinema may become all that its well-wishers desire. So far, its short career of some twenty years is a tale of splendid achievement. Its creative power is incalculable, and its service to the theatre is nothing less than the preparation of vast, new audiences for the time when plays shall be accessible at possible rates in every square mile of a town. How many people, including the repentant writer, has it already restored to the playhouse?

Vol. I, no. 2   August 1927

CONTINUOUS PERFORMANCE

II

MUSICAL ACCOMPANIMENT

Our first musician was a pianist who sat in the gloom beyond the barrier and played without notes. His playing was a continuous improvisation varying in tone and tempo according to what was going forward on the screen. During the earlier part of the evening he would sometimes sing. He would sing to the sailing by of French chateaux, *sotto voce*, in harmony with the gently flowing undertone that moved so easily from major to minor and from key to key. His singing seemed what probably it was, a spontaneous meditative appreciation of things seen. For the Gazette he had martial airs, waltzes for aeroplanes. Jigs accompanied the comic interludes and devout low-toned nocturnes the newest creations of fashion. For drama he usually had a leit-motif, borrowed or invented, set within his pattern of sound moving suitably from pianissimo to fortissimo. He could time a passage to culminate and break punctually on a staccato chord at a crisis. This is a crude example of his talent for spontaneous adaptation. As long as he remained with us music and picture were one. If the film were good he enhanced it, heightened its effect of action moving forward for the first time. If it were anything from bad to worst his music helped the onlooker to escape into incidentals and thence into his private world of meditation or of thought.

The little palace prospered and the management grew ambitious. Monthly programmes were issued, refreshments were cried up and down the gangways and perfumed disinfectants squirted ostentatiously over the empty spaces. The pianist vanished and the musical accompaniment became a miniature orchestra, conspicuous in dress clothes and with lights and music stands and scores between the audience and the screen, playing set pieces, for each scene a piece. At each change of scene one tune would give place to another, in a different key, usually by means of a tangle of discords. The total result of these efforts towards improvement was a destruction of the relationship between onlookers and film. With the old unity gone the audience grew disorderly. Talking increased. Prosperity waned. Much advertisement of 'west-end successes' pulled things together for a while during which the management aimed still higher. An evening came when in place of the limping duet of violin and piano, several instruments held together by some kind of conducting produced sprightly and harmonious effects. At half-time the screen was curtained leaving the musician's pit in a semi-darkness where presently wavered a green spot-light that came to rest upon the figure of a handsome young Jew dramatically fronting the audience with violin poised for action. Fireworks. Applause. After which the performance was allowed to proceed. Within a month the attendance was reduced to a scattered few and in due course the hall was 'closed for decorations', to reopen some months later 'under entirely new management', undecorated and with the old pianist restored to his place. The audience drifted back.

But during the interregnum, and whilst concerted musical efforts were doing their worst, an incident occurred that convinced me that any kind of musical noise is better than none. Our orchestra failed to appear and the pictures moved silently by, lifeless and colourless, to the sound of intermittent talking and the continuous faint hiss and creak of the apparatus. The result seemed to justify the curses of the most ardent enemies of the cinema and I understood at last what they mean who declare that dramatic action in photograph is obscene because it makes no personal demand upon the onlooker. It occurred to me to wonder how many of these enemies are persons indifferent to music and those to whom music of any kind is a positive nuisance.

If ever films are made to sound, if not only the actors, but the properties, street traffic, cooking-stoves and cataracts are given voices as are already in some cinemas the bombs and thunderstorms falling upon the dumb players, musical accompaniment will be superfluous whether as a cover for the sounds from the operator's gallery and the talking of the audience, or as a help to the concentration that is essential to collaboration between the onlooker and what he sees. For the present music is needed and generally liked even by those who are not aware that it helps them to create the film and gives the film both colour and sound. In our small palace we object to any sound coming from the screen. We dislike even the realistic pistol-shot that was heard once or twice during our period of great ambitions. With the help of the puff of smoke and our pianist's staccato chord we can manufacture our own reality.

And since the necessary stillness and concentration depend in part upon the undisturbed continuity of surrounding conditions, the musical accompaniment should be both continuous and flexible. By whatever means, the aim is to unify. If film and music proceed at cross purposes the audience is distracted by a half-conscious effort to unite them. The doings of an orchestra that is an entertainment in itself go far in destroying the entertainment one came forth to seek. I saw in Switzerland a number of films whose captions were in columns and bi-lingual and whose appearance was the signal for a chorus of linguists making translations for the benefit of less gifted friends. But the strife of tongues on and off the screen was less disturbing than the innocent doings of the orchestra which opened proceedings before the lights were lowered with a sprightly march and went into the darkness with it and played it until the end of the reel, which had shown us a midnight murder on a moor, and then became visible, lights up, cheerily playing yet another martial air. They continued throughout the performance, vanishing and reappearing and playing, regardless of what might be going forward upon the screen, 'band music' with a perfect mechanical precision.

But orchestral music, whether at its worst or at its best is unsuited to any but the largest halls where perhaps, though a concert grand can supply all needs, an orchestra, that has rehearsed, with the film, music written or arranged for that film until the two are one, is the ideal. Short of that the single player at his best is not to be beaten.

Vol. I, no. 3 September 1927

CONTINUOUS PERFORMANCE

III

CAPTIONS

Experience has taught us to disregard placards. So we enter the hall in innocence and give ourselves to the preliminary entertainments. They are always very various, and whether good or bad we charm them, powerfully or feebly according to our condition, with the charm of our confident anticipation. A good mood will fling some sort of life even into the most tasteless of the local advertisements that immediately precede the real business of the evening, beginning when at last we are confronted with a title, set, like a greeting in a valentine, within an expressive device. We peer for clues. Sometimes there is no clue but the title, appearing alone in tall letters that fill the screen, fill the hall with a stentorian voice. Thrilling us. We know we are being got, but not yet at what vulnerable point and we sit in suspense while the names of author, adapter, producer, art-director, photographer and designer come on in curly lettering and singly, each lingering. Then there is a screenful of names, the parts and their players, also lingering and perhaps to be followed by further information. We do not desire it but may not now turn away from the screen. At any moment the censor's permit will appear and whether lingering or not – usually by this time the operator has gone to sleep in his stride and it lingers – this last barrier must be faced for the length of its stay or we may miss the first caption. At one time we used to pay devout attention to the whole of these disclosures. They were a revelation of the size of the undertaking and our wondering gratitude went forth to the multitude of experts who had laboured together for our enterprise. But after a while the personal introduction of all these labourers became a torment. We grudged the suspense exacted by what might prove to be a record of wasted effort.

In due course and as if in awareness of our overtaxed patience the preliminaries were reduced to title, name of author, or a star or so, official permission, each hurrying by, hurrying us towards the caption that should launch us on our journey: a screenful of psychology, history, or description of period and locality. There is eager silence in the hall during the stay of the oblong of clear print whether beginning: 'Throughout the ages mankind has—' or 'Avarice is the cruellest—' or 'In a remote village in the Pyrenees, far from—'. When we have read we know where we are supposed to be going; we have grown accustomed to finding our places in the long procession of humanity, to going down into the dread depths of our single selves, to facing life in unfamiliar conditions. But we do not yet know whether our journey is to be good. Whether there is to be any journey at all. So we are wary. We remember films whose caption, appearing in instalments at regular intervals, has been the better part, presenting, bright and new, truths that in our keeping had grown a little dim, or telling us strange news of which within reason we can never have too much. We have come forth, time and place forgotten, surroundings vanished, and have been driven back. Very often by people whose one means of expressing emotion is a vexed frown, or people whose pulpy rouged mouths are forever at work pouting, folding, parting in a smile that laboriously reveals both rows of teeth. These people, interminably interfering with the scenery, drive us to despair. Sometimes we are too much upset to battle our way to indifference and see, missing what is supposed to be seen, anything and everything according to our mood; it is difficult to beat us together. We remember films damaged by their captions. Not fatally. For we can substitute our own, just as within limits we can remake a bad film as we go. With half a chance we are making all the time. Just a hint of *any* kind of beauty and if we are on the track, not waiting for everything to be done for us, not driven back by rouged pulp and fixed frown, we can manage very well. For the present we take captions for granted. But we are ready to try doing without them. Now and again a film gathers us in without any clear hint beyond the title. This we love. We love the challenge. We are prepared to go without a hint even in the title. We are prepared for anything. We trust the pictures. Somewhere sooner or later there will be a hint. Or something of which we can make one, each for himself. The absence of any hint is a hint we are ready to take.

Perhaps the truth about captions is just here: that somewhere, if not in any given place then all over the picture, is a hint. The artist can no more eliminate the caption that he can eliminate himself. Art and literature, Siamese twins making their first curtsey to the public in a script that was a series of pictures, have never yet been separated. In its uttermost abstraction art is still a word about life and literature never ceases to be pictorial. A work of pure fantasy bears its caption within. A narrative, whether novel, play or film, supplies the necessary facts directly, in a novel either by means of the author's descriptive labels or through information given in the dialogue, in the play by means of that uncomfortable convention that allows characters to converse in anachronisms, in the film by means of the supply of interlarded words. And if the direct giving of information in captions is the mark of a weak film, the direct giving of information in a play or novel is the mark of a weak novel or play. There are masterpieces enough to flout the dogma.

Nevertheless the film has an unrivalled opportunity of presenting the life of the spirit directly, and needs only the minimum of informative accompaniment. The test of the film on whatever level is that the wayfaring man, though a fool, shall not err therein, though each will take a different journey. The test of the caption is its relative invisibility. In the right place it is not seen as a caption; unless it lingers too long upon the screen.

Vol. I, no. 4   October 1927

CONTINUOUS PERFORMANCE
IV
A THOUSAND PITIES

It was the winter's strangest happiness, coming into mind with autumn's first dead leaves and forgotten only at the budding of the new green. Its great day brought together by magic a concourse of people to sit in wedding garments at the gate of heaven, blithely chattering until the golden air became moonlight and a breathless waiting for the swish of curtains gliding open upon heaven itself. Sometimes puzzling but always heaven and its inhabitants celestial; save at those moments when one of the blessed, turning from his blissful mystery, came down to the footlights and sang at us, incomprehensible songs that quenched the light and brought strange sad echoes such as we knew on earth. Heaven recovered when the celestial being went back into his place, and was lived in until the end, incalculably far away. And after the end there was a fresh beginning, a short scene made of swift and dreadful moments, charm and mystery and shock, just outside heaven's closed gates. A little troop of beings, half-earthly, born of the earlier scenes, romped close at hand in a confined space before a façade of earthly houses. Harlequin, lightly leaping, snaky, electric, sweetly-twirling Columbine, lolloping Pantaloon with sad, frightened mouth. Swish-whack. Shocks unfortellable. Bangs of exploding fleas. Ceaseless speechless movement, swift leaping, whirling, staggering, light and heavy together making strange shapes in the diminished light until the immortals vanished and we were down on solid earth with the largefooted policeman, the nursemaid and the perambulator and infant, funny and dreadful on a scene where the power of the vanished immortals still worked and brought us joyous moments: the moment of the falling of a house-front, the squashing and the sight, a moment later, of the squashed, flat upon the centre of the stage.

We knew that everything happening after the immortals had vanished was out of place and if the mortals in their foolishness had been all that we saw, the scenes no matter how short, meaning nothing, would have brought weariness. But we gazed without weariness because we saw somewhere within the stilted speechless pasteboard movements something of the glory that had passed. Our eyes were still full of the last scene in heaven from which the lively celestials who came down to dance in the street had been created, the opening of the heaven of heavens in the Transformation Scene where everything and everyone had assembled in a single expanded shape, shimmering, flower-like, that slowly moved in changing form and colour, stretching out attention to the uttermost lest some lovely thing be missed. It foretold the end of beauty but was itself endlessly beautiful, holding us to its eternity by its soundlessness. If any part of it had broken into sound, its link with us would have been snapped, its spell broken. Of its moving stillness and our own that it compelled was born something new, a movement of our own small selves. Only because in its continual movement it was silent did it reach the whole small self. It demanded less than the rest of the performance and much more. Taking part in that we had been everything by turns, keyed up to the limit of our green faculties, living rapidly, thinking thoughts, going beyond ourselves, moving now here now there, loving and hating, laughing, shrieking aloud at need. But the appeal of the Transformation Scene was not to single faculties in turn but to all at once, to the whole spirit gathered at home in itself. Stilled stage, stilled music gave the surrounding conditions.

So with the film, whose essential character is pantomime, that primarily, and anything and everything else incidentally. But primarily pantomime. Vocal sound, always a barrier to intimacy, is destructive of the balance between what is seen and the silently perceiving, co-operating onlooker. It is no accident that the most striking and most popular film success to date is that of a mime. This man was the first to grasp the essential quality of the medium, to see what to do and what to avoid to reach the maximum of collaboration with the onlookers. His technique admits sound, but only of things and that sparingly. Himself and his assistants dispense as far as possible with the appearance of speech. The language of his films is universal. And though the world-wide success of this d'Artagnan of the gutters rest partly upon shameless gaminerie, perpetually defying even the most dignified slings and arrows of outrageous fortune with perpetual custard pie, its securest prop is his unerring art. His use of the film as a medium. Wealth of imaginative invention is held together by simplicity of design, the fullest use is made of the thoughtlike swiftness of movement made possible by the film. His small grotesque figure, whether going with incredible swiftness through its clever, absurd evolutions, or a motionless mask of ever-varying expressiveness, or geometrically in flight down a long vista, was the first to exploit these possibilities. Rudimentary in material, his work is sound in foundation and structure, an advance sample of what the film, as film, can do.

Poetry, epigram, metaphor, chit-chat social, philosophic or scientific are the reactions and afterthought of spiritual experience, are for the stage. And even upon the stage the actual drama moves silently, speech merely noting its moment. The 'great dramatic moments' are speechless. The film at its best is all dramatic moment. The film is a spirit and they that worship it must worship it in spirit and in truth. Like the garish Transformation Scene and the debased Harlequinade of the old-fashioned pantomime, the only parts remaining true pantomime, its demands are direct and immediate, at once much more and much less than those of the vocal stage-play. And its preliminary demand is for concentration. Given favourable surrounding conditions for concentration, the film's power of making contacts are, so long as it remains consistent with itself, a hundred to the one of the theatre: the powerful actor, the stage play's single point of contact with the 'audience', with those who are indeed, though not hearers only, throughout the course of the collaboration largely concentrated on listening.

The sounds that have so far been added to the film, of falling rain, buzz and hoot of motors, roll of thunder, pistol-shots and bombs, are sometimes relatively harmless. And if they were an indication of experiment, suggesting that sound is to be tested and used with discrimination, their presence might cease to be disturbing. But they are being introduced not in any spirit of experiment or with any promise of discrimination. They are there because they are easy to produce. More sound is promised as soon as the technical difficulties shall be overcome. The bombs are the fore-runners, evidence of a blind move in a wrong direction, in the direction of the destruction of the essential character of the screen-play.

Vol. I, no. 5   November 1927

CONTINUOUS PERFORMANCE

V

THERE'S NO PLACE LIKE HOME

Short of undertaking pilgrimages we remain in ignorance of new films until they become cheap classics. Not completely in ignorance for there is always hearsay. But these films coming soon or late find us ready to give our best here where we have served our apprenticeship and the screen has made in us its deepest furrows. It is true that an excellence shining enough will bring out anywhere and everywhere our own excellence to meet it. And the reflected glory of a reputation will sometime carry us forth into the desert to see. But until we are full citizens of the spirit, free from the tyranny of circumstance and always and everywhere perfectly at home, we shall find our own place our best testing-ground and since, moreover, we are for THE FILM as well as for FILMS, we prefer in general to take our chance in our quarter, fulfilling thus the good bishop's advice to everyman to select his church, whether in the parish or elsewhere close at hand, and remain there rather than go a-whoring after novelties. The truly good bishop arranges of course that the best, selected novelties shall circulate from time to time.

Meanwhile in the little bethel there is the plain miraculous food, sometimes coarse, sometimes badly served, but still miraculous food served to feed our souls in this preparatory school for the finer things that soon no doubt will be raising the level all round. And we may draw, if further consolation be needed, much consolation from the knowledge that, in matter of feeding, the feeder and the how and the where are as important as the what.

Once through the velvet curtains we are at home and on any but first nights can glide into our sittings without the help of the torch. There is a multitude of good sittings for the hall is shaped like a garage and though there are nave and two aisles with seats three deep, there are no side views. Something is to be said for seats at the heart of the congregation, but there is another something in favour of a side row. It can be reached, and left, without squeezing and apologetic crouching. The third seat serves as a hold-all. In front of us will be either the stalwart and the leaning lady, forgiven for her obstructive attitude because she, also an off-nighter, respects, if arriving first, our chosen sittings, or there will be a solitary, motionless middle-aged man. There is, in proportion to the size of the congregation, a notable number of solitary, middle-aged male statues set sideways, arm over seat, half-persuaded, or wishing to be considered half-persuaded. Behind there is no one, no commentary, no causerie, no crackling bonbonnières. The torch is immediately at hand for greetings and tickets and, having disposed ourselves and made our prayers we may look forth to find the successor of Felix making game of space and time. Hot Air beating Cold Steel by a neck, or, if we are late, an Arrow collar young man, collarless, writhing within ropes upon the floor of the crypt whose reappearance will be the signal for our departure. Perfection, of part or of whole, we shall rarely see, but there is no limit to vision and if we return quite empty-handed we shall know whose is the fault. The miracle works, some part of it works and gets home. And sometimes one of the 'best' to date is ours without warning.

For any sake let everyman have his local cinema to cherish or neglect at will, and let it be, within reason, small. Small enough to be apprehended at a glance. And plain. That is to say simple. The theatre may be as ornate, as theatrical as it likes, the note of the cinema is simplicity. Abandon frills all ye who enter here. And indeed while dramatic and operative enterprise is apt, especially in England, to be in part social function the cinema, though subtly social, is robbed by necessity of the chance of becoming a parade ground. One cannot show off one's diamonds in the dark. Going to the cinema is a relatively humble, simple business. Moreover in any but the theatre's more vital spaces it is impossible to appear in an old ulster save in the way of a splendiferous flouting of splendour that is more showy than diamonds. To the cinema one may go not only in the old ulster but decorated by the scars of any and every sort of conflict. To the local cinema one may go direct, just as one is.

For the local, or any, cinema the garage shape is the right shape because in it the faithful are side by side confronting the screen and not as in some super-cinemas in a semi-circle whose sides confront each other and get the screen sideways. The screen should dominate. That is the prime necessity. It should fill the vista save for the doorways on either side whose reassuring 'Emergency Exit' beams an intermittent moonlight. It is no doubt because screens must vary in size according to the distance from them of the projector that the auditorium of the super-cinema (truly an auditorium for there is already much to be heard there) is built either in a semi-circle or in an oblong so wide that the screen, though proportionately larger, looks much smaller than that of a small cinema, seems a tiny distant sheet upon which one must focus from a surrounding disadvantageously-distributed populous bigness. The screen should dominate, and its dominating screen is one of the many points scored by the small local cinema.

For the small local cinema that will remain reasonably in tune with the common feelings of common humanity both in its films and in its music, there is a welcome waiting in every parish.

Vol. I, no. 6   December 1927

CONTINUOUS PERFORMANCE

VI

THE INCREASING CONGREGATION

It is the London season. Not a day must be lost nor any conspicuous event. And the cinema, having been first a nine months wonder and then, almost to date, a perennial perplexity, matter for public repudiation mitigated by private and, with fair good fortune, securely invisible patronage, is now part of our lives, ranks, as a topic, alongside the theatre and there are Films that must be seen. We go. No longer in secret and in taxis and alone, but openly in parties in the car. We emerge, glitter for a moment in the brilliant light of the new flamboyant foyer, and disappear for the evening into the queer faintly indecent gloom. Such illumination as there will be, moments of the familiar sense of the visible audience, of purposefully being somewhere, is but hail and farewell leaving our party again isolate amidst unknown invisible humanity. Anyone may be there. Anyone *is* there and everyone, and not segregated in a tier-quenched background nor packed away up under the roof. During the brief interval we behold not massed splendours bordered by a row of newspaper men, but everyone, filling the larger space, oddly ahead of us.

'What about a Movie? That one at the Excelsior sounds quite good.' Suggestions made off-hand. A Theatre is a rarity, to be selected with care, anticipated, experienced, discussed at great length, long remembered. But a film more or less is neither here nor there. May be good may be surprisingly good in the way of this strange new goodness provided for hours of relaxation and that nobody seems quite sure what to think of. It will at least be an evening's entertainment, a welcome change from talk, reading, bridge, wireless, gramophone. And the trip down town revives the unfailing bright sense of going out, lifts off the burden and heat of the day and if the rest of the evening is a failure it is not an elaborately arranged and expensive failure.

There's pictures going on all over London always making something to do whenever you want to go out, specially those big new ones with orchestras. Splendid. It's the next best thing to a dance and sure to be good you can get a nice meal at a restaurant and decide while you're there and if the one you choose is full up there's another round the corner nothing to fix up and worry about. And it's all so nice nothing poky and those fine great entrance halls everything smart and just right and waiting there for friends you feel in society like anybody else if your hat's all right and your things and my word the ready-mades are so cheap nowadays you need never go shabby and the commissionnaires and all those smart people about makes you *feel* smart. It's as good an evening as you can have and time for a nice bit of supper afterwards.

It is Monday. Thursday. The pence for the pictures are in the jar beside the saucer of coppers for the slot metre. But folded behind the jar are unpaid bills. In the jar are threepence and six halfpence ... 'Me and 'Erb tonight, then we'll have to manage for Dad and Alf Thursday and then no more for a bit. ... Whatever did we used to do when there was no pictures? Best we could I s'pose and must again.'

'Never swore I wouldn't go again this week. Never said swelp me. Might be doin' worse. It's me own money anyway.'

'Goin' on now. This minute. Pickshers goin' on now. Thou shalt not ste.... . Goin' on and me 'ere. It won't be, if I pay it back ...'

And so here we all are. All over London, all over England, all over the world. Together in this strange hospice risen overnight, rough and provisional but guerdon none the less of a world in the making. Never before was such all-embracing hospitality save in an ever-open church where kneels madame hastened in to make her duties between a visit to her dressmaker and an assignation, where the dustman's wife bustles in with infants and market-basket.

Universal hospitality. See that starveling, lean with loathing, feeding his unknown desperate longings upon selected books, giving his approval to tortoiseshell cats. He creeps in here. Braving the herd he creeps in. His scorn for the film is not more inspiring than the fact of his presence.

And that pleasant intellectual, grown a little weary of the things of the mind, his stock-in-trade. He comes not for ideas, but to cease in his mild circling, to sue the cinema as a stupefier, forty winks for his cherished intelligence. He will go away refreshed to write his next article.

Happy youth, happy childhood, weary women of all classes for whom at home there is no resting-place. Sensitives creep in here to sit clothed in merciful darkness. See those elders in whose ears sound always the approaching footsteps of death. Here, now and again, they are free from the sense of moments ticked off. See the beatitude of the stone-deaf. And that charming girl lost, despairing in the midst of her first quarrel, who would no more go to an entertainment alone than she would disrobe herself in the street. But this refuge near her lodgings opens its twilit spaces and makes itself her weepery.

Refuge, trysting-place, village pump, stimulant, shelter from rain and cold at less than the price of an evening's light and fire, drunkenness at less than the price of a drink. Instruction. Peeps behind scenes. Sermons. Homethrusts for hims and for hers, impartially.

School, salon, brothel, bethel, newspaper, art science, religion, philosophy, commerce, sport, adventure; flashes of beauty of all sorts. The only anything and everything. And here we all are, as never before. What will it do with us?

Vol. II, no. 1   January 1928

CONTINUOUS PERFORMANCE
VII
THE FRONT ROWS

As the heavy drops fell and the first cannonade rumbled through the upper layers of the heat-wave I saw close at hand garish placards and wide open doors. Entering, following the torch on and on through the darkness until we could go no further, [I] was for retreating and spending the hour elsewhere. But as the torch-bearer stood aside for me to pass to a seat, the light of the screen fell full upon the occupants of the front row: three small boys, one collapsed in the attitude of sleep, and indeed, I saw as I sat down, soundly sleeping, propped against the shoulder of my neighbour whose thin face, sheened by nervous excitement, lifted a foolish gaze towards the glare. Here was the worst. Here indeed was 'the pictures' as black villainy. I remembered all I had heard and tried hard to forget on the subject of the evils of the cinema, as it is, for small children and especially for the children in the front rows. All the week these boys were penned in stuffy class-rooms. And this was their Saturday afternoon, their time to reverse engines and go full steam backwards into savagery, make their street a jungle and learn from each other the lessons of the jungle. Or perhaps their time for becoming boy scouts. And here they were, 'ruining nerves and eyesight and breathing stifling air' and learning either less than nothing or more than was good.

But the air was not stifling. In spite of the weather the place had a certain coolness and when I raised my eyes to the screen I had no sense of blinding glare or effort to focus. There was indeed no possibility of focusing a scene so immense that one could only move about in it from point to point and realise that the business of the expert front-rower is to find the centre of action and follow it as best he can. Of the whole as something to hold in the eye he can have no more idea than has the proverbial fly on the statue over which he crawls. But at least as far as I could tell there was no feeling of glare or of eyestrain. Though it may be that the interest of making discoveries put the censor off guard. It seemed at any rate that unless it be bad for young eyes to gaze for three hours at a large mild brilliance close at hand, the eye-strain alarmists were disposed of. And if indeed it is bad, it is for the public health people to legislate for an increase of the distance between the screen and the front rows. But supposing the worst to exist only in the imaginations of the officiously fussy, what I wanted if possible to discover was just what it was these three boys got from the discreet immensity so closely confronting us. The one nearest to me certainly nothing more than unhealthy excitement, but he poor soul whether pent in school or ramping in alley, called for special help before he could get anything anywhere and was therefore disqualified to act as a test. Left to himself the poor moth was fated merely to gravitate.

The enormous bears moved in foolish gravity upon their cliffs in a scene too dispersed to be impressive. But they were of course bears, real bears. Bears in movement. They passed and soon we were looking at the deck of a ship in mid-ocean. Crew, deeds, drama, a centre of action moving from point to point. Suddenly, before the weight of a funny man in difficulties and at bay, a portion of the gunwale swung round in the manner of a gate upon its hinges and held him dangling in mid-air above the seething main. From the end-most boy, the one beyond the sleeper, came a shriek I can never forget. It filled the silent hall, one pure full high note that curved swiftly up to the next and ceased staccato; blissful terror in a single abrupt sound. People behind craned forward hoping for a happy glimpse of the face of a child in transport. The man on the ship swung back to safety and out again and again the cry pealed forth. This time I caught sight of the blood-thirsty little villain. A perfect gamin, rotund. Clear-eyed, clean-skinned, bolt upright with pudgy fists on knees to watch the event. We had that yell four times, the outflung utterly unselfconscious being of a child attained, the kind of sound Chaplin listens for when he is testing a film.

It changed the direction of my meditation on the front rows.

Since that far-off incident I have seen and heard a good deal of the front rows and much as I should like to see widened the gap between them and the screen I no longer desire to send the juvenile front rowers to amuse or bore themselves elsewhere. Thinking them back into a filmless world and particularly into filmless winters, I am glad of their presence on the easy terms that are compensation for their inconveniences. Presently no doubt there will be children's cinemas with films provided by the good folks who like to believe they know both what children need and what they like. Before this prospect I hesitate thinking of the children's hour upon the wireless. But such films, any films put together for children regarded as dear little darlings, inviting their own fate will have their little day and cease to be. Most children unless forcibly excluded from all other films, will refuse to sit them out. There are plenty of people about whose love for children is tinctured with a decent respect. Let us hope that some of them are even now meditating possible films.

Meanwhile the front rowers of all ages, the All-out responsive pit and gallery of the cinema are getting their education and preparing, are indeed already a little more than prepared for the films that are to come. Anyone visiting from time to time a local cinema whose audience is almost as unvarying as its films, cannot fail to have remarked on the development of the front rowers, their growth in critical grace. Their audible running commentary is one of the many incidental interests in a poor film. It is not only that today the lingering close-up of the sweet girl with tragically staring tear-filled eyes is apt to be greeted with jeers, and the endless love-making of the endless lovers with groans. It is not only that today's front rowers recognise all the stock characters at a glance and can predict developments. It is that the quality of the attention and collaboration that almost any stock drama can still command is changed. For although attention never wavers and collaboration is still hearty and still the sleek and sleekly-tailored malefactor is greeted at his first and innocent seeming entry as a wrong'un and the hero, racing life in hand through a hundred hairbreadth escapes to the rescue is still loudly applauded and applause breaks forth anew when the villain is flung over the cliff, the front rows are no longer thrilled quite as they were in their earlier silent days by all the hocus-pocus. They come level-headed and serenely talking through drama that a year ago would have held them dizzy and breathless. Even a novel situation does not too much disturb them. They attend, refuse to be puzzled, watch for the working out. And films 'above their heads', if the characters are fairly convincing, the acting fairly good, and the whole fairly well-knit, do not bore them. They see, possibly not all that is intended, but if quality is there, they see and assist. It is never the goodish to good film that produces fidgets, giggles, audible yawns, wailings and gnashing of teeth. Only to the film that is half maimed and blind, no matter what magnificence it may present, will these tributes be paid. In the film as in life, the what matters less than the how. All this of course within reasonable limits. There are certain films that front rows prefer above all others. And of some kinds they can apparently never have too much. Comics for instance. And family drama of all kinds. Family drama must be very feeble indeed to fail to capture. This is hardly surprising. There is very little about family life the front rows do not know. Animals too, tame or wild, are greatly beloved though there is no longer a thrill to be got from the seedy old lion trotting half-heartedly from room to room after prey known to be in no danger. And the American language. Once it was part of the puzzles and bewilderments of 'the pictures', but is there now a child in London who cannot at the right moment say: 'Oh, *boy*' and read and delightedly understand each idiom, and grin through the Hollywood caption that is metaphor running amuk and crammed with facetiousness?

They are there in their millions, the front rowers, a vast audience born and made in the last few years, initiated, disciplined, and waiting.

Vol. II, no. 3   March 1928

CONTINUOUS PERFORMANCE
VIII

(*Animal impudens* ...)
(Early Father, conditioned reflex of,)

Amongst the gifts showered upon humanity by the screen and already too numerous to be counted, none has been more eagerly welcomed than the one bestowed upon the young woman who is allowed to shine from its surface just as she is. In silent, stellar radiance, for the speech that betrayeth is not demanded of her and in this she is more fortunate than her fellows upon the stage. Yet even they – even those who are mere stage effects, a good deal less than actors and, since they are ambulatory, rather more than properties – are, for some of us, magical and songworthy. And to those film-stars who are just ambulatory screen effects many of us have paid homage to the point of willingness to die for their sweet sakes, and all of us, partly on account of their silence but largely for the Film's sake, have suffered them more or less gladly.

But it is not only upon the screen that this young woman has been released in full power. She is to be found also facing it, and by no means silent, in her tens of thousands. A human phenomenon, herself in excelsis; affording rich pasture for the spiritual descendants of Messrs Juvenal and Co. And thus far the lady is beneficient. But there are others together with her in the audience. There are for example those illogical creatures who, while they respectfully regard woman as life's supreme achievement, capping even the starfish and the stars, are still found impotently raging when in the presence of the wonders of art she remains self-centred and serenely self-expressive. Such, meeting her at her uttermost, here where so far there is not even a convention of silence to keep her within bounds, must sometimes need more than all their chivalry to stop short of moral homicide.

I must confess to having at least one foot in their camp. I evade the lady whenever it is possible and, in the cinema, as far as its gloom allows, choose a seat to the accompaniment of an apprehensive consideration of its surroundings, lest any of her legion should be near at hand. Nevertheless I have learned to cherish her. For it's she at her most flagrant that has placed the frail edifice of my faith in woman at last upon a secure foundation. For this boon I thank her, and am glad there has been time for her fullest demonstrations before the day when the cinema audience shall have established a code of manners.

That day is surely not far off. One of the things, perhaps so far, the only thing, to be said for the film that can be heard as well as seen is that it puts the audience in its place, reduces it to the condition of being neither seen nor heard. But it may be that before the standard film becomes an audible entertainment it will occur to some enterprising producer, possibly to one of those transatlantic producers who possess so perfectly the genial art of taking the onlookers into their confidence and not only securing but conducting their collaboration, to prelude his performance by a homily on the elements of the technique of film-seeing: a manual of etiquette for the cinema in a single caption, an inclusive courteous elegant paraphrase of the repressed curses of the minority:

Don't stand arguing in the gangway, we are not deaf.
Crouch on your way to your seat, you are not transparent.
Sit down the second you reach it.
Don't deliver public lectures on the film as it unfolds.
Or on anything else.
Don't be audible in any way unless the film brings you laughter.
Cease, in fact, to exist except as a contributing part of the film, critical or otherwise, and if
    critical, silently so.
If this minimum of decent consideration for your neighbours is beyond you, go home.

An excellent alternative would be a film that might be called *A Mirror of Audiences*, with many close-ups.

Meanwhile here we are, and there she is. In she comes and the screen obediently ceases to exist. If when finally she attends to it – for there is first her toilet to think of, and then her companion, perhaps not seen since yesterday – she is disappointed, we all hear of it. If she is pleased we learn how and why. If her casual glance discovers stock characters engrossed in a typical incident of an average film, well known to her for she has served her enthralled apprenticeship and is a little blasé, her conversation proceeds uninterrupted. And to this we do not entirely object. The conversation may be more interesting than the film. But, so long as she is there, gone is the possibility of which any film is so delightfully prodigal: the possibility of escape via incidentals into the world of meditation or of thought. And, whatever be the film so long as she is close at hand there is no security. Odd fantasy, a moving drama well acted, a hint of any kind of beauty, may still her for a while. But there is nothing that can stem for long the lively current of her personality. Her partner follows her lead after his manner, but quietly, unless his taste is for commentary displaying his wisdom or his pretty wit.

Let us attend to her, for she can lead her victim through anger to cynicism and on at last to a discovery that makes it passing strange that no male voice has been raised save in condemnation, that no man, film-lover and therefore for years past helplessly at her mercy, has risen up and cried Eureka. For she is right. For all her bad manners that will doubtless be pruned when the film becomes high art and its temple a temple of stillness save for the music that at present inspires her to do her worst, she is innocently, directly, albeit unconsciously, upon the path that men have reached through long centuries of effort and of thought. She does not need, this type of woman clearly does not need, the illusions of art to come to the assistance of her own sense of existing. Instinctively she maintains a balance, the thing perceived and herself perceiving. She must therefore insist that she is not unduly moved, or if she be moved must assert herself as part of that which moves her. She takes all things currently. Free from man's pitiful illusion of history, she sees everything in terms of life that uncannily she knows to be at all times fundamentally the same. She is the amateur realist. Not all the wiles of the most perfect art can shift her from the centre where she dwells. Nor has she aught but scorn for those who demand that she shall be so shifted. And between her scorn and the scorn we have felt for her who shall judge?

Down through the centuries men and some women have pathetically contemplated art as a wonder outside themselves. It is only in recent years that man has known beauty to emanate from himself, to be his gift to what he sees. And the dreadful woman asserting herself in the presence of no matter what grandeurs unconsciously testifies that life goes on, art or no art and that the onlooker is a part of the spectacle.

Vol. II, no. 4   April 1928

CONTINUOUS PERFORMANCE
IX
THE THOROUGHLY POPULAR FILM

The moment those crudish, incessantly sparking, never-to-be-forgotten photographs, setting the world in movement before our enchanted eyes, made way for the elaborate simplicities of the aesthetically unsound film play, there descended upon the cinema and all its works a blast of scorn so much more withering than any that has fallen to the lot of other kinds of popular entertainment that its sheer extremity calls to the disinterested observer – or, since it is claimed that such is not to be found under the sun, let us say to the relatively disinterested observer – for ampler justification than is supplied in the ravings of the ebullient critics: the desire to nip in the bud a virulently poisonous growth.

For this justification is acceptable only if we can bring ourselves to believe that the prophetic critics wholeheartedly credited their vision of the cinema as embarked upon an orgy of destruction that would demolish the theatre, leave literature bankrupt and the public taste hopelessly debauched. And, if we bring ourselves so to believe we land in the conclusion that these prophets are futility personified. A most uncomfortable conclusion. For surely even an alarmist, even the most wildly rocketing fanatical prophet of disaster must, so long as he is sincere, be something more than a waste product. He is usually a being of acute perceptions and abnormally long sight. A wise, superior person. And if they are right who define wisdom as the darker side of God he is presumably the Devil, and far from futile. But is he? For with perfect unanimity, from age to age, mankind ignores him and goes its way and none may know whether it is the certainty of neglect that endows the prophet with his fury or his fury that shocks humanity into the averted attitude. What is he therefore? Where, we are compelled to ask, does he come in?

Authentic fury is at best a regrettable spectacle. But perfect futility is an intolerable spectacle, a spectre at the feast to be exorcised at any cost, even at the cost of snatching from under the nose of the satirist a most succulent morsel. Can it be done? Can we perhaps transform the wrath of those who fell tooth and nail upon the cinema by interpreting it as a kind of paternal shock, a fury of desire for what was actually in being before their eyes, the thing of beauty promised by the hideous infant? So to do is not to claim superiority of vision. It is indeed to leave vision in their hands who sensitively shrieked the moment they were hurt – for we, the general public, were not looking for beauty. We were knocked silly by the new birth, were content to marvel at the miracle.

That babe is now a youth, a thing of beauty creating disturbances, precipitating recantations right and left. And though scorn still breathes its would-be withering blast, the blast is directed now to concentrate upon the youth's ill favoured twin, the movie in excelsis. Here at least say the critics you will admit that we were right. And there is no sound nor any that answers. But there is an epithet, a single word, half awestruck and respectful, half hilariously mocking, coined in the largest nursery of the new civilisation, by some citizen of the lower world wandered by chance into alien territory: highbrow.

These contrasted territories are not of course neatly separated. They are linked by a wide dim region inhabited by half-castes whose brows are neither out-size nor yet low. And inhabiting both the upper and the nether aesthetic worlds are the lost and strayed who would be happier elsewhere and everywhere are those who could be happy in either, were tother fair charmers away. Roughly nevertheless there are the two main territories, the territory of the Films and the territory of the Movies. The films climb, austere and poverty-stricken while the Movies roll in wealth upon the lush floor of the valley. And there is small reason to anticipate an immediate relief for those so narrowly existing on the heights. It is however interesting to speculate as to what would happen if the economic security of the Movies were suddenly withdrawn, what would happen if films were made only by those desiring to make them and ticketless audiences trooped in at ever open doors. Cinemas would be packed, but would the anaesthetic, a psychological immoral unwholesome popular film cease to exist? Would anything cease to exist but that which is at present to be laid to the account of speculation as to what the public wants, what that is to say, it will pay for? Would there not still be the innocent enthusiastic artificer whole-heartedly producing the bad, beloved films? It may be urged that in such a world everyone would be educated away from infantile tastes. But there are limits, even to education. Much may be taken over by one person from another, but there will be no likeness between them unless they are one in spirit. And contemplation of these two worlds, the aesthetically adult and the others, reveals a something that a never so generously contrived education is powerless to change: a fundamental difference of approach. There is a larky something behind the veil that offers, on behalf of everything under the sun, a choice of interpretations. It is this lark, this salt of the journey that drives the truly dogmatic dogmatist to present his dogma as something no intelligent person can deny. But there is always an alternative interpretation. Everything is in pairs, though not everyone is ready to echo the commis voyageur's *hourrah pour la petite différence*.

Let us by all means confess our faith. In this case faith in Art as an ultimate, a way of salvation opposed, though not necessarily contradictory, to other ways of salvation, Religion, Ethics, Science rather existing independently and though aware of them regarding them only as making for the same bourne by different routes. And if at once we have to remind ourselves that life is an art, and the evangelist, moralist and big man of science all imaginative artists, well that is a pleasant holiday for our minds that so easily grow a shade too departmental. Art by all means. Let us live and die in and for it. But when we condemn the inartistic let us beware of assuming aesthetic excellence as always and everywhere and for everyone the standard measure. If we feel we must condemn popular art let us know where we are, know that we are refusing an alternative measure and interpretation of the intercommunications we reject.

As a rule the dogmatic, so rightly dogmatic, aesthete cannot bring himself to glance at the possibility of an alternative measure. So great is his anger and dismay that he is fain to curse and go on cursing. It is however to be remarked of the dogmatic aesthete that he is commonly rather a guardian of the temple than himself a creator. Is not one of the incidental delights of voyaging amongst the records left by the creators the discovery of their quaint tastes in art, their psalms in honour of contemporaries whose long-forgotten work, displaying a perfect inanity, doubtless performed miracles in its own day?

Meanwhile the philistines go their way. They go on cherishing films whose characters, situations and sentiments are said to stand condemned by every known test. And we would like to claim on behalf of even the worst of them, even those that would make a cat laugh and draw tears of agonised protest from a stone, that the condemnation can never be more than relative. We would like to suggest, for example, that the judges live in a world where such characters and situations and sentiments do not exist, in a different dimension of the spirit, and that they have therefore no experience that can illuminate for them the deadly depths. The cause of their horror lies not in what they see but in their way of seeing. It is possible that they are immensely above and beyond the world they condemn. It is certain that they are too far removed from it to get behind its conventions.

Take any of the stock characters of whom it is said that they never existed on land or sea. The poor dear sheik, for example, the man who can kill, can magnificently adore the beloved carried upon his shield high above his head, can dominate, and kneel. Yet he exists. Even in Tooting under a bowler hat. The heroine, the emotional lovely damsel guarding the pearl of price that is but once bestowed. She perhaps is to be met only by those who can create her in her fulness. Then the good ending. In some respects the worst criminal of all and certainly a thing-in-itself. It is demanded absolutely. They won't, we are told, stand anything else. But there is good reason for their refusal, for their stern convention. Is it or is it not, the good ending, the truth, perhaps crudely and wrongly expressed, of life, and their refusal to have it outraged based deeply in the consciousness of mankind? They welcome even the most preposterously happy ending not because it is in contrast to the truth as known in their own lives, but because it is true to life. The wedding bells, the reconciled family, the reclaiming of the waster, all these things are their artistic conventions and the tribute of love paid to them by the many is a tribute to their unconscious certainty that life is ultimately good.

Vol. II, no. 5   May 1928

CONTINUOUS PERFORMANCE
X
THE CINEMA IN THE SLUMS

At the moment of reaching perfection as territory sacred to horror, slumdom produced a novelist who featured with all his mind and all the heart and all the soul the lives of its inhabitants, awakening official expediency and unofficial solicitude and driving the oblivion of the general public into a timely grave. And the day that saw compulsory education snatching the children for a while from the worst, saw also philanthropy grown fashionable, slumming adding meaning to the lives of the charitable unemployed and bands of devoted people weaving a network of settlements, missions, and institutions of all kinds over those areas of the larger cities that hitherto had been left undisturbed, save for an occasional forced raid, even by the police, and unproductive save for their disproportionate contribution of disease and crime and the endless procession of half-starved labourers of all ages and both sexes available for exploitation in the basements supporting the British empire.

But slumdom, though not quite what it was, continues to flourish and will continue, however rehoused and state-aided and generally disciplined, if they are right who see its problem as a biological problem, its habitants as a recruited army, an army ceaselessly recruited from above and to disappear only when we make up our minds to weed out undesirable types. And though wonders have been worked, as all may see who can remember the children haunting the by-ways even twenty years ago, there is still a vast army living, except for the all-too-short school years, in a state of mental and moral constriction, pressed upon and paralysed by circumstance, and there is its off-shoot, the battalion of half-crazed intelligentsia dreaming of salvation to be reached one by a banding together for destruction.

All these people like all the rest of us are preached at by doctrinaires of all kinds and mostly by heavily interested doctrinaires who from the midst of ease – though many of them are hard workers, at jobs chosen and beloved – rate these state-pampered idlers for their thriftlessness, quote the perilous budgets of exceptionally heroic family chancellors – oh those budgets detailed from margarine to skimmed milk – upon which appears no single one of the necessary superfluities whose rôle in creating the cheerfulness of the complacent judges is ignored by them because it is permanent.

And almost everything that comes to this segregated army from without, teaching, preaching, state-aid, welfare-work, art-galleries and suchlike cultural largesse is tainted more or less, not always hopelessly but always tainted, by the motive of interest. Is not, cannot be, entirely above suspicion. Even the most devoted resident missioners are there with an aim, the confessed aim of betterment, of bringing light into darkness and comfort where no comfort was. It would be monstrous to attempt to decry the motives and the labours of these noble people and absurd to deny their great fruitfulness. And though there may be amongst them numbers of pitying souls who would be left at a loss if there were no one to rescue, there are also those whose labours are carried on in the spirit of an invitation to the dance of life. These bring charm. But their power is akin to that of the kindly host. Contact with them may be for the lost a tour of paradise; but it is a conducted tour.

And now, as it were over-night, there has materialised a presence subsuming all these others and, by reasons of its freedom from any ulterior motive beyond that of its own need to survive, immeasurably more powerful as a civilising agent than any one of them. It says of course aloud for all to hear as it opens its doors conveniently in the manner of the gin-palace at every corner: it's your money we want. It does not say we want to help you. Yet it offers as many kinds of salvation as all previous enterprises combined and offers them impersonally, more impersonally than even the printed page. It illustrates. And its illustrations are encountered innocently, unguardedly, in silence and alone.

It is said that the cinema offers nothing to nobody save spiritual degradation. There are clamourings too, and secret whisperings of the enormous power of the film rightly used, used that is to say according to the speaker's idea of what is right. But both these claims ignore what is inherent in pictures, ignore that which exerts its influence apart from the intention of what is portrayed. Mankind's demand for pictures, like the child's demand, is much more than a childlike love for representation. There is in the picture that which emerges and captures him before details are registered and remains long after they are forgotten. And this influence, particularly in the case of the contemplators we are considering, is exercised as potently by a photograph as by a 'work of art' and by a moving photograph, if it be the work of an artist, much more potently. Imagination fails in attempting to realise all that is implied for cramped lives in the mere coming into communication with the general life, all that results from the extension of cramped consciousness. But it is not merely that those who are condemned, with no prospect of change to a living death, are lifted for a while into a sort of life as are said to be on the great festivals the souls in hell. It is that insensibly they are living new lives. Growing. Gathered spontaneously and unsuspecting before even the poorest pictures, even those that play deliberately upon the passions of the jungle, the onlookers are unawares in an effectual environment. While they follow events they are being played upon in a thousand ways. And all pictures are not bad or base or foolish. But even the irreducible minimum of whatever kind of goodness there is in any kind of picture not deliberately vicious, is civilisation working unawares.

Vol. II, no. 6   June 1928

CONTINUOUS PERFORMANCE
XI
SLOW MOTION

No one who heard the hysterical laughter that greeted the first slow-motion pictures can fail to be struck by the quiet bearing of the average audience of today when confronted by these strange transformations. And were it not for a haunting suspicion of the part played by mere familiarity with the spectacle, it would be possible to claim this change of attitude as the surest direct evidence of the educative power of the film. But if familiarity alone is responsible for the change, then that dreadful laughter, coming after years of experience of what the film can do, must stand, a mocking mark of interrogation over against the articles of our faith. Yet since there is other evidence, and particularly the mass of evidence accumulated in the minds of those who have experience of the evolution of single local audiences in regard to 'the pictures', to confirm that faith, we may take courage to assume that from the first, behind the laugher, recognition was there and has grown. If now it is present, it was there from the first, for without its work there would be no second seeing. Each seeing would have been a first and the laughter would have continued.

And yet, recalling that first revelation, doubt creeps in on behalf of just this one of the many offerings of the film. Can anyone forget the revelation, the two revelations, of beauty upon the screen and the beast confronting it? Has that particular beauty conquered the beast, become a joy forever, or just passed into nothingness? Indeed it is difficult to say. For there must have been incidents. Indignant people must have hushed the gigglers. Sensitive people must have cried out in ecstatic appreciation and produced wonder that upon the next opportunity turned to attention hopeful of discovering the hidden charm.

Experience gathered in one small local cinema would hopefully suggest that the first laughter for the first slow-motion picture is partly to be credited to the nature of the movement and the manner in which it was offered. For it was a picture of runners at close quarters to each other upon the last lap of a mile race. The three figures, first shown moving at normal pace were in desperate competition, agonised heads thrown back, open mouths agasp at the last effort for supremacy; not a pleasing exhibition. It flashed away and a caption spoke: 'Now see what our slow-motion camera can do', an invitation to watch a conjuring trick, preparation for something that was to impress by its cleverness. And it is possible that if we had been shown stills of these men caught in the various attitudes born of movement, beauty might clearly have emerged. But though it was there in the balanced movement of the athletes advancing as if through resistant air, there was also a sharp touch of the grotesque as these figures with arms arched, and rigid, air-clutching fingers, slowly, goose-steppingly lifted leaden limbs in shorts. The anxious faces, the air of infinite caution, were legitimately funny and the avalanche of laughter may be interpreted as joyous welcome for yet another revelation of the comic possibilities of the film.

The next slow-motion exhibition was of horses clearing a hedge and ditch in a steeple-chase, and throughout the majestic spectacle, from the moment the great beasts slowly rearing left the earth until again they lightly, as if weightlessly, touched it in descent, there was nothing that could even remotely appeal to the eye on the look-out for pretexts for mirth. But the laughter came, for the slowness, the anomaly. There were those no doubt who held breath in wonder and delight. But the result, regarding the audience as one person, was, as before, registration of a freakish incidental of the new entertainment.

The first slow of these early days that failed to precipitate either the avalanche of derision or the chorus of sniggers was of a man taking a high jump. And here perhaps all lesser emotions were submerged in that of stupefaction at the sheer marvel of the levitations. It was offered simply for what it was, Mr Jones winning the high jump, without preparative suggestion. We saw Mr Jones run and lightly leap and clear, and reach the ground in an athletic sprawl. And then again there were the high posts and the bar and the relatively small man held to earth by a pointed toe, who rose as if dreaming, slowly through the air upon which as he cleared the bar he lay sideways in repose, on his face the look of blissful concentration given in religious art to saints whose battles are won, indolently stretching one limb to slant downwards beyond the bar and bring its fellow following and the whole elastic body to move poised in the air upon the outstretched toe that sought and lightly found the earth. Perfect silence greeted this revelation of the miraculous commonplace. It won. Was bound to win. Its beauty and its wonder were imperious demands, overwhelming.

And the revelation bestowed by the ecstatic face, of the spirit withdrawn, within the body it was operating, to the point of perfect concentration, showing this business of athletic achievement as one with every kind of human achievement, with that of the thinker, the artist and the saint, is one of the most priceless offerings to date of the film considered as a vehicle for revealing to mankind that in man which is unbounded. If tomorrow every vestige of this new art were swept away save just one slow of a human body hoisting itself over a high bar, the film would not have existed in vain.

Vol. III, no. 1   July 1928

CONTINUOUS PERFORMANCE
XII
THE CINEMA IN ARCADY

Hedge-topped banks form a breezeless corridor upon whose floor, white with dust, the sun beats down. Dust films the edges and most of the flowering things that brought forgetfulness of the hidden distances have fled. We trudged averted from beauty defaced, hearing bird-song in the unspoiled hedges of fresh invisible fields and watching for the bend of the long lane and the reward: shelter or high trees that there begin their descending march and, for our shaded eyes, the view of the little grey harbour town at our feet screened by misty tree-tops of spring, the wide estuary beyond it, sapphire backed by golden sand-dunes, miniatures of the tors standing in distant amber light along the horizon. The bend came and the twin poplars that frame the prospect for which our waiting eyes were raised; to see, fastened from trunk to trunk an obliterating sign-board: *Come to the Pictures*.

Jealously the year before we had resented the walls of the small palace rising in unearthly whiteness at the angle of a grey ramshackle by-street. And even while we knew that what we were resenting was the invasion of our retreat by any kind of culture and even while we were moved by the thought of the marvels about to appear before the astonished eyes of villagers and fisherfolk, we still had our doubts. And this placard defacing the loveliest view in the neighbourhood seemed symbolically to confirm them. We doubted because we had found in these people a curious completeness; wisdom, and a strange sophisticated self-sufficiency. We told ourselves that they were an ancient aristocratic people and made romantic generalisations from every scrap of favourable evidence. And though it may perhaps fairly be claimed that these lively, life-educated people of the coast villages and fishing stations do not need, as do the relatively isolated people of crowded towns, the socialising influence of the cinema, we were obliged in the end to admit that our objections were indefensible.

There, at any rate, the cinema presently was. We ignored and succeeded in forgetting it until the placard appeared and in imagination we saw an epidemic of placards, in ancient hamlets, in meadows, on cliffsides and we sent forth to battle. We battled for months for the restoration of the hillside landscape. In vain. Urban district councillors were sympathetic and dubious. The villagers were for living and letting live and the harbour towns-folk would not come out against a fellow townsman. Generally our wrathful sorrow provoked a mild amusement. The placard was regarded as a homely harmless affair as inoffensive as a neighbour's out hung washing, except by those few who were voluble in execration of the cinema and all its works. From these we collected evidence recalling the recorded depredations of strong drink amongst primitive peoples. Crediting all we heard we should see the entire youthful population of the parish, and many of the middle-aged, centred upon the pictures, living for them. We heard of youths and maidens once frugal, homely and dutiful, who now squander their earnings not twice weekly when the picture is changed, but nightly. Of debt. Of tradesmen's bills that mount and mount unpaid as never before. The prize story is of a one-time solid matron now so demoralised that rather than miss a picture she will obtain groceries on credit and sell of them to her neighbours.

It is clear that down here amongst these full-living hard-working landspeople the enchantment has worked at least as potently as in the towns. And reflection suggests an explanation that would apply equally to almost any rural district where life is lived all the year round in the open or between transparent walls, lived from birth to death in the white light of a publicity for which towns can offer no parallel. Drama is continuous. No day passes without bringing to some group or member of the large scattered family a happening more or less shared by everyone else and fruitful of eloquence. Speech is relatively continuous. Solitude almost unknown. And these people have turned to the pictures as members of a family who know each other by heart will turn to the visitor who brings the breath of otherness. And whereas in the towns those who frequent the cinema may obtain together with its other gifts admission to a generalized social life, a thing unknown in slum and tenement, lodging-house and the smaller and poorer villadom, these people of village and hamlet, already socially educated and having always before their eyes the spectacle of life in the raw throughout its entire length, the assemblage of every kind of human felicity and tribulation, find in the cinema together with all else it has to offer them, their only escape from ceaseless association, their only solitude, the solitude that is said to be possible only in cities. They become for a while citizens of a world whose every face is that of a stranger. The mere sight of these unknown people is refreshment. And the central figures of romance are heaven-born, are the onlookers as they are to themselves, heroes and heroines unknown to their neighbours. To cease for a moment to be just John or Mary carrying about with you wherever you go your whole known record, to be oblivious of the scene upon which your life is lived and your future unalterable cast, is to enter into your own eternity.

It is not possible perfectly to disentangle from that of the wireless, the popular newspaper and the gramophone, the influence of the cinema in rural districts. Certain things however, emerge more or less clearly. There is for example no evidence, at any rate down here in the west, of any increased desire for town life. Rather the contrary, for the prestige of that life has suffered more than a little as a result of realistic representation and the strongest communicable impression whether of London, New York or other large city – all much of a muchness and equally remote, though not more so than Plymouth – is that of insecurity. Neither in railway station, hotel, or crowded street is either money or life for a single moment free from risk. And the undenied charm of the Far West is similarly overshadowed: you must be prepared either to shoot or be shot. And although condemnation goes hand in hand with envy of the apparently limitless possibilities of acquisition and independence, the vote on the whole goes steadily for the civilisation and safety of rural conditions.

Melodrama and farcical comedy are prime favourites and an intensity of interest centres about the gazette, the pictures of what is actually going on in various parts of the world. That there is always something worth seeing and that the music is 'lovely' is almost universal testimony. It is probable that the desire for perpetual cinema will presently abate. A year of constant film-seeing is not overmuch for those without theatre, music-hall or any kind of large scale public entertainment. Meantime one clearly visible incidental result of this intensive cultivation is to be noted: these people, and particularly the younger generation, have no longer quite the local quality they had even a year ago. They are amplified, aware of resources whose extent is unknown to them and have a joyful half-conscious preoccupation with this new world that has been brought into their midst, a preoccupation that on the whole, and if one excludes the weaklings who would in any case be the prey of desirable or undesirable external forces, serves to enhance the daily life. They no longer for one reason and another, amongst which the cinema is indisputably the foremost, … [f]it to their local lives as closely as of yore. Evidence of this change is to be found even in their bearing. The 'yokel' is less of a lout than he was wont to be and the dairymaid even on workdays is indistinguishable from her urban counterpart. And though doubtless something is lost and the lyric poet is shedding many an unavailing tear, much undeniably is gained. These youths and maidens in becoming world citizens, in getting into communications with the unknown, become also recruits available, as their earth-and-cottage-bound forebears never could have been for the world-wide conversations now increasingly upon us in which the cinema may play, amongst its numerous other rôles, so powerful a part.

Vol. IV, no. 1   January 1929

~~~~~~

CONTINUOUS PERFORMANCE
PICTURES AND FILMS

American films, sharp as steel, cold like the poles, beautiful as the tomb, passed before our dazzled eyes. The gaze of William Hart pierced our hearts and we loved the calm landscape where the hoofs of his horse raised clouds of dust.

Quite so. True, true, perfectly true. Something, at any rate, *did* pierce our hearts, and we *did* love the calm of the landscape whereupon the wild riders flew, the dust-clouds testifying to their pace. Just those things and as they were, unrelated to what came before and after. And to whatever it might be that had preceded, and to whatever it was that might follow, the splendid riding of the vast landscape and the wild riding and all the rest passing so magnificently before our eyes.

But however devout our feelings it did not occur to us to express them quite so openly and prayerfully. And, I *beg* of you … has not the quoted tribute a strange air? An air at first sight of being an extract from an out-of-date hand-book on the year's pictures, part of whose compilation had been entrusted to a youth with literary ambitions, and a somewhat exotic youth at that, and therefore a youth who properly should not have been the prey of the wild west film? And yet here most certainly is *cri du cœur*, with no question of tongue in cheek.

But young Englishmen of no period, and under no matter what provocation, are to be found gushing in these terms. Gush they may. But not quite in these terms. A young Englishwoman, then? An aspiring and enthusiastic young Englishwoman writing to suggest to other aspiring and enthusiastic young Englishwomen exactly what they think about the movies, and well understanding the heart-piercing and the adoration of the landscape.

But though the sentiments may be thus accountable, the expression of them remains a little mysteriously not an English form of expression until – turning the page to discover in whose person it was that *The Little Review* at any point in its thrilled and thrilling career should have waxed lyrical over the movies in their own right, as distinct from their glimpsed possibilities – one finds the signature of a French writer, one of the super-realists who had hoped the war would have rescued art from romanticism, had been disappointed and, having enumerated the few artists who in Europe were giving the world anything worth the having, looked sadly back upon the movies in their pristine innocence.

With the strange unsuitability of the English garb to the sentiments expressed thus cleared up by the realisation that the article was a literal translation, one could give rein to one's delight in the discovery of this genuine feeling of the day before yesterday, even though immediately one was forced to reflect that this wistful young man, given the circumstances and the date, could not possibly have seen any FILMS.

Accepting, therefore, its French reading, I have set down this tribute in the manner of a text, first because with an odd punctuality it came to my notice immediately on my return, from a first visit to London's temple of good films, to get on with the business of extracting forgotten treasures from a packing-case, and also because its sentiments chimed perfectly with certain convictions floating uninvited into my mind as I talked, on matters unrelated to the film (if, indeed, at this date any matters can be so described), with a friend encountered by chance on my way home from The Avenue Pavilion.

I had seen, in great comfort, and from a back seat whose price was that of the less valuable portions of the average super-cinema, *The Student of Prague*. This film, I am told, though excellent for the date of its production, a good play, well acted and likely to remain indefinitely upon any well-chosen repertory, has been out-done and left behind by films now being shown in Germany and in Russia. It is approved by the film intelligentsia, including psycho-analysts who delightfully find it, like all works of art, ancient and modern, fuller of wisdom than its creator clearly knows. And it was most heartily approved by a large gathering of onlookers, revealed when the lights went up, as consisting for the most part of those kinds of persons to be seen scattered sparsely amongst the average cinema crowd.

For me, personally, and before the human interest of the drama began to compete with whatever conscious critical faculty I may possess, it joined forces with the few 'good' films I have seen at home and abroad in convincing me that the film can be an 'art-form'. There is much in it I shall never forget, and that much was supported and amplified in a way that no conceivable stage setting can compete with. The absence of the spoken word was more than compensated. Captions there may have been. I remember none. Clear, too, was the role of the musical accompaniment, though this was now and again a little obtrusive, and one grew intolerant of the crescendo of cymbal-crashing that accompanied *every* great moment instead of being reserved for the post-script, the final discomfiture of the wonderful devil with the umbrella, surely one of the best devils ever seen on stage or film? The same uniform cymbal-crashing did much, a week or so later, to spoil the revival of Barrymore's Jekyll and Hyde, first seen in England to the tune of the Erl-könig, itself a work of art and fitting most admirably to Barrymore's achievement.

But the rôle of the musical accompaniment was clear, nevertheless, its contribution to the business of compensating the absence of the spoken word, its support and its amplification that joins the many other resources of the film in deepening and unifying and driving home all that is presented. Conrad Veidt on any stage would be a great actor. Conrad Veidt moving voicelessly through the universal human tragedy in surroundings whose every smallest item 'speaks to the occasion', has the opportunity that at last gives to pure acting its fullest scope.

I left gratefully anticipating such other good films as it may be my fortune to see. Yet within and around my delights there were, I knew, certain reservations at work waiting to formulate themselves and, as I have said, taking the opportunity, the moment my attention was busy elsewhere, of coming forward in the form of clear statement.

The burden of their message was that welcome for the FILM does not by any means imply repudiation of the movies. The FILM at its utmost possible development can no more invalidate the movies than the first-class portrait, say Leonardo's of the Lady Lisa, can invalidate a snap-shot.

The film as a work of art is subject to the condition ruling all great art: that it shall be a collaboration between the conscious and the unconscious, between talent and genius. Let either of these elements get ahead of the other and disaster is the result, disaster in proportion to the size of the attempt.

The film, therefore, runs enormous risks. Portraits are innumerable. The great portraits produced by any single nation are very few indeed. And the portrait that is merely clever or pretentious, be its technique what it will, is no food for mankind. But the snap-shot, and the movie that offers to the fool and the wayfaring man a perfected technique, is food for all. It can't go wrong. It is innocent, and its results go straight to the imagination of the onlooker, the collaborator, the other half of the game.

The charm of the first movies was in their innocence. They were not concerned, or at any rate not very deeply concerned, either with idea or with characterisation. Like the snap-shot, they recorded. And when plot, intensive, came to be combined with characterisation, with just so much characterisation as might by good chance be supplied by minor characters supporting the tailor's and modiste's dummies filling the chief rôles, still the records were there, the snap-shot records that are always and everywhere food for a discriminating and an undiscriminating humanity alike. 'Sharp as steel, cold like the poles'; of landscape calm or wild, of crowds and all the moving panorama of life, of interiors, and interiors opening out of interiors, an unlimited material upon which the imagination of the onlooker could get to work unhampered by the pressure of a controlling mind that is not his own mind.

I was reminded also that the Drama, for instance, the Elizabethan drama, became Great Art only in retrospect. Worship of Art and The Artist is a modern product. In the hey-day of the Elizabethan drama the stage was despised, the actor a vagabond and a low fellow.

It may be that the hey-day of the film will come when things have a little settled down. When the gold-diggers, put out of court, shall have ceased to dig, when the medium is developed and within reach of the vagabonds and low fellows, when writing for the film shall no longer offer a spacious livelihood. Then, by those coming innocently to a well-known medium, the World's Great Films, the Hundred Best Films, will be produced. And, since history never repeats itself, they will probably be thousands, some of which, it would seem, have already been made in pioneering Russia.

But the movies will remain. The snap-shots will go on all the time. And there will always be people who infinitely prefer the family album of snap-shots to the family portrait gallery. And this is not necessarily the same as saying that there will always be irresponsible people, people who are happy merely because they are infantile. Much has been said, by those who dislike the pictures, of their value as evidence of infantilism. It is claimed that the people who flock to the movies do so because they love to lose themselves in the excitements of a dream-world, a world that bears no relationship to life as they know it, that makes no demand upon the intelligence, acts like a drug, and is altogether demoralising and devitalising.

Such people obviously know very little about the movies. But even if they did, even if they cared to take their chance and now and again submit themselves to the experience of a thoroughly popular show, it is hardly likely that they would lose their apparent inability to distinguish between *childishness*, the quality that has of late been so admirably analysed and presented under the heading of infantilism, and *childlikeness*, which is quite another thing. The child trusts its world, and those who, in all civilisations and within all circumstances, in face of all evidence and no matter what experience, cannot rid themselves of a child-like trust are by no means to be confused with those who shirk problems and responsibilities and remain ego-centrically within a dream-world that bears no relation to reality.

The battles and the problems of those who trust life are not the same as the battles and problems of those who regard life as the raw material for great conflicts and great works of art. But only such as regard the Fine Arts as mankind's sole spiritual achievement will reckon those who appear not to be particularly desirous of these achievements as therefore necessarily damned.

Vol. IV, no. 6   June 1929

CONTINUOUS PERFORMANCE
ALMOST PERSUADED

Never having experienced a Talkie, having sustained – in merely imagining a film breaking into speech, wrecking its medium, its perfection of direct communication – a shock comparable to that we should receive if our favourite Botticelli began throwing stones, we spent, far from films, a winter whose severity was the bitterer for our woeful apprehensions.

Every reading of a daily brought bad moments: cowardly avoidance of suspicious columns, alternating with shuddering sallies in search of facts.

March arrived heralding spring and with it the news that Mr Wells had at last come forward not only to hail the film as the art-form of the future, but also to name this child with his happy aptitude for epithet.

In remarking that it is only at long last that Mr Wells comes forward we do not attempt to suggest the impossible: Wellsian dilatoriness. Wells was amongst the first film-fans, Chaplin-fans. One of the first to see some of the possibilities and it would hardly be fair to label his predictions, though coming at a time when so many possibilities are already realised, prophecies after the event.

Our delight of course was born of the name chosen by Mr Wells for the art of cinematography: Music-Drama. And so great is our faith in Wells' perceptiveness, in regard to anything he may scrutinise leisurely and at first hand, that we immediately cried, 'Ah-ha. What price Talkies now?' and hugged more closely than ever our prejudice in favour of musical accompaniment, whether 'Home, Sweet Home' on a cottage piano or cunningly adapted orchestral effects. For, if music be there, the screen must be more or less silent. Unless indeed the stars break into song … Wagnerian films … Film imitating opera side by side with film imitating theatre. These for the vulgar, pot-luck-taking continuous performance public of which we are a member, and beyond them FILMS, developing and developing and developing?

In the March issue of *Close Up*, we again met Mr Wells, this time quoted as telling us with what extraordinary reluctance, if at all, we had been brought to admit the film's power of excelling the written word. Here it would seem that in deciding formally to sponsor the film – and good, for the prospects of the English film proper, was the day upon which he decided so to do – he deems it best to tell the world more than it can actually believe in the interest of making it believe that it believes something. For it is hardly possible to suppose that Wells sees in the arrival of the film the departure of literature.

Certain kinds of writing, the directly tendencious, the propagandist and much of the educational it may in the end supplant to the extent of compelling the theorist, the reformer and the teacher to produce their wares in a form suitable for translation into film. Meanwhile the film to date has created more readers than it has destroyed, if indeed it has destroyed any, and is more likely, as it progresses, to achieve for all the arts renaissance rather than death. In literature alone it is creating a new form. For just as the stage play created a public for the written play and many are the unplayable plays that are eminently readable and quite numerous those who in any case would rather read a play than see it acted – so will the practice of film-seeing create a public for the film literature of which, if we except the miniature scenarios from time to time appearing in periodicals, Mr Wells' own book is characteristically enough, the first example.

But our delight in the hailing of the film as the art-form of the future, not this time by the bold editors of *Close Up* who so hailed it two years ago when they were voices crying in the wilderness of a filmless England, but by a prophet whose least word is broadcast over the planet – in so far as it was founded upon the development of the generous pronunciamento into specification of a form for that art that appeared to exclude Talkies – was short-lived. A moment's reflection told us that even Mr Wells cannot stampede humanity by suggestion. The multitudes agog for novelty at any price will demand Talkies because they are new.

So we returned to the scanning of *Close Up*, and in a moment we were devoutly attentive. Here was Mr Herring breathlessly falling over himself in exposition of Pudovkin's idea of the use of sound on the film. And when Mr Herring grows breathless it is time to hold one's breath and listen hard to what he has to say. We listen for several pages to his eager voice vividly interpreting, and return to a world that will never be quite the same again. (It never is, of course, from one moment to another.) For we have heard the crashing of a barrier against which modern art has flung itself in vain. The barrier Antheil drilled holes in when he 'composed' mechanisms (did not one of his works require sixteen pianos and a screen?) and Dos Passos splintered when he described a group of straight-faced elderly relatives arrived in mourning garb at a house of death for funeral and reading of Will, gravely *jazzing* through the hall, and other American writers, have severely shaken by their unashamed metaphoricality, and all those novelists have fist-punched who in pursuit of their particular aims, produced texts retrospectively labelled cinematographic.

Is not Wells' dirge then justified? (Did not he too, time and again, cry out within his text upon the limitations of the printed page?) Has not literature, for so long prophesying unawares the fully developed film, had its day?

No. The film is a social art, a show, something for collective seeing, and even in the day that finds us all owning projectors and rolls of film from the local circulating filmery it still will be so, a small ceremonial prepared for a group, all of whom must adjust their sensibilities at a given moment and at the film's pace. Reading, all but reading aloud, is a solitary art – is this why it has been called the unpunished vice, and ought we to scrap these pages and swear only that we hope Wells might be right about the alleged competitor? – and the film can no more replace it than the Mass can replace private devotions. What film, to take a simple, current example, could supplant *Im Westen Nichts Neues* (recently translated, *All Quiet on the Western Front*) whose poetry both forces and enables the years of day-to-day unforgettable experience lived through in six or seven hours of reading. A stereoscopic film, complete with sound imagery might enormously enhance and deepen typical episodes and, by generalising the application of the whole, shock whatever onlooker – for a moment – into horrified recognition. But for that onlooker there would not be the intimate sense of having shared an irrevocable personal experience that is the gift of Remarque's quiet book.

The film is skyey apparition, white searchlight. The book remains the intimate, domestic friend, the golden lamp at the elbow.

'Think', pursues Mr Herring, 'of sound-imagery in Pudovkin's terms, and thank yourself you are alive.' We do, thank *you*, Mr Herring. We think, wishing the while that the whole of your exposé could be broadcast daily for weeks, printed and circulated with every Talkie programme, of angry man and lion's roar preceding, of fire-engine bells announcing devastating lady and all the subtleties made possible by the composing of sound, the direction of sound-imagery, director using sound like a musical score. Unifying sound and spectacle.

So we could mark time more than happily through Herr Meisel's certainties as to the marriage he is arranging between film and music and give full rein to our glee over his inclusion of the tinkling cottage piano which once we heard do some excellent sound-imagery in single notes for a Chaplin grotesque.

The sound-film then, and music drama, and, moreover, the stereoscopically three-dimensional ...

For these we are almost persuaded we would abandon our silent screen. In spite of the risks. For the risks, like the difficulties and the triumphs, will be enormous. Between success unprecedented and failure more disastrous than the failure of the worst soundless film there will be less than a hairsbreadth.

Yet we hesitate. Even while hailing expression not only free from certain of the cramping difficulties of dramatic and literary art, but able to convert these difficulties into so many glorious opportunities. Hallelujah. Amen.

Why do we hesitate? Is it that the interference between seer and seen is to be too complete? The expressionism, the information, the informatory hint altogether too much of it? The onlooker too overwhelmingly conducted? It is said that the audiences of Russian films have to be held down in their seats. Excitement, collective. This is of the theatre. Would a single soul seeing his film in silence and alone have to be so held down? Here, in living sample is all the answer we need to any question as to the future of literature and some would say, denying that wild eye and torn hair are ever the signs of the presence of great art, a question set to the film. But such perhaps forget that so far in the world's history the birth of an art has not been a public affair, though the inhabitants of Cimabue's native town beholding the first painted picture, *did* carry him in triumph through the streets.

If, beside the film grown solid and sounding the silent magic lantern show persists as we are told it will. ... But will it, for example pay? Is it not already old-fashioned? We are reminded of a lady who remarked on hearing that Paderewski had played 'The Bee's Wedding', 'That old thing? Why Winnie could play that when she was eight!' Alas, alas, alas.

Vol. V, no. 3   September 1929

CONTINUOUS PERFORMANCE
DIALOGUE IN DIXIE

Meekly punctual, clasping our prejudice in what might just possibly prove to be a last embrace, we entered the familiar twilight: the softly-gilded interior twilight, the shared, living quietude, still fresh and morning-new in their strange power. We could not be cheated altogether. We might be about to enter a new kingdom. Curiosity joined battle with fear and was winning when upon the dark screen appeared the silent signal: the oblong of rosy light, net-curtained. In a moment we were holding back our laughter: rueful laughter that told us how much, unawares, we had been hoping. For here was fear to match our own: the steady octopus eye, the absurdly waving tentacles of good salesmanship. The show was condemning itself in advance. We breathed freely, we grew magnanimous. We would make allowances. We were about to see the crude, the newly-born. We grew willing to abandon our demand for the frozen window-sill in favour of a subscription for a comfortable cradle. Ages seemed to have passed since we sat facing that netted oblong, ages since the small curtains had slid apart to the sound of a distressingly animated conversation. We had wandered, moralising; recalled the birth of gramophone and pianola, remember that a medium is a medium, and that just as those are justified who attempt to teach us how to appreciate Music and the Royal Academy, and Selfridge's so most certainly, how certainly we had not until later any conception, must those be justified who attempt to teach us how to hear Talkies. We remembered also Miss Rebecca West's noble confession of willingness to grow accustomed to listening to speakers all of whom suffer from cleft-palate ...

Cleft-palate is a fresher coin of the descriptive currency than the 'adenoids' worn almost to transparency by the realists. Nevertheless adenoids, large and powerful, at once mufflers and sounding-boards, were the most immediate obstacle to communication between ourselves and the semi-circle of young persons on the screen, stars, seated ostensibly in council over speech-films. Their respective mouths opened upon their words widely, like those of fish, like those of ventriloquists' dummies, those of people giving lessons in lip-reading. And the normal pace of speech was slowed to match the effort. The total impression was strong enough to drive into the background, for clear emergence later, our sense of what happened to film upon its breaking into speech, into no matter what imagined perfection of clear speech. For the moment we could be aware only of effort.

The introductory lesson over, the alphabet presumably mastered and our confidence presumably gained by the bevy of bright young people with the manners of those who ruinously gossip to children of a treat in store, we were confronted by a soloist, the simulacrum of a tall sad gentleman who, with voice well-pitched – conquest of medium – but necessarily (?) slow and laboriously precise in enunciation, and with pauses between each brief phrase after the manner of one dictating to a shorthand-typist, gave us, on behalf of the Negro race, a verbose paraphrase of Shylock's specification of the claims of the Jew to be considered human. He vanished, and here were the cotton-fields: sambos and mammies at work, piccaninnies at play – film, restored to its senses by music. Not, this time, the musical accompaniment possessing, as we have remarked before, the power, be it never so inappropriate provided it is not obtrusively ill-executed, to unify seer and seen and give to what is portrayed both colour and sound – but music utterly lovely, that emerged from the screen as naturally as a flower from its stalk: the voices of the cotton-gatherers in song. Film opera flowed through our imagination. Song, partly no doubt by reason of the difference between spoken word and sustained sound, got through the adenoidal obstruction and because the sound was distributed rather than localised upon a single form, kept the medium intact. Here was foreshadowed the noble acceptable twin of the silent film.

The singing ceased, giving place to a *dead* silence and the photograph of a cotton-field. The gap, suddenly yawning between ourselves – flung back into such a seat of such a cinema on such date – and the instantly flattened, colourless moving photograph, featured the subdued hissing of the projector. Apparatus rampant: the theatre, ourselves, the screen, the mechanisms, all fallen apart into competitive singleness. Now for it, we thought. Now for dialogue. Now for careful listening to careful enunciation and indistinctness in hideous partnership. A mighty bass voice leapt from the screen, the mellowest, deepest, tenderest bass in the world, Negro-bass richly booming against adenoidal barrier and reverberating: perfectly unintelligible. A huge cotton-gatherer had made a joke. Four jokes in succession made he, each smothered in sound, each followed by lush chorus of Negro-laughter, film laughter, film-opera again, noble partner of silent film.

And so it was all through: rich Negro-laughter, Negro-dancing, of bodies whose disforming western garb could not conceal the tiger-like flow of muscles. Pure film alternating with the emergence of one after another of the persons of the drama into annihilating speech. Scenes in which only the natural dramatic power of the actors gave meaning to what was said and said, except by a shrill-voiced woman or so and here and there the piercing voice of a child, in a way fatal to any sustained reaction: slow, enunciatory, monstrous. Perhaps only a temporary necessity, as the fixed expressionless eyes of the actors – result of concentration of microphone – may be temporary?

But the hold-up, the funeral march of words, more distracting than the worst achievements of declamatory, fustian drama, was not the most destructive factor. This was supplied by the diminution of the faculty of *seeing* – cinematography is a visual art reaching the mind through the eyes alone – by means of the necessity for concentrating upon hearing the spoken word. Music and song demand only a distributed hearing which works directly as enhancement rather than diminution of the faculty of seeing. But concentrated listening is immediately fatal to cinematography. Imagine, to take the crudest of examples – the loss of power suffered by representations of passionate volubility – the virago, the girl with a grievance, the puzzled foreigner – if these inimitable floods of verbiage could be heard. ... In all its modes, pure-film talk is more moving than heard speech. Concentration upon spoken words reveals more clearly than anything else the hiatus between screen and stage. In becoming suddenly vocal, *locally* vocal amidst a surrounding silence, photograph reveals its photographicality. In demanding for the films the peculiar attention necessary to spoken drama all, cinematographically, is lost; for no gain.

The play featured the pathos and humour of Negro life in the southern States and was, whenever the film had a chance, deeply moving; whenever these people were acting, moving, walking, singing, dancing, living in hope and love and joy and fear. But the certainty of intermittent dialogue ruined the whole. When it was over the brightness of our certainty as to the ultimate fate of the speech-film was the brighter for our sense of having found more in a silent film – seen on the pot-luck system the day before – that happened to be in every way the awful irreducible minimum, than in this ambitious pudding of incompatible ingredients.

The photography was good to excellent, actors all black and therefore all more than good. A satisfying, sentimental *genre picture* – genuinely sentimental, quite free from sentimentality – might be made of it by cutting out the speeches which served only to blur what was already abundantly clear, and substituting continuous obligato of musical sound.

If the technical difficulties of speech are ultimately overcome, the results, like the results of the addition to silent film of any kind of realistic sound, will always be disastrous. No spoken film will ever be able to hold a candle to silent drama, will ever be so 'speaking'.

'As we are going to press', the August *Close Up* came in and we read Mr Herring's notes on *Hearts in Dixie*. Mr Herring bears a lamp, a torch, electric torch kindly directed backwards, as boldly he advances amongst the shadows of what is yet to be, for the benefit of those who follow *rallentando*. We respect his pronouncements and are filled, therefore, with an unholy joy in believing that for once-in-a-way we may blow a statement of his down the wind, down a north-easter, *sans façon*. One does not need to temper winds to lambs with all their wool in place. Therefore: As a fair-minded young Englishman, Mr Herring is for giving the Talkies their chance and their due even though his conscience refuses to allow any claim they may make for a place in the same universe as the sound-film proper. He has taken the trouble to consider their possibilities. One of these he finds realised in *Hearts in Dixie* at the moment when the white doctor, having drawn the sheet from the body of the mother who has been treated by a Voodoo woman, and bent for a moment, scrutinising, stands up with his declaration: 'All the time,' says Mr Herring, 'we see his face. Then his words cut across, "she's been dead three days". Now, in a silent film, the visual thing would have been broken' and he concludes his remarks on the incident by describing it as 'the odd spectacle of talkies assisting visual continuity'.

We do not deny the possibility here suggested, but if this incident is to stand for realisation then the possibility is not worth pursuing. For though not quite the stentorian announcement of the guest-ushering butler, the doctor's statement inevitably had to be announcement, clear announcement in the first place to us, the audience, and incidentally to the sorrowing relatives to whom, in actuality let us hope, he would have spoken rather differently. The shock got home, not because its vehicle was the word spoken with the tragic picture still there before our eyes, but by virtue of its unexpectedness. It would have lost nothing and, relatively to the method of carefully-featured vocal announcement, have gained much by being put across in sub-title. But since Mr Herring objects that sub-title would have interfered with visual continuity, we must remind him that the right caption at the right moment is invisible. It flows, unnoticed into visual continuity. It is, moreover, audible, more intimately audible than the spoken word. It is the swift voice within the mind. 'She's been dead three days' was dramatic, not cinematographic, and the incident would have gained enormously if the white doctor had acted his knowledge of the unknown death, if he had reverently replaced those sheets and shown his inability to help. To be sure we should not have known about the three days. What matter?

Vol. VII, no. 3   September 1930

CONTINUOUS PERFORMANCE
A TEAR FOR LYCIDAS

During last year's London season we saw and heard on Talkie, *Hearts in Dixie* and wrote thereof in *Close Up* and foreswore our sex by asserting, in bold, masculine, side-taking, either-or fashion, that no matter what degree of perfection might presently be attained by the recording apparatus we were certain that the talkie, as distinct from the sound-film, will never be able to hold a candle to the silent film.

This year, therefore, though we knew there must be small local halls still carrying on, and hoped that our own little Bethel, which we had left last autumn ominously 'closed for repairs', might have taken courage to re-open, we felt that we were returning to a filmless London. Resignedly.

There was, there always is, one grand compensation: we came fully into our heritage of silent films. 'The Film', all the films we had seen, massed together in the manner of a single experience – a mode of experience standing alone and distinct amongst the manifolds we assemble under this term – and with some few of them standing out as minutely remembered units, became for us treasure laid up. Done with in its character of current actuality, inevitably alloyed, and beginning its rich, cumulative life as memory. Again and again, in this strange 'memory' (which, however we may choose to define it, is, at the least, past, present and future powerfully combined) we should go to the pictures; we should revisit, each time with a difference, and, since we should bring to it increasing wealth of experience, each time more fully, certain films stored up within. But to the cinema we should go no more.

Arriving, we found our little local hall still wearing its mournful white lie. All over London we met – there is no need to describe what we met, what raucously hailed us from the façade of every sort of cinema. Our eyes learned avoidance, of façade, newspaper column, hoarding and all the rest.

But ears escape less readily and we heard, as indeed, bearing in mind the evolution of pianola and gramophone, we had expected to hear, of the miracles of realism achieved by certain speech-films. Of certain beautiful voices whose every subtle inflection, every sigh, came across with a clarity impossible in the voice speaking from the stage. People who last year had wept with us had now gone over to the enemy and begged us to see at least this and that: *too* marvellous. Others declared that each and every kind of speech film they had seen had been *too* dire.

We accepted the miracle so swiftly accomplished, the perfected talkic, but without desire, gladly making a present of it. Wishing it well in its world that is so far removed from that of the silent film. Saw it going ahead to meet, and compete with, the sound-film. Heard both rampant all over the world.

Driven thus to the wall, we improvised a theorem that may or may not be sound: that it is impossible both to hear and to see, to the limit of our power of using these facilities, at one and the same moment. We firmly believe that it is sound.

The two eloquences, the appeal to the eye and the appeal to the ear, however well fused, however completely they seem to attain their objective – the spectator-auditor – with the effect of a single aesthetic whole, must, in reality, remain distinct. And one or the other will always take precedence in our awareness. And though it is true that their approximate blending can work miracles the miracle thus worked is incomparably different from that worked by either alone.

Think, for example, of the difference between music heard coming, as it were out of space and music attacking from a visible orchestra. Recall that an intense concentration on listening will automatically close the eyes. That for perfect seeing of landscape, work of art, beloved person, or effectively beautiful person, we instinctively desire silence. And agree, therefore, that there neither is, nor ever can be, any substitute for the silent film. Agree that the secret of its power lies in its undiluted appeal to a single faculty.

It may be urged that to the blind the world is a sound-film whose images must be constructed by the extra intelligent use of the remaining senses helped out by memory, while to the deaf it is a silent film whose meaning cannot be reached without some contrived substitute for speech. That deaf people are more helpless and are usually more resentful of, less resigned to, their affliction than are the happier blind. And that therefore the faculty of hearing is more important than that of sight: the inference being that the soundless spectacle is a relatively lifeless spectacle.

Those who reason thus have either never seen a deaf spectator of a silent film or, having seen him, have failed to reflect upon the nature of his happiness. For the time being he is raised to the level of the happy, skilful blind exactly because his missing faculty is perfectly compensated. Because what he sees is complete without sound, he is as one who hears. But take a blind man to a never so perfect sound-film and he will see but little of the whole.

In daily life, it is true, the faculty of hearing takes precedence of the faculty of sight and is in no way to be compensated. But on screen the conditions are exactly reversed. For here, sight *alone* is able to summon its companion faculties: given a sufficient level of concentration on the part of the spectator, a sufficient rousing of his collaborating creative consciousness. And we believe that the silent film secures this collaboration to a higher degree than the speech-film just because it enhances the one faculty that is best able to summon all the others: the faculty of vision.

Joris Ivens's *Rain*
(Vol. V, no. 3,
September 1929).

Rain (ibid.).

Yet we have admitted, we remember admitting, that without musical accompaniment films have neither colour nor sound! That any kind of musical accompaniment is better than none. The film can use almost any kind of musical accompaniment. But it is the film that uses the music, not the music the film. And the music, invisible 'coming out of space', enhances the faculty of vision. To admit this is not to admit the sound-film as an improvement on the silent film though it may well be an admission of certain possible sound-films as lively rivals thereof.

Life's 'great moments' are silent. Related to them, the soundful moments may be compared to the falling of the crest of a wave that has stood poised in light, translucent, for its great moment before the crash and dispersal. To this peculiar intensity of being, to each man's individual intensity of being, the silent film, with musical accompaniment, can translate him. All other forms of presentation are, relatively, diversions. Diversions in excelsis, it may be. But diversions. Essential, doubtless, to those who desire above all things to be 'taken out of themselves', as is their definition of the 'self'.

Perhaps the silent film is solitude and the others association.

* * *

Wandering at large, we found ourselves unawares, not by chance, we refuse to say by chance, in a dim and dusty by-street: one of those elderly dignified streets that now await, a little wistfully, the inevitable re-building. Giving shelter meanwhile to the dismal eddyings and scuttlings of wind-blown refuse: grey dust, golden straw, scraps of trodden paper. Almost no traffic. Survival, in a neglected central backwater, of something of London's former quietude.

Having, a moment before, shot breathlessly across the rapids of a main thoroughfare, we paused, took breath, looked about us and saw the incredible. A legend, not upon one of those small, dubious façades still holding their own against the fashion, but upon that of the converted Scala theatre: Silent Films. Continuous Performance. *Two Days. The Gold Rush*.

Why, we asked, stupefied, had we not been told? Why, in the daily lists, which still, hopelessly hopeful, we scanned each day, was there no mention of this brave Scala?

A good orchestra. Behind it the heart of Chaplin's big wandering film: the dream wherein the sleeping host entertains his tragically absent guests with the *Oceana Roll*, showing itself to an empty house.

To the joy of re-discovering a lost enchantment was added strange new experience. Within us was all we had read and heard and imaginatively experienced of the new conventions. All that at moments had made us sound-fans. Enhancing critical detachment. We were seeing these films with new eyes. They stood the test. These new films, we said, may be the companions, they can never be the rivals of the silent film. The essential potency of any kind of silent film, 'work of art' or other, remains untouched.

Later we saw *The Three Musketeers* and agreed, perhaps with Fairbanks, we trust with Fairbanks, that if melodrama be faithfully sought all other things are added unto it. And we were looking forward to *Metropolis* and *The Circus*, when suddenly the theatre closed.

The experiment, we gathered, had not been a success.

But what, we would respectfully enquire of the Scala management, what is the use of winking in the dark? What is the use of having a silent season, in an unfrequented by-street, and leaving London's hundreds of thousands of silent-film lovers to become aware of it by a process of intuition? Advertisement is surely less costly than an empty house. And we are prepared to wager that any house bold enough to embark on a silent season and to advertise it at least to the extent of listing it in the dailies will gather its hundreds for each showing.

[Humble apologies to *The Boltons* cinema in Kensington and the Palais de Luxe in Piccadilly; of whose current loyalty to the silent film the writer is informed too late for tribute in this article.]

Vol. VIII, no. 3   September 1931

CONTINUOUS PERFORMANCE
NARCISSUS

Discontent may be rooted in the contempt of one who believes mankind to be on its way to a better home and thinks, or most oddly, appears to think, that he honours that home by throwing mud at his. Or it may be just the natural mysterious sense of in-completeness haunting those for whom at times, haunting even those for whom all the time, life is satisfying beyond measure. More generally it is the state of having either lost or never fully possessed the power of focussing the habitual.

From this kind of discontent, escape by flight is impossible. Another house, another town, country, planet, will give only a moment's respite, for each in turn, and each with more swiftness than the last, will close in and become odious while, perversely, those left behind will mock the fugitive by revealing, with an intensity that grows as it recedes further and further into the distance, the qualities that once had charmed him.

It is customary to account for this distressing experience by the part played by distance, to say that distance lends enchantment and to talk of the transforming power of memory.

But distance *is* enchantment. It is a perpetual focus. And escape from the obstructive, chronic discontent we are considering, the state of deadness to the habitual, whether that habitual to good or bad, is possible only to those who by nature or by grace have the faculty of ceaseless withdrawal to the distance at which it may be focussed.

Some kind of relinquishment is implied: an abandonment of rights that reproduces on a very humble level the saint's *salto mortale*. Something of the kind must take place before surroundings can be focussed. It may be enforced. By illness, for example. The sick man, recovering, returns from his enforced detachment to a world transformed. But his freshness of vision is for a while only, unless his experience has taught him the secret of withdrawal. Or by a disinterested observer, through whose eyes what had grown too near and too familiar to be visible is seen with a ready-made detachment that restores its lost quality.

An excellent illustration of the operation of this casual gift is afforded by the story of the man who grew weary of his house, put it up for sale and, soon after, reading in his newspaper amongst descriptions of properties on the market a detailed account of a residence whose enumerated features, attracting him more and more as he read on, presently forced upon his attention the fact that it was his own house he was contemplating, was filled with remorse and telephoned to the agent to cancel the offer.

And what has all this moralising to do with the film? Everyone knows that amongst its thousand and one potentialities the film possesses that of being a mirror for the customary and restoring its essential quality. But must we not, to-day, emerge from our small individual existences and from narcissistic contemplation thereof? Learn that we are infinitesimal parts of a vast whole? Labour and collaborate to find salvation for a world now paying the prices of various kinds of self-seeking? And, for the re-education of humanity, is any single instrument more powerful than the film that is here offered merely as a provider of private benefits?

True. But the everlasting WE who is to accomplish all this remains amidst all change and growth a single individual.

Even so, is this so obvious mirror-focus quality a point worth insisting upon in relation to an art that has now passed so far beyond photographic reproductions of the familiar and, in so far as it remains documentary, registers – if we except Dziga-Vertoff [Dziga Vertov] and his followers engaged in directly representing anything and everything without selective interference beyond that dictated by the enchanted eye – only 'interesting' or 'instructive' material?

I believe it is immensely worth making and insisting upon. I believe that mirroring the customary and restoring its essential quality is and remains the film's utmost. Remains *Borderline*'s utmost as well as that of *The Policeman's Whistle*.

An early 'animated picture,' a little fogged and incessantly sparking, of a locomotive in full steam making for the enchanted spectator, a wild-west film complete with well-knit story on a background that itself is an adventure, a psychological drama all situations and intensities, a film that concentrates on aesthetic beauty or on moral beauty, an abstract film that must be translated by the mind of the onlooker, a *surréaliste* film produced by the unconscious alone, all these, every imaginable kind of film, talkies included in their utmost nearness to or distance from stage-plays, reduces or raises, as you please, the onlooker to a varying intensity of contemplation that is, in a way that cannot be over-estimated, different from the contemplation induced by a stage-play just because, whatever the ostensible interest of the film, it is arranged and focussed at the distance exactly fitting the contemplative state.

And this is not only because it is a finished reproduction that we are seeing, so that part of our mind is at ease as it can never be in the play that is as it were being made before our eyes in a single unique performance that is unlike any other single performance, and the faculty of contemplation has therefore full scope, but also because in any film of any kind those elements which in life we see only in fragments as we move amongst them, are seen in full in their own moving reality of which the spectator is the motionless, observing centre.

In this single, simple factor rests the whole power of the film: the reduction, or elevation of the observer to the condition that is essential to perfect contemplation.

In life, we contemplate a landscape from one point, or walking through it, break it into bits. The film, by setting the landscape in motion and keeping us still, allows it to walk through us.

And what is true of the landscape is true of everything else that can be filmed.

Vol. VIII, no. 4   December 1931

CONTINUOUS PERFORMANCE
THIS SPOON-FED GENERATION?

When, not so very long ago, Everyman's earth was motionless and solid beneath his feet, his immediate concerns were apt to fill and close his horizon. He knew, dimly and forgetfully, that his world, inhabited by foreigners as well as by the English, was engaged in hurtling through space at unimaginable speed and had possibly heard that the solid part of it was but a thin crust. But he thought in terms of solidity, and his universe was a vague beyond that mattered but little in comparison with his personal beyond, the stable world of daily life whose ways he knew and whose unchangeability.

Each generation, it is true, has had in turn to experience the break-up of a known world. The remotest historical records yield anathema, that might have been written yesterday, on modern noise and hustle, on new-fangled ideas and the perilous paths pursued by the ignorant young; and wistful longings for the good old days.

But until to-day Everyman remained relatively self-contained, and could plan his life with fair certainty in a surrounding that could be counted upon to remain more or less in place. Himself, his house, street, town, nation, all were stable; and beyond these secure stabilities his imagination rarely wandered.

The normal moral shocks awaiting him came gently. They were called disillusionments: change and decay, the loss, with age, of the sense of personal stability and personal permanence. But the solid earth remained unchanged, and one of the consolations of the elderly sane was the enchantment, growing in proportion to their own detachment, of the distant view of life, focussed now for the first time and free from the fret of immediacy, taking on an ever more moving beauty and intensity.

But to-day, it is not only that science, from whom had come the news of the tumultuous movement of everything, has begun to doubt the sufficiency of its methods of approach to render any exact account of the ultimate nature of reality, but also that its news, all the latest news, that to-morrow may be contradicted, is now common property almost from the moment of its arrival.

Everyman lives in a world grown transparent and uncertain. Behind his experience of the rapidity and unpredictability of change in the detail of his immediate surroundings is a varying measure of vicarious experience of the rapidity and unpredictability of change all over the world, and a dim sense that nobody knows with any certainty anything whatever about the universe of which his world is a part.

A new mental climate is in existence. Inhabited not only by those few whose lives are spent in research and those who are keenly on the lookout for the results of further research, but also in their degree by the myriads who have been born into the new world and can remember no other. Uncertainty, noise, speed, movement, rapidity of external change that has taught them to realise that to-morrow will not be as to-day, all these factors have helped to make the younger generation shock-proof in a manner unthinkable to the majority of their forebears.

And more than any other single factors (excepting perhaps Radio through which comes unlocalised, straight out of space, music with its incomparable directness of statement, and news forcing upon his attention the existence of others than himself and his relatives, friends and enemies; and knowledge, if he have the taste for it, and a truly catholic diversity of stated opinion) has the Cinema contributed to the change in the mental climate wherein Everyman has his being.

Insidiously. Not blatantly, after the manner of the accredited teacher is the film educating Everyman, making him at home in a new world.

And this it is, this enlightenment without tears, that makes so many of those who were brought up under a different dispensation cry and cry without ceasing against both Radio and Cinema as spoon-feeders of an Everyman who becomes more and more a looker and a listener, increasingly unwilling to spend his leisure otherwise than in being entertained.

Up hill and down dale we may criticise both Radio and Cinema. Nothing is easier. Nor is it other than desirable that the critical faculty should play freely upon these purveyors of Everyman's spiritual nourishment. But it is surely deplorable that so many people, both good earnest folk and the gadfly cynic, should be so busy in and out of season with the parrot-cry of 'spoon-feeding'? Deplorable that the Cinema, in the opinion of these pessimists, should be the worst offender. Radio, they declare, is sometimes, astonishingly and inexplicably, turned on as an accompaniment to occupation. But to 'the pictures' everything is sacrificed; home, honour, mind, body, soul and spirit. So they allege.

Is there an atom of justification for these wild statements? Do they not melt like morning mists before the sunny power of even half as much imaginative attention as the navvy may give to the average picture-show?

Cut out good films, instructional films, travelogues and all the rest of it. Leave only the average story-film, sensational or otherwise, the News Reel and the comic strip. Judge, condemn, all these, right and left. Is it possible to deny, even of this irreducible minimum of values, that it supplies to the bookless, thoughtless multitude the majority of whom do not make even that amount of unconscious contact with aesthetic and moral beauty that it is implied in going to church, a civilising influence more potent and direct than any other form of entertainment available in their leisure hours and sufficiently attractive to draw them in large numbers? Is a man spoon-fed the moment he is not visibly and actively occupied?

Is there not a certain obscenity, a separation of the inner spirit from the outer manifestation thereof, in regarding pictures we despise and audiences we loftily look down upon in the momentary relationship as we imagine it to exist in the accursed picture-house? Should we not rather set ourselves the far more difficult task of conjuring up the pre-picture outlook on life of those who make no contact with art in any form, and then try to follow out in imagination the result of the innumerable gifts of almost any kind of film, bestowed along with it, unawares, and therefore remaining with the recipient all the more potently: the gift of quiet, of attention and concentration, of perspective? The social gifts: the insensibly learned awareness of alien people and alien ways? The awakening of the imaginative power, the gift of expansion, of moving, ever so little, into a new dimension of consciousness?

Surely those positive cultural activities are more than enough to balance the much-advertised undesirabilities and to disqualify the verdict of 'spoon-feeding.'

The scaremongers would perhaps cease to wail if the film-fans, deserting the cinemas, battered down the closed doors of museums and picture-galleries and spent their evenings in silent contemplation not of lively human drama, and lively human nonsense and the living news of the changing world, but of the immortal frozen records of the things of the spirit that are unchanged from age to age.

Has it occurred to them to reflect that film-audiences, popular picture audiences, growing by the bread they have eaten, are maturing, are themselves cultivating and improving the medium from which they have drawn life? And that these audiences seen in the bulk, disregarding single, exceptional individuals, are much more capable of appreciating the wares of museum and gallery than were, in the bulk, their pictureless predecessors?

Vol. IX, no. 1   March 1932

CONTINUOUS PERFORMANCE
THE FILM GONE MALE

Memory, psychology is to-day declaring, is passive consciousness. Those who accept this dictum see the in-rolling future as living reality and the past as reality entombed. They also regard every human faculty as having an evolutionary history. For these straight-line thinkers memory is a mere glance over the shoulder along a past seen as a progression from the near end of which mankind goes forward. They are also, these characteristically occidental thinkers, usually found believing in the relative *passivity* of females. And since women excel in the matter of memory, the two beliefs admirably support each other. But there is memory and memory. And memory proper, as distinct from a mere backward glance, as distinct even from prolonged contemplation of things regarded as past and done with, gathers, can gather, and pile up its wealth only round universal, unchanging, unevolving verities that move neither backwards nor forwards and have neither speech nor language.

And that is one of the reasons why women, who excel in memory and whom the cynics describe as scarcely touched by evolving civilisation, are humanity's silent half, without much faith in speech as a medium of communication. Those women who never question the primacy of 'clear speech', who are docile disciples of the orderly thought of man, and acceptors of theorems, have either been educationally maltreated or are by nature more with the man's than within the women's camp. Once a woman becomes a partisan, a representative that is to say of one only of the many sides of [the] question, she has abdicated. The batallions of partisan women glittering in the limelit regions of to-day's world, whose prestige is largely the result of the novelty of their attainments, communicating not their own convictions but some one or other or a portion of some one or other of the astonishing varieties of thought-patterns under which men experimentally arrange such phenomena as are suited to the process, represent the men's camp and are distinguishable by their absolute faith in speech as a medium of communication.

The others, whom still men call womanly and regard with emotion not unmixed with a sane and proper fear, though they may talk incessantly from the cradle onwards, are, save when driven by calamitous necessity, as silent as the grave. Listen to their outpouring torrents of speech. Listen to village women at pump or fireside, to villa women, to unemployed service-flat women, to chatelâines, to all kinds of women anywhere and everywhere. Chatter, chatter, chatter, as men say. And say also that only one in a thousand can *talk*. Quite. For all these women use speech, with individual differences, alike: in the manner of a façade. Their awareness of being, as distinct from man's awareness of becoming, is so strong that when they are confronted, they must, in most circumstances, snatch at words to cover either their own palpitating spiritual nakedness or that of another. They talk to banish embarrassment. It is true they are apt to drop, if the confrontation be prolonged, into what is called gossip and owes both its charm and its poison to their excellence in awareness of persons. This amongst themselves. In relation to men their use of speech is various. But always it is a façade.

And the film, regarded as a medium of communication, in the day of its innocence, in its quality of being nowhere and everywhere, nowhere in the sense of having more intention than direction and more purpose than plan, everywhere by reason of its power to evoke, suggest, reflect, express from within its moving parts and in their totality of movement, something of the changeless being at the heart of all becoming, was essentially feminine. In its insistence on contemplation it provided a pathway to reality.

In becoming audible and particularly in becoming a medium of propaganda, it is doubtless fulfilling its destiny. But it is a masculine destiny. The destiny of planful becoming rather than of purposeful being. It will be the chosen battle-ground of rival patterns, plans, ideologies in endless succession and bewildering variety.

It has always been declared that it is possible by means of purely aesthetic devices to sway an audience in whatever direction a filmateur desires. This sounds menacing and is probably true. (The costumiers used Hollywood to lengthen women's skirts. Perhaps

British Instructional, with the entire medical profession behind it, will kindly shorten them again.) It is therefore comforting to reflect that so far the cinema is not a government monopoly. It is a medium, or a weapon, at the disposal of all parties and has, considered as a battlefield a grand advantage over those of the past when civil wars have been waged disadvantageously to one party or the other by reason of inequalities of publicity, restrictions of locale and the relative indirectness and remoteness of the channels of communication. The new film can, at need, assist Radio in turning the world into a vast council-chamber and do more than assist, for it is the freer partner. And multitudinous within the vast chamber, as within none of the preceding councils of mankind, is the unconquerable, unchangeable eternal feminine. Influential.

Weeping therefore, if weep we must, over the departure of the old time films' gracious silence, we may also rejoice in the prospect of a fair field and no favour. A field over which lies only the shadows of the censorship. And the censorship is getting an uneasy conscience.

Vol. X, no. 2   June 1933

CONTINUOUS PERFORMANCE

One can grow rather more than weary of hearing that the Drama is on its death-bed. For although there is no need to listen to them, it is not easy to escape the voices of the prophets of woe. They sound out across the world at large, and each little world within it has private vocalists. And there is a certain grim fascination in the spectacle of their futility. What are they? What purpose, since no one heeds their warnings, can they possibly serve? Are they the lunatic fringe, the outside edge of common prudence, the fantastic exaggeration that alone seems able to command fruitful attention? But they don't, in their own day, command fruitful attention, nor do all of them exaggerate. 'Oh, Jerusalem, Jerusalem, thou that slayest the prophets, hadst thou but known in this thy day the things that belong unto thy peace!' Woe over tribulation that might have been averted if the prophets had been listened to. But in the little world of The Drama, the mourning prophet, true or false, gleams with a perfection of meaninglessness. If his word be false, what does it matter? If true, what can be done? For though cascades of tears may relieve the hearts of those at the bedside, they will not restore the patient.

Meanwhile Drama, variously encumbered, goes its way. And from time to time a play appears – either refreshingly of its time or, equally refreshingly, standing well back within one or other of the grand traditions – and deals with its audiences much as did, when first they dawned, the plays that now are classics, assembled in groups under period labels.

Yet still the prophets howl. And so monotonous is their note, that it is a relief to hear one howling with a difference. Lo, says this newcomer, the drama is starved for lack of good new dramatists, but all is well with the theatre, since it can carry on with revivals. Triumph-song of an inheritor. Drama comes and drama goes, but the stage goes on for ever. Selah. No matter that one disagrees with his diagnosis. One can stand at his side and drink to the drama in general, date unspecified.

But this prophet has not done with us. Having passed sentence on The Drama, and forthwith commuted it on account of past achievements, he turns to the Film. We learn that the Cinema, like the stage, is starving for lack of good writers. Unlike the stage, it has no classics to fall back upon and must therefore starve to death. Result: the days of the Cinema are numbered.

Why, it may well be enquired, since everyone knows that there is, the world over, a sufficiency of good films to keep going for an indefinite period the cinemas run for those who prefer good films and more than a sufficiency for those who prefer other films, why tilt at such a preposterous windmill? Why not enquire, with trans-atlantic simplicity, 'What's biting you?' And why not politely indicate one or two recently-appeared masterpieces and point out that they could be exhibited in the world's leading Cinemas simultaneously, whereas the Stage –

Quite. But there is in this prophet's outcry something more than a pessimism so neat and so mathematical as to have the air of a pastime not unlike a jigsaw puzzle. And while indeed it might be a pastime to oppose the statement on its own ground, in the accredited heavy-weight boxing style of the debating-society, by retorting that if the Stage can worry along on classics, so can the Cinema, by filming these classics, it may not be out of place to take a look at the unconscious assumption underlying this prophet's neat equation. The assumption that the Cinema is merely the Stage with a difference. For this assumption is one that the general public, including ourselves, is daily more and more inclined to make. Growing talkie-minded, we increasingly regard the Film in the light of the possibilities it shares with the Stage.

For Stage and Screen, falsifying the prophecies of those who saw in the Talkies the doom of the Theatre, have become a joint-stock company, to the benefit of both parties. They, so to speak, try things out for each other. Successful plays are filmed, successful films are made into plays. Insensibly therefore, the screen's patron, the general public including ourselves, while more or less constantly aware of the ways in which Stage outdoes Film and gets the better of Stage is apt increasingly to regard the Film as the Purveyor of Drama.

We hear of a good film. Born as a film. Or as the brilliant by-product of an obscure novel. Or as the screen equivalent of a good play. The organiser of the cinema showing this film obligingly indicates the times at which it may be seen. We look in. See our play and come away. We are play-goers.

But cinema could subsist without these events. And could make us attend to it. And even these are ultimately dependent, for their pull on us, upon the peculiar quality of the film's continuous performance, the unchallenged achievement that so overwhelmingly stated itself when the first 'Animated Pictures' cast their uncanny spell with the dim, blurred, continuously sparking representation of a locomotive advancing full steam upon the audience, majestic and terrible.

It was the first hint of the Film's power of tackling aspects of reality that no other art can adequately handle. But the power of the Film, or Film drama, filmed realities, filmed uplift and education, all its achievements in the realm of the Good, the True and the Beautiful, appealing to the many, and in the realm of the abstract, appealing only to the few, rests alike for the uninstructed, purblind onlooker and the sophisticated kinist [cineaste], upon the *direct* relationship, mystic, joyous, wonderful, between the observer a continuous miracle of form of movement, of light and shadow in movement, the continuous performance, going on behind all invitations to focus upon this or that, of the film itself. And if to-morrow all playwrights and all plays should disappear, the Film would still have its thousand resources while the Stage, bereft of its sole material, would die. Except, perhaps, for ballet?

Vol. VIII, no. 4   December 1931

Reviewed by W. B.

DAWN'S LEFT HAND, BY DOROTHY M. RICHARDSON, PUBLISHED BY DUCKWORTH, 7S. 6D.

It is not possible to forget the first meeting with Miriam, the heroine of Miss Dorothy Richardson's many volume novel, *Pilgrimage*. Our own memory goes back to *Backwater* in 1916. It was a moment when normal adolescence ceased, and although the suppression was accepted, it was a violently imposed external barrier and actual impulses made themselves felt in a hidden way, through delight in small events that made the days endurable or despair that was as old and barren as the press communiqués at night. There were food queues, there was no heat in winter-damp rooms. Against this cold, and never ending anxiety, a searchlight swung in black sky. Into this suspended moment came *Pilgrimage*, and in its pages growth was possible.

It was a peculiar sensation, to be conscious that development was barred not because of any inward conflict, but for sheerly external reasons imposed by war. Reading *Pointed Roofs* and *Backwater*, not one but many, were able to resume for a few hours, the growth proper to their age. It was not escape, but an actual sense of movement.

Perhaps it is for this reason that Dorothy Richardson seems to express, more than any other writer, the English spirit. Her books are the best history yet written of the slow progression from the Victorian period to the modern age. She is the English Proust and like him, has written for the few, but her understanding of character is much deeper and she sees so universally that her books belong most to the circles of workers where for some inexplicable reason, her work is little known.

Miriam becomes a teacher, in Germany and England, then a governess, then a secretary. She has a brief holiday in Switzerland, occasional country weekends, the ordinary average life of hundreds fifteen years ago, of thousands now. But this *Turksib* of a worker's years is set against the background of the emerging of the modern world and of her own view of life. Unless, she says the human being is often alone, it is impossible to appreciate the richness of human individuality; London or the countryside are only fully to be enjoyed in contrast one with the other.

What a film her books could make. The real English film for which so many are waiting. Apart from Miriam herself, the pages are filled with people, men and women who resume their whole thought and vocabulary in a few phrases or a few actions, immediately to be recognised, for they are to be met every day. *Dawn's Left Hand* begins (as perhaps films should) in a railway carriage. Miriam returns from a holiday in Switzerland: the London year goes by, apparently nothing happens, underneath the surface an epoch of life, of civilisation, changes. She leaves a flat and the narrow boundaries of a social worker's mind for the communal richness of the boarding house, familiar to readers of previous volumes. She meets a friend, refuses to marry a doctor, her own development progresses. And in each page an aspect of London is created that like an image from a film, substitutes itself for memory, to revolve before the eyes as we read.

This volume, the tenth in the series, is probably the finest written by Miss Richardson to date.

Dorothy Richardson, by John Cowper Powys (Joiner and Steele, 3/6) is an excellent study of Miss Richardson's methods, though not all readers will agree with his conclusions. It is, however, particularly to be commended to those who hesitate to begin *Pilgrimage*, because they have not read all the previous volumes.

PART 5

Borderline and the POOL Films

INTRODUCTION

Anne Friedberg

It will mean, concerning cinematography, new beginning ...

POOL advertisement, *transition*, July 1927

The POOL group produced three short films – *Wing Beat* (1927), *Foothills* (1929) and *Monkey's Moon* (1929) – before it mounted its most ambitious project *Borderline* (1930), a feature-length film 'starring' Paul Robeson and H.D.[1] *Close Up*'s first issue dramatically heralded the first POOL film. A full-page ad announced:

ON THE WAY

WING BEAT

A POOL film. A study in thought.

The screen has had all these equivalents:

the epic,

the novel,

the chronicle,

the fantasy,

the play.

But no free verse poem. WING BEAT is the first.

Wing Beat, 'a study in thought', deployed its images in poetic association, sought visual strategies to present 'a film of telepathy'.[2] In an unpublished essay on *Wing Beat*, H.D. expanded the ornithological metaphor ('a bird in the brain, that is what this film seems to me') and called for the cinema that would present the 'vast areas of consciousness that cannot be caught in cages'.[3] One remaining fragment of *Wing Beat* demonstrates how the film attempted to approximate thought. A sequence which cross-cut between three different shots - a shot of Macpherson reading a paper headlined 'Talking Book', a shot of a young man (John Ellerman Jr – Bryher's younger brother) dancing a jitterbug and a close-up of a spinning phonograph disk – culminates in a triple superimposition. This three-layered palimpsest renders – in purely visual terms – Macpherson's growing irritation with the disturbance of the music's volume and the vibrations of the dance.[4] It is unclear whether *Wing Beat* was

'One of Nature's film-stars.' Still from *Monkey's Moon*. Directed by Kenneth Macpherson (Vol. V, no. 1, July 1929).

ever completed or shown publicly. In the *Borderline* pamphlet (reprinted here), H.D. seals its fate: 'Kenneth Macpherson turned a personal little film in 1927. It is carefully packed away and he shows it to no one.'[5]

The next POOL film, *Foothills*, was shot in the winter and spring of 1928 in the village of Veytaux, near Territet. Shot on a small budget, using panchromatic film, a number of 'Jupiter' twin carbon arc lamps and the same Debrie model L camera used in *Wing Beat*, *Foothills* was a tale of a city woman (H.D.) who visits the countryside and grows quite bored. Macpherson acknowledged that this scenario was not completely original. F.W. Murnau's *Sunrise*, released in late 1927, had a similar plot. In the March 1928 issue, the *Close Up* critic Robert Herring – who also appears in *Foothills* – complains about the much-heralded *Sunrise*: 'There is no psychology, no insight, nothing we have been waiting for.'[6] *Foothills* tried to supply these missing elements. In a not-so-humbly-titled account of the production, 'Wie ein Meisterstuck enstand' ('How a Masterpiece Is Made'), Macpherson described every technical difficulty as a determinant for an aesthetic choice:

> I was conscious that my critical view of cinematography would become deeper through a film on which I myself had to be an electrician, cameraman, director, and occasionally performer ... if every critic would just do this, our film criticism would be completely different.[7]

When Macpherson and Bryher were in Berlin in August 1928 they showed *Foothills* to G. W. Pabst, who responded enthusiastically.[8] 'Here and there the work was excellent,' writes H.D. about *Foothills* in the *Borderline* pamphlet. But, she continues, the film was 'commented on too generously, Macpherson feels, by certain of the German and French and English critics. But he himself was not satisfied.'[9]

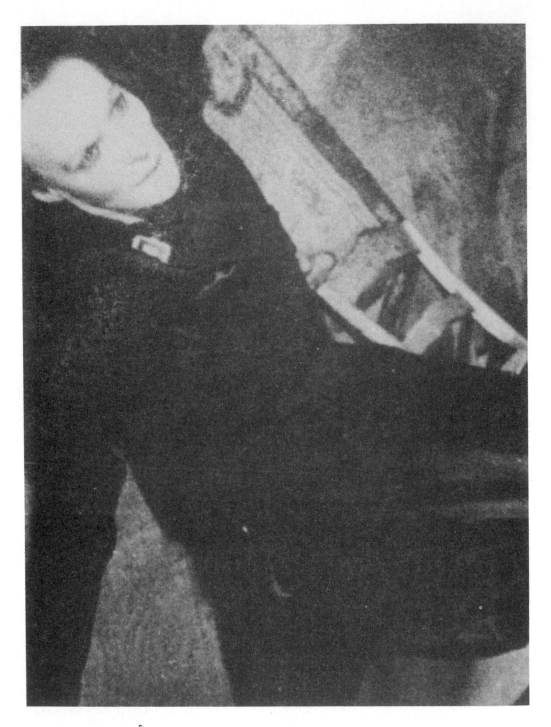

H. D. in
Borderline:
'Helga Doorn
gives her
interpretation
of those little
deaths we die'
(Vol. VII, no. 2,
August 1930).

Foothills,
directed by
Kenneth
Macpherson
(Vol. V, no. 1,
July 1929).

Eslanda Robeson in *Borderline* (Vol. VII, no. 4, October 1930).

Borderline: 'Paul Robeson enjoying his self-ordained canonization' (Vol. VII, no. 2, August 1930).

The third POOL film, *Monkey's Moon*, was heavily announced in the July 1929 issue
of the journal. The cover brandished a still of the film's protagonists – Macpherson's
pet douracoulis monkeys – and inside there were four more stills, with the caption: 'A
film now nearing completion by Kenneth Macpherson.' Stills from *Monkey's Moon*
peppered the pages of the July, September, October and December 1929 issues.[10]

Like the other POOL films, the feature-length *Borderline* was most visible in the
stills and advertisements that crowded the pages of *Close Up*.[11] The participation of
Paul Robeson was a coup for the POOL group. Robeson had appeared in only one
previous film – Oscar Micheaux's 1924 *Body and Soul* – and his presence in the
POOL film seemed guaranteed to draw attention to it. By the spring of 1930,
Robeson's concert and stage career had brought him a notable celebrity in Europe.[12]
Yet because *Borderline* was made by ardent partisans of silent film-making, the film
only used Paul's imposing visual presence, effectively muting his prodigious voice.

A film of roughly seventy minutes, *Borderline* was a complex experiment,
meticulously planned, story-boarded in nearly a thousand sketches specifying camera
angle and movement.[13] 'The Story' to *Borderline* was told in an accompanying printed
'libretto', a necessary key to the otherwise disjunctive and elliptical narrative. In a
'small "borderline" town anywhere in Europe', Adah (Eslanda Robeson) has been
'involved in an affair' with Thorne (Gavin Arthur) and is 'staying in rooms with' the
white couple, Thorne and Astrid (H.D.). Adah does not realize that her husband Pete
(Paul Robeson) is in the same town working in a hotel-café run by a cigar-smoking
proprietress (Bryher).[14] A quarrel between Astrid and Thorne results in Astrid's
'accidental death'. As the programme note tells it: 'The negro woman is blamed …
Thorne is acquitted … the mayor, acting for the populace … ordered Pete … to leave
town. Pete goes … a scapegoat for the unresolved problems, evasions and neuroses for
which the racial "borderline" has served justification.'[15]

The racialized sexual politics of the film operate within the binary metaphor of
borderline – white/black; hetero/queer – presenting a complex matrix of racial and
sexual tensions. The white heterosexual couple (Astrid and Thorne) are cast as unstable
neurotics, and yet they remain the film's central subjectivities.[16] H.D.'s pamphlet on the
film demonstrates the ambition to permeate all levels of the project – production,
montage style, even spectator position – with the borderlines of black and white, male
and female, borders of nation and class, psychic borderlines. *Borderline* contained
everything that seemed important to the POOL group, combining, as it did, the
psychological realism of Pabst, the psychoanalytic insights of Hanns Sachs and the
montage theories of Eisenstein. In this regard, the film emerged out of an unprecedented
liaison between cinematic and psychoanalytic theory: the alliance of Sachs's
Freud-driven theories of the figurational processes of the unconscious and Eisenstein's
theories of intellectual montage. Macpherson described his intentions for *Borderline*:

> instead of the method of externalised observation, dealing with objects, I was
> going to take my film into the minds of the people in it, making it not so much a
> film of 'mental processes' as to insist on a mental condition. … It had not been
> done, had not been touched except in Pabst's frankly psychoanalytic film,
> *Secrets of a Soul* …[17]

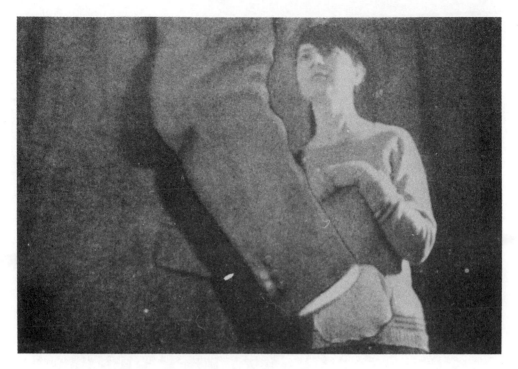

Bryher in *Borderline* (Vol. VII, no. 4, October 1930).

Invoking *Secrets of a Soul*, Macpherson aligned his project with Sachs's proviso to 'make perceptible ... invisible inward events'.[18] In 'Film Psychology', Sachs praised Soviet film-makers' particular adeptness at manifesting psychic events on film. But Sachs's insights lacked cinematic specificity. While citing examples from *Potemkin* and *Mother*, he failed to acknowledge the role that montage played in 'dissecting' the everyday event and evoking its revelatory power. It was Macpherson who made the link between Sachs's description of the spectator's unconscious response and Eisenstein's theories of the overtone and intellectual montage. In his December 1929 'As Is', Macpherson wrote:

> We must go to psychoanalysis to understand that action is the modified outgiving of interacting conscious and unconscious adjustment ... We are not watching something happen to somebody else, we are experiencing our own reaction to something which *has been dissected and spread out for the precise purpose of our comprehension and unconscious participation*.[19] [emphasis added]

As *Close Up* began to embrace Eisenstein – to translate his theories – Macpherson's appeal to the 'unconscious participation' of the spectator took a new, more precise, direction. *Borderline* was forged in this rare crucible.

The planning for *Borderline* began in May 1929 when, as Macpherson claimed, 'Europe was unaware, and so was I, of Eisenstein's now commonly accepted though little understood theory of overtonal montage.'[20] In the May 1929 issue *Close Up* published the first translation of Eisenstein's work, 'New Language of

Cinematography', an essay which marked the beginning of his speculation on an 'intellectual cinema'.[21] In March 1930 (the same month that *Borderline* was shot) *Close Up* published the first translation of 'The Fourth Dimension in Kino', wherein Eisenstein proposed a 'higher category' of montage, 'not of roughly physiological over-tone(s)' but 'overtones of an intellectual order'.[22] 'The intellectual Kino', Eisenstein wrote, 'will be the Kino which resolves the conflict-conjunctions of the physiological and intellectual overtones.'[23] In a lengthy (ten-page) introduction to the Eisenstein essay, Macpherson cited a long passage from Sachs's 'Film Psychology', making it apparent that he saw Eisenstein through the lens of Sachs.

H.D. compares the editing of *Borderline* to the 'lightning effect of repeated firing' in Eisenstein's *October*. ('The almost instantaneous effect was Eisenstein's meticulous innovation – the cutting and fitting of minute strips of soldier, gun, gun-fire, soldier, gun.'[24]) In *Borderline*, when Pete and Adah embrace in the Swiss countryside, the image of Pete is intercut with the flowing rapids of a waterfall to give the effect of Eisensteinian 'clatter montage',[25] an effect H.D. writes, 'almost that of super-imposition but subtly differing from it ... achieved by the meticulous cutting of three and four and five inch lengths of film and pasting these tiny strips together.'[26]

Borderline 'dissects' everyday events and, in their recombination, invests them with psychoanalytic import. 'The welding of the psychic or super-normal to the things of precise every-day existence', writes H.D. in her generous paean to Macpherson, 'is Kenneth Macpherson's rare gift.'[27]

Borderline was shown at a limited number of *ciné-club* and film society screenings – at the Academy Cinema in London in October 1930, the Second International Congress of Independent Cinema in Brussels in November 1930, at a *ciné-club* in Catalonia in January 1931 and the Rote Mühle in Berlin in April 1931. Screenings were intended for America, but for reasons that remain unclear, in October 1931 the film was impounded by US customs and refused entry.

Critics complained of *Borderline*'s 'obscurity' and its 'chaotic' structure.[28] In the end Macpherson stridently insisted it was 'the only really avant-garde film ever made'.[29] He compared British audiences, who were consistently condemned in the pages of *Close Up*, to Germans whose 'minds ... worked differently':

> They [the British] reject *Borderline*, not because it is complex – for its power is its complexity, its unexplainedness – like something seen through a window or a key-hole; but because it is a film of subconscious reasoning. And if, among the English, the subconscious is ruefully admitted, for some definitely social reason, it is not to be condoned.[30]

The critical failure of *Borderline* – the only POOL film with a record of public screening – produced a *crise du cœur* for Bryher, Macpherson and the other *Close Up* writers associated with it. The 'new beginning for cinematography' that POOL so valiantly declared in 1927 seemed to have met a dead end, foreclosed by the intransigence of the cinema world they had hoped to transform.

BORDERLINE: A POOL FILM
WITH PAUL ROBESON

H.D.

In the Cast:

Pete (A Negro)	Paul Robeson
Adah (His Wife)	Eslanda Robeson
Astrid	Helga Doorn [H.D.]
Thorne (Helga's Husband)	Gavin Arthur
The Café Manageress	Bryher
The Barmaid	Charlotte Arthur
The Pianist	Robert Herring
The Old Lady	Blanche Lewin

I

Borderline is chosen as the name of this new film; clarid sequence of ideas will show why.

There are in Europe, many just such little towns as this particular borderline town of some indefinite mid-European mountain district. There are trains coming and trains going. One of these trains has already deposited the half-world mondaine Astrid with Thorne, her lover. They have come here because of some specific nerve-problem, perhaps to rest, perhaps to recuperate, perhaps to economise, perhaps simply in hope of some emotional convalescence. They live as such people do the world over, in just such little social borderline rooms as just such couples seek in Devonshire, in Cornwall, in the South of France, in Provincetown, United States. They are borderline social cases, not out of life, not in life; the woman is a sensitive neurotic, the man, a handsome, degenerate dipsomaniac. Thorne has not reached the end of his cravings, may step this side, that side of the border; Astrid, the white-cerebral is and is not outcast, is and is not a social alien, is and is not a normal human being, she is borderline. These two are specifically chosen to offset another borderline couple of more dominant integrity. These last, Pete and his sweetheart Adah, have a less intensive problem, but border; they dwell on the cosmic racial borderline. They are black people among white people.

Though in this specific mid-Europe, there is nothing intrinsically disharmonious in that, their situation is a sort rarely, if ever, touched on, in film art. Their problem is not dealt with as the everlasting black-white Problem with a capital. It remains however a motive to be counted on; though threads are woven in and through the fabric, white into black and black into white, Pete and Adah must inevitably remain 'borderline', whether by their own choice and psychic affiliation or through sheer crude brute causes.

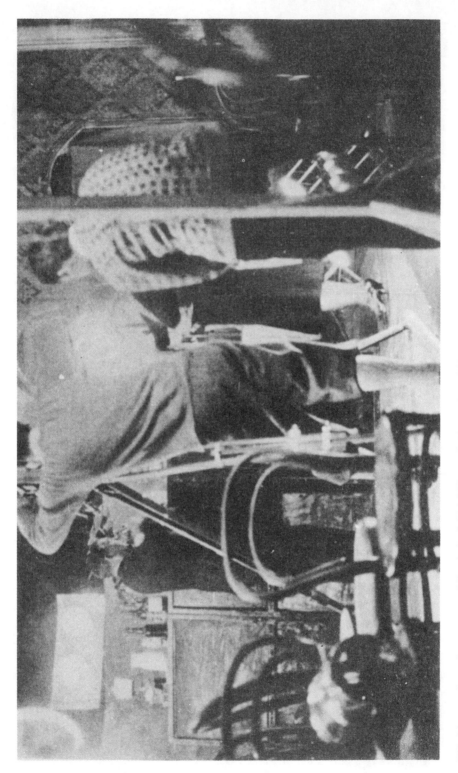

'Working on the cafe sequence of *Borderline*' (Vol. VII, no. 5, November 1930).

Mr Kenneth Macpherson is himself, you might say, borderline among the young cinema directors. He is not at all allied with the ultra-modern abstract school of rhomboid and curve and cross-beam of tooth pick or coal shovel. I do not mean that Mr Mapherson is out of sympathy with any form of realistic cinema abstraction, I simply quote him, remember his saying in casual conversation, 'why should one trouble to photograph a match stick when a birch tree is so interesting?' Mr Macpherson finds a white birch tree as interesting, as abstract, as some people find a tooth-brush. But he is also interested in toothbrushes. In their place. There are moments, in Mr Macpherson's sequences, when a flash of white hand or the high lights across the knuckles of a black hand become, you might say, as 'sterile' as certain much-vaunted 'effects' of sieve, tooth-pick, or cullander. But when Mr Macpherson plays upon abstraction, it is in reference to some other abstraction. A telephone receiver of usual form and literacy, is dealt with, as abstraction, though it merges to the concrete when applied to succeeding abstraction of a stern chin line. The method of Mr Macpherson is admittedly an 'abstract' method, but he is only satisfied when abstraction coupled with related abstraction makes logical dramatic sequence. A little oil can, for instance (concise modernistic abstraction) relates to a giant negro shoulder. Oil and heat are related to a dark brow, that great head that bends forward, very earth giant. While light and air, indication in an inblown curtain, link on to the Victorian abstraction of a stuffed dead sea-gull and thence, by swift flashes of inevitable sequence, to a weathered woman-face. That face beats through the film like the very swift progress of those wings, doomed it is evident, and already extinguished in this 'borderline' existence.

Mr Kenneth Macpherson is 'borderline'. In Germany, among German appreciators, there is an odd phrase, though one must learn to accept it: 'ach, so English, sehr English'. In England, the inevitable reaction to this abstract and formalized intellectuality, is to say 'absolutely influenced by the Germans'. Both of these are and are not true. Mr Macpherson is nordic, is English in general European terminology, though obviously his intense specialized inspiration is that of the northern Celt. His fine fibre is nordic, is celtic, his types therefore, conforming to physical outward symbol (European or African), are used, regardless of the feelings of his audience, to propound some 'runic' problem. These people are the riddles, they ask 'why' and they ask 'what' and they say 'when is this or that not that or this?' When is an African not an African? When obviously he is an earth-god. When is a woman not a woman? When obviously she is sleet and hail and a stuffed sea-gull. He says when is white not white and when is black white and when is white black? You may or may not like this sort of cinematography. This is no concern whatever of your young director. He does not care for you, he does not care for me, he does not care, it is obvious, for his carefully chosen and meticulously directed cast of mixed black and white, of mixed professionals and 'amateurs'. He *does* care and he does not care. The riddle, when is an amateur not an amateur, might be aptly propounded at this moment. The answer to that rune is comparatively easy. There is, under proper directorship, no such thing as an amateur. Certain of the German and Russian directors claim that some of their most poignant effects have come from people who have stepped for the first time before a camera. In that, Mr Macpherson follows the 'foreign' tradition. And in this again, Mr Macpherson is borderline, working as he does with German-Russian approach yet with keen knife-blade of indigenous intrepidity.

Again Mr Macpherson's company is borderline, not only in that it is racially mixed but also because of the relative professional experience and inexperience of its members. Mr Robeson, we all know as an artist of high repute. His wife, Eslanda Robeson, has not appeared, to my knowledge, on the stage or screen. She moves, 'emotes', reacts in uncanny sympathy to the ideas of her director. Mr Robeson had only to step before the camera and the theme flowed toward him as many small streams toward that great river. Mr Robeson is obviously the ground under all their feet. He is stabilized, stable, the earth. Across Mr Macpherson's characterisation of Pete, the half-vagrant young giant negro, the fretting provincialism of small-town slander and small town menace move like shadows from high clouds. The giant negro is in the high clouds, white cumulous cloud banks in a higher heaven. Conversely, his white fellow-men are the shadows of white, are dark, neurotic; storm brews; there is that runic fate that 'they that live by the sword shall perish by the sword'. Or as here applied, 'they that live by neurotic-erotic suppression shall perish by the same'. This is not so precisely stated. But it is the white woman and the white man who are victims, when there is the final test of man and nature.

Here again, Mr Macpherson is 'borderline'. He is, in no way whatever, concerned personally with the black–white political problem. As an artist, he sees beauty, 'take it or leave it', he seems to say again and again, and, 'I'm not busy with party politics.' Nevertheless, in his judicious, remote manner, he has achieved more for that much mooted and hooted Problem (with a capital) than if he went about to gain specific sympathy. He says, 'here is a man, he is black', he says 'here is a woman also of partial African abstraction'. He says, not 'here is a black man, here is a mulatto woman', but 'here is a *man*, here is a *woman*'. He says, 'look, sympathize with them and love them' not because they are black but because they are man, because they are woman. This race presentation will be no palliative for a decadent palate. Mr Macpherson does not even hint or suggest any aesthetic compromise. He simply states his riddle, answers his riddle, says 'see and love and if you see and do not love, that is no concern of mine'. Mr Macpherson is the artist par excellence, he sees with the eye and what he sees, he portrays. He cares no more for you or me than Leonardo did for King Francis or the merchant husband of Mona Lisa.

II

Juxtaposition of 'Leonardo' with 'modern screen art' is neither as inept nor as ironical as it may seem at first glance. This name connotes mechanical efficiency, modernity and curiosity allied with pure creative impulse. The film *per se* is a curious welding of mechanical and creative instincts. Yet, you may ask, granted that, what has Leonardo, demi-god of accepted intellectuality, to do with this gutter-offshoot of modernity? What has that steel blade to do with harem beauties in bathing costumes and with sugar and spice and everything that is nice and must, *must*, MUST remain nice in the commercially constituted realm of so-called cinematography? You say 'what indeed?' We answer, 'do you know your Leonardo? Do you know your film world?' Leonardo, you say, is a text-book, high-water mark of Renaissance painting, someone dead long ago. Cinema art, you will repeat, is a present-day gutter offshoot of the stage, having to do with ladies and laddies and gentlemen with gardenias and crooks and safety vaults. We must answer, 'that is all true'.

Yet we may ask, have any of you gentlemen tried to use a camera? How many of you take photographs, even passably good ones, of suns and sunsets, of ladies among water-lilies? Have you any idea of the technical difficulties to be surmounted in dealing even with a newsreel? Have any of your creative artists who paint passable pictures ever mixed your own colours, have you cut apart dead arms and dead hands to see what nerve centres really do look like, and have you probed down and down with a little sharp implement, perhaps the very little knife you just now scraped your palate with, to see if you can discover by its valve formation, why the human heart should beat so? Have any of you writers invented personal secret script, written mind and soul secrets in that? Was writing so dear to you that you ever wrote with NO eye to any ulterior auditor, for yourself only? If you have done some of this or sympathised with some of this, then you may be said to know your Leonardo; if you have done some of this or sympathised with a little of it, then you may be said to be prepared to approach your new mechanical-creative film art.

You may deliberate over a few technical mechanical art problems; you may or may not accept them as applicable to the film. If, in yourself, there is no grain of this divine Leonardo–like curiosity, of this intensive Leonardo–esque modernism, then the screen can be of no use. Leonardo did not say, 'there is no hope in painting, look at Giotto'. Young Lindenberg did not say, 'many brave hearts lie asleep in the deep, so beware, beware'. Mr Macpherson does not say, 'there is no use doing this, I sweat blood for what use, if I ever do get across no one will understand me', he just goes on, his cadaverous frame getting more thin, his grey-steel eyes getting more glint and fire, his hands steady and his mind stable though his knees are shaking. It is funny to watch him work if you have a mind for just that sort of humour. Like watching a young gunner alone with his machine gun. It is as if one knew all the time the sniper would at the last get him. But it is a privilege, in no small way, to stand beside just such rare type of advanced young, creative intellectual, waiting for the sniper to get oneself too. Pro patria indeed, if that pro patria is a no-man's land, an everyman's land of such plausible perfection. Mr Macpherson, like Mr da Vinci, is Hellenic in his cold detachment, his cool appraisal, his very inhuman insistence on perfection.

Well, what anyhow is perfection? There is your perfection, there is my perfection, there is the perfection of Mr da Vinci as well as that of Mr Lindenberg and of Tom, Dick and Harry. Your perfection may be this or this, a cigar in a club window or a gardenia in a buttonhole or a pair of translucent gold-silk stockings or the talk that goes with that or the legs that go with this or a volume of de Maupassant. *Chacun à*, we are told, *son goût*. Mr Macpherson's is admittedly a peculiar pleasure. He stands, after any human being would drop dead of fatigue, casually with his elegant Debrie, machine man with it. He directs an elaborate serious of overhead and side and ground lights, he writes a script which he meticulously illustrates with a series of some 1,000 pen sketches, he chooses his troop of players, he poses them, he all but acts for them, he directs from behind the camera while all the time he himself is concerned with the elaborate one-man mechanism of various stops, different focuses, indeterminate 'pans' up and down, and the ever tricky job of the sheer turning. Did I say the camera was a one-man job? I spoke hastily. I have watched three men in one of the biggest studios of Germany hold up Mr G. B. Pabst himself while all three gesticulated as to the proper focus, lens, distance, stop and rate of 'turning'. The camera is no one-man job. It takes half a dozen in the usual professionally equipped studio to wield this bulky monster. The sheer physical Macpherson, it seems, sometimes may just snap off somewhere about his elongated middle. But something else keeps him. It is that terrible thing, rare in any art, rarest of all in the new bastard, machine created film art, *creative impulse*. Divine creative instinct enslaves that monster, beautiful as a model air-ship, that renowned Debrie that is all sinew and all steel. The cinema-camera is a renaissance miracle or a final miracle, that delicate crystal lense. But what good is all that lacking even more divine impulse to enslave it? The camera has for the most part been the property of monsters, like those three Gorgons in the waste-land, holding a precious legacy, one human EYE between them. Would it be altogether inept to say that Mr Macpherson and his young colleagues are just the least bit like the Perseus who snatched the EYE from the clutch of the slobbering and malign Monsters? Well, yes, perhaps that is a little silly. Kenneth Macpherson, at work, is a hard-boiled mechanic, as if he himself were all camera, bone and sinew and steel-glint of rapacious grey eyes.

III

This then is the miracle, this curious atavism, the relationship so dramatically stressed between the ultra-modern, and the ultra-classic. The aim of the Renaissance of quattrocento Florence was to bring the classic vibration into line with its own day. A renaissance is admittedly that. To-day those that scoff at film-art and its possibilities are as old-fashioned as the later retrogressives who burnt their Hesiod and then their Savonrola [Savonarola] who had maligned him. There is no such thing as any fixed art standard. This is beautiful, this was beautiful, this may be beautiful. There is one beauty, it is the beauty of belief, of faith, of hope. And if that beauty is allied to sheer grit and technical efficiency, you get a new sort of art creation.

There is beauty, there has always been beauty. The problem in every art period is to present that beauty in a form allied to its environment and its time. No one can paint like Leonardo, no one can draw like Dürer, no one to-day can satirize like Hogarth nor blow wind in tree-tops like Corot. No one man can hope to sculpt and make music and design air-ships in any one lifetime. This is, we are told, an age of specialists. Leonardo, however, the world's greatest 'artist' must have a try at everything. Moreover, convention of his period forced this on him. In his apprentice days, he had to gild statuettes, paint in shadows, daub out shadows, sculpt, smear on colour, hammer gold leaf. He had at the same time to be politically and socially, an entity, scholar, musician, diplomat, soldier. An 'artist' to-day is apt to be either a bit of a social pariah or a bit of a snob. There remains one world where a true artist may still demand and still attain something of that quattrocento ideal. An advanced and intellectual film-director must be mechanic, must be artist, must be man, must be warrior. He can be no spiritual anaemic, no physical weakling. He may not himself, personally, draw, paint, sculpt, yet instinctively in his outlook, he must maintain sympathy with all these art-facets and with music, drama, and every form of writing. For in the film alone to-day, may these allied arts be welded.

Light flows over a face. That means nothing or little to you. There is a bronze forehead and the eye sockets are gouged out just this way; there is a concentration of shadow here, a plane of light here. You see a face, perhaps at most you see a pleasing portrait. You may even murmur 'Gauguin'. You think, no doubt, that this is clever posing or perhaps delightful portraiture. You do not realise that that face has been moulded, modelled by an artist, that those lights have been arranged, re-arranged deliberately focussed. Those who know anything, even of the technique of mere photography, realise that Macpherson sculpts literally with light. He gouges, he reveals, he conceals. All this not by accident, not automatically but with precision and deliberate foresight. Mr Macpherson worked over his 1,000 little sketches for some months before he began to 'turn'. There was not one angle of a face, scarcely a movement of a hand or fold of drapery that he had not pre-visualised. The ordinary director leaves much to chance. He has 'takes' and 'retakes', leaves much of the visual construction in the hands of his camera-men, of his light effects in the hands of his elaborate staff of mechanics. Macpherson had one electrician who helped him shift incandescents. He had the delicate and competent assistance of John Macpherson with the spot-lights. Mr John Macpherson, delicate portrait painter, with sure artistic instinct, did much to assist Kenneth Macpherson in some of the more conventionalized poses. But the whole conception was already, as I say, pre-arranged in the curious and amazing visual memory of his son.

A man has two hands. With one of his two hands, Kenneth Macpherson turned with steady even pressure, adjusted with the other, this or that spot, this or that delicate change of focus, like a sensitive violinist. The hands of John Macpherson, allied to the sympathetic mind, worked a spot light as his son directed. Back of the camera, facing his models, not eye to eye, as in the case of the usual director, but THROUGH THE LENS Mr Macpherson gave definite and sustained direction. His 'stand, now move, a little slower, not so sullen, that light a little higher', were uttered with assurance and received the immediate response that the ordinary director gets only at long range and after untold rehearsals. It stands to reason that the sheer pictorial quality of Mr Macpherson's work (apart from the dramatic and rhythmic) must be unique among his contemporaries.

He achieves almost without exception, arresting and surprising effects, not only in the legitimate film sense, but in actual, historic, conventional 'art' values. It is strange to see delicate screen tree-tops etched against a screen sky, that Corot would acclaim. It is odd to associate Botticelli with the cinema but that association is inevitable in some of the interior scenes for instance of Astrid and her shawl. It is unusual to weld the idea of bronze with movement, but a head is sculptured, gouged out in planes and focus of light and shadow and inset with eyes like those Mena period Egyptian heads with amber glass, yet that head moves. It is difficult to imagine Hogarth, Fragonard, Botticelli, Egyptian bronze and Greek marble all allied and welded, a unit and that unit modern. In this film, you get all these; the line of trees too in the long popular avenue down which Thorne wanders as in some astral dream, bring to mind the high spaces of the Karnak temple. Trees are foundations, pillars of gigantic temple, they are delicate too, as remote and ethereal as the trees of Corot. Men are men, in everyday clothes, in everyday existence, and women are women with petty jealousies and nerve-reaction and erotic-cerebral modern complexes. Men are men but they are as well, black and white, carved massive intimate stone and bronze portraits. Women are women, but they are embroidered with delicacy, as that head of Adah against rock-flowers, like an Asiatic on a screen, or they are fine with some 'French' sophistication as the frivolous and Fragonard-like moments of the girl in the café or they are gouged out with a white lightning fury, like the tragic face of Astrid, from white marble. Mr Kenneth Macpherson is rooted firmly in the bed-rock of recognized and recognizable beauty; he reaches forward (strange contradiction) toward the lean skyscraper beauty of ultra-modernity. In this there is no forced note, no note of falsity because that beauty and the beauty of Mena period Egypt, of Hohkousai ([Hokusai] Japan, of quattrocento Florence, of Hogarth and of Fragonard and of Botticelli of pre-Phidian Athens, of Ionian Ephesus are all one. Mr Kenneth Macpherson has some obvious affinity with all these facets of past beauty. But this is his uncanny legacy. He brings all these high powered vibrations of past static art conception into direct line with modern problems, with modernity and with the most modern art of portraiture in movement.

IV

I have said that Kenneth Macpherson touches the various 'stops' and focus appliances of his beautiful camera like a violinist. And that presents another parallel. I have said that in the film alone can the pictorial arts be welded. They can in addition be *wedded* and to a separate art form. And that form, music.

But here we are on difficult ground; speaking of one art in terms of another always seems the hall-mark of the 'nineties' or of facile dilettantism. Yet it is perhaps as necessary to-day for the modernist artist to endeavour to shock weary sensibilities as it was for the so-called 'effete' of that generation. Whistler says 'Symphony in B flat' or 'Harmony in F major' or whatever it was he did say, and the mutton-sleeves raised lorgnettes and the gardenias leaned a little nearer to these bizarre effusions of black and white and pallid purples on small canvas. We have grown so used to that sort of juxtaposition of terms of art form and music, that we hesitate before elaborating on the obvious affinity between film and music. Though we should not hesitate. There is mechanical parallel as well as emotional to uphold us. The film relates to set measures and beat; it moves rhythmically or unrhythmically to certain measures, one-two-three or one-two-three-four or one-one or two-two etc. etc. We used to set our metronomes when we pounded away at Czerney [Czerny], to those various necessities. In the same way, it appears, some of the most spontaneous effects of the innovators of the Russian school of montage, were gained by being actually cut, re-cut, measured and re-measured with infinite pain and patience until just the desired time-element was hit upon. It is needless to point out that metronome-cutting in the hands of a mere mechanic, becomes tedious and meaningless in the extreme. While in the hands of a creative artist, *any* desired emotion effect can be achieved. The range is unparalleled and the best part of it all is, that film montage as *per se*, an art, stands at the moment, with a few brilliant exceptions, almost unexploited.

Yet people still say 'a picture' and 'a moving picture' with different pitch of voice as inevitably as a scholarly Chinaman can tone his actual vowels to mean things entirely different. To–day a 'moving picture' is still something indelibly linked with gutters and safety vaults and thrillers, in general, of the lowest order. Why not, instead of maligning this perfect instrument for the projection of a new and entirely complete 'art form', don't we get together and try to invent some way of getting something across that we may not be ashamed to confess openly we were 'thrilled' about? Why indeed? Have you for one, ever stopped to try it? Artists of this and this denomination step forward, patronage in gesture, brotherhood in bearing. Take the writer, he has a 'story', a drama, why don't we do this or this, why don't we do the other or that, why don't we, in other words listen to his receipt for reform of this malignity, film art? The professional writer, seldom if ever stops to puzzle out the difficult reasons for time–limits, effect of light and shadow that may or may not mean to him what it must inevitably mean to the director or the man behind the camera. Certain juxtaposition of event or character, he may insist, is inevitable to this or that effect. He will not and indeed can not, stop to realize that the film, rightly presented, is not a matter of one effect but many, nor of any one art but many. There is the actual drama presented through the actual people. But there is, odd anomaly, the camera man or the director again behind him, to play upon those presented and discussed persons of the drama, like a musician actually on a flute, an organ or a violin cello. Just to arrange characters and leave the effect to chance or some obsolete idea of stage acting, is, as we all know, fatal. A sensitive director must, it is obvious, have perfect instruments to play on. The great task is the finding of those instruments, but at last analysis, it is the director himself who does more than half the acting. The novice must learn primarily not only not to over–act, but actually you might almost say, not to act. To be able to strike a balance between inanition and subtle transference of the director's ideas into sympathetic action is no easy task. If the greatest actors have not yet appeared on the screen, it is not because the screen is not the perfect medium for the perfection of their art, or perhaps we should say, of a new, infinitely more subtle rendering of their art.

The modern film director does rely actually on musical notation. He wants an effect of ponderous stolidity. Well, what easier? He turns his camera (timed metronome beat) to get a man who is walking at normal pace, to walk faster or much, much slower. We all know something of those effects from the 'comics' which at least have made applicable the scherzo and allegro con molte [*sic*] of our old friend the comic–villain, hurled headlong over a precipice and a scherzo–ing down a sand bank. We have the precise staccato of the mincing step of the dandy or the billowing of the heroine's rallentando at the Blue Danube ball; she does not really dance as a rule to waltz time. To quote the much–quoted Pabst, speaking of a then little known, now over–acclaimed film star, 'she never walked slowly enough, she was too nervous. I had to make the whole cast suit their step to hers, then get the cameras to turn faster.' Here we have an actual demonstration of the film director's affinity with the concert meister's. G. W. Pabst beat out, like an orchestra conductor, a time for his cast and his staff to follow. This is perhaps an exotic instance. However it illustrates exactly the relationship between musical notation and film notation.

These are all somewhat superficial examples of the primary relationship of the film to music – the mere turning is a thing that can be regulated as well as the primary movements of the actors in the same way, I repeat, that you regulate a metronome to a certain dance or song time or that dance time to the metronome. The actual montage is a more subtle matter.

Screen montage or mounting is a difficult thing to talk of even to those who know everything about it. As we all know, the film is taken on long strips, miles long in certain exaggerated studios, much modified under saner American and European directorship. To boast of the miles of film used in certain pictures is to boast ignorance and waste. A normal director can get his effects by three or four 'takings'. Many for matters of economy and expediency, less. Most of Mr Macpherson's shots in *Borderline* were done once.

In the actual taking of the film and its actual normal projection, we can easily trace the one-two-three, or the one-two-three-four time or the largo or the allegro, the fortissimo or the piano–piano. Anyone with any normal sense of rhythm and balance can do that. The difficult thing to explain is the thing easy to see, that thing so apparently artless, that the spectator is often not even conscious of the vast and breakneck process of the achievement, nor the actual skill back of it. The minute and meticulous effect for instance that Mr Macpherson achieves with Pete, the negro and the waterfall, or the woman Astrid with the knife, are so naturalistic, I should say so 'natural' that they seem to the uninitiate, sheer 'tricks' or accidents. The effect of the negro, Pete, against the waterfall is achieved by a meticulous and painstaking effort on the part of the director, who along with the giants of German and Russian production is his own cutter and will not trust his 'montage' to a mere technician, however sympathetic.

Mr Macpherson, it is true, can not possibly, under his present working conditions, achieve the prolonged rhythms of many of the more commercial productions. It must be realized however that he himself is doing the actual work of montage, just as he has done the camera work and the scenario. The effect of the negro and the waterfall seems at times a mechanical super-imposition of short shots. It is not. An effect almost that of super-imposition but subtly differing from it is achieved by the meticulous cutting of three and four and five inch lengths of film and pasting these tiny strips together. The same sort of jagged lightening effect is give with Astrid with her dagger. The white woman is here, there, everywhere, the dagger is above, beneath, is all but in her heart or in the heart of her meritricious lover. This effect of immediacy is not achieved by a facile movement of a camera; that would be impossible. It is attained by the cutting and fitting of tiny strips of film, in very much the same manner that you would fit together a jig-saw puzzle. There is much of meticulous jig-saw puzzle technique in the best of the advanced German and Russian montage, though the uninitiated would not think of it as that.

It is easy to see that this form of montage required subtle alliance of patience, ingenuity, mechanical knowledge, *plus* the creative impulse. That combination of psychological opposites is rare. The most perfect and now almost historical example of creative originality plus technical ingenuity is that in *Ten Days*, the soldier, the gun, the lightning-like effect of repeated firing. The lift, fire, pause, lift, fire, etcetera, were repeated in metronomic precision. The almost instantaneous effect was Eisenstein's meticulous innovation – the cutting and fitting of minute strips of soldier, gun, gun-fire, soldier, gun.

My images and my explanations must be of necessity obvious. I only want to get across something of this musical affinity. I am sure that every one of us, however, has had this, so to speak, reversed and in the most excruciating manner. We all know what Miss Dorothy Richardson means when she speaks of the 'parish' cinema. We sometimes get, in these little out of the way houses, especially abroad, astonishingly up-to-date productions. Take a newer film rhythm, Continental, British or American and watch that run off to the tune of the old cow died of, played competently by the ex-policeman or the ex-convict or the post-master's daughter. Your eyes and ears are tortured, you execrate life and the weather, you manage either to dull out your perception or you rush out into a blinding snow-storm or a hail-storm or a volcanic eruption in preference.

In a word, you know exactly when film rhythm is NOT allied to music.

V

There is still another of the arts that is of necessity bone and fibre and nerve tissue of the film. The art of the drama, obviously. People come, go, enter rooms, pass through doors, look out of windows. The film has spoiled many of us for even competent stage production. We are not satisfied with a man and a window, or a woman and a door. We must see a man at a window and then a view of the man from the point of view, for instance, of someone *outside* that window. We must see a woman at the foot of a staircase, Lulu, for instance, in Pabst's *Pandora's Box*, and then we must see the entire stair case, perhaps slightly tilted, to give effect of dizzy eminence or of the state of mind of that woman, say, in the case of Lulu, waiting to fly up it.

We take so for granted the use of the term for instance, 'flying upstairs', that we do not realize how apt and arresting that phrase really is, until the camera again shows us that, actually, in vision or in retrospection or in anticipation, we 'fly' upstairs at a given warning or a given signal. So we can 'swim' in ecstasy and 'drown' actually in happiness.

I mean words, as such, have become weathered, the old stamp is obliterated, the image of king or of olive wreath or the actual stars or the actual oak branch have been worn off the coin. Words are all alike now, the words even one feels sometimes of a foreign language have lost 'virtue'. The film brings words back and how much more the actual matter of the drama. Words become again 'winged' indeed. We 'fly' upstairs with Lulu.

Man's first attempt at art was, as we all know, the famous 'picture' writing. We who have read and written until the sight of a printed page can give us cholic or delirium tremens can yet sit peacefully in the dim penumbra of a movie theatre. We go to the film now, on the whole, as a sort of sedative. When we get past this sedative period, we will perhaps begin, 'write' our novels and plays in 'pictures'. That is the aim psychologically to be striven toward. And this is why Kenneth Macpherson, as an innovator, is valuable. I do not mean for one moment to compare him with the magicians of the present-day screen. He can not compare with Pabst, Eisenstein, King Vidor or Pudovkin. He is a still younger man, he derives from these earlier sources. But he has contributed to the film in a lesser but perhaps finer way, as much as any of these masters. He has what not one of them has. His work is of necessity more restricted, but he himself strives toward the renaissance ideal and within his narrow limits, he attains it. He is writer, painter, mechanic, actor and trained camera man.

'*Borderline*', he said to me, 'has its striking defects, but it is not amateurish.' Kenneth Macpherson turned a personal little film in 1927. It is carefully packed away and he shows it to no one. A year later with the assistance of Bryher and some of the present *Borderline* group, notably Miss Blanche Lewin and Mr Robert Herring, he turned a full length five reel film. Here and there the work was excellent. That film has been shown privately and commented on too generously, Macpherson feels, by certain of the German and French and English critics. But he himself was not satisfied. There were high water marks that equalled much of the more advanced film work, there were gaps however, woeful discrepancies in style. Different styles of acting, camera work and projection grated on this sensitive critic, Kenneth Macpherson, and he abandoned *Foothills*. Soon after, he 'turned' a less ambitious film, a document of commercial lengths of his two pet Douracouli monkeys, and in 1930, the film *Borderline* which he confesses, within its limits, satisfied him. We say advisedly, 'within its limits'. We must insist on that qualification. The 'limits' are imposed by Macpherson on this very renaissance ideal. To begin, he could not possibly direct a large cast in a large setting and do his own camera work. Later he no doubt will widen out his horizon, his technique will gain and his technique will suffer. This we can safely certify. There is no modern film director who has at his finger tips the technical mastery of a half dozen arts.

It may be argued, of course, that this is no advantage, that a man can do one thing only with full technical efficiency. That is our present attitude, it has been carried to excess and it should be pointed out again and again, that the greatest artists of all time, those of renaissance Italy and quattrocento Florence in particular, argued differently.

If Mr Macpherson were a dilettante in any of the branches of the allied arts, the specialists' argument might hold. But he, oddly, is not nor is his film art a 'phase', though it must be remembered that Macpherson is the author of two creditable novels and critical essays of value. His actual 'trade' at one time was that of pen and ink designer. He considers drawing as the most natural medium, he drew prematurely as another child might pick out letters. He drew as another child might pick out sentences from books which he was told not to read. His mother had a quaint way of saying 'one artist is enough in the family'. He drew little pen and ink sketches on his school books and surreptitiously designed art and craft sort of posters and costumes behind locked doors at home. He had five years of creditable work in an office in the city, before he learnt that actually his poster and advertisement designs, were, practically speaking, of more value as a sheer commercial asset. He has been craftsman and designer. But his actual beginnings were those of the born 'artist'.

There was nothing, however, self-conscious or 'arty' about the child-Macpherson's attitude to these things. They were play to him and a little bit, rebellion.

VI

Borderline is a dream and perhaps when we say that we have said everything. The film is the art of dream portrayal and perhaps when we say that we have achieved the definition, the synthesis toward which we have been striving. Film is art of another dimension, including not only all art but including all life. Art and life walk hand in hand, drama and music, epic song and lyric rhythm, dance and the matter of science here again, as in some elaborate 'allegory' of the Florentines, take hands, twine in sisterly embrace before their one God, here electrically incarnated, LIGHT. Before the high-powered effect of [the] lamp (most modern expression of voltage and amperes) we have the whole run of antiquity, the whole run of nature, the whole run of modernity. Step into your dream and everything evolves, simplifies; the conglomerate experience of a day, of an hour, of a lifetime meet, rehearse some little scene of life or death or mimicry. We are not surprised, in a dream, to find Grandmama and our latest lover conversant over a forgotten sand heap. We are not surprised when our lost toy-boat swells to Lithuania proportion and when that dream symbol floats majestically across a field of blossoming clover. It does not surprise us to greet an incarnation of our tailor or our modiste in a little college class room, struggling with us, in past anxiety, over a page of logarithms long ago 'forgotten'. Nothing in a dream is forgotten. The film as Macpherson directs it, seems almost just some such process of 'remembering'.

The men and women in *Borderline* move, speak, turn, act, in set formula to a set rhythm. They are real people, terribly incarnated. In the little café through which Pete stalks and his mistress turns, gazing with great eyes at a vague conglomeration of whites, we have something of the nightmare that we would image [*sic*] a sensitive negro might have, on facing a room full of antagonistic presences. Adah is real, Pete is real, vital dynamic, indifferent in his giant mastery. Nevertheless, there is dream in them, nightmare, and that dream-nightmare permeates our consciousness although we may not know what it is or why. Pete and Adah escape from their little room and stand on a hill slope. Like a dream, the great negro head looms disproportionate, and water and cloud and rock and sky are all subsidiary to its being. Like a personal dream, gone further into the race dream, we see (with Pete) hill and cloud as, on that first day created. Dream merges with myth and Pete, regarding a fair heaven far from the uncreated turmoil of that small-town café, says quite logically, 'let there be light'. Light has been, it is obvious, created by that dark daemon, conversant with all nature since before the time of white man's beginning.

His small sweetheart in her little shop-bought, pull-on soft hat is complement to this radiant figure. She has sinned, she is not altogether god-like, but she is created on the hill-slope with him, apart from the nightmare of the uncoordinated white-folk.

The white-folk, of necessity, in this film take subsidiary value. Macpherson has decreed this with delicate irony and foresight. One wonders, watching the group (barmaid, café manageress and white demented Astrid) to which one of these three furies one would give the vote if called on. For a moment, the barmaid seems more degrading, with her slack morality and sweet gone stagnant. Then one sees at heart, she is a 'good sort' and one turns to the companion figure. The manageress, chewing her gum-drop in the face of the dæmonic fury of the deserted white woman, is callow, impervious to anything but double column of debit and credit; she is thinking not of Astrid and her fury nor of the black-white problem in any of its phases but simply, one feels, 'will Pete and that woman pay for their rooms'. Nevertheless, we must confess, 'business is business'; what of this third fury? Astrid, whose intemperate fury has lashed itself almost to dementia, screams ' it has all happened because these people are *black*'. Then for some inhuman sort of distinction, we let *her* go. It is impossible to choose between them.

The excellent characterization of the white lover, sensitively depicted by Mr Gavin Arthur, stresses again nightmare. He enters the café bar and the three café furies, above enumerated, are on an instant frozen from animation into noncommittal attention. We see these three figures, not as in themselves people or even symbols, as we ourselves might see them. We see them through the eyes of Thorne, whose dark sweetheart has been alienated from him, he imagines by the machinations of these three. The three women, barmaid, manageress, and mistress, become fixed symbols in his, in our minds. They become obvious allegory of drink, you might say, sordid calculation and unbridled jealousy. So for a moment ... then as in a dream, the scene shifts. Astrid rises in abstraction of fiend-rage and claws the air shouting, 'nigger-lover'. Thorne, her faithless lover, by dream juxtaposition is seen posed as if a noose were dangling him from a floor, which we feel reel beneath his feet by this parallel of contraries. A small touch perhaps, to be noticed by a few only, but bound to have subconscious significance. Macpherson, it is obvious, in just that flash is demonstrating a tardy aphorism. If a black man is hanged for loving a white woman, why should not a white man be likewise lynched for loving a black one? Dream, I say. These conclusions happen only in the higher fantasy of dream value and of ultimate dream justice.

VII

Then what is this film about and where does it lead us? Is it about two negroes in a small Continental mid-European town, who cross a back-water of small-town vice and malice and leave it cleansed and hallowed for their passing? No, it is nothing so defined, nothing so logical, nothing of such obvious sociological importance. Then what is this film about? Is it a series of psychological interpretations of white and white, neurotic and super-neurotic, lounge lizard and stalesweet of small-town Messalina? No, there is nothing so logical, nothing so dramatic, nothing so consistent. It is not about any of these things. There is no actual acute moment of crisis in a series of lightning-like 'flashes' where each, from the first moment of Astrid's frenzied entrance to the last beneficence of the giant-negro on the hill-top, is equally a crisis. Film and life are or should be indisseverable terms. In this modern attempt to synchronize thought and action, the inner turmoil and the other, the static physical passivity and the acute psychic activity, there is hardly one moment, one dramatic 'sentence' that outweighs another. Kenneth Macpherson has indeed achieved a sort of dynamic picture writing. His camera has recorded his pen and ink sketches with fluidity and precision. He 'wrote' his scenario in a series of some 1,000 pictures, the actual directions for each special picture read like captions. His script, in this, is unique and in itself a work of art. His is an innovation in the manner of approach to 'film art' that can not be over-estimated. He writes (I choose at random):

13.   Interior. Astrid's Room. Close up. *Fade in.* A door is flung open, and for a fraction of a moment, *Astrid's* shadowy face is seen. The impression must be of covertness and speed. Her hand rises across her face, and—

14.   Interior. Astrid's Room. Close up. *Panning.*—plunges forward through the room, past furniture to grasp—

15. Interior. Astrid's Room. Close up.—at a telephone receiver.

To the right of these little paragraphs, you must imagine delicate pen and ink drawings with arrow indications of direction; first a wild face, then a poised, tenuous hand, then the same hand lowered.

Or:

441. Interior. Pete's Room. Close up. *Pete's head,* still and dark, watches with wide eyes. Presently the tiniest confirmative nodding takes place. The eyebrows move, the eyes do not blink. He smiles.

442. Pete's Room. Close up. *Thorne* feels the tremendous healing of Pete's immense personality. The inner conflict is marked in nervous twitchings, amazement and unbelief that Pete is not gibing.

443. Interior. Pete's Room. Semi-shot. *Pete* lets his hand fall along his arm. He is still watching the conflict in Thorne. *Adah background.*

We have here an exquisite pen and ink sketch of a negro head almost filling the space of the little frame allotted. (There are usually about six of these drawings to a page.) Below it, three quarters, gazing out of the opposite side of the following 'frame' or 'shot', we have a balancing white face, suggesting almost equal mobility and suggestiveness. Beneath that again is the semi-shot of the standing negro, with suggested café-background and an indefinite woman form.

I have chosen at random these six descriptive captions. There are exactly 910 of them in the finished script. This does not include numerous side drawings of exterior effects, of 'repeats' and so on. I do not think there can be any doubt in the mind, even of the most sceptical, that film, in this case at any rate, is allied in the most obvious manner to two of the giant 'arts'. Kenneth Macpherson's mastery of both descriptive writing and drawing can not be deprecated. Nor can you for one moment be in doubt of the intense value of the dramatic directorship. Pen and ink sketches cannot actually and psychically move nor can words. There can be no doubt that Macpherson's film does. So dynamically does it move that it seems, at times, as if he had almost over-stepped the bounds even of the most exaggerated screen values. His posed figures are seething with mental turmoil and with psychic discord. They seem sometimes, at rest, to be about to fall forward and annihilate us with their intensity as glacier edge may give some sort of warning to those attuned to natural premonitions. Macpherson seems at times, in fact, to overstep the bounds of even the most intense screen dynamics. As one of his German contemporaries remarked, on seeing a hurried informal 'showing' of the film at Territet, 'you have achieved a nightmare and a dream. I congratulate you'.

You may consider yourself justified in remarking 'and is that achievement?' I may consider myself justified in answering, 'the greatest'. Ibsen achieved that same effect of dream and nightmare. Certain of the Russain dramatists have done so. This quality is rare in all art. The welding of the psychic or super-normal to the things of precise every-day existence is Kenneth Macpherson's rare gift. His is no cheap conjurer's box of super-imposition and shadow-ghost. An Ibsen introduces no Ghost into his drama of that name. Nor does Macpherson any actual 'borderline' case into his film *Borderline*. Astrid, the woman, terribly incarnated and wracked with the most banal of feminine vices, jealousy, yet achieves through the careful lighting, posing and camera-work of Macpherson, an entity, we might almost say, did we not feel it necessary to fight shy of that word, 'astral' in its effect. His deserted white woman as she moves among odd pieces of lodging house furniture, sits at a table, listens at a door or runs across a room to fall, draped in the most obvious of imported London or Paris embroidered shawls, is a woman of the drama, of the screen, yet like the Hedda of Ibsen or any of the Hildas or Hedwigs, she achieves through the actual fitness of her materialized setting, furniture, blowing window curtain, stuffed gull and overcrowded mantle-piece, something more obviously out of the world than any pantomime effect of cloud spook off could ever hope to attain. Even that marvellous playing with distorted personalities in the *Student of Prague*, for instance, startling and dramatic as that was, seems in retrospect, facile and obvious. Macpherson does not need to superimpose figure and shadow figure as has been so excellently done in some of the Swedish and German productions. The camera 'truquage' would be, in his case, a kind of psychic cheating. Kenneth Macpherson's figures move consistently, as in a dream or nightmare, because of some intrinsic dynamic virtue of his own inner vision.

Vol. VII, no. 5   November 1930

~~~~~~

Kenneth Macpherson

AS IS

Talking about one's own work is a bore – especially when that work lies behind, completed, and therefore, to oneself, no longer living. This funny business about *Borderline*. The reviews have been coming in, and there seem to be deductions worth making in respect of film criticism in general. But first it will be necessary to go back, and that is a pity. Please do not think I wish to impose myself or my personal ideas on you or on anybody. It is simply that the two sides which we know every question has, are here remarkably manifest, with rather surprising results.

Borderline began to be composed about eighteen months ago. It was finished in June of this year. Eighteen months ago Europe was unaware, and so was I, of Eisenstein's now commonly accepted, though little understood, theory of over-tonal montage. Eighteen months ago I decided to make *Borderline* with a 'subjective use of inference'. By this I meant that instead of the method of externalised observation, dealing with objects, I was going to take my film into the minds of the people in it, making it not so much a film of 'mental processes' as to insist on a mental condition. To take the action, the observation, the deduction, the reference, into the labyrinth of the human mind, with its queer impulses and tricks, its unreliability, its stresses and obsessions, its half-formed deductions, its glibness, its occasional amnesia, its fantasy, suppressions and desires.

Could this be done. Eighteen months ago I said firmly; Yes, it can. And to-day, having made *Borderline*, I repeat, yes, it can. It had not been done, it had not been touched, except in Pabst's frankly psycho-analytical film, *Secrets of the Soul*, which met with, if anything, greater derision among experienced critics. And there, again, it had been treated objectively, from outside, from the clinical point of view. There was something of it in *Uberfall* (*Accident*), which has also been known as *Assault and Battery*. Suggestion dominated this film. Suggestion dominated *Borderline*. *Borderline*'s suggestion, however, was of conflict, of mental wars, of hate and enmity. *Borderline* was to be jagged. *Uberfall*, a much shorter film, was simplified. It dealt with one emotion only – that of fear.

Eighteen months ago everybody was saying the silent film had reached perfection. It had no further to go. When in reality it had only reached the first stage in an intensive development. And oddly enough, it was not until after the talkies had swept the silent film out of existence, that *Borderline*, perhaps the only really 'avant-garde' film ever made, came about. I say this deliberately, and without false pride – indeed without any pride. I have said that *Borderline* has many faults. How idiotic to pretend that it has not. Traversing new ground, it had all the rawness of a pioneer. But pioneer it was. And as I have said to my critics, in ten years time, the 'obscurity' of which they complain will be plain as punch. And I think it will take ten years for them to recognise it.

But the faults of *Borderline* are not the faults that have been complained of. As a matter of fact some of what I call its faults have been condoned or praised. And what I know to be good has been almost unanimously ignored or condemned. But that was as I expected. I know what my purpose was and I know exactly where I have achieved it. You must give me credit for that amount of integrity after these intensive years of study and analysis. You may argue that even if I have achieved my purpose, is it worth while when the result is only partly comprehensible? For that I have no answer vehement enough. Yes, yes, yes. Comprehensibility. What is it? A demand for concessions. Simplicity, what is that? A demand for concessions. Simplicity is for children. Simplicity is for tired people. And everything in life is done for them. Everything is made more ordinary, more shallow, more trivial for these souls who demand facile understanding. *Everything in life is done for them!* And the result is we stand quite still and our minds lie fallow and soggy with traditions – more concessions – and wonderful innovations come about and we have neither the will nor wit to use them. I say that the essence of film art is not and can never be so simple as 'simplicity'. These rudimentary 'power-illusions' are for the weakest of the weak. Simplicity is easy to cope with, and sometimes and often it has a rightful place. But the film, to me, and to anybody who bothers to think twice, is *life*, and breathes with the breath of life, and life is not simple, and life cannot be kept within the shallow limits of form or formulae.

Borderline, then, whether you like it or not, is life. To a mind unaware of *nuance*, to a one-track mind, it would naturally appear chaotic. I do not deny for a moment that it is chaotic. It was intended to be. But over this chaos rings and reverberates one pure, loud, sullen, note. I had no specific name for it, but now we know it is overtone. Some of the strips contain pictures so simple, so almost uninteresting, that alone they would seem to have no justification. But, nevertheless, they have. Some, again, are pictorially luscious. These images have never 'just happened'. It was not for nothing that I made a thousand or more drawings. I worked in terms of *tension*. My drawings, and my images were composed to have no static value. As I have said in an article in *The Architectural Review* for November, the film unit, or in this case, film strip, or scene, cannot be thought of as a static quantity. Its essential character is *transferential*, and it is this transferential character which alone has informed the structure. Static forms have been used, certainly. And very often. But solely to drive forward the mental impetus.

And, what is interesting to me, *Borderline*, with its 'meaningless obscurity', it's 'vague symbolism', etc. etc., has met with none of these objections among the Germans. Their minds, it is true, work differently. They are attuned to the mental, especially in its more sombre aspects. But among quite undistinguished Germans there has been an appreciation that has been lacking in the most enlightened English. I think some of my friends in England are honestly abashed by it. Kindly enough, I think they feel I have let myself down and even displayed some ignorance or foolishness. So many of them have evaded me since it was shown, or made some fleeting allusion. And this has interested me keenly. I do believe that England has definitely not the approach to things of the mind that one or two other peoples have, notably the Germanic countries and the Jews. The mental sciences, psycho-analysis, for example, seem not quite happy in their growth, somehow climatically softened and changed. The Englishman rejects too much of his emotional being, and is embarrassed if he has to be brought face to face with it. His fear of 'morbidity' and the neurotic is a race neurosis which sets him at a disadvantage when it comes to emotional, or mental-emotional experience. This attitude is clearly evident among my critics. They reject *Borderline*, not because it is complex – for its power is its complexity, its 'unexplainedness' – like something seen through a window or a keyhole; but because it is a film of sub-conscious reasoning. And if, among the English, the sub-consciousness is ruefully admitted, for some definitely social reason it 'is not to be condoned'!

Drama, of which only part filters through. That, to my mind, alone constitutes drama. There is much more to it than is ever seen – as there would be in life. Film, stage and literature have made bed-rock of the false principle of *complete enaction*. There is no complete enaction in life. There are hundreds of layers, inferences and associations, enmeshing everything into everything. Germany understood this. The lovely words of Pabst have invalidated all destructive carping. 'You must be proud of your work!' – and to my abashed 'I had not thought of it like that', 'You *must* be proud!'

PART 6

Cinema and Psychoanalysis

INTRODUCTION

Laura Marcus

The intimate, and intricate, connections between psychoanalysis, film and film theory begin with the emergence of both psychoanalysis and cinema at the end of the nineteenth century – twin sciences and technologies of fantasy, dream, virtual reality and screen memory.[1] *Close Up*, whose project was substantially informed by psychoanalytic thought and theory, played a significant role in the development of this symbiotic relationship. Macpherson, Bryher and H.D. were all committed to psychoanalytic ideas before they founded the journal. H.D. and Bryher had undergone formal analysis in the 1920s and were close to the psychologist and sexologist Havelock Ellis.[2] Their interests in film were strongly guided by their particular approaches to psychoanalysis. Macpherson's two early novels, *Poolreflection* and *Gaunt Island* (both published in 1927), for example, are studies of 'abnormal' family relationships and incestuous desires.[3] Their techniques are in large part modelled on H.D.'s prose writing, with its explorations of mirroring relationships and its palimpsestic 'superimpositions' of different times and spaces.[4] These forms had their cinematic counterpart in Macpherson's POOL films.

Where H.D. found in psychoanalysis and film a means of access to hidden, 'occulted' realities, Bryher was more concerned with psychoanalysis, cinema and education or, in her terms, 'development'.[5] In her writings, psychoanalysis is presented as a way of freeing individuals and cultures from their stultifying histories and readying them for modernity; she believed that psychoanalysis should inform teaching at all levels. Bryher represents her analysis with Hanns Sachs, undertaken between 1928 and 1932, as a further adventure in an adventurous life: 'We tried to dig down to the bones of the past and to excavate memories in the process. Sometimes an episode came to light, then there would be dreary weeks when the grains of sand we sifted had no meaning.'[6]

Bryher's meetings with the 'masters' of psychoanalysis are, indeed, represented as the happy outcome of her embrace of modernity, with its excitement and dangers. 'I met Freud through flying and not through any serious considerations of the soul!', she writes, describing the plane journey she and Macpherson took from Venice to Vienna in May 1927 in the early days of air travel.[7] A trip at the end of that year to Berlin resulted in an invitation to Pabst's house, where Bryher met the 'quiet, almost Eastern-looking figure sitting in one corner who was afterwards to be my analyst, Dr. Hanns Sachs', who 'had recently been acting as adviser on the first attempt to make a psychoanalytic film, *Secrets of a Soul*'.[8] The encounter with the analyst takes place, then, in the context of film and, moreover, in the context of a film about psychoanalysis.

Pabst's *Secrets of a Soul* is itself a key moment in the relationship between cinema and psychoanalysis. In 1925 the Freudian analyst Karl Abraham was approached by

Eric Neumann of Ufa about the possibility of a film exploring psychoanalytic concepts. Letters between Abraham and Freud chart Abraham's growing enthusiasm for the project and Freud's continuing resistance: 'My chief objection is still that I do not believe that satisfactory plastic representation of our abstractions is at all possible.'[9] By mid-1925, Hanns Sachs had, along with Abraham, become centrally involved in the making of the film, and it was he who wrote the pamphlet which accompanied it and explained some of the psychoanalytic concepts it explored.[10] The production of an accompanying, explanatory monograph was taken up by the POOL group in 1930, when H.D. wrote the pamphlet intended to both publicize and explain the film *Borderline*, defined by Macpherson as an attempt at something which 'had not been done, had not been touched, except in Pabst's frankly psychoanalytic film, *Secrets of a Soul*'.[11]

Hanns Sachs thus influenced *Close Up* at many crucial points. Bryher's analysis with Sachs lasted for almost the entire duration of *Close Up*'s existence, moving between Berlin and Switzerland, in a pattern which also governed Bryher's, and to a certain extent H.D.'s and Macpherson's, reception of cinema. As Anne Friedberg shows, Macpherson's 'take' on Eisenstein's work, the core of *Close Up*'s theoretical project, was mediated largely through Sachs's Freudian theories, with Macpherson using Sachs's reading of a sequence from *Potemkin* to illustrate the concept of 'overtonal montage' in his introduction to Eisenstein's 'The Fourth Dimension in the Kino'.[12]

Sachs discusses Eisenstein's film in the first of the three pieces he wrote for *Close Up*, 'Film Psychology', as an example of the way in which a seemingly insignificant detail becomes an 'indispensable means of expression'.[13] The interest of the episode from *Potemkin* is in part that it contributes to the film's powerful affect not through the depiction of a facial expression but by means of a gesture or a reflex, the guard's turning of his head to watch the proceedings which 'betrays, however slightly, his character of a human-being'. The face of things, Sachs suggests, is revealed not through facial expression, as it is for the actor in the theatre, where the face 'works', as the phrase has it, in the expression of emotion, but in the equivalence between the film actor and 'inanimate' things.

The term 'betrays' relates Sachs's article to the accounts of unconscious gestures and 'symptomatic acts' that run throughout Freud's writings, as in the following passage from his case-history '*Dora*':

> When I set myself the task of bringing to light what human beings keep hidden within them, not by the compelling power of psychosis, but by observing what they say and what they show, I thought the task was a harder one than it really is. He that has eyes to see and ears to hear may convince himself that no mortal can keep a secret. If his lips are silent, he chatters with his finger-tips; betrayal oozes out of him at every pore. And thus the task of making conscious the most hidden recesses of the mind is one which it is quite possible to accomplish.[14]

The chattering fingertips to which Freud calls attention are strongly reminiscent of the language of gesture in the silent cinema and of the workings of the close-up in film aesthetics more generally. The film, Sachs suggests, is 'revealed as a kind of time-microscope, that is to say, it shows us clearly and unmistakably things that are to be found in life but that ordinarily escape our notice'.[15]

Sachs's discussion in this article also echoes the theories of a number of the most influential cultural and film critics. The cinema's (and, more specifically, the close-up's) revelations of the 'hidden mainsprings of a life which we had thought we already knew so well'[16] appear frequently, for example, in the work of the Hungarian film theorist Béla Balázs, whose first writings on cinema were published in the early 1920s. Balázs's expressive, 'physiognomic' aesthetics are substantially concerned with cinematic representations of 'the face of man' and 'the face of things'. In *Theory of the Film*, a summation of earlier writings, Balázs writes of Eisenstein's use of 'metaphors' in *Battleship Potemkin* – the 'gesture' made by small sailing-boats to the battleship, and the 'physiognomy' of objects:

> In the immortal scene in Eisenstein's *Battleship Potemkin* where dead and wounded are lying on the great flight of steps, the set-up shows bloodstained and tearstained human faces. Then it shows the Cossacks who fire on the crowd. But it shows only their boots. Not men, mere boots trample down those human faces. The boots have such oafish, stupid, base physiognomies that the spectator clenches his fists in anger. Such is the effect of picture-metaphors.[17]

In a section on 'microphysiognomy' in his writings of the 1920s, Balázs's physiognomic aesthetics is given a distinctly psychoanalytic inflection:

> But the camera moved closer and, behold, within the face it reveals partial physiognomies which betray something different than the total expression had tried to suggest. In vain he knits his brow and flashes his eyes. The camera moves in even closer, isolating his chin, showing him as a coward and a weakling. A delicate smile governs the total expression. But nostrils, earlobes and neck have their own face. And shown in isolation, they betray a hidden crudeness, a barely disguised stupidity. In such detailed analysis, the 'general impression' will not cover up ... The camera close-up aims at the uncontrolled small areas of the face; thus it is able to photograph the subconscious.[18]

Balázs's reflections here, as Gertud Koch notes, probably inspired Walter Benjamin's speculations on the relationship between the 'optical' and psychoanalytic unconscious.[19] In 'A Small History of Photography', Benjamin writes: 'Photography, with its devices of slow motion and enlargement, reveals the secret. It is through photography that we first discover the existence of this optical unconscious, just as we discover the instinctual unconscious through psychoanalysis.' Even, or especially, in scientific photography, photography reveals 'the physiognomic aspect of visual worlds which dwell in the smallest things, meaningful but covert enough to find a hiding place in waking dreams'.[20] 'The work of art in the age of mechanical reproduction' explores the power of film, substantially through the devices of the close-up and slow motion, to reveal both the known and unknown aspects of the phenomenal world:

> Evidently a different nature opens itself to the camera than opens to the naked eye – if only because an unconsciously penetrated space is substituted for a

space consciously explored by man. ... The camera introduces us to unconscious optics as does psychoanalysis to unconscious impulses.[21]

For Siegfried Kracauer, whose *Theory of Film*, published in 1960, recapitulates many of his earlier responses to the cinema, the 'revelations' of which film is capable include: the 'possibilities' inherent in inanimate objects, discovered primarily through the close-up;[22] the depiction of the transient and fleeting, 'the least permanent components of our environment';[23] the familiar made strange, 'virgin impressions emerging from the abyss of nearness',[24] 'rendering visible what is normally drowned in inner agitation'.[25]

A psychoanalytic emphasis on the revelation of the habitually concealed or occluded is thus combined with a political focus, developed in Russian Formalist and Brechtian theories, on the role of art in 'making strange' the familiar word and world, and on art's 'alienation' effects. In writing about film, such theories become intimately linked with the concept of the 'close-up' which, in Benjamin's words, 'burst asunder' the 'prison-world' of the habitual 'by the dynamite of the tenth of a second'.[26] Kracauer makes a very similar point in *Theory of Film:*

> Huge close-ups reveal new and unsuspected formations of matter ... Such images blow up our environment in a double sense: they enlarge it literally; and in doing so, they blast the prison of conventional reality, opening up expanses which we have explored at best in dreams before.[27]

The close-up, like the dream-work for Freud, thus effects something like a 'transvaluation of all values', making the invisible visible, the familiar unfamiliar, the distant proximate.[28] The habitual scale of values is also overturned because film, like the unconscious, does not know the 'trivial' detail; each image captured by the camera or the memory speaks its own truth or conceals another.[29] '*Dream-displacement* and *dream-condensation* are the two governing factors to whose activity we may in essence ascribe the form assumed by dreams,' Freud writes in *The Interpretation of Dreams*.[30] In his account of Lubitsch's *Drei Frauen* Sachs finds the equivalent to the 'displacement' of the Freudian dream-work in a further 'symptomatic act':

> The woman says: 'Undress yourself', and the man 'I don't want to', but the treatment is so contrived that both can act as if the behaviour of the other were simply the playfulness of idle fingers. ... For [the onlooker] the proceedings are clear enough, and this 'displacement' is exactly one of those means of expression, to which Freud first called attention, used by the unconscious everywhere, for instance, in dreams and in jest, to elude conscious recognition. The film seems to be a new way of driving mankind to conscious recognition.[31]

The relationship between unconscious and conscious knowledges is one of Sachs's preoccupations in his film articles. He is at pains to note that directors and spectators do not normally construct and recognize Freudian structures and concepts as a result of awareness of psychoanalytic theory; the work of symbolic and symptomatic representation rather inheres in the gesture or object itself. In 'Film Psychology' Sachs suggests that the film-work functions not only by analogy but by contrast with the dream-work. While the dream disguises unconscious wishes and desires as a way of eluding the censor, the film reveals them. In this sense, the film could be said to be closer to dream-interpretation, with its emancipatory potential, than to the dream itself.

The plethora of psychoanalytic and psychological writings on dreams and dream-life in the early twentieth century found new forms of assocation and analogy in film. For the Surrealists, film both simulated dreams and brought dream-life into waking life. In 1930 Antonin Artaud wrote: 'If the cinema is not made to interpret dreams or what pertains to the realm of dreams in conscious life, it does not exist.' [32] This formulation is echoed in H.D.'s claim, in 'The *Borderline* Pamphlet', that 'the film is the art of dream portrayal and perhaps when we say that we have achieved the definition, the synthesis toward which we have been striving.'[33]

Hanns Sachs's introduction to psychoanalysis had come with his reading of Freud's *The Interpretation of Dreams* in 1904. He abandoned his law career in its early stages and followed Freud into psychoanalytic work, initially through writing and editing, and, in 1920, through the training of analysts. Freud's 'dream-book' remained a key text for him, as did Freud's essay 'The Creative Writer and Day-dreaming' (1908 [1907]). Fascinated by the applications of psychoanalysis to the creative process and to the reception of works of art, and by the concept of the work of art as a 'collective day-dream', Sachs explored the idea of 'day-dreams in common'.[34] His starting-point was Freud's speculation that literary works (more particularly, popular and genre narratives) are disguised versions of egoistic daydreams and fantasies and that 'the essential *ars poetica* lies in the technique of overcoming the feeling of repulsion in us which is undoubtedly connected with the barriers that rise between each single ego and the others'. 'It may even be', Freud suggested, 'that not a little of this effect [catharsis] is due to the writer's enabling us thenceforward to enjoy our own day-dreams without self-reproach or shame.'[35]

These arguments clearly inform Sachs's article on 'Kitsch', in which he translates Freud's ideas about popular fiction into an account of popular film, and Freud's assertion that 'a happy person never phantasies, only an unsatisfied one', into the statement that 'Kitsch is the exploitation of daydreams by those who never had any.' The distinction between Kitsch and film as art is thus to be most reliably drawn, Sachs argues, as a question of the artist's relationship to his or her material:

> The artist, so much we believe ourselves to know, is impelled to creative activity by the sense of guilt attached to his day-dreams. Any one who produces Kitsch obviously has no such sense of guilt to contend with, he is freer in relation to the fantasy contents of his production: that is to say, he is bound to it by far less inward sympathy.[36]

Sachs's earlier writings on daydreams and the creative process focus on the human desire to collectivize the burden of primal, Oedipal 'guilt', overcoming, in Freud's words, 'the barriers that rise between each single ego and the others'. In the early 1930s Sachs shifts Freud's arguments to suggest not only an absence of 'guilt' on the part of the producer of kitsch but a cynical manipulation of fantasy. (There are echoes here of Siegfried Kracauer's claim, in his 'The Little Shopgirls Go to the Movies', that 'stupid and unreal fantasies are the *daydreams of society*, in which its actual reality comes to the fore and its otherwise repressed wishes take on form.'[37]) The public which receives kitsch films is, Sachs suggests, largely drawn by 'the borrowed class idea'; he uses the example of German military farces to explore the ways in which 'the lower, suppressed classes, in so far as they are not educated to independent class-consciousness, accept and firmly adhere to the ideals of the higher class which governs them'. Hesitant of 'suggest[ing] that the explanation is to be sought in the political temper, which is responsible for these and many other aberrations', Sachs nonetheless alludes to the political dangers of kitsch, with its refusal to recognize mental and ethical conflict, ambivalence and choice. In 1932, the year in which his article on 'Kitsch' was published, Sachs left Germany for the United States, where he lived until his death in 1947.

The relationship of cinema to other kinds of dream and fantasy is the subject of the remaining articles in this section. Barbara Low, one of the first British Freudians and an analysand of Sachs, was a friend of Bryher's and Dorothy Richardson's. Her book *The Unconscious in Action*, which explored the applications of psychoanalysis to education, was published in 1928.[38] While Bryher and Richardson viewed film as a potentially beneficial educational medium, Low's 'Mind-growth or Mind-mechanization?' is highly critical of the cinema and sceptical of its educational values.[39] Where Robert Herring celebrates the 'magic' of the cinema, Low sees this as its most dangerous aspect, prolonging 'the period of unconditional omnipotence' and threatening the necessary transition (for the individual in 'civilization') from the pleasure to the reality principle:

> It is the *method* of the moving picture which brings about so vividly the sense of wish-fulfilment as if by magic ... the Film's simplifications and problem-solving creates the fantasy that the spectator's wishes are or can be, fulfilled, and this helps to maintain his omnipotence and narcissism, leading to a regressive attitude.[40]

Low's equation of the child and the 'primitive', with their belief in 'magic', is made by a number of commentators at this time, who represent the new medium of the film as more 'primitive' and childlike than the arts of civilization which it has overtaken in the popular imagination. The result of technological progress, in this account, is psychical regression.[41]

In their articles for *Close Up* (reprinted here), L. Saalschutz and C.J. Pennethorne Hughes pursue, more positively, the idea of film as mass fantasy, collective daydream and the 'transmuted and regulated dream life' of the people. Saalschutz attempts to map Freud's model of the dream-work onto film techniques. Silent cinema, he suggests, represents unconscious life; sound film, consciousness. 'The film is the dream of the post-war world,' Pennethorne Hughes writes, suggesting not only that films and dreams are analogous structures, but that the film has in some sense replaced the dream in and for the twentieth century. If the film stands in for the dream, he argues, it must replicate its structures; the analogy is thus used as an argument against the incursions of polychrome and of sound into the silent, monochromatic, two-dimensional world of the film. The model of the dream, then, becomes the necessary control upon technological madness. Conversely, while dreams themselves for the most part elude manipulation, the film, it is suggested, is a dream which can be shaped to new ends, transforming 'the subconscious ... of the people', turning their bad dreams into good ones.[42]

Vol. I, no. 3   September 1927

Barbara Low

MIND-GROWTH OR MIND-MECHANIZATION?
THE CINEMA IN EDUCATION

An interesting viewpoint which, though not altogether in accordance with our own beliefs, yet states one side of the educational question with thoroughness and insight. Miss Low is a Member of the British Psychological Society, Hon. Secretary to the Educational Section of the British Psychological Society, Executive Member of the Committee for Psychological Research and the Author of 'An Outline of the FREUDIAN THEORY', etc. etc.

The art of the Cinema and its swift development may be ranked as one of the most remarkable features of our latter-day civilization. No one can dispute, nor would even wish to, the enormous hold the 'Pictures' exert upon the minds and interest of the adult population – whether white, black, or of any intervening shade – the world over; nor can there be a question as to the new spheres of experience opened up by means of this medium; nor the high degree to which human skill and creative power have developed in this connection. Whether we appreciate it or not, this fact is overwhelmingly established, that the Cinema-art has made a place for itself as a rival to – it may be a triumphant victor over – all the various other arts which make appeal to mankind, and has even surpassed in strength and extent that appeal to a degree hitherto unknown. So far, so good; or, if not so good in all eyes, it is a situation to be accepted, studied, and turned to the very best account. Humanity, in all ages, has pursued its pleasure and will continue so to do, in the mass aiming at the greatest amount of satisfaction with the least output of effort, a goal most satisfactorily achieved via the path of the 'Pictures'. If in addition, wider experience, more accurate realization of life in its various manifestations, more ready power of contact can be obtained, few will deny the legitimacy of this form of pleasure-getting by the adult man or woman;— the *adult* – and here we are face to face with the problem: is the adult's fare necessarily nourishment for the *child*?

The idea of the child as the 'little man' – the adult in a backward stage – has long been abandoned by all who can observe and judge, and the profounder aspects of mind which the psychology of the unconscious has revealed must convince us that the child has its own destiny to fulfil, and if it misses essential phases of childhood-development it will inevitably suffer loss, and may be, serious disharmony, when adult. The truth grasped by the Jesuits, namely, that the early years are all-important in shaping character-trends, has been so amply reinforced by modern science that we are forced to value educational methods and agencies according as they help or hinder the developing mind; yet it is notable that such a valuation has hardly been considered by the enthusiasts, educational and 'lay', who wholeheartedly welcome the cinema for educational usage.

Perhaps the first problem is to understand the meaning of the demand for the Cinema-entertainment, to what this is a reaction. Some answer is afforded by study of adult modern communities in which we see a widespread demand for easy and effortless entertainment characterized by incessant variety and sensationalism. The vastly popular variety entertainment, the cabaret show, the jazzband, the modern dance, much of the drama of the moment, pictorial art and literature, and, above all, the contemporary Press bear the characteristics already mentioned. In the individual we can note much the same: that is the demand for, and enjoyment of, sensationalism, alternating with a negativism or so-called cynicism covering a strong but repressed emotional attitude. Thus we may see in the excessive demand for the Cinema, both a *symptom* of this prevalent attitude, and a *gratification* of the wishes creating that attitude: it is by investigating along these lines that we may come to understand some of the deeper significance of the problem.

But before dealing with these more complex issues let us consider a moment the more obvious aspects. Everyone agrees on certain predominant characteristics of the Cinema-entertainment: Its overpowering appeal to the eye and correspondingly small demand upon intellectual processes; its arbitrary and therefore false, simplification; its confusion of values; the film knows no light and shade; features which are striking to the eye, however superficial or trivial in content, however subsidiary to the main theme, may equal in value or even submerge the really significant aspects; its perpetual variety; and finally the illusion of timelessness due in the first place to the fact that real human beings are never present, only simulacra, and in the second place to swiftly culminating happenings without intermediate phases of slow elaboration.

In the face of this we must ask, is this type of experience, with such characteristic features, suited to either the demand of the child-mind or to its harmonious development? The child as such must learn to develop beyond its purely visual pleasures – a pleasure which along with taste and touch predominates in the first stages of life; it must gain power of concentration, of continuity of interest, in place of the appeal made by variety. As a child it is incapable of a true sense of proportion or understanding of slow development leading towards a wished for goal: but it is just these capacities we must seek to develop if the child is to become adult in the true sense of the word, instead of that product so prevalent in the modern world, the Peter Pan type, the man with the child-mentality.

And now to return to those influences and reactions which are still more significant – concealed from ordinary observation. In the human being's development, one of the most important stages is that of belief in magic, a stage characteristic of the infant, the very young child, the primitive and to some extent, though disguised, of the 'Civilized' adult. It is the stage named by Ferenczi, the famous Hungarian psycho-analyst, 'the period of unconditional omnipotence': a period wherein life and all its dearest needs and wishes are maintained from some mysterious external source, without human effort. It is clear that such a condition is an actuality in the earliest months of life; a little later this stage is sadly left behind and the child must learn through bitter necessity that achievement is reached only through effort; yet there remains still, and throughout life, some of this 'omnipotence' wish (manifested for instance, in such forms as the universal interest in gambling, in fortune-telling, in prophecy, in 'luck'). Now it is a matter vitally affecting harmonious development how far such an attitude becomes dominant, for it is one based on the pleasure-principle and antagonistic to reality. Those who cling to their 'Omnipotence' stage with the accompanying egocentricity, never get reconciled to the renunciation of their unconscious irrational wishes and 'on the slightest provocation feel themselves insulted and slighted and regard themselves as step-children of fate, because they cannot remain her only or favourite children'.

It is not difficult to see that the characteristics of the Cinema referred to above are just those which must foster and develop this magic 'omnipotence' sense, to a greater degree than is possible in the case of fairy-tale, novel, drama, or picture, and does so independently, to a large degree, of the *theme* dealt with by the film. It is the *method* of the moving picture which brings about so vividly the sense of wish-fulfilment as by magic. The Cinema's business is to give a solution to all problems, an answer to all questions, and a key to every locked door. Real life is complex, unselective, often baffling to our curiosity and regardless of our desires; the Film's simplifications and problem-solving creates the fantasy that the spectator's wishes are or can be, fulfilled, and this helps to maintain his omnipotence and narcissism, leading to a regressive attitude: That is to say a return to the pleasure-seeking infancy with its magically fulfilled desires, since it is always easier for the Ego to retread known paths which have already yielded pleasure than to go forward on paths yet untried and calling for effort. But this latter process is essential to the child's development and through it alone can he attain to mental maturity. An even more serious consequence is the disintegration which must result from the failure of the pleasure-impulse to reach to, and co-operate with, the level of development attained by the rest of the personality – that 'split' which is so marked a feature of the neurotic. By an emotional expenditure of an infantile nature only (that is, narcissistic emotion unrelated to external reality and very easily obtained) the emotional life remains undeveloped: inadequate and extravagant at one and the same time.

It will, perhaps, appear startling to class together those films which are true to human and scientific reality and the crudely false melodrama or romance. Undoubtedly there is a world of difference as regards the consciously-felt effects, but it is possible for the same unconscious effects to be produced in both cases since the mechanism at work is identical. In the film of the Scott Expedition, than which nothing could be more beautiful and more moving as far as the pictures themselves are concerned, all the elements of magic achievement, of simplification, of rapid solution are present just as in other films. And this criticism holds good, though to a far less degree, in nature films, geographical films, and films illustrating mechanical processes. A small investigation recently carried out among school children of different types, and of ages varying from eight to twelve, revealed interestingly the child's capacity for distortion: seventy per cent of the children believed that such processes as the development of the chick from the egg, of the fish from the spawn, of the pearl within the oyster, of nest-building and so forth, took just the time which elapsed in the showing of the films, even though each step in the process was elaborated. And this is inevitable since the film, operating in a mechanical universe, fills the gaps, rounds all corners, and presents persons and events in the neatest way, like so many brown paper parcels; as [a] result, there is lack of emotional contact both in the production and the spectator. Closely related to the above is another aspect of the film which has much significance for the deeper human impulses, namely its relation to time. Research into the unconscious of man has revealed that the idea of time (and its twin-companion death) is among the most deeply-repressed material of the mind, and it is only by the process of becoming adult that a realization and acceptance of time becomes possible. If from a very early stage the child is strengthened in his repression so much the more difficult for him is recognition of reality. Bearing upon another of the most powerful impulses is that character of the film, already referred to, which demands from the spectator an almost exclusive visual attention. The powerful rôle played by curiosity in the early life of the child, developed and gratified by seeing and looking, is maintained by means of the films' dominant appeal, and in thus obtaining and continuing his gratification he is assisted in remaining at the infantile curiosity-level.

In the light of such effects, conscious and unconscious (and I have here space to touch upon a few only), produced by the film it is surely worth while to consider whether, and to what degree, we are prepared to make it a part of our educational system. The adult, educated or ignorant, in virtue of being adult must be free to chose his own pursuits and pleasures, but in educating the child we are forcing upon him experience which he is not in position to evaluate: the justification is if our wider and deeper experience convinces us that what we offer will assist the best and truest development of the child.

Can we be satisfied that the Cinema is a method of promoting mind growth rather than one of mechanizing mentality?

Vol. III, no. 5   November 1928

~~~~~~

Hanns Sachs

FILM PSYCHOLOGY

The plot, whether of a novel, play or film, consists of closely interwoven psychological coherencies. The film can be effective only in so far as it is able to make these psychological coherencies visible; in so far as it can externalise and make perceptible – if possible in movement – invisible inward events.

Psychic events are most freely outwardly perceptible when mirrored in facial expression. The obvious procedure for the film, therefore, was to build itself up upon the actor's power of facial expression. This procedure soon demonstrated its futility; for man expresses his emotions and passions far more powerfully and explicitly by word of mouth than by movement and facial expression. The film that is built up on mimicry is simple dumb-show, pantomime, and absurd hybrid, powerless either to reproduce or to develop itself. What, then, can we substitute for these so severely limited mimetics? To make human beings artificially dumb is not the proper business of the film, but things *are* dumb and we do not need to close their mouth by force if we are able to make them express psychic acts, which find their outlet through them, around them, or because of them.

This is amply demonstrated by the modern films in which the Russians, and notably Eisenstein in *Panzerkreuzer Potemkin* [*The Battleship Potemkin*], have gone furthest and most successfully.

Mimetic expression is here only one amongst many means of enhancing an effect already created from another source. The actor stands on an equality with inanimate things. Like them, he can embody the movement of the drama, but only so far as his embodiment is of such psychic events as are before or beyond speech; by this means, reflexes – and, above all, those small unnoticed ineptitudes of behaviour described by Freud as symptomatic actions – become the centre of interest.

According to Freud these so small, and in themselves so trivial and insignificant movements – as, for example, the dropping or losing of an object, the thoughtless toying with some small article, the forgetting or omitting of some action usually carried out with mechanical ease – are in the highest degree indicative of the inner experiences of the subject, of his desires and emotions, and exactly of those desires and emotions of which he himself is unaware. Accepting the inherent condition of the technique of cinematography, all discriminating producers have used details of this kind as indispensable means of expression; most of them, certainly, without having the smallest theoretical knowledge of their actual significance.

The agreement existing between the artists and poets of all periods and the principles of psycho-analysis has long been known to us, and it is not at all surprising that the film, after its own fashion, should take over and carry on the great tradition.

1. *Panzerkreuzer Potemkin*

A friend who had just seen Eisenstein's film for the third or fourth time, explained to me that at one point in the representation he had been very strongly moved without being able to discover what it was that had moved him. On each occasion this experience came to him at the moment when, by the captain's command, the sail-cloth is being carried on board. In the midst of this operation the head of the fugleman of the guard called up for the shooting emerges clearly for a moment, turned to watch. This watching head seems to have no particular expression, and any expression it might bear would, owing to the fractional time during which it appears in the picture, be lost upon the spectator.

As my friend is a particularly intelligent and experienced film-professional, I felt urged to discover the solution of the riddle, and when next I saw the film I paid particularly close attention to the scene that had so profoundly impressed him and that yet in itself seemed so slight and so incidental. Picture the situation: on the one hand the guard standing to attention, firm, stern, mechanised by discipline – on the other, the sailors driven hither and thither in the maze of the conflicting emotions of rage, despair and long-practised obedience.

When the captain has the sail-cloth brought along, tension rises to its height and our sympathies are concentrated upon the question as to which will be the stronger, human pity or the force of discipline. Will the guard shoot or refrain? When at this moment one of the guard – whom so far we have considered as a creature bereft of individuality by drilling, a mere mechanically functioning unit – is dissociated from the group and, by means of a movement (independent and not dictated by discipline), by looking round at the sail-cloth as it is being carried past, betrays, however slightly, his character of a human-being involved in the proceedings, our question begins to be answered. We know that even the guard, in its totality an unfeeling machine, is made up of men capable of sympathy, and we begin to hope.

In order to produce this moment of extreme tension it was of the highest importance that the transformation should appear suddenly and unexpectedly at the moment of greatest danger, at the sounding of the word of command: 'Fire!' Only thus could come about the powerful release carrying each spectator along with it. But for this operation, sudden only in its arrival, the spectator's mind must be cunningly prepared. Something within him must have desired, surmised, anticipated an event which otherwise would remain outside him, strange, a rescue from the clouds, the work of a *deus ex machina*. The sense of a strong psychic release is to be attained only in the case of a sudden ending of a painful to-and-fro between hope and fear. The onlooker must anticipate the turn of affairs without himself being aware of his anticipation. This suddenly seen head of the leader of the guard is to be counted amongst the things that assist his unconscious expectation. Certainly only a few of the millions who have seen *Potemkin* will have even noted the movement of the head, but upon all it will have worked as powerfully as upon my friend. The film is thus revealed as a kind of time-microscope, that is to say, it shows us clearly and unmistakably things that are to be found in life but that ordinarily escape our notice.

2. *Mutter*, by Pudowkin [Pudovkin]

Here, too, everything turns upon the effectual preparation of a moment of tension. The son is in prison, the mother hopes to hand him secretly, during the visitor's hour, a scrap of paper which will show him the way to freedom. The two are talking to each other through a grille and the mother's attention is concentrated on smuggling the paper into her son's hands unnoticed by the authorities. Two officials are present. From one, seated near her at a table, she has nothing to fear. He is fulfilling the duty of all overseers: he is asleep! But on the other side of her stands with stiffly-planted gun the guard who brought her son to the meeting-place and will take him away again: a yokel with expressionless features who, for lack of something more interesting to contemplate, stares steadily at the floor. Now the director might create the sense of tension by allowing the mother to make several attempts to pass the paper through the grille, and in each case to draw back her hand. This effect he might heighten by close-ups of the hand. But he has invented a far more ingenious method. Near the guard stands a bowl of milk, and here a subject is introduced which draws the guard's attention. A cockroach has crawled into it and is trying to get out again. The guard sees it just as it is reaching the end of its efforts, the safe rim of the bowl. Grinning, he extends a finger and pushes it back again and while this happens the mother pushes the scrap of paper into her son's hand. Here the tension is enhanced by means of shifting it to a secondary incident, to something apparently trivial and of no consequence upon which yet hangs the life of a man. And how ingeniously is the incident devised! It gives us a complete miniature of the horrible conditions of prison life, where food is befouled and infected; it also repeats, as if accidentally, the main movement of the drama: here, as there, we are faced by a prisoner who strives to free himself and is thrust back. But that which brings destruction to the one is to the other the first step towards freedom. Here we see not only a contrast, but at the same time a presentiment. The son has fallen into hands from which there is no rescue, hands which pitilessly push back him who thought himself already rescued. Thus is this episode a prelude, for the son falls later under the bullets of the soldiers just as he has escaped from prison. But the relationship of the two episodes goes even deeper. It reaches to a depth where not the intelligence but only the feeling of the onlooker can follow. The milk symbolises the mother in its character of being her first and most important gift to her child, a gift linking together forever the giver and the receiver.

The insect drowned in the milk indicates not only that there is to be for the son no escape, but also that he will die, not in the harsh besoiled prison, but as a free man in the arms of his mother. Thus, through a mere piece of by-play is the deep intrinsic emotional value of this work of art both epitomised and anticipated.

3. *Drei Frauen*, by Lubitsch

A young worldling has become, for the sake of her money, the lover of an elderly woman. Having achieved his expectations he no longer considers it worth while to go on convincing her of his love. She has no suspicions, refuses to have any, and perpetually offers herself to the reluctant lover. The situation is delicate, one not easy to represent even upon the stage; upon the film where things appear without the mitigating veil of words, in all their brutal reality, its representation would appear to be an insoluble problem. How has the producer found it possible to film this situation without sacrificing anything of its poignancy?

The two are sitting side by side upon a sofa. The woman leans against the man, caresses him, toys with his clothing. She flings her arms round his neck. Playfully she plucks at his tie and at last draws it out so that it hangs over his waistcoat. The man restores it to its place and is once more irreproachably correct.

In this case the representation is simple and short. There is no question of creating a tension, only of making the inexpressible expressible by means of displacement onto a small incidental action. The woman says: 'Undress yourself', and the man 'I don't want to', but the treatment is so contrived that both can act as if the behaviour of the other were simply the playfulness of idle fingers. The man does not choose to understand what the woman wants, the woman will not see that the man does not choose to understand, but the onlooker gives to the little episode its true value and knows in a moment more than could be revealed to him by means of a long caption. For him the proceedings are clear enough and this 'displacement' is exactly one of those means of expression, to which Freud first called attention, used by the unconscious everywhere, for instance, in dreams and in jest, to elude conscious recognition. The film seems to be a new way of driving mankind to conscious recognition.

In his *Traumdeutung*, page 263, Freud gives an explanation of the symbolic meaning of the tie, which, certainly, neither the onlookers of the film, nor the director, who created it, knew. But, all the same, it fits exactly into the thinly-veiled meaning of the 'slip action'.

Vol. V, no. 5   November 1929

Oswell Blakeston

FREUD ON THE FILMS

Far away back in April (1929) *Close Up* welcomed Metzner's *Uberfall*, and described it as 'a beautiful flow of images without break or jerk, catching the essence of Freudian nightmare'. Later, L. Saalschutz, in a most interesting article, discussed the film in its relation to the unconscious. There remains Germaine Dulac's *The Sea-Shell and the Clergyman*.

When Mr Stuart Davis, the enterprising [...], had it brought hopefully to London, we hastened to investigate.

Now that so many stage plays are being screened it was good to see a psychoanalytical exposition of thought, for the stage cannot show the layers upon layers of simultaneous consciousness. The stage cannot acquire the mobility of the subconscious, or put over as effectively the utter grotesqueness, so essential to dream states, which trick photography can capture on the screen. Piscator, and others, have tried by splitting the proscenium into sections, but the results have always been ponderous, they lack this flow, this ebb, this rhythm of the cinema.

Germaine Dulac's picture begins with a door, a high and narrow slit of a door, casting a shaft of light on to the floor of blackness. Here is the same lesson that I found in *The Eleventh Year* (*Close Up*, vol. V, no. 2), that light is creating, that light is doing something on the screen. All put, in cinematic terms, very neatly. See, there is a square door and a round pool of light. How you have to watch for the little things in this kind of picture! There are no laws in this fourth dimension, just light doing things. Square door, round pool.

The clergyman sits at a table, pouring liquid, from a shell, into a series of retorts, which, after he has filled, he throws to the ground. Symbolism, obvious.

Smoke flows over the fragments of glass.

A man appears in the cell, he comes through a gaping door; an intruder wearing a uniform, standing for Authority. He arrests the cleric in his monotonous actions. The setting of the cell makes it clear that these are the things the clergyman has shut away in his mind, and Authority, or Public Opinion, forbids him to dwell on them. The unfortunate falls to the floor. He creeps about feeling so much less than the others, he has his vow of celibacy.

Startling change from the studio set, he is crawling down a real street. In his life, as distinct from his suppressed desires, he feels inferior.

Houses are placed over one another by quick mixes.

The groveller notices Authority driving, in a cab, with a woman. It infuriates the clergyman to think that this man may have, lawfully, that which is denied to him by his vows. He chases the couple, and tracks them down in a church. In slow motion, the movement of a dream state, he approaches. This is his territory, the church.

Always the woman's face is shown as a chocolate-box type. She gazes on vaguely while the clergyman strangles her partner.

A close up shows the face of the attacked. Threads of blood trickle down the nose; threads that become wires to pull the face into two parts. Nightmare. Poetical waters of horror fill the screen. The clergyman is revealed with the other floating in his arms. (Under the water sensation.)

A great quarry. The clergyman on the skyline. His old enemy appears at his side, frenzied he hurls him to destruction in the waters beneath.

The water motif over, space is bridged with the rapidity of the unconscious. Back in the church the clergyman tears the clothing from the woman's breasts. Shells appear to cover her breasts.

Men and women dance crazily in a room; the candelabra spins madly. Authority and the woman enter and mount a throne. Materializing from space the clergyman, who is holding a shell in his hand, watches the dancers embracing. Hurling the shell to the floor he sees it explode in smoke.

The tails of the clergyman's frock grow into flowing trains: his rank, his vows.

Down corridors, and by a stream he pursues the woman. The woman turns and jeers. She puts out her tongue.

Lights in a crystal globe remind of lights in the retorts. He beckons for the woman to come and look in the globe, she refuses. Symbolism, obvious.

He has a key in his hand. He swings the key in a complicated figure. Opening door after door he finds the rooms empty.

At rest in a hammock, while Authority sits in a warehouse, the clergyman yet manages to watch the woman materializing from the sky. There are no laws of time and space. Now the clergyman feels that he could kill the capricious woman. Between his hands models of houses and castles are superimposed: symbols of his burning wishes for domestic happiness. Follows pure imagery. Ships, with beautiful sails, float on a sea so still that only the imagination could see it. Silver curtains, ships.

Maids clean the floor. Starting a new phase. The crystal stands in the room. Men enter. The clergyman is married to the woman by Authority dressed as a parson. Castles, houses, boats, and silver nets. The crystal grows larger, crashes to the floor. In the wreckage the face of Authority.

The scenario was written by Antonin Artaud. If one could do it justice in mere words it would not be such a good film.

Vol. V, no. 1   July 1929

L. Saalschutz

THE FILM IN ITS RELATION TO THE UNCONSCIOUS

I am going to treat the Film from the standpoint of the Freudian Psychic Life. The other standpoint, namely that of the conscious perceptual reality, has resulted in the Optophonic Cinema.

Night dreams, day dreams, fantasies, delirium, are according to Freud direct manifestations of the Unconscious.

With these I class the direct visually-excited mass fantasy of the Cinema.

When an audience weeps, that is mass-fantasy affecting the lacrymal glands causing tears. When an audience feels Fear, that is mass-fantasy affecting another set of glands causing a feeling of fright. Intellectual processes are only partially present.

Let us examine the Dream; see if we can really *apply* its mechanisms to support our theory of the Relation of the Film to the Unconscious. Maybe we shall discover something new.

What gives the Dream its content, shape, and expression is a conflict between primitive psychic wishes and the sublimated (disguised) impulses. In Dream-making proper, intellectual processes are non-existent, whereas in the Fantasy, Reverie, and the Day-dream, there is a definite content of intellectual conflict with the emergent (censored) unconscious. This applies to the Cinema in so far as it is considered purely as a mass fantasy, but the whole question is one of degree.

The triteness of our phrases requires a certain amount of qualification before we may proceed.

The film is a visual reality ... light patterns on a screen. But the content of the cinema is fantasy.

We know well that there is no need to feel sorry for the Hall Porter in *The Last Laugh* ... no need to let tears of the sublimest emotion well into our eyes when the unearthly purity of the blind girl (who we *know* is *not* blind) threatens to be defiled in *Jeanne Ney*. At some time or other I have repressed sorrow and tears. Pabst who understands me and you, brings them to the surface in association with the creatures of his own conception, to give me, strangely enough, intense joy. Pabst transforms and transmutes my complexes at will, but always into something of great beauty.

* * *

Firstly, we will speak of the 'content' of the film. This I liken to the 'Manifest Content' or 'Dream-Narrative' of the Dream (in its wider inclusive sense).

The visual, perceptual film-narrative, obviously resides totally in the conscious ego ... only to be forgotten slowly.

But manifest content is not the major importance of the 'avant garde' cinema. And our theory helps us in determining what *is* this major importance, and in what manner ... by what mechanism, is it to be achieved.

We turn then to the 'Latent Content' ... to something which I hold is entirely a function of the Unconscious and Pre-conscious.

There is none of this mechanism of the psychic processes about which we speak, without these two parts: manifest content and latent content, and their inter-relation. So the name of this article 'The Film in Relation to the Unconscious' springs from this consideration.

Three very important psycho-mechanisms are 'Condensation', 'Displacement', and 'Dramatization' ... the same three mentioned by Freud as Dream-mechanisms.

'Condensation' is a term applied to the process whereby various elements in the latent content become fused together in the manifest content, and finds its parallel in the 'mix', 'composite-shot', and sometimes in the 'dissolve' of the cinema.

The separate latent thoughts of the 'mix' are sorted out by the unconscious (not without further complexities, let it be mentioned) and retained as associated yet distinct entities. Only in the manifest content is there mixture.

I suggest that a 'mix' of the more directly associative elements of parallel-action is superior to rapid cutting, in that an inherent disjointedness of the latter method is avoided, and provided other features are carefully directed, the 'condensation' may be of extra value as a psychological means of creating an associative tension between the separate thought-entities, far surpassing even the Russian method.

Again in the 'composite-shot' I see a mechanism of abstraction that centres perhaps four or five distinct trains of thought, which run their course in the pre-conscious. At the same time a valuable associative complex is set up in the unconscious which can be utilised later to telling effect in the narrative.

The 'dissolve' is generally badly used. A momentary condensation of a train of thought which has served its purpose with another which has not yet begun its purpose, is something which requires careful handling.

Generally it is used, this so called 'lap dissolve', to associate the old with the new shot, and is in a narrow sense successful in this aim. At best elementary, there is a better use.

The material in the finished train of thought (a) should be condensed momentarily with the raw visual (manifest) material in (b) for the sole purpose of associating the latent content of (a) with the manifest content of (b). This (b) has as yet no latent content. Therefore, the dissolve should be used purely as an associative technique connecting the latent content of narrative-reality with the symbolism of visual 'imagery'.

I prefer a technique more innately fluid for the purpose of purely narrative fluidity, and suggest the quick de-focus-cut-re-focus, which I have seen only once or twice, and then badly applied. There is no condensation and defective intention is avoided.

There has been much spoken about 'imagery', and for me it is nothing more or less than 'symbolism'. It depends on the intellectual elevation of the composer whether it be subtle or merely obvious symbolism. Money-lenders always have been and always will be fat spiders to American Cinema, but occasionally a Seastrom gives us symbolism of the subtle kind seen in *Wind*.

Presently we shall consider this subject in its fuller aspect, that of the sublimation of unconscious material ... the 'raison d'être' of all symbolism.

'Displacement', the second mechanism, is an agent whereby psychic importance is shifted from a given element in the latent content, to another unrelated element in the manifest content. This seems to be bound up with 'camera angle' and its purpose.

A film with a theme of thwarted love for its latent content, rises to a physical climax. In itself the manifest physical climax is not over impressive ... but added psychic tension is brought to bear upon it by displacement from 'thwarted love'. Exactly how to induce 'displacement' we shall touch upon later in connection with 'Manifest Repression'.

The third mechanism known as 'Dramatization' is simple, and of greatest importance.

The visual form, a scene of action, time sequence, etc., are given to the elements of the latent content.

We have met this before under the name of 'literalness'. It was employed in *The Street*. The wayward clerk sees his wife's image going away from him ... as he looks at his wedding ring before staking it in the gambling hall.

Symbolism? No ... for no symbol was employed. Therefore, not 'imagery' either. This visualisation was a literal translation of the latent content ... his wife would be separated further and further away from him. An abstract mental process converted into its primary perceptions. Such indeed, is the definition of 'Dramatization' in the Freudian sense.

In general, of course, manifest content is a dramatization of the latent content ... but not invariably.

Where is the direct 'dramatization' of latent content in a sequence heavily charged with dramatic irony? The irony arises from the fact of that complete variance or absence of dramatization between latent and manifest content. This point has probably never been stated in psychological terms before.

Every abstract mental process is capable of a purely visual Dramatization. Of any associated ideas connected with the essential latent thoughts, such ones that will permit of visual representation are preferred. This is definite ... psychologically innate in man.

Therefore I contend that silent cinema is hampered in no way, and will remain superior to optophonic cinema.

The mind prefers a visualisation to anything else. Even if the latent thought is inflexible, the mechanisms we have reviewed are sufficient to recast it into another if more unusual visual form. When successfully recast and treated more unusually the work is called 'advanced art'.

The sound element will rob the film of much of its fantasy, its mechanisms will be rendered almost meaningless, and therefore, its psychological appeal will dwindle.

En passant, I do not think there is any meaning in 'counterpoint' in connection with fantasy ... but will not say definitely.

Before passing on to a discussion of Repression in the cinematic sense, we may first liken the film generally to the dream process called Regression. 'The dreamer is usually looking on at the dream enactments as a spectator surveys the stage' ... and this is called Regression by Freud; we call it cinema. And the more careful use of dream-mechanism will produce the more perfect cinema.

Pandora's Box:
'Lulu and Jack'
(Vol. IV, no. 4,
April 1929).

Regression will cease when the camera acquires a personality.

'Cinematic Repression' is of the kind seen in *Uberfall*. The footpad's blow is vividly hinted ... it is not seen ... therefore, latent content is hightened by the Repression of certain manifest elements (their absence).

If the blow were to be manifest, the latent content would be resolved, there would be no Repression of a brutal thought and it would suffer from lack of psychic tension.

'Displacement' may be induced by means of deliberate repression of this kind. Very often the psychic tension may be usefully transferred (displaced) to the symbols employed. Again: Seastrom ... who generally transfers to some natural force which was a subtle symbol all the time.

It was hoped that this theory of Cinema would serve as a lead and a Statement to a New English Cinema ... one with courage in its conviction that 'talkies' shall find no place in its heart ... and moreover one with a purpose.

This brings me to Purpose. Viewed in the light which it is hoped has been cast upon it, its Purpose appears to be the Sublimation and De-sublimation of certain mass repressions and complexes which may go to isolate the Englishman from the world.

Certainly the only instrument capable of such a forlorn task, is the instrument of mass fantasy ... the Cinema.

Vol. VII, no. 2   August 1930

C. J. Pennethorne Hughes

DREAMS AND FILMS

The advocation of another theory of the cinema may appear, at the moment, to be futile: a voice crying hopelessly in the wilderness of vulgarity. Everyone is talking at once, and a bewildered public floods stickily to the appalling attraction of the Latest. Yet there is a hypothesis which might help to co-ordinate the scattered tags of cinematic theory, and which should therefore be urged, even at the risk of adding another note to the prevailing discourse.

The film is the dream of the post-war world. It is this not only in the obvious sense that it expresses many of the sub- or barely conscious aspirations of the generation, but also in its machinery. It is suggested here that a true line for the development of the film is that it should attempt to intensify this, so that a picture should be, in appearance, an interesting dream, perfectly remembered and artistically presented.

The more the analogy of the true film and the dream is pursued, the more numerous the points of affinity appear, whilst they are practically unopposed by points of obvious difference. First, the dull subfusc tinting generally adopted for films, until the last year, gives uniformity. This is true even of the more dazzling treatment accorded to what is wide, open or spacious. Now it is extremely rarely that colours appear in dreams.

If, in dreams, we are conscious of a colour at all, it is usually as an intellectual appreciation – that particular hair is red, or fields are brown. A very few people seem to possess chromatic sense in dreams, but as a general rule it does not exist, and the values are purely those of relative clearness or depth, as in the world through a camera. The screen world, too, is still essentially a shadow world, for the latest polychromatic spectacles are monstrosities, superimposed upon the wave of successful vulgarity, and completely out of the true line of development. The ability to combine rhythmic movement of forms with a concentration upon particular points is an advantage which the film is the only medium to possess, and this can be achieved by purely tonal effects far more easily and clearly than with the aid of any pseudo-realistic additions. And in a film, as in a dream, two dimensions are enough.

The love of analogy shown in dreams, which turns a row of sheep into a row of soldiers, the soldiers into Buckingham Palace, and Buckingham Palace into the Palace Music hall, is also one of the most familiar possessions of the cinema. Havelock Ellis has shown, and Lewis Carroll illustrated, that a similarity of form immediately suggests, to the unconscious, a transition from the one idea to the other. So the fusion obtained by the camera's 'mix' gives a transition of interest, and the desired speed, through a similarity of forms: as when the hand of the light woman, holding a cigarette, fuses to that of the heavy villain, holding a dagger. Actually, the trick has been strained and overdone until good-mannered directors are frightened of it. But it remains one of the great advantages of the medium, nevertheless.

The film, better than any other form of artistic expression can give the terrible Alice and the Red Queen feeling of exertion without progression, that of complete paralysis, or that of falling from an immense height, all so frequent in dreams. Flux and fusion, vague but important irrelevancies, and a constantly rising and falling rhythm, the film alone can visually portray. It can do it so well, moreover, even already, that audiences interested in the development of a picture often react to it by making the same strangulated gestures, to help the protagonists on the screen, as those made by people sleeping, and experiencing particularly vivid dreams. The reaction to a film play by Vertoff [Vertov] may be as strong, but as removed from the conscious intelligence, as that to any nightmare. Whilst the desirability of artificial nightmares is perhaps dubious, the ability so to produce them is at least interesting.

It is a peculiar quality of dreams that, as they are hardly ever coloured, so they scarcely ever employ the aural mechanism. We are conscious of what people wish to express, but usually intuitively, or Belshazzar-like. Words are actually heard occasionally, but rather as a theme, a refrain, than as continuous dialogue. And here again cinematic practice must comply. It is already being seen how barren is the purely naturalistic speaking film. If sound is to be used, it should be selected and emphasised words, or carefully and sensitively synchronised music, and chromatic and vocal effects should be used only where tremendous emphasis is desired. In this respect, as in others, the film might copy the dream.

Of course all this has been noticed, and partially attempted. And of course it would be horrible to think of audiences miserably attending cinemas to study the disclosure of their own or anyone else's unconscious. The present generation, as Mr Aldous Huxley reiterates, is already sick with the overcontemplation of its own psychology.

Yet despite these two facts – that the dreamy film is now out of fashion (it *was* messy, and it is a fairly justified maxim that 'thou shalt do no Murnau') and that healthy audiences do not demand cinema, but movies – the dream film hypothesis is worth study. Freud, Man Ray, and others, may have played at it, and in *A Sheep in Wolf's Clothing* the idea was definitely and consciously exploited. But up to now it has hardly been formulated clearly. And the present is a blare of sound.

As a footnote to the secondary and obvious idea of the film as the expression of the national subconscious, it may be noticed that already this quality has been generally shown. And this before the complete arrival of the talkie has made the geographical distribution of films, temporary at all events, a necessarily national affair. America produced for years romances dealing with that Wild West which is the spiritual heritage, commercially repressed, of every 75 per cent American. England produced, for years after the war, the sentimental apple-blossom stuff which then seemed so particularly remote from a depressing and reconstructive reality. France produced, in an interminable parade of fancy dress, the national picaresque. Germany, where conscious and unconscious are more obviously coincident, produced increasingly mechanised pictures. For the ordinary man visits a cinema to 'get outside himself'; that is, [to] get *inside* himself. What pleases him is the display of lavish wealth and spurious luxury of an incredibly High Life. He loves, too, the extravagant sentiment which commerce officially rejects. He loves the sexual preoccupations which are considered vicious in his own environment. He loves what he can't get. This love finds its outlet in the natural medium of dreams and the artificial one of the cinema. Each man and each nation has a different technique.

The film, then, is to some extent the subconscious – the transmuted and regulated dream life – of the people. As most peoples have at the moment mainly bad dreams, and the transmuting alchemists are avowedly out for gold only, the results are rather depressing. But, if only it were realised that the film, by adopting and exploiting the mechanism of the dream, could give itself fuller realisation and so greater success, something might yet be done.

The theory is an incomplete one, here imperfectly and only most briefly outlined, and I do not claim too much for it. But it is a theory. And, in the present welter of unorganised vulgarity, Heaven, not alone, knows that one is wanted.

Vol. IX, no. 3   September 1932

Hanns Sachs

KITSCH

Against the attempts of psycho-analysis to solve aesthetic problems the objection is urged that a persistence bordering on monotony that it is all very interesting, stimulating and even fruitful, but really quite hopeless, for aesthetics fixes values, whereas psycho-analysis, being a pure natural science, must, as a matter of course, desist from any attempt at valuation. This assertion is true, but the objection deduced from it is false. Rather, from the successful achievements of psycho-analysis – for instance, from Freud's 'Wit and its Relation to the Unconscious' – one ought to draw the conclusion that aesthetics too comprises a domain in which, though it does not fix values, it tries to investigate the laws controlling the genesis and decline of the psychical reactions subject to aesthetic valuations. Also, with all due deference to aesthetics as a fixer of values, one ought not to forget how sadly its judgments have proved wanting up to now. The wisest systems are reduced to helpless silence so soon as an unaccustomed phenomenon confronts them – an original work, a new line or even a new species of art, such as the film. We have not yet progressed very far beyond the Nestroyan: 'Yes, if this is beautiful, it is of course beautiful.'

So long as there were closed cultural circles and so far as such still exist, it was or is quite idle to deduce valuations from a theory. Everyone knew what was beautiful: namely, what gave pleasure to himself and his compatriots or compeers: the unfamiliar was rejected without much effort of thought. With the Renaissance began the process of linking up the various nations; owing to the new means of production the closed cultural circles were more or less thoroughly broken up, deprived of their insular character and dissolved into a general human mass. And here begins the necessity and at the same time the problem of aesthetic valuations. (This is, of course, only a fraction of the total development, which operated similarly in the domains of religion, ethics and social questions.) The capacity for aesthetic experience is incomparably wider in the modern man than at any earlier epoch. He is sensible of the beauty of the sea and of wild, lofty mountains, which was imperceptible to the ancients; he feels the charm of the machine with its power and purposefulness, which was denied by the romantics; he is able to appreciate deeply and sympathetically both Greek statues and negro masks, both the Gothic and the East Asiatic. This abundance necessarily produces some confusion, and the multitudinous diversity engenders a superficiality which prevents anything from penetrating very deeply; thence a lack of judgment and, as a protection against the perpetual readiness to succumb to an impression, a craving for a fixed theoretical criterion of value. As, at the same time, artistic, like every other, output has, as a result of the new technical resources, assumed a hitherto undreamed of scope and character, our age is confronted with a new problem, which had scarcely any importance for the men of the closed cultural circles – with the question: 'Do I really like what I like? Or is my dislike the proof of a new and stronger quality which I am not yet able to appreciate? Is it really the herald of a more profound liking?' In other words: 'What is Kitsch?'

Having forced our way to our subject through the crowded and terrible straits of argumentation, we may now repeat the question as to the sphere of validity of psycho-analysis. Kitsch is not one of the eternal problems; it is sprung mainly from the peculiarity or, if you like, the lack of peculiarity of the aesthetic culture of our age. The determination what is Kitsch and what is not cannot, therefore, be deduced from the fundamental laws of psychic processes which psycho-analysis is investigating. From one point of view, however, psycho-analysis can contribute something towards the solution. Associated with Kitsch is a quite special form of mass reaction, and what psycho-analysis teaches about these things and about the emotional basis of mass formation is the more applicable since a number of connections with the problem of art have already been established here.

We shall have to disregard the need for a definition of what constitutes 'Kitsch'. Its main characteristics are usually thought to be sugary sentimentality and omission of the painful and disgusting sides of reality, but this does not by any means exhaust the whole conception, for in addition to rose-coloured Kitsch, there is a savage, brutal as well as an 'originality Kitsch' and also a 'refined Kitsch', which seems to satisfy all the higher claims. Nor is it helpful to refer to lack of true originality as the distinctive feature, for that is only substituting one ignorance for another. Judged by present-day notions of intellectual property Shakespeare would rank as the most shameless plagiarist.

Moreover analysis of the contents which lie at the base of a work – day dreams or unconscious fantasies – cannot offer the slightest clue; they are far too typical in character to afford any criterion. The talentless product of a puberty conflict is just as much built up on the Oedipus complex as is *Hamlet*, and the story of the foundling who is ultimately restored to his parents has given rise to just as many magnificent myths as it has to Kitsch films. The difference lies not in the subject but in the manner in which it is treated; the work of art creates new hitherto unknown possibilities of inner experience, new approaches to the unconscious base. Kitsch relies on safe and long familiar effect: A tree in blossom under a spring sky is beautiful, the death of a child is touching – that we have long known and no new feature is added to this knowledge. But perhaps a little bit of known fact may be inserted here. The artist, so much we believe ourselves to know, is impelled to creative activity by the sense of guilt attached to his day-dreams. Any one who produces Kitsch obviously has no such sense of guilt to contend with, he is freer in relation to the fantasy contents of his production: that is to say, he is bound to it by far less inward sympathy. One might – with some exaggeration but with essential justice – hazard the formula: Kitsch is the exploitation of daydreams by those who never had any.

Consequently, a work which in itself can only be accounted Kitsch may produce on one person or another a very deep impression such as is generally only produced by a genuine work of art – if, that is to say, the daydreams and with them the 'complexes' of the person receiving the impression are so disposed that they happen to coincide exactly with what is offered by the work in question. I once observed an effect of this nature during an analysis where I was quite able to understand it. The person I was analysing had been deeply and lastingly stirred by the film *The Fiddler of Florence* which, despite the acting and some interesting details, must certainly be ranked as Kitsch. The film described, in fact, almost the whole evolution of her suppressed childhood; it dealt with and solved her unconscious conflicts: the craving for sole possession of the widowed father, the fear of losing him by his second marriage, the attempted flight into masculinity in order to escape disappointment, and the final reunion with a new, rejuvenated father and discarding of the masculine disguise.

The remoteness of Kitsch from the unconscious and the daydreams of its author may therefore be non-existent for the person succumbing to its influence; such a case is, however, an exception, and the question is: what is the rule? Can we make any pronouncement as to the way in which Kitsch produces an impression on the average public, the 'many-headed multitude?'

Instead of stopping short at the platitude that Kitsch and multitude belong together, we will proceed from a little peculiarity which to an attentive observer must seem rather remarkable. Among the German films of last year, for example, were those military farces which for a considerable time enjoyed such boundless popularity with the public that it was by no means easy for the film-lover to avoid them. These films, like the army itself, comprise two different worlds: officers and men. In the officers' world there would be a surly-tempered colonel and, above all, an intolerably smart lieutenant – anything from a count upwards – who loves a girl belonging to the world of the privates and is loved by her in return, until they give each other up and the lieutenant marries his exquisitely lovely and virtuous bride – anything from a princess downwards. In the world of the private soldiers there is less that is noble and enviable; here too, there is indeed a sergeant-major with a rough exterior, but above all there is an orderly who is lazy, awkward, greedy or vicious, and who gets well paid-out for it. Apparently, it is easier to ridicule these stock figures than to replace them by new ones, for, with slight modifications, they have touched and amused the public again and again. But what is this public which identifies itself so promptly and readily with the protagonists in a world of officers and princesses and is so delighted by ridicule of the common man? One might imagine it to consist only of men of the 'upper circles,' men who might have been lieutenants and girls who might at least have carried the bridal train of the princess. As we know, however, this is by no means the case; the success of these films with the big public is sufficient proof that the overwhelming majority of their admirers are men who might have become orderlies and girls who might at best have been deserted by a lieutenant, and these are the people who take an enthusiastic interest in this sort of thing. It might be suggested that the explanation is to be sought in the political temper, which is responsible for these and many other aberrations. But we find the same thing elsewhere, though not with equal crassness. Let us take a typical example of American Kitsch: *Shanghai Express*. Does the female portion of the American film public (incidentally this film has also had a great success in Germany) consist to a noteworthy extent of girls who may hope to be one day transformed into courtesans of stainless virtue, who are at first loaded with presents and elegant toilettes and are finally led to the altar by some heroic soul?

To such questions we may find a reply first of all from the sociological point of view, namely, that the lower, suppressed classes, in so far as they are not educated to independent class-consciousness, accept and firmly adhere to the ideals of the higher class which governs them. This sociological fact has a very obvious psychological background which appertains to our theme. Undoubtedly, where alien ideals are borrowed and imitated the possibility of Kitsch is particularly imminent. It would be interesting, however, to find out something more about the mechanisms by which, whatever the situation – and it is certainly not exclusively a matter of the borrowed class idea – the fantasy emotional response or, in other words, the satisfaction of aesthetic needs is, as a mass phenomenon, most readily accomplished by way of Kitsch.

If a man wants to fall in love or become a hero or be otherwise impressive and interesting in accordance with the ideals of a way of life that is alien to him, he will undoubtedly find this more difficult than if he were moving in his own familiar, everyday sphere. A crowd composed of such individuals needs, therefore, a larger measure of help, and will be grateful if the course of its emotional response is plainly indicated. The tendency to win this special kind of gratitude from the public is the infallible road to Kitsch, although, of course, it may be realized by very various means – more subtle or more gross as the case may be. It is always a matter of introducing unmistakably clear indications, plainly legible signposts, as it were, which are scattered through the whole work from beginning to end and steer the possibilities of emotional response along definite channels. For instance, the public can only successfully identify itself with definite figures and from a definite point of view – but with these it can identify with the greatest ease. Who or what is good and beautiful or ugly and reprehensible, who is suffering in an enviable and who in only a comical way must be made so emphatically obvious as to be comprehensible to the dullest intelligence. Obviously well-tried methods and familiar standards lend themselves best to this purpose. For the ends of Kitsch, therefore, anything new or bound up with the spiritual experience of the author is not only superfluous, as has already been shown, but absolutely prejudicial; he must not merely be content not to seek it, but must take pains to avoid it at any cost. There must be no hint of the diverse possibilities of psychic decisions, through which in a work of art first the creator and then – in a less degree – the person responding to the work must force his way; there must be no mention of doubt or of the awful question: 'Soul, whither has thou led me – what has become of me?' Or, should it, none the less, be voiced, the reassuring answer must follow promptly and plainly: 'Among good people.'

For all this, we must not over-estimate the importance of obvious 'signpost' technique as an objective aid towards classification as Kitsch. The boundaries separating the artistic urge towards clarity and form from the signpost methods proper to Kitsch are very often debatable in the individual case. Perhaps it may help us to arrive at the determining characteristics if we consider the effect produced in one or other case on an eagerly receptive crowd.

From the point of view of the public, Kitsch has the advantage that it renders their enjoyment as effortless as possible and guards them against uncertainty and allusions to unpleasant recollections. It is no wonder if most prefer it unreservedly – yet certain limitations and weaknesses are inseparably bound up with this advantage.

Owing to the skill with which the distribution of emotions is anticipated, the public are indeed saved a good deal of worry, including that of choice, but at the same time the free development of their emotions is restricted; the possibility of lifting them by degrees out of the unconscious and letting them have free play is done away with. The process must involve the minimum of psychic activity and must never be arrested. Hence it is that Kitsch, which mainly relies on the old and well-tried, cannot dispense with the attraction of the new or ultra-new: one popular song succeeds another, each season brings its operettas and revues; in one's recollection they all seem indistinguish-ably alike. But the film-producers, if they are ambitious, search for an 'original milieu'.

The action of Kitsch on an eagerly receptive public is, therefore, easily characterized: it begins promptly and is soon over. The emotions released are so universal and superficial as to be independent of the individual work. It is applauded and forgotten, like its predecessors, and its successor has a like fate: indeed all of them taken together have only the emotional value of a single work. The influence of a work of art need not necessarily operate slowly, but it may do so, and where it has once been achieved it is indestructible. Nothing less than a total transformation of the personality – apart from variations of intensity – is required in order to extinguish the impression left by a work of art; the changes it has wrought are too considerable for it ever again to become a matter of indifference. That it may even be added that this fact, as is common knowledge, is reflected in the larger dimensions of historical happenings. The appreciation accorded to a work of art and the capacity to respond to it emotionally are not diminished by the passing of the centuries. Kitsch no more finds a permanent resting-place in its age than it does in the soul of the individual.

PART 7

Cinema Culture

INTRODUCTION

James Donald and Anne Friedberg

One thing which *Close Up* had in common with the radical British film journals of fifty years later – *Screen*, *Afterimage*, *Framework*, *Undercut* and the others – was a commitment not only to writing about cinema but also to creating a radical film culture. The situation in the 1970s was, however, very different from that in the 1920s. Two factors in particular account for the change. One was the existence of new institutions which were able to give limited support to the production of independent films and the creation of a film culture, but which also skewed them in particular directions. The British Film Institute came into being in 1933, just as *Close Up* ceased publication. In the 1970s and early 1980s, the BFI sponsored a network of institutions for film production, distribution, exhibition, debate and education which were marked by a degree of aesthetic and/or political radicalism. The Arts Council of Great Britain's Film Department was perhaps more sympathetic than the BFI to avowedly avant-garde film-making. The second factor was that, by the 1970s, the political economy of intellectual work had been transformed, with the critical work previously done by small privately funded magazines like *Close Up* being incorporated more and more into an expanding higher-education system.

Both these changes entailed a professionalization not apparently envisaged by *Close Up*. In the 1920s, its attempts to create an independent film culture were built on the enthusiasm and work of people who were, in the best sense, amateurs. For all *Close Up*'s declared commitment to 'theory and analysis', Kenneth Macpherson would have hated the deliberately academic emphasis of the 1970s – its academicism, he would no doubt say. 'Theory made too precise can only impoverish,' he wrote in December 1929. But the demand for systematic cultural policies and the construction of bodies of theory as a foundation for a new university discipline of Film Studies would have been temperamentally as well as intellectually at odds with *Close Up*'s amateur ethos. That ethos is manifest in a thread of reports, comment, discussion and debate that runs through the magazine's pages and reveals its readers' practical engagement with the issues we look at briefly in this section: film production; the distribution and exhibition of films; and film censorship.

Production

We have already commented on the significance of the 1929 Independent Cinema Congress (as it is called here) held at La Sarraz. What is striking about the report for *Close Up* by the normally sceptical Jean Lenauer is his optimism that it might be possible to create a subsidized enclave in which films could be produced and distributed for an exclusive public 'already educated and intelligent'. With hindsight, of course, most film historians see La Sarraz as an end rather than the beginning envisaged by Lenauer.

Largely through the work of Bryher, *Close Up* encouraged a broader range of film production than the elite niche contemplated at La Sarraz. Increasingly, its pages of notes and comments were taken up with reports from local film-making societies around Britain. What some of them were up to can be gleaned from the exchange between the enthusiastic amateur Orlton West, of the Film Guide of London, and Ralph Bond, an increasingly frequent contributor to the magazine, a leading Communist, and a film and union activist from the 1920s until well into the 1970s.

Distribution and exhibition

Close Up also encouraged the creation of alternative means for disseminating and showing non-mainstream films. Ralph Bond was one of the key figures behind its backing for the creation of a Workers' Film Movement, designed in the first instance to make a wider range of films available for exhibition through a national network of film societies, but with ambitions to move into politically engaged production and to rival the equivalent organizations in Continental Europe. Bryher wrote frequently and practically on the importance of amateur involvement in film societies and film exhibition. She was one of many authors to discuss the potential role of film in education, and both she and Dorothy Richardson wrote on the need for high-quality films for children. Richardson gives her rather eccentric views on how film exhibition could be improved, to the evident consternation of the editor, in her 'A Note on Household Economy'. We also reprint an article about the Academy in Oxford Street, which remained London's best-known art cinema until its closure in the 1970s.

Censorship

Close Up's most focused political campaign was its petition for reforms to the United Kingdom's film censorship laws. At the time *Close Up* appeared, these were being imposed in a manner which was both politically partisan and aesthetically boorish. Pabst's films were routinely hacked about. As the caption to stills from *Potemkin* in the February 1928 issue of *Close Up* notes, despite the international fame of the film, many of the magazine's readers would not have been able to see it, as public screenings were banned. A later issue of the journal prints the memorable rejection slip for Germaine Dulac's *Le Coquille et le Clergyman* (1926): 'This film is so cryptic as to be meaningless. If there is a meaning, it is doubtless objectionable.'

The legal basis for this censorship was laid down in the Cinematograph Act of 1909. The Act had been passed in the wake of the Charity Bazaar fire in Paris. Local authorities were granted licensing powers to establish safety regulations for lighting and exits in order to protect British audiences against similar disasters. The wording of the Act was so vague, however, that local authorities could in effect censor films by granting or withholding these licences.

In 1929, Ivor Montagu's pamphlet *The Political Censorship of Films*, published by Gollancz, showed how the 1909 Act was being used to censor Soviet films in England. Macpherson and Bryher bemoaned censorship restrictions from the first issues of *Close Up* onwards, but the magazine's campaign did not really get going until late 1928. In the January 1929 issue, a formal petition was enclosed in the back pages. The form was to be signed and returned to the *Close Up* offices, with the signatures being added to the formal petition to be presented to Parliament.

Much of the February 1929 issue was devoted to the question of censorship. In his editorial, Macpherson is at his most scathing and condescending as he mockingly itemizes the list of criteria used by the British Board of Film Censors. Although nominally a trade body similar to the Hays Office of the MPPDA, its appointees were more directly political, and there was active collusion between the BBFC and the Home Office:

> If you read through their various proclamations, decrees, ultimatums, threats, brags and promises, you become more and more dizzy with the boggy confusion of their innuendos. The list ... is so indecent that if it came from any but a recognised public society for protecting people's morals, this issue of *Close Up* would be burnt by the common hangman, without a doubt.[1]

Articles by Robert Herring and Oswell Blakeston offer more detail on the British situation. Lenauer, Kraszna-Krausz and Chevally report on French, German and Swiss censorship policies. At the back of the issue, with an evident degree of ironic satisfaction, a *Daily Express* report about *Close Up*'s role in the anti-censorship campaign is quoted: '[There is] a pro-Russian propagandist organization operating from Territet, Switzerland to remove the ban imposed by the Government and the British Board of Film Censors on about forty Russian propagandist films now in cold storage in this country.'[2]

Much of the practical work in organizing the petition was undertaken by Dorothy Richardson. Looking back on the ultimately unsuccessful campaign a year later, in January 1930, she reflected on its two main aims. In order to overcome 'the mutilation to the point of destruction of almost all foreign films shown in this country, and the customs duties whose rage is prohibitive for all but those films which are certain of a large commercial success', the petition had made two main requests:

> The petition appealed ... primarily for the creation, on behalf of films of artistic scientific and educative value, of a special category; a category independent of the two already in existence into which all films whatsoever are dropped, after censorship and resultant cutting down to the measure of the rules – those considered unsuitable for children going into A (Adults) category, and all the rest into U (Universal). In the second place it was pleaded that the board of censors should include persons capable of judging artistic and scientific films on their intrinsic value rather than their commercial possibilities, and it was further suggested that such films, when released for limited showing, should be automatically entitled to a large rebate of customs duties and reduction of entertainment tax.[3]

The petition was couched in terms designed to appeal to British Imperial pride. 'Such restrictions are harmful,' it read, 'not only because British films have not attained a standard sufficiently high to establish them firmly in world markets, but also because of the tendency of those in the industry with intelligence and initiative to go abroad when the opportunity presents.' It emphasized that British films were 'lacking in standard and technique' and complained about the impossibility of experimental work in England.

The petition was lost in the dog days of a Parliament after a general election had been called. One MP's last effort to have it considered was greeted with the official response that this was a matter for local authorities, not government. 'This quiet remark', laments Richardson, 'falls upon our effort with the effect of a dismissing smile.'[4] As the articles by Hanns Sachs and Ralph Bond testify, the pressure continued. In 1937, however, the President of the BBFC was able to declare with smug satisfaction that 'there is not a single film showing in London today which deals with the burning issues of the day'. Sixty years on, United Kingdom film censorship law remains largely unchanged.

Vol. V, no. 4   October 1929

~~~~~~

Jean Lenauer

THE INDEPENDENT CINEMA CONGRESS

An international congress of the independent cinema was held from the second to the seventh of September at the château of Madame de Mandrot at la Sarraz.

S. M. Eisenstein was present as delegate from Russia. He came at the last moment (the other two delegates not having been able to obtain the Swiss visa), accompanied by his assistant G. Alexandroff [Alexandrov] and his cameraman E. Tisse, Alberto Cavalcanti, Leon Moussinac, Janine Boussounouse, J. G. Auriol and Robert Aron (who was president of the congress) represented France; Walter Ruttmann, Hans Richter and Béla Balazs [Balázs] came from Germany (Pabst was prevented from being present); J. Isaacs and Ivor Montagu from England; Montgomery-Evans from the United States; F. Rosenfeld from Austria; Prampolini and Sartoris from Italy; M. Franken from Holland; Moituro Tsuytja and Hijo from Japan; Caballero from Spain; and from Switzerland Guye, Schmitt, Kohler and Masset.

There were several difficulties at the beginning. The nature of the independent film (formerly *avant garde* film) was not understood in the same way by different members of the Congress. Thus, for example, Hans Richter was rather perturbed that Pabst had been invited for, said he, Pabst made 'spielfilms', that is films with plot and action, with professional actors. It was clear that Richter understood that only absolute and abstract films could be denominated independent films.

It has often enough been pointed out that the absolute film is definitely a genre of cinema interesting in itself, but at once an error if it is considered as the only possible manifestation of cinema, that is to say as soon as cause and effect are confused. It seems to me negligible and of secondary importance whether a film is made with living or inanimate objects if it has its own integrity.

At last a basis was found. And practical discussions became possible. The results of this discussion are the creation of an International League of Independent Cinema and of a co-operative of production. The League will have for its principal aim distribution among the already existing clubs (such as the Film Society or Film Liga) and the creation of films of note. Naturally the films produced by the co-operative will be contained in the programmes of these clubs. The League will also distribute current films which for one reason or another could not be released in the commercial theatres, on the condition, of course, that their cinegraphic value justifies the idea.

Most important, though not always of the most practical value, is the contact of various groups all over the world whose aim is the furtherance of good films.

It was decided also to send a petition to the Institut International Intéllectuel at Rome, asking for favourable conditions in respect of censorship and quota for films of

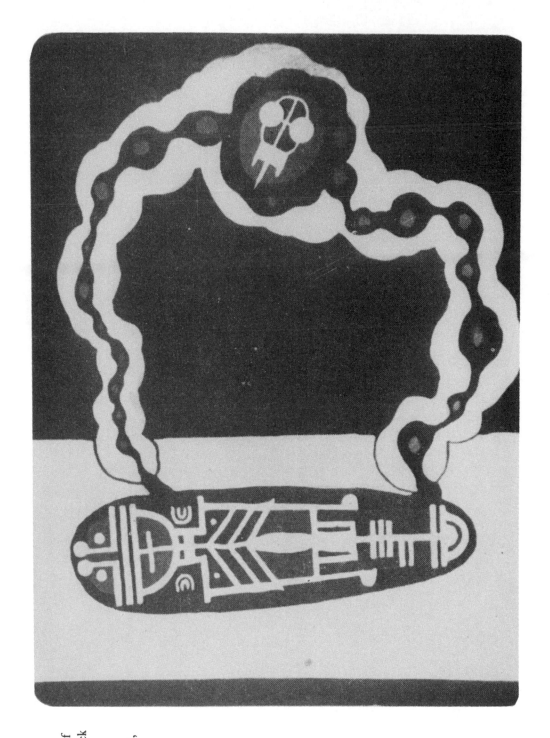

Tusalava, a film by Len Lye: 'A film of life cells, attack and repudiation' (Vol. VI, no. 2, February 1930).

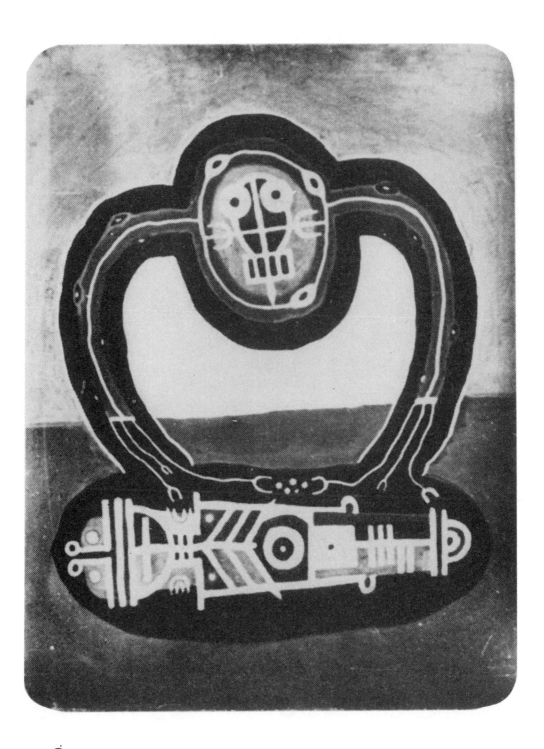

Tusalava (ibid.).

the co-operative and those which the League will distribute; a justifiable demand, since these productions will be confined to a public already educated and intelligent, and able to furnish sufficient guarantee of moral responsibility.

The big event was the arrival of S. M. Eisenstein, who the next day made a little film, in which all members of the congress played a rôle, a short comedy which will incidentally be the first production of the co-operative.

The enthusiasm of Eisenstein was so infectious that all the serious minded were tempted to forget their dignity and do as he instructed.

I shall not speak here of Eisenstein himself, who so greatly changed the aspects of the congress, but I should in any event like to proclaim my admiration for this splendidly youthful man who has to his credit *Potemkin*, *Ten Days* and *The General Line*.

We must now wait for the results of the congress. But in spite of a vivid scepticism which I maintain always towards any sort of congress, very little was said (which is well enough, since it at least prevents the usual *bêtises*) and it is to be hoped that the goodwill of all these different beings, who all more or less pursue the same ends, will lance itself strongly enough to be a real creative force.

Vol. IV, no. 6   June 1929

Orlton West

RUSSIAN CUTTING

'We will do some Russian cutting on those scenes!' (yards, or rather inches, of it) ... The phrase sounds clever. It has a magic significance for many amateurs, whom, as yet, seem to have devoured but the skin from the milk. They have missed the meaning of Russian film *construction*.

Take a dozen shots from an express train, or, should road traffic fill you with keener delight, of taxis, omnibuses, and 'One Way Street' signs. Sprinkle a liberal dose of 'unusual angles' over the conglomeration, measure your film to the nearest centimetre, and stick the pieces together. You have achieved 'Russian Cutting'.

But have you?

Take a couple of close shots showing just how angry two people can become with each other, cross cut them at an increasing tempo to suggest the rising excitement of fury – and you have achieved 'Russian Cutting'.

But again, have you?

Not at all. This kind of thing is merely clever. Do we not strive to be something more than clever? We must get beyond the stage where we utilise a mechanical device, which, like the automatic telephone, becomes ordinary, accepted fact, as soon as the polish of its novelty has worn off.

We can blame our own mechanical age for the fact that, as soon as a technical development in films arrives, its mechanical or 'clever' aspect is seized upon, while its intellectual depths remain untouched. And so we get 'rhythm cutting' on traffic, cross-cutting of train and car chases, and summer lightning displays of close shots.

True, Russian film construction is built upon a foundation of psychology, yet many really keen amateurs are unacquainted with the words of such thinkers as Freud. ... The psychological processes of symbolisation and association are mostly *visual* (as a film thinking friend has pointed out to me), and therefore one of the highroads to intelligent cinemas. A little reading of Freud, and a little more thought in the application of his principles to film construction, together with a course of really good films (Shaftesbury Avenue Pavilion) and one suddenly sees light and feels brilliantly rewarded. 'Russian cutting' no longer remains a magic phrase, but comes to signify a developed cinema.

Let us then cut out some of these traffic shots, releasing ourselves from these playful externals, which mean nothing. Let us, instead, try joining up our shots in a form with which the human brain would, or might, associate its mental visions, then we shall begin to achieve meaning.

Before we commence, we must know what psychological effect we aim at achieving, or what our definite idea is, then we can construct our film on its foundation, as Pudovkin has said, and done. Our idea need not be anything so tremendous as a new social order, it may be simply to convey a certain state of mind. It may be to present an aspect of modern life, to compare the dash of the City with the calm of the Countryside, and here you do not need much traffic, but persons, symbols with a meaning, associations, sudden little comparisons, all working towards – and directed by – your definite idea.

The definite aim, a little knowledge of psychology, a few good films, seen in a new light as a result of the psychology, that is the diet which, I am sure, many amateurs will find as nourishing as I myself have found it to be.

Vol. V, no. 5   November 1929

~~~~~~

R. Bond

'THIS MONTAGE BUSINESS'

The Film Guild of London, an amateur organisation, is suffering from a bad attack of 'this montage business'. The phrase in quotes is not mine; one of the members of the Guild aptly but thoughtlessly employed it at their meeting last month when several recent productions of the Guild were screened.

Chief among these was *Waitress*, produced on 9mm stock by Mr Orlton West. *Waitress* is a bad film, very bad. Originally it was made as a one-reeler, but after he had made it Mr West went to the Continent and saw the work of Vertof [Vertov]. He was

Eisenstein's
*The General
Line* (Vol. III,
no. 3,
September
1928).

so impressed with Vertof's montage that he came back, added another reel to his film, and endeavoured to cut the whole production in the Vertof manner.

Now cutting, or montage as some people prefer to call it, is something more than clipping every possible shot to a couple of frames. Cutting should be composed, and Mr West has neither composed his film nor his cutting. The result is a striving after effect purely. If the director had paid a little more attention to his lighting and photography (which were terribly poor), and to his story construction, and less to stunts, *Waitress* might have been a better film. The very long and almost unintelligible double exposure sequence which attempts to express the mental collapse of the girl in the café could well have been dispensed with, or, at least, shortened considerably.

This desperate endeavour to be clever in order to be different also spoilt *Fade Out*, a first effort by Miss Norah Cutting. (The name is quite genuine, I believe!) This short has possibilities, but again is almost ruined by 'this montage business'. Its climax, when the man who is helping an amateur company on location falls from the tree and dies, is killed by a rapid succession of closely cut shots which the mind positively refuses to follow. The weather conditions under which the film was made were obviously bad, and this should have been taken into consideration when *Fade Out* was edited. If Vertoff [Vertov] had been working under similar conditions, he would never have attempted to do what the director of *Fade Out* has done. Film Guilders, please note!

In case I be misunderstood, let me say that the members of the Film Guild are honestly endeavouring to do good work, but they are afflicted with an attitude which can best be described as posing. Everybody recognises the difficult conditions under which the British amateurs have to work to-day. But these difficulties cannot always be used as an excuse for careless work. Carelessness is impermissible in amateur production.

The Guild is certainly working towards something, and most of its work is experimental, but in doing so it is wasting a terrible amount of time and energy. *Gaiety of Nations*, an amateur film reviewed by me in *Close Up* last month, took over six months to make, and it was worth it. I am not suggesting that every amateur film should take a similar length of time, but the lesson to be learned from *Gaiety of Nations* is that adequate care, thought and attention must be given to all amateur productions if the British amateur film movement is to compete successfully with similar movements on the Continent and in the U.S.A.

Hastily conceived and shoddily constructed work will only bring discredit.

Vol. VI, no. 1   January 1930

R. Bond

FIRST STEPS TOWARDS A WORKERS' FILM MOVEMENT

The organisation of a Workers' Film Movement in Britain is an event of some importance; the fact that the movement is meeting with the most encouraging response, and achieving positive results, is of even greater importance.

In matters of this kind Britain – as in so many other things connected with the Cinema – has been very backward. In Germany the proletarian film movement is firmly established and has intimate contact with hundreds of Trade Unions and other mass working class organisations. In France and Austria, in the Scandinavian countries, and in America, similar movements have been undertaken with varying degrees of success.

But in Britain, up to a month or two ago, nothing practical had been accomplished. In November of last year, however, a group of enthusiasts got together, and laid the foundations for an organisation which, within a very short space of time, got things done.

A Federation of Workers' Film Societies was launched, with the object of encouraging the formation of local Workers' Film Societies on a private membership basis, arranging to supply films and apparatus to the local societies, and encouraging the production in Britain of films of value to the working class.

The Federation is governed by a large and representative Council, with a working Executive which included John Grierson, Henry Dobb, Oswell Blakeston, Ivor Montagu, Ben Davies and the present writer.

London, naturally, was the first centre upon which the Federation concentrated its activities, and a London Workers' Film Society was formed. This Society has for its object, the private exhibition of films of outstanding technical, artistic, educational and other merit which are not easily accessible to workers. The lowest practicable subscription was fixed (13/- per season), and in order that workers should not be debarred through economic reasons from joining, provision was made for the subscription to be paid in monthly instalments.

The response was magnificent. Several hundred members were secured in the first few weeks. The initial performance was arranged for a Sunday afternoon in November, but a week before the date arranged the London County Council stepped in and refused permission for the Cinema to be opened on a Sunday afternoon! Hurried alternative arrangements had to be made and the performance was held in a Co-operative Hall on a week-night. Five hundred members and guests gave an enthusiastic reception to a programme which included Stabavoi's *Two Days*, Florey's *Skyscraper Symphony*, and *Garbage* (*La Zone*) by Lacombe.

Both before and after London's first performance, the Federation had been receiving letters from enthusiasts in many provincial towns, and from workers in the mining areas of South Wales and other coalfield districts. The Federation is now busily engaged in assisting these workers to organise local societies on a similar basis to the London Society. Early results are anticipated from Belfast, Cardiff, Edinburgh and other centres.

One of the first problems that had to be tackled by the Federation was a supply of suitable films. Some of the Russian productions were available, but a wider range was desired. Negotiations with the German workers' film movement produced gratifying results, and the Federation has now at its disposal several films from this quarter, including *Shanghai Document*, *Shadows of the Machine*, and *Hunger in Waldenburg*. This latter film, re-edited, and re-named *The Shadow of the Mine*, was shown with great success at the second performance of the London society.

But the greatest difficulty of all was the Censorship (O Blessed Word!) and the licensing conditions. It cannot too often be said that the regulations governing private film performances are ridiculous and barbaric. Nearly all the local licensing authorities stand by the decision of the British Board of Film Censors, *both for public and private* performances. If a private Society in London wants to show an uncensored film to its own members in an ordinary licensed Cinema or Hall, it must obtain the sanction of the London County Council. If the film were to be exhibited without or against this sanction the license of the Cinema would be endangered. If a private film Society in London wants to show a programme of *censored* films in a Cinema on a Sunday afternoon (which is invariably the only time available) it cannot do so without the sanction of the L.C.C.!

The London Society duly made an application to the L.C.C. for the necessary permit, and was met with a refusal! No reasons were given. The existing Film Society has a permit to exhibit uncensored films and to give Sunday afternoon performances, but apparently a workers' society must not have the same privileges.

The Federation urgently needs finance to develop its work. In the early stages some assistance must be given by the Federation to the local Societies, particularly in many of the industrial areas where economic standards are low. The offices of the Federation at 5, Denmark Street, London, W.C.2 will gladly welcome donations from friends anxious to help in its work.

While, for the time being, the work of the Federation and its affiliated Societies will be mainly in the field of exhibition, it is firmly intended to undertake the production of suitable films in Britain at a later stage. The possibilities, and the material, for production work by a workers' film movement are immense.

Vol. III, no. 2   **August 1928**

Dorothy M. Richardson

FILMS FOR CHILDREN

The failure of the theatre to provide for juveniles anything more than the annual Christmas pantomime, or Blue Bird or Peter Pan, is presumably to be accounted for by the assumption that upper and middle class children are excluded from evening outings, except during holidays, and that in the long summer vacation they are away from town. But, as a matter of fact, few children are rigorously excluded for the whole of term-time from evening entertainments, and an adequate Juvenile Theatre could count upon a daily audience during the season, even if only a percentage of the available children paid each a single visit – and it is to be remembered that children are the best of advertising agents. Again, there is no reason why a summer holiday season should be less successful than that of the winter pantomime. For though most of the patrons are away for a part of the holiday, few are away for the whole of the six weeks, and all are in the privileged position of having earned relaxations.

But if it is strange that no one has yet risked the safe experiment of a Children's Theatre, it is far stranger that we have to date no Children's Cinema. For children of all classes and ages go all the year round to the cinema. And if it is the truth that the trade fears to specialise, fears to do anything but cater all the time for a mixed house, then the waiting opportunity calls aloud to the enterprise of the amateur association.

Meanwhile educated adults discussing the desirability of films for children have fallen into three groups: the *pros*, the *contras*, and those who, regretfully accepting the fact that the film has bolted with humanity and is by no means to be restrained, urge on behalf of the juveniles a restriction to the severely instructional. Most educationalists who believe in the film come heavily to their support. Comparatively few consider its artistic possibilities. Amongst these few is conspicuous Mr Hughes Mearns, who, in his interesting contribution to the May *Close Up*, demonstrated the use of the film as artistic experience, as a means by which children may be trained to discriminate, to detect the commonplace in style and in sentiment, to reach, for instance, the point of blushing with shame for a poet who offer them 'the heart of a rose'. His plea is, in fact, for the children's film regarded as an elevator of the taste of the rising generation.

Training in taste is incontestably an admirable ideal for those whose business it may be to select films for the use of schools – provided the children are not too overtly acquainted with the nature of the intended process. Much, if not everything, that the film can do is at stake the moment the onlookers are aware that they are being challenged to judge, and particularly is this the case with children of normal egocentricity and love of power. A large, perhaps the larger, part of 'education' is unconscious, its vehicle a wholehearted irresponsible collaborating enjoyment. In proof, let any adult recall his early experience and compare his response to those things that were presented to him with credentials from above with that called forth by what he discovered 'accidentally' on his own account. To admit the superiority of the latter is not to attempt to decry systematized education. It is merely to note that even the best efforts of the accredited teacher cannot achieve the overwhelming influence of what offers itself without the taint of ulterior motive. Train up a child in ... by all means, and the obligations of the school screen are inexorable to the limit of the term. But however psychologically enlightened our schools may become, however imbued with the spirit of free collaborations between teachers and taught, they will remain schools, training-grounds for youth that must recognise its state of pupillage. And there is that in every man which not only revolts against the state of pupillage but ceaselessly is outside it, is born adult and more than adult. And it is to this free persistent inner man that art in all its forms is addressed, that the art of the children's cinema will address itself and will do so freely only in circumstances allowing the children to feel themselves simply an audience in surroundings to which they innocently betake themselves for recreation and delight.

All over the world this young audience is now waiting in its millions, and there are almost no films available for it beyond those of its beloved Clown and his imitators. This audience may, and can and does, together with its elders, reap the many gifts offered by the film independently of what is represented. But its individual needs are ignored as they are in no other branch of contemporary art. There are, it is true, the films, many of them excellent, issued by the *British Instructional* for use outside the theatre. Most of these are directly instructional, some only incidentally so. Very many of them might serve as items in public programmes for children. Apart from these and the selection that might be made of the films already publicly exhibited, there is to hand no material wherewith to draw up programmes for children's shows.

It may not unreasonably be objected that the children themselves do not want children's shows, that a cinema for juveniles equipped with no matter what enticements would be tarred for the average child with the same brush as is every institution, educational or otherwise, supposed to be adapted to its needs, and that unless they were denied admission to other cinemas children would treat the newcomer with contemptuous neglect. Some of them would. Many would not. Most parents of cinema-visiting children would rally round the experiment. Those who doubt its final capture of the children may be invited to consider the case of the child amongst his favourite books. For the relationship between child and film finds its nearest parallel in that between child and picture-book. Children's films, in nearly all their desiderata, are akin to children's books, with the difference that the film, with its freedom from the restrictions of language, is more nearly universal than the book and can incorporate, for the benefit of the rest, the originality of each race unhampered by the veil of translation.

Apart from racial divergencies, films for children, like children's books, call for certain common characteristics. The child has ceased to be a born criminal, a subject for continuous repression and admonition, and is ceasing to be a toy adult, a person whose mind is a small blank sheet upon which the enterprising elder may inscribe what he will. Something of these he still is, but the something else, the unlimited opportunity he represents, overshadows the rest. And films for children are, as Mr Mearns points out, the film's great opportunity. An opportunity that can be used to its utmost only by such films as may operate upon the child without need of adult intervention. Films are by their nature precluded from emulating those children's books, many of them excellent, which are intended to be read aloud and expounded. And the pull of the film is just here, in its unsupplemented directness, in the way it can secure collaboration in independence of the grown-up medium who may so easily, by the business of exposition carried too far, inhibit, or at least retard, in the child, the natural desire to explore on its own account. Interpretation should be, as far as possible, implicit. A good picture will tell its own story. The caption, at its utmost only the passing shadow of intervention, is usually indispensable, particularly for the instructional film, which at present is apt to be rather insufficiently captioned. Psychologists have quite justifiably protested in horror and dismay at the way the average 'nature' film lends to the depicted natural processes an unnatural smooth swiftness and unreality that the child's lack of experience renders it unable to correct. Most of these films appear to have been devised merely to astonish, to give sensational exhibitions of 'the wonders of nature'. Inadequate captioning leaves these marvels to lie about in the child's mind unrelated to any kind of actuality. The chick emerging from its shell with the ease and swiftness of a conjuring trick is a well-known example of a method of presentation whose evil can be mitigated only by careful captional commentary.

But, in the child's film proper, as distinct from the instructional film, captions should be reduced to the minimum and should remain impersonal, avoiding intrusion, running commentary, any kind of archness or the 'roguery' so detested by children even while they politely respond to it, avoiding any steering of the onlooker's thoughts or emotions – everything but necessary statement or indication. The child's note is sincerity, and a steadiness that its immature physical and mental gestures fail, to its own vast annoyance, to convey. Only an immense steadiness through thick and thin, a complete serenity of presentation of no matter what, will secure its full collaboration.

Technically, just as its book should be clear in type and easy to read, its film should be clear, avoiding complications – though the child's passion for detail is not to be forgotten – unhurried, and not afraid of repetitions. Youthful eyesight is to be considered and the fact that children look chiefly at, and only very slightly through, what they see, only through within the limits of their small experience. Presentation should incline therefore to the primitive, avoiding highly elaborated technique. The late and deeply lamented 'Felix' has revealed the enchanting possibilities of the drawn film. Let us pray that an artist may arise who will be moved to produce, with all the magic there is for children of five and of fifty in primitive drawing, film fantasies, grotesques, burlesques and what not.

The available subject matter for children's films is, of course, inexhaustible. World history, travel, adventure in all their guises and gradations, stories grave and gay. Satire is acceptable if quiet in tone and matter-of-fact. For the young child, dreams are inestimable treasure. To it, as to God, all things are possible. Its animism is normal and beneficent and at least as 'true', regarded as interpretation, as the varying descriptions of the nature of existence that later take its place. It may be well in the case of elder children to anticipate the strange embarrassment awaiting them in the discovery of themselves as more or less central. But the young child's rose should be allowed to keep its heart. If you strike, it is not at the imagined heart of the rose, but at that of the child, who gave the rose its heart. Let it keep the magic garden, the dreams and fantasies and fairytales, to which eternally it belongs, together with the city of familiar life within which soon enough it must learn its place.

Most children, like most adults, object to being preached at. Yet direct moral teaching has its place, and what a priceless chance here has the film as against the moralising author, who must make his voice between fable, sly parable and sermon. Author, as preacher, is in a dangerous situation unless he be part artist and part saint. But the picture is impersonal. The children sit before it as ladies and gentlemen of the jury. Æsop and La Fontaine, remaining because they are works of art, offer admirable material. So does Strewelpeter, which contains the makings of enchanting grotesque moral films.

Vol. II, no. 3   March 1928

Bryher

WHAT CAN I DO?

What a pity it is that the type of letter most often repeated is the following:

'Being alone here I should like to go often to the movies but they show such dreadful rubbish that it is only once in a while I make up my mind to go. How interesting *Jeanne Ney* sounds from your description but I suppose it will never be shown down here.'

A lot of the letter is true. What one regrets is the attitude behind it. Because it is precisely the sort of people who write such letters *who could do so much for the cinema*.

But they say, what can we do? How can we, a group of three or four at most, help cinematography in a tiny country town?

Well, first they can keep in touch with the progress of cinema all over the world. CLOSE UP will do this for a shilling a month. Then they can go regularly to the cinema even if the films are bad. For one thing there is quite a lot to be learned even from a bad film: how not to light a set, exactly what not to do. But the chief reason for going regularly is that the owners of most local cinemas are willing enough to discuss their programmes with *regular* patrons.

If a copy of a good film is known to be in England, ask for it to be shown. And as there is more chance of its being rented if thirty people ask, interest your friends. Talk to people about the cinema. In the bookstore, the station, the post office, the bank, the grocer's shop, there will be film fans; people who have grown up with the cinema and are ready for more than they are given only do not know what to ask for by themselves. A little propaganda of the right kind, a few good films and there will be a demand (as there now is in Germany) for the better psychological type of picture.

Of course all this means trouble but it means interest as well. I saw last summer in London so that they must be showing somewhere in England, *White Gold, Out of the Mist* (a very beautiful film of the German mountains), *Saucy Suzanne* (some amusing scenes with Ellen Richter), and *Secrets of the Soul* (mutilated beyond recognition and yet here and there with flashes of wonderful photography that all the cutting had not quite destroyed). If enough people in any town ask for them, these films can be seen. And by way of arousing more general interest why not form a cinema library with books such as *The Motion Picture Cameraman* by Lutz, or *The Anatomy of Motion Picture Art* by Elliott to explain the way films are made; Robert Herring's *Films of the Year* to remind them of what has been accomplished, and volumes such as *Grass* to tell more fully the story of expeditions that have brought back moving pictures of little known races and customs. There are some excellent cheap French books on different branches of cinematographic art and American magazines such as *Asia* or the *National Geographic*, often have articles on the taking of such pictures as *Moana* or *Chang*. Then a weekly trade paper is helpful for it would make the group realise among other things the average attitude of the buyer of pictures in the cinematographic world. It need not be an expensive matter, a library; all that is required is a few enthusiasts, a bookshelf, and two or three pounds for books and magazine subscriptions, collected in small sums.

From the library and discussion of films the next step would be to organise a monthly showing of interesting but non-commercial films. It is said that it costs about ten shillings a head in Paris for a group of thirty to hire for a single showing almost any Russian, German or French film, not of purely commercial appeal. I have not been able yet to find out the English cost. But there are fifty or more good foreign films in Wardour Street that will probably never be shown generally. There should not be any insuperable difficulty connected with the hiring of them for a single showing. Possibly the groups from several neighbouring towns could unite for this purpose once a month. The important thing would be to keep the costs as low as possible, for the enthusiast is likely to be someone – schoolteacher, writer, or adolescent – with much interest but little money.

There are now several inexpensive projectors on the market, mainly intended for school use. They usually need a slight knowledge of mechanics if they are to be worked successfully. And it is said that copies of old films can be bought quite cheaply. These would have a certain interest but would be too scratched probably, for serious showing and there are regulations to be observed with regard to the storing of films of an inflammable nature. (Most of the new films are printed on non-inflammable stock.) In time no doubt some substance will be discovered that will enable people to buy prints of their favourite films at a reasonable cost, as now books are bought.

Interest, enthusiasm, vitality; these rather than money are the chief factors. Suppose you take a hundred people who all say 'we would go to the cinema if there were better films' and reply 'there *are* better films and they can be shown to you. Which ones do you want to see?' How many of the hundred would be able to give a single name in answer?

There are films now made. Psychological films. Films of great beauty. Copies of them are in England. They will be shown if people ask for them. When enough people hold together against the mutilation of films and the re-titling of them, these abuses will stop. Only it is really time that people stopped saying 'I would go to the movies if ...' because the matter, perhaps the very future of cinematography, is in their own hands.

Advertisement for the 'Jacky' projector (Vol. VI, no. 3, March 1930).

Advertisement for Bryher's *Film Problems of Soviet Russia* (Vol. IV, no. 3, March 1929).

Vol. II, no. 6   **June 1928**

Bryher

HOW I WOULD START A FILM CLUB

A film club will be of no real service to cinematography unless based upon the following principles.

No censorship.

Films to be shown in the original version as cut by their directors.

Two thirds of the films shown each season should be new, for six months in the cinema may mean revolution of lighting or photographic method.

Abroad it is usually easy to hire a local cinema cheaply at a convenient time but this is difficult in England for the following reasons: a Film Club will be obliged to arrange its meetings chiefly in the evenings or on Sundays. Evenings are out of the question as the local cinema will have its ordinary programme. Most country cinemas have no Sunday license. And I must confess that to date I have been able to obtain no reliable information as to exactly how the censorship rules apply to private film shows. Many of the films shown at the London Film society are cut. Whether this has been done at the request of members or of the L.C.G. I do not know. But to avoid all risks it will probably be better for English Film clubs to buy their own projectors.

It is possible that there are films which it may be unwise to show a general audience, though it is doubtful whether any film can do the harm that people say, but still it is reasonable to bar certain films from universal showing. But if an adult is not intelligent enough to see *Potemkin*, *La Tragédie de la Rue*, or *The End of St Petersburg*, in their original uncut form, then he is not intelligent enough to be in a film society. His want can be catered to by any cinema showing the ordinary Hollywood films. Therefore the first essential of a film club is *no censorship*.

It is possible to buy a good projector in France for thirty pounds and one that will give results equal to any in a small local cinema for sixty. The prices may be higher in England on account of the duty. Or there may be English projectors on the market that will give satisfactory results. But as I have no personal experience of them (where I have seen the French ones used constantly), I will not attempt to deal with the English makes.

From thirty to sixty pounds is a large item at the start though it would probably be cheaper spread across several seasons, than hiring the local picture house. It is hard to say what the electrical cost would be in England. Here in Switzerland, it works out at about sixpence to a shilling for an evening. Probably an arrangement could be made in England to have the projector working 'on power' in the same way that an electrical fire or cleaner is worked. And this is a much cheaper rate than lighting.

There is another point. The Ursulines advertises that it will send out a man, projector and film to any house on payment of costs and a moderate fee. It might be worth while for several small Film Clubs in the same district to unite and buy one projector and employ one man, between them.

Then with regard to choice of film. The Ursulines have arranged to send their programme to Belgium and Switzerland as well as to towns in France. By this means small Film Clubs can afford to see *new* films. Naturally it costs more to hire a new film than an old one but if a central cinema can take it for an initial run and then pass it on to a number of smaller clubs the expense being divided among so many will amount to the same as if each one had hired separately some old films. By this means in time a circle of small cinemas will evolve which will guarantee a showing to new intelligent films, with fair profit on both sides. But for the moment practically the only way in which a good programme will be financially possible will be some sort of amalgamation of clubs who will share together the expense of one *complete and good programme*.

Of course there are a number of foreign films in London that were excellent in their original form. But the foreign trade papers quite cynically print warnings that in England only a 'happy ending' is possible and the versions sent to Wardour Street usually arrive with their continuity destroyed. One good point made by the French quota was that films must be submitted in the form shown in the country of their origin. It is a pity that this rule is not enforced in London for friends who have seen both English and German versions tell me that *Jeanne Ney* and *Am Rande de Welt* have been cut so badly that continuity and balance are broken. And it is useless stating that a film is of value to students of cinematography *and then showing it in a mutilated form*. Therefore the ideal must be direct importation from abroad.

But where in this discussion, is the place of English films? Are there no English films to fill the programme? I do not think there are. Not to come up to the standard of Pabst, Pudowkin [Pudovkin], Bruno Rahn, Czinner and half a dozen others. And if we are to evolve standards of criticism in England and the capacity to make films as great, we have got to see the *best*. And the best at the moment means foreign films.

But then, someone will say, is there not a danger that the film club will become as exclusively foreign as, it was alleged the commercial world was exclusively Hollywood? If it did for a few years it would not matter. Directly the English made similarly good films, these will get shown. (At present it would probably mean that if someone did make a true and psychological film, in England, the only chance for that film would be to show it abroad.) As matters stand it is doubtful if anyone compelled to remain in England can more than surmise and grope after the real developments of modern cinematography. *Mother, Potemkin, The End of St Petersburg, Bett und sofa, Tragédie de la Rue*, and others as great have never been shown publicly in England. *Joyless Street* and *Nju* were shown by the Film Society for one performance, *Joyless Street* in a mutilated form. *Jeanne Ney* and the *Violinist of Florence* to choose at random have been horribly cut. In Paris, in Berlin, in even the smaller towns in Switzerland it is possible to see a programme almost weekly including such a film. IN ENGLAND THEY ARE NEVER SEEN AT ALL. Yet until we know what cinematography has already achieved how can we hope to evolve standards of comparison and criticism?

I have noticed in connection with this point that several educated English people who go occasionally to the cinema come abroad and are frankly baffled by such a film say as *Mother* or *Sühne*. But the people here as they sell one potatoes or newspapers will quite often discuss the same film quite intelligently. They have been trained by several years of good among bad films (for there are bad films shown here as well as elsewhere). But frequently the English are so accustomed to a Western or to sob-stuff that directly they are faced with straight psychology they are uncomfortable. The same applies to America.

It is the duty therefore of the small Film Clubs to build up an audience of intelligent spectators. And here for a start are a few suggestions.

1. Collect as many people as possible who will be intelligently interested but don't for the sake of numbers include those whose presence will prevent the showing of films not in accordance with *their* convention of morality.

2. Decide upon the relative advantages and disadvantages of buying a projector or hiring the local cinema.

3. Take in a trade paper from England, France or Germany and borrow a corner of a room from some member where it may be read. It is valuable to have a trade paper for the following reasons. It will give the commercial viewpoint in the terms of 'tie-ups' with groceries, zoos, aeroplanes, silk stockings, and other commodities. It lists films to be trade shown or released so that people will know what films to look for or demand. It will often include a good technical article on photography, projection etc. Their reviews of films are based naturally on whether the said films are suitable for 'family halls', 'safe booking for sophisticated patrons', 'useful booking for uncritical patrons' or 'sound entertainment on popular lines'. But this straight negation of all artistic merit is perhaps preferable to the half hearted literary criticisms one too often reads which try to fit films into outworn dramatic formulas with which cinematography has no concern.

4. Keep the costs as low as possible as the people who are usually interested in films are young and have little spare money.

5. Get in touch with Film Clubs abroad who will help you to keep up to date with programmes and with other small Film Clubs in England with a view to co-operation. Providing space permits, *Close Up* will be pleased to print names and addresses of any Film Clubs formed.

In time perhaps some kind of central distributing trade show might be arranged for film clubs only. In France there is said to be an excellent system applicable to all films. Copies of a foreign film are sent 'en douane'. That is they are kept at a customs depot provided with projection room. Prospective buyers may view the films there and if they like them, the duty is paid and until the establishment of the quota, the films were allowed to enter. If on the other hand they have not been bought within a reasonable time they are returned to their owners in their country of origin with no duty other than a small fee. Some such system should be arranged in England so that the best foreign films could be seen by representatives of Film clubs who might buy copies for private showing.

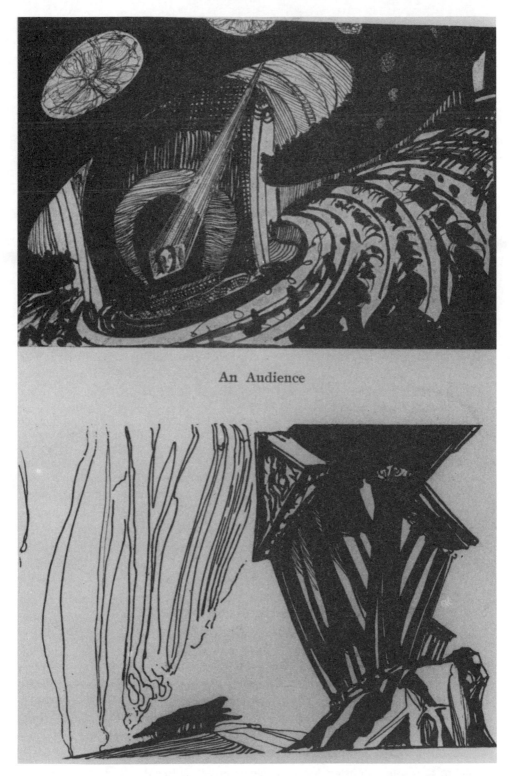

An Audience

'Sketches for studio sets', by Kenneth Macpherson (Vol. I, no. 3, September 1927).

Vol. II, no. 2   February 1928

~~~~~~

Dorothy M. Richardson

A NOTE ON
HOUSEHOLD ECONOMY

(Here the problem of the film theatre is discussed. It raises points that have probably occurred to all film goers. The solutions suggested have of course been applied in many of the larger and more up to date cinemas in England and abroad but the suggestion that the audience should enter from the front, that is, from somewhere beside the screen instead of from behind might prove anything but a remedy. Suggestions on this point are invited [Ed.])

Of the two lions upon the path of those using the film as an art-form, the expense of production and the certainty of mutilation, one has been tethered. Screen plays are being made that both by reason of their subjects and the spirit in which they are handled may be called relatively cheap. Several of these plays have been released, and most film-lovers are under the impression that they have seen certain of them. It now transpires that what has been seen is the remains of the originals after they had been absurdly and pathetically and shamefully mauled by lion number two who is being hauled into the market-place in the hope of some kind of lynching, in the hope that an indignant public will at least make an effort to capture and bind the beast, at least rise up and declare that the mutilation of a film is on a level with the mutilation of a picture or a statue and must cease.

Suppose it does. Suppose that in the fairly near future the film as it stands, to be taken or left, is regarded as the sacred property of its maker. Is the way then clear? Is there not a third lion waiting just round the corner and so far unperceived because we have been thinking of the film-play in terms of the stage-play? Where are these hopeful films to be housed? How are they to gather profitably together the enormous public that we know is ready and waiting for them? For it is not waiting in a theatre. It is waiting for the most part in buildings only half of whose seating capacity offers an acceptable view of the performance. And while for a good stage-play the theatre-loving public will sit or stand in any part of the house, for a film they will take only those seats from which it is possible to see. And in most cinemas such seats come to an end about half-way down the hall. Can the new producer concentrating his attention on the business of turning out a good film afford to ignore the front rows? Big Business will never consent to ignore them or any part of the economic problem of film production that is so fundamentally different from that of the producer of plays whose house consists of several parts related to each other as good, better, and best. The film-producer's house is sharply divided into two or at the most three parts, related to each other as good, fairly good and impossible. And thus it is that to date the economically sound films are films capable of attracting together with those who pay for good seats, those who will pay for a view that relatively is no view at all.

And to admit that good films if they are to pay their ways must either be subsidized or housed in halls all of whose seats are good seats is not to admit that the front rows cannot assimilate good films, [and] will not pay for bad views of good films as they pay for their bad views of the average film to date. They can and will. There are good films whose appeal is universal and safely collects those who customarily sit in front. But it is probable that the average good new film will tend for some time to come to select its company from the habitual back rowers. Which is to say that good films, if for no other than economic reasons, need houses all of whose seats are decent seats.

Everything seems to point directly to the many-tiered semi-circular auditorium, a disposition of the audience which for reasons already noted elsewhere is vastly inferior to the rectangular disposition of the early, garage-shaped cinemas. The alternative is lateral extension. A good side view is after all a view, and anything is better than being an inch too near. In either case if the forward space is counted out, and in time in all decently run cinemas it most surely will be counted out, the utmost possible lateral extension becomes an economic necessity. And it is only owing to unreflecting conformity with theatrical tradition that the majority of our cinemas fail to exploit the possibilities of lateral extension. The majority of our cinemas are necessarily oblong in shape. Wide frontages, except for very big business are hard to come by and expensive in the upkeep. But it is the unimaginative handling of these oblongs, relatively so easy to build or acquire, that, in placing the screen after the manner of a stage upon the narrower, end wall opposite the entrance instead of upon either of the longer, side walls, has secured a high percentage of bad seats and sacrificed so many good ones. The extremest side views from the middle and back rows of the average cinema are excellent and an extension of these rows would yield places with views vastly better than those to be had from any part of the front rows.

There is a further possibility applying to every type of cinema and whose neglect is directly due to thoughtless imitation of play-house procedure. The theatre has its main entrance and houses its general paraphernalia in the less valuable part of the house, the part furthest from the stage. In the cinema, though the relative values of the parts are exactly reversed the disposition of the etceteras is not. They face the screen instead of being behind it or at its sides. Why should not the screen be immediately inside the main entrance, either backing or set sideways to it, and its attendant staff of torch-bearers and other indispensables facing the house instead of occupying space that should be a solid mass of good seats? The only space needed by the management in that portion now so lavishly and lamentably squandered is accommodation for the operator and his fire-extinguishers. No one leaving a cinema in the midst of a play and pausing behind the end barrier for a last glimpse can have failed to notice the excellence of his view. Views almost equally excellent are to be had behind the side back-rows where at present torch-bearers and attendants hang about and chat. The greater part of that hindmost region of barriers, curtains, draughts, arrivals and departures, that should be the ultimate, undisturbed wall-backed paradise of the film-lover, is sheer waste land.

Vol. X, no. 2   June 1933

E. Coxhead

TOWARDS A CO-OPERATIVE CINEMA
THE WORK OF THE ACADEMY, OXFORD STREET

I

Everyone knows the Academy Cinema. When we say Academy, it is as often as not (and how shocked our grandfathers would be to hear it) that one we mean. It is more than a cinema; it is a policy, a promise, a guarantee. Something one has in common with other people, a topic of conversation, a means of making friends.

To understand the Academy and its aims, one has to go back more than three years: back, in fact to 1916, when Elsie Cohen, a young woman fresh from college, and rather interested in films, found Wardour Street open to women, as so many fields were then which now are not. She walked into a post on the *Kinematograph Weekly*, and began, from the excellent vantage-point of a technical paper, her apprenticeship to the oddest trade in the world.

She soon observed that there were a good many interesting film happenings in other countries beside America. There was Germany, for instance, and there was also Holland, where a small company was making films specifically for the English market. The difficulty of getting information about them suggested to her that the company needed a good publicity manager. She wrote offering her services, and by return – those were the happy, haphazard days – was invited.

Her work for this company included, in the end, everything except actual direction. She managed the studio, sold films, travelled everywhere, even getting to the States and selling her first European film. When the company was dissolved, she already knew her way about the film world; she went to Berlin, coming in at the end of the great silent period. She stood over *Vaudeville* and *Manon*, and had her fingers in many interesting pies. So far, just the chequered career anyone might have in the Trade.

But already she saw in it more than a trade. She grew yearly more convinced that the most important film work was scarcely heard of in England, let alone seen; but that there were people at home who would be interested, people who never went to films at all, but would be won over by the new kind of film, which struggled for a footing against the old. The audiences of Germany and France appreciated and understood; and so would the right audience in England.

She came home, and found films in a state of apathy. For a time she worked as floor-manager in English studios, but the lack of organisation made a too painful contrast with those of Germany. Everyone, she said, spent their time hanging around waiting.

The idea of catering for an intelligent film public was growing in her mind. People seemed interested. She was constantly asked about her experiences in Germany, about the new films from Russia, about the chances of getting old films revived. Only the Trade was not interested at all. She could find no one to finance her.

For years she waited, being discouraged and laughed at with a dreary persistence. It was not till 1929 that she had any kind of opportunity; the little Windmill Theatre fell vacant for six months, and she was allowed to try out a highbrow season which was a success. But then the theatre was taken for other purposes, and her pilgrimage in the Trade wilderness began again. Finally she secured the support of Eric Hakim: in 1931 the Academy opened with *Earth*. Everyone gave the scheme a six weeks' run. But it seems likely that of all London's film policies, it will have the longest life.

II

The policy of the Academy, like all living ideas, has developed since its birth and one change is notable. At first it was definitely a repertory cinema, and showed interesting pictures without regard to their age or the number of times they had been seen before. The audience clamoured for revivals, and the difficulty of seeing again in an ordinary cinema a picture one had once liked was, and for that matter still is, acute. The Academy worked off a good many of the great silent pictures during 1931, and then the audience began to show an interest in new work and to ask for it. This accorded with Miss Cohen's own desire to encourage fresh ideas, and the Academy changed over to a policy of premieres and longer runs. The new sound films *West-front 1918*, *Kameradschaft*, *The Blue Express* were shown, and their immense success established the cinema as important. Even the Trade noticed it, and was uneasily stirred.

From the beginning, Miss Cohen realised that the ordinary clamorous methods of film publicity were useless; the public she worked for had long been deafened by them; it had to be approached quietly, rationally, told the really important thing about each new picture, the director, the technical staff, the country and place of origin, the artistic aim. Only circularising could convey all this information. She started a mailing list, quite a small one. The names on it now run into thousands and a good many of them are people who live far away, but like to know what is going on and come up to London specially for a particular film. Ten of the Academy circulars are posted each week to China. The recipients intend to come up too, in time.

So the co-operative spirit of the Academy began. The audience began to write in its turn, asking for this and that, criticising and suggesting. Gradually the Academy became a nucleus of intelligent film thought, a meeting-ground and a clearing house for ideas. All the interest which had been floating in the air for a year or more before it opened, it gathered, and in some sense interpreted by its programmes. It was a very great service to the cinema. Small groups and film societies, valuable though they are, cannot by their very nature do such a work; because their members constitute, finally, a clique, and a clique, do what it may, is always in the end driven into an attitude of intellectual conceit; and also because they are so often dominated by one strong personality. The

Academy has been broad enough to escape intellectual snobbery, and Miss Cohen sufficiently wise, experienced and wholehearted to efface herself and see her audience as whole. Her years on the Continent and up and down Wardour Street did that for her; they fitted her to guide, and to guide impersonally, what is fast becoming a national movement.

The Academy films have included three Pabsts, five Clairs, the Dutch *Pierement*, the Swedish *En Natt*, the American *Quick Millions*, the Russian *Blue Express* and *Road to Life*, the German *Hauptmann von Köpenick*, *Mädchen in Uniform*, *Barberina*, *Emil and the Detectives*; that gives some idea of the breadth of choice. Not all these films have pleased everyone; they have not all pleased Miss Cohen equally; but that is the point. Each one had some new and particular merit, and for that it was shown, regardless of the prejudices of any particular section of the audience. Only by encouraging a wide appreciation can such work as the Academy keep its educative value.

On the other hand, its relations with the amateur film societies all over the country have been more than friendly; in many cases it has kept them alive. Miss Cohen is at present acting as a quite unpaid agent and source of supply to these rather bewildered amateurs; she passes on to them her films, supplies them with endless information and advice regarding the securing of films, and listens with amazing patience to all their long and often unreasonable demands. As she is very well aware, the new intelligence and understanding of cinema which they represent is tremendously valuable to her. It is preparing the ground for a chain of Academies in every big town, and this, of course, is her ideal. Not until her work is national can it really be said to have succeeded. When she can again find the capital and the encouragement, this chain will be established, for her plans have a way of working themselves out. The further plan of a film club and social centre at the Academy itself is at present held up for lack of space; but the need for it is great, and Miss Cohen is undoubtedly the person to carry it through.

Of course there has been criticism of her programmes; but apart from her deliberate policy of broad-mindedness, the extreme difficulty she finds in getting the right films at the right time must be taken into account. Her market is the whole world, and this gives plenty of room for the rapaciousness and obstinacy which seem everywhere to characterise the renter of films. Over and over again she is held up in the most urgent negotiations, because huge sums are demanded for first British rights of films which would have no appeal in the ordinary commercial market. A chain of cinemas would, of course, help matters here.

In my opinion, the greatest work of the Academy is the establishment of quite new relations between exhibitor and audience. As its ideas spread, the theatre itself will become less important; it will end as just one of a wide circle of theatres working on the same plan. But the spirit of co-operation which it has fostered will increase; the ideal of a thinking audience, as opposed to an audience which is spared all thought by the exhibitor's own policy, may finally become the most powerful factor in the Trade. And it will be high time. Not until that happens can we expect a consistently high standard of film production. For we know well enough that in the last instance it is the audience, not the artist, that makes the film; the artist can only supply a demand which is already there. The film is our responsibility, and the co-operative film theatre our best way of creating a film that is worth while.

Vol. IV, no. 5 May 1929

~~~~~~

Hanns Sachs

MODERN WITCH-TRIALS

A further article from the pen of Dr Hanns Sachs, eminent Viennese psychoanalyst, dealing with the question of censorship. His thousand words of scientific examination are more than enough to puncture the ponderous bladder and deflate it of its copious hot-air!

A few months ago I read about a trial against a book describing a form of human love not acknowledged hitherto either by acts of parliament or by popular story writers: the love relations between two women. A modern witch-trial is bound to have its modern ways: the attorney for the prosecution admitted that the book in question was a serious work of art, far from frivolity or lasciviousness, but – and in this culminated everything that was said in favour of the prosecution – we must think of those who are in danger of falling, those who waver between virtue and vice and may, by the impression of such a book wrought on their weak minds, be tempted away from normality and flung into everlasting perdition. Judge and jury and the court of appeal applauded this sane argument and damned the book unhesitatingly – which, I sincerely hope, has done something to enlarge its circulation. Anyhow, the thesis of the danger of the unprotected ones who may get lured into vice – a moral or political one – by a book or a picture is the main stronghold of the formidable fortress: censorship. It's worth while to try out how this will apply to film censorship.

Exposed to danger are, as far as the film is concerned, mainly the children and half the adults of the urban proletariat – in rural conditions the film is no factor and the young ones of the middle classes are safeguarded by their families. Now, I don't think that any person who has a glimmering of a notion about the conditions of family life among the proletariat – as depending on the housing problems – will assert that an average proletarian child can ever see in a film anything showing sexuality in such a gross and coarse way as it is shown to it daily – or nightly – at home and near home. True, the American film 'demi-mondaines' of the movies are far more attractive and tempting than the real ones whom the child sees, so to speak, 'in the flesh' – but then these real ones are far less chaste and virtuous. It will take a long way of amelioration of the conditions of the working classes till the film may be considered in the light of a danger to the morality of their offspring.

Let us take another point of view. Those who had reached an age of discretion 25 years ago will remember the strong and protracted outburst of public feeling in England against the government methods in Russia about the time of the Russo-Japanese war and shortly afterwards – at the epoch of pogroms and 'black hundreds'. Had at this time a film art existed and had there been an English director with the gift of expressing his views in a vigorous and virile fashion, had this director taken the revolt of the Black Sea fleet as a subject and treated it according to the universal feeling of his countrymen – the result of his endeavours would have been a film exactly on the lines of *Potemkin*; there is no doubt whatever that it would have aroused the frantic acclamations of every true and staunch English audience, that it would have been considered as appealing to the best traditions and the sounded instincts of the British nation – hate of oppression and corruption, sympathy with the weak and so on. But to-day *Potemkin* is banned, Englishmen must be protected from falling into the bottomless pit of Bolshevism. The contrast becomes still more glaring in Germany where *Potemkin* has been shown innumerable times to enthusiastic audiences; the persons protesting vehemently against this enthusiasm as 'unpatriotic' are absolutely identical with those who only twelve years ago would have considered it downright defeatism to depict a Russian army or navy officer as anything else but a brutal and inhuman monster, hated to death by his inferiors.

A third case: A short time ago in Berlin was shown an American film which I don't hesitate to call the worst of its class. *The Man who Laughs*. A work without any artistic ambition, appealing only to the densest – especially sadistic – emotions. In this film is shown a woman in her bath and at the subsequent toilet as being observed through the key-hole by two men. True, the naked body is never shown entirely, only various and sundry appetizing bits of it, some directly, some indirectly as silhouettes or mirror-reflection. The tendency of this scene which has nothing whatever to do with the plot is plainly to give the audience cheap erotic sensations – absolutely the same as in any pornographic picture. And yet it seems that this scene passed censorship even in chaste U.S.A. from whence it comes – whereas many pictures of 'Ways to Strength and Beauty' which certainly were not intended to stir sexual reaction and could hardly do so, had to be cut out because the beautiful athletic bodies were 'stark naked'. How about the 'danger problem' here?

I trust I have made it clear that this 'danger' business is shear bunk being just a thin disguise of something else, to which disguise cling many well intentioned persons who ought to know better. The tendency of censorship as shown above is simply to deny the existence of certain facts which are not in accordance with the code of life which censorship tries to uphold as the only existing one. In print, especially in scientific discussion they may be admitted, in the movies, which appeal to the emotional side of an indefinite number of people they are to be treated as if they don't exist. This 'as if' is the centre of the problem; the true meaning of censorship is nothing more or less than the maintaining of a fiction – the queer idea that things are not what they are as long as you don't say so.

The psychoanalyst knows a mechanism which works exactly the same way in the individual mind and plays a great part in early development. The child, as long as its personality is still weak and undeveloped, has not the weapons of experience and judgment to defend itself against untoward emotions and to solve the many and grave conflicts in its mind. In face of these indissoluble difficulties it resorts to a more primitive way of reaction: it 'represses' those facts – emotions, recollections, phantasies, whatever they are, – which are contradictory to its newly acquired standard of personality; i.e. it tries to make out, – and succeeds by and by, – that these facts don't exist – never existed. Of course every individual pays a high price for this falsification, becoming unable to face certain realities of life and to deal with them adequately.

Censorship is only the social repetition of this individual process of regression, of the most primitive and infantile way [of] reacting to a conflict. The child, as it grows up, learns to use better methods, to see problems and grapple with them successfully.

How long has a nation to resort to these infantile methods which are outgrown by every reasonable member of it?

Vol. VI, no. 4   April 1930

~~~~~~

R. Bond

ACTS UNDER THE ACTS

Friends and foes who feared (or hoped, as the case may be) that after the rejection of the *Close Up* petition nothing more would be heard for some time about the Film Censorship in Britain, will rejoice (or curse) in the knowledge that this question has suddenly become a storm centre of heated discussion and fierce controversy.

So numerous and involved have been the incidents of these last few weeks that it will do no harm to get some little order out of the chaos.

Act 1

It is now well known that in November 1929 the London Workers' Film Society applied to the London County Council for a licence to exhibit privately uncensored films on Sunday afternoons. The application was summarily rejected without explanation or reason despite the fact that the Film Society had long enjoyed these same privileges. The Workers' Film Society said that the L.C.C. decision was actuated by class bias; that they were not far wrong will shortly be seen.

In January 1930 the Workers' Film Society again applied to the L.C.C., this time for a permit to show *Potemkin* on one specified occasion to its members. The L.C.C. replied saying that the Council had decided that under no circumstances could *Potemkin* be shown in any Cinema licensed by them under the 1909 Act. Back went a letter pointing out that *Potemkin* had been exhibited by the Film Society as recently as November 10th, 1929 in premises licensed by the L.C.C. under the 1909 Act. Would the L.C.C. please explain?

No explanation was forthcoming. Another letter was sent. This time the L.C.C. replied dealing with another matter altogether and strangely enough completely omitting any reference at all to *Potemkin*!

Act 2

The Film Society announces that it will show *Storm Over Asia* at the Tivoli on February 23rd. Great sensation. The Lord's Day Observance Council is very upset and calls on

the L.C.C. to prohibit the exhibition. The audience at the Tivoli is assembled. A copy
of a letter received by the Tivoli management from the L.C.C. is flashed on the screen.
Fearing the worst, and straining our eyes we read:

> Clause 8 (a) of the Rules of Management, etc., etc.
>
> No cinematograph film shall be exhibited which is likely to be injurious to morality
> or to encourage or incite to crime, or lead to disorder, or to be in any way offensive in the
> circumstances to public feeling or which contains any offensive representation of living
> persons.
>
> I am to add [proceeds the letter] that should any disorder occur at the premises during
> the exhibition of *Storm over Asia* the Council will hold the licensee of the premises
> responsible.
>
> I am Sir,
Your obedient servant.

The Film Society laughed. So would a cat. But can you beat it?

Act 3

The I.L.P. Masses Stage and Film Guild announces that it will show *Mother* in a
London cinema on March 2nd. An application for the necessary permit is confidently
sent to the L.C.C. A week or so before the date of the proposed exhibition the Council
in full session assembled rejected the application.

The Masses Guild then says that it will show *Mother* in the Piccadilly Theatre, a
theatre licensed by the Lord Chamberlain.

Theoretically, this is possible. The L.C.C. has no control over this theatre, and the
Lord Chamberlain, it was assumed, had no authority to prevent any film being shown
in one of his theatres on a day when his licence was not operative.

But prevent it he did. Nobody seems to know why, and it would appear that the
Chamberlain himself is not very sure of his grounds for it is expected in some quarters
that he will lift his ban. By the time this article appears he may have done so.

Act 4

Meantime, Miss Rosamund Smith, Chairman of the Theatres and Music Halls
Committee of the L.C.C. has been giving the low-down on the whys and wherefores
of the decision of that remarkable body. It all boils down to the fact that the minimum
subscription to the Film Society is twenty-five shillings, whereas anyone can join the
other Societies on payment of one shilling. Which means, according to Miss Smith, that
any member of the general public can join these latter societies. You see, if you pay
twenty-five shillings to the Film Society, you are not a member of the general public.

Class bias? Oh, no! Anyway, the combined entrance fee and subscription to the
Workers' Film Society for a season of eight performances is 13*s.*, which is just about
half that of the Film Society, so when is a member of the general public not a member
of the general public? Answer – twelve bob!

Act 5

These extraordinary events, following so rapidly one upon the other seem at last to have convinced various people that the British censorship and its attendant licensing regulations are the most reactionary in Europe. It takes a long time to get some people moving, but an all-Party Committee has been organised and has promised to raise the whole question of the censorship in the House of Commons and in the L.C.C.

The first step of this Committee of M.P.s was to arrange for a deputation to the L.C.C. to ask for a change in regulations governing private societies.

For this meeting the Theatres and Music Halls Committee of the Council prepared a special report. From this it appears that they asked the Board of Censors whether in its opinion the films *Mother*, *Potemkin*, *Storm Over Asia* and *Modern Babylon* are provocative or likely to cause a breach of the peace if shown (a) publicly, or (b) privately. 'The Board's opinion is definitely in the affirmative', we are told.

Well we all know the Board of Censors. (The Company controlling *Modern Babylon* recently re-submitted it to the Censors who rejected it on account of its 'constant alternation of brutality and bloodshed, with scenes of licence in many cases', and 'indecency'.)

The Committee recommended to the full Council that no permission be given for the private exhibition of *Mother* and the report was couched in such terms as to suggest that the Film Society itself might have its privileges withdrawn.

The reference back of the Committee's report was defeated by 69 votes to 38!

So there you are. Comment seems quite superfluous; it is quite painful enough merely to record such events as these.

One other thing. A certain film critic on a London newspaper, who is famous for his admiration of Russian films and for his complementary remarks concerning Russian film directors, professes to see the whole business as part of a 'well concocted scheme' to undermine the censorship. Almost a Bolshevik plot, in fact, with Ivor Montagu as the chief conspirator and villain of the piece!

This gentleman rushed in to assure the great British public that (1) the cinema industry is perfectly satisfied with the present system (which may or may not be true, but has nothing to do with this case), and (2) that if Moscow's propaganda films are rigorously excluded, their directors may eventually be persuaded to make films of a 'more commercial and entertaining character'.

Which, when you come to think of it, is a very significant remark. What a pity that our friend is going to be disappointed.

PART 8

Fade

Vol. X, no. 2   June 1933

Bryher

WHAT SHALL YOU DO
IN THE WAR?

To be a Jew is bad, and to be a Communist is worse, but to be a pacifist is unforgivable.

—Popular German slogan.

A year ago this June I returned from Berlin. I came from a city where police cars and machine guns raced about the streets, where groups of brown uniforms waited at each corner. The stations had been crowded: not with people bound for the Baltic with bathing bags, but with families whose bundles, cases or trunks bulged with household possessions. (The fortunate were already going into exile.) Everywhere I had heard rumors or had seen weapons. Then I crossed to London and to questions 'what is Pabst doing now' or 'will there be another film like *Mädchen in Uniform?*' I said 'I didn't go to cinemas because I watched the revolution' and they laughed, in England.

But the revolution is a fact now even to people quite uninterested in politics. The *Manchester Guardian* and the *Nation* printed a little of the truth. They have been banned in Germany. Mowrer in *Germany Puts the Clock Back* quoted documents and they tried to turn him out of the country. Actually the real news of the rebellion could not be printed in any newspaper. Tortures are freely employed, both mental and physical. Hundreds have died or been killed, thousands are in prison, and thousands more are in exile.

A great number are Jews. Six hundred thousand, many of them men who were among the finest citizens Germany had, peaceful and hard working, are to be eliminated from the community. In future no Jew is to have the rights of an ordinary citizen. He may be made to fight for Germany but his children are to be denied an education. But besides these Jews, and in a way in even worse plight (for they have no other country to which to turn), are the hundreds of liberal minded Protestant Germans who are accused of trying to build up an alliance with France.

'To be a Jew is bad, to be a Communist is worse, but to be a Pacifist is unforgivable.' This very popular slogan sums up the revolution. For it is a revolution against the whole conception of peace.

Germany says that she does not want war. This is probably true as far as the statement applies to the present year. She would like first to re-train, re-equip and re-arm the entire folk. But unless her pre-war territory be handed back to her, it is doubtful she will content herself with any peaceful protest.

This is not a place to discuss the complicated question of treaty revision. It must be remembered, however, that 'two wrongs do not make a right' and that it would not be honorable on the part of Europe, to transfer populations to a land that has denied equal rights of citizenship to many of its most loyal families.

For twelve years a liberal and moderate minded section of the German people fought a losing fight. They won popular opinion in England and America over to their side. Treaty revision and the German right to re-arm were discussed in a manner impossible anywhere some years ago. German goods were bought, German films shown and books read, and Germans were welcomed abroad as students and tourists. In exactly three weeks the national socialists smashed what it had taken twelve years of patient and unrewarding work to build.

Think of their blunder! Only a government wilfully ignorant of English conditions or extremely afraid, would ban a paper that has the *Manchester Guardian*'s reputation for honesty and impartial criticism. How was it possible for them not to realise that Protestant and Catholic alike would react with horror to their boycott of inoffensive Jews.

Books by Heinrich and Thomas Mann, Remarque, Arnold Zweig, Stefan Zweig, Tucholsky, Feuchtwanger, Schnitzler, Glaeser, and many other authors, together with foreign translations have been taken from libraries and publicly burnt. The writers themselves have been forced into exile and in many cases, their possessions in Germany confiscated.

Heinrich and Thomas Mann both come from a north German non-Jewish family and their work has contributed more than is realised to the overcoming of hostility towards German intellectual life at the end of the war. Heinrich Mann was, we believe, the first German writer to be invited to visit a group of French authors after the Armistice and both his books and those of his brother enjoy an international reputation.

Schnitzler died before the present conflict and was never a political writer. Several of the other authors are banned merely because they wished to help towards a better feeling for France.

Pabst, who did more than any one to open the cinemas of the world to German films, has been exiled and it is said a price has been put on his head should he approach a German frontier. They will never forgive him the fraternising of French with German workmen in *Kameradschaft*. *All his films have been banned in Germany*. The men who worked with him and under him, have been scattered across Europe. It is said in fact, that barely ten per cent of the workers in the German studios of last year are left.

Hundreds of Jewish doctors have been forbidden to practise and have been dismissed from the hospitals. They are unable to obtain work and in several cases known to me personally, they have been left to starve. Einstein and many of their best scientists are in exile. Those who waited too long, or could not afford a railway ticket, are shot or are in prison.

It is quite possible that a lot of German citizens do not realise what is happening. If a man complains of his treatment or of the new laws, he is beaten to death or sent to a concentration camp. Should he escape across the border, his nearest relative or a friend pays the penalty for him.

It is also extremely probable that English tourists staying at hotels frequented by foreigners in the main cities will see little of what is happening. Last June, I walked down the Kurfurstendamm amongst a number of people shopping and staring quietly at the windows of the various stores. One street away, several men were killed and injured in a so–called political row. The average tourist knowing little of the language would never have heard of it. As for the English speaking people there for trade or study, they have either to accept the present regime, even to the point of saying in their letters how wonderful it is, or a pressure of small events will combine to force them to departure. They may talk when they get back to England but they won't while they are there.

For the last fifteen years people have used the words peace and war so much that the sound of them means nothing at all. They have read war books, said 'how terrible' and gone on to read accounts of life in the south seas or on a farm or stories of a feudal castle, as if all were equally real or perhaps better, unreal. They have signed resolutions and exchanged armistice memories and sighed (if they are old enough) for 'the good old days before the war'. But very few have ever made a constructive attempt to prevent the months of 1914 from being repeated on a larger and worse scale.

I do not think a pacifism of theories and pamphlets is of any use. The mass of the people desires action. In this respect both fascism and communism alike respond to primitive psychological needs. Ninety per cent of any nation wants deeds and not ideas.

If this point of view is to govern the world, then we can hope only for war, with intervals of peace. But in one of these upheavals (and in spite of speeches how near we are to it at present) the whole of civilisation may disappear. And we shall not return to the Utopia of the machine-less savage, so often evoked by romantic writers, because the native of the Congo say or the south seas is a product of an elaborate scheme of life that has taken generations of peace to evolve. The barbarism to which we should return would be something so cruel and so stark that only the very cunning or the very strong could hope for survival. It would be comparatively easy even to–day for half Europe to perish from starvation.

It is said that in the Balkan countries not a child is adequately fed, but every third person is in uniform. They do not organise their food supplies but they find money for their armies. One rash move on the part of desperate young boys, might loose war right across Europe.

I believe peace still to be possible. But on condition only that we fight for it now as hard as we should fight in war.

If we want peace, we must fight for the liberty to think in terms of peace, for all the peoples of Europe. It is useless for us to talk about disarmament when children are being trained in military drill and when every leader of intellectual thought in Germany is exiled or silenced.

Democracy may have many faults but the democracies that have been longest established have the least record of wars. Look at Switzerland and the United States. The Crimea apart, we had for almost a century no European fighting. Autocracy (and autocracy can come from a system as well as from an individual) breeds discontent. Discontent discharges itself in war.

Whether the danger come from a repressed and irritated people or whether it be deliberately provoked by a group, we are faced at this moment with a danger greater than at any time since 1918. Do not let the lessons of the last war be lost. Remember if mass excitement is loosed, few of us will be able to retain clear judgment or to stand against the pressure of mass feeling. Make your decision now while you still have time to work for whatever you believe.

And remember that Austria, though a German speaking country, is struggling still to preserve her independence and that one should differentiate between the two countries and not group them together because of a language similarity.

If one believes that there is never a justification for war, then it is one's duty to join a peace organisation and fight for peace, not through the signing of resolutions but through an attempt to help those who are now suffering because they believed in peace. One should try to spread the knowledge of other nations among the many English in outlying villages who still believe a foreigner to be not quite as human as themselves. Remember that abstract words about peace mean very little; and that the first impressions that a child receives about another country will be lasting. If you know children, find out if their geography lessons are interesting and what they think about other nations.

But it would be advisable to join an organisation and keep in touch with it, not to come with conscientious objections discovered only on the outbreak of war.

On the other hand, those who think that there are times when a resort of arms is justified, should decide what to do if there were war. What training have they? Do they know anything of modern warfare?

Remember that the last war proved to us that we have no right to demand a man who does not believe in war, to be a soldier, for we failed in our war and we have all but failed in our peace. But we have the right to demand that everyone shall choose now, and not when the struggle is upon us, whether he or she will fight or not. And if one does not wish to fight, one must think if all is being done now that can make peace possible?

What I write applies to women equally with men. They will be conscripted in the next war; already there is labor conscription for them in Germany and it is said that a similar law would be applied upon the outbreak of hostilities in France.

Let us decide what we will have. If peace, let us fight for it. And fight for it especially with cinema. By refusing to see films that are merely propaganda for any unjust system. Remember that close co-operation with the United States is needed if we are to preserve peace, and that constant sneers at an unfamiliar way of speech or American slang will not help towards mutual understanding. And above all, in the choice of films to see, remember the many directors, actors and film architects who have been driven out of the German studios and scattered across Europe because they believed in peace and intellectual liberty.

The future is in our hands for every person influences another. The film societies and small experiments raised the general level of films considerably in five years. It is for you and me to decide whether we will help to raise respect for intellectual liberty in the same way, or whether we all plunge, in every kind and colour of uniform, towards a not to be imagined barbarism.

APPENDIX 1

The Contents of *Close Up*, 1927–1933

ROTHA; Bits and Pieces, ORLTON WEST.

Vol. V, no. 4, October 1929
As Is, KENNETH MACPHERSON; The Independent Cinema in Belgium, CARL VINCENT; Going Talkie, ERNEST BETTS; Reasons of Rhyme, ROBERT HERRING; Lachman and Others, HUGH CASTLE; A Tragedy, HAY CHOWL; Heavy Stuff, OSWELL BLAKESTON; Epoch, ROGER BURFORD; Pour la Défense du Cinéma Artistique, FREDDY CHEVALLEY; The Independent Cinema Congress, JEAN LENAUER; News of the Soviet Cinema, P.A.

Vol. V, no. 5, November 1929
As Is, KENNETH MACPHERSON; Mechanisms of Cinema (contd), L. SAALSCHUTZ; SuPeRpRoDuCeR [*sic*], MICHAEL STUART; *Stump of an Empire*, P. ATTASHEVA; Over the Moon, ROBERT HERRING; Kino and Lichtspiel, H.A. POTAMKIN; Freud on the Films, OSWELL BLAKESTON; Making a Film of the Actual, JOHN GRIERSON; Loss and Profit, CLIFFORD HOWARD; Finds, D.L.H.; 'This Montage Business', R. BOND; Voir et Entendre, FREDDY CHEVALLEY.

Vol. V, no. 6, December 1929
As Is, KENNETH MACPHERSON; Stuttgart and Its Effects, A. KRASZNA-KRAUSZ; Vertoff, His Work and the Future, JEAN LENAUER; Talk on Technique, OSWELL BLAKESTON; Second-Rate Sex, NORMA MAHL; The Amateur Convention, R. BOND; A Certificate of Approval, BRYHER; Turksib, H.D.; Movie: New York Notes, H.A. POTAMKIN; Dental Dilemma, HUGH CASTLE; L'Esprit Moyen et le Cinéma, FREDDY CHEVALLEY.

Vol. VI, no. 1, January 1930
As Is, KENNETH MACPHERSON; The Censorship Petition, DOROTHY M. RICHARDSON; In the Land Where Images Mutter, H.A. POTAMKIN; Old Moore's Fourth Dimension, HUGH CASTLE; Three More Russian Films, OSWELL BLAKESTON; Pre-View of The General Line, BRYHER; 'Not Yet To Be Seen!' K.M. & B.; Pre-Script for The London Review, ROBERT HERRING; Casparius: A Name in Film and Photo, K.M.; Menace around the Corner, CLIFFORD HOWARD; First Steps Towards a Workers' Film Movement, R. BOND; Mickey Virtuose, F. CHEVALLEY.

Vol. VI, no. 2, February 1930
As Is, KENNETH MACPHERSON; The Japanese Cinema, W. RAY; Movie: New York Notes, H.A. POTAMKIN; Twenty-Three Talkies, ROBERT HERRING; A German School Film, BRYHER; In Praise of Simplicity,

JEAN LENAUER; The Cinema in the Argentine, H.P. TEW; Ah Oui! Le Cinéma!, F. CHEVALLEY; An Outburst on an Old Subject, D.L.H.

Vol. VI, no. 3, March 1930
As Is, KENNETH MACPHERSON; An Introduction to 'The Fourth Dimension in the Kino, Part I', S.M. EISENSTEIN; Filmic Art and Training (an interview with Eisenstein), MARK SEGAL; Scenario-Writer, MICHAEL STUART; Present Tense, L. SAALSCHUTZ; Super Film, OSWELL BLAKESTON; Movie: New York Notes, H.A. POTAMKIN; A New Commission, BRYHER; Light Rhythms, O.B.; Here Endeth the First Lesson, B. DE LA V., H.A.M., P.R.

Vol. VI, no. 4, April 1930
As Is, KENNETH MACPHERSON; The Fourth Dimension in the Kino, Part II, S.M. EISENSTEIN; The English Censorship, ROBERT HERRING; It Rests with the Local Authorities, L.B. DUCKWORTH; Acts under the Acts, R. BOND; Paris Hears Eisenstein, S. BRODY; The Personality of the Player, H.A. POTAMKIN; In the Old Days, CHARLOTTE ARTHUR; Mechanisms of Cinema, L. SAALSCHUTZ; Our Literary Screen, OSWELL BLAKESTON; Production, Construction, Hobby, A. KRASZNA-KRAUSZ; Mutter Krausen's Fahrt ins Gluck, TRUDE WEISS; News from the Provinces, JEAN LENAUER; Horloge Magique, F. CHEVALLEY; Obituary, H.A. MAYOR.

Vol. VI, no. 5, May 1930
As Is, KENNETH MACPHERSON; Stereoptimism I, ERIC ELLIOTT; Geometric Criticism, HUGH CASTLE; Cinema Circus, ROBERT HERRING; In the Old Days, CHARLOTTE ARTHUR; The Art Director and the Composition of the Film Scenario, PAUL ROTHA; Everywhere the Same, A. KRASZNA-KRAUSZ; It Still Rests with the Local Authorities, L.B. DUCKWORTH; Talk and Speech, CLIFFORD HOWARD; Book Review, OSWELL BLAKESTON; Ciné Club de Genève, FREDDY CHEVALLEY.

Vol. VI, no. 6, June 1930
As Is, KENNETH MACPHERSON; Stereoptimism II, ERIC ELLIOTT; All Singing, All Dancing, All Nothing, ERNEST BETTS; London Looke Backe, ROBERT HERRING; Phases of Cinema Unity, H.A. POTAMKIN; How I Turned *Quand les Epis Se Courbent*, JEAN DREVILLE; Film Criticism, H.A. MAYOR; This Year's Sowing, OSWELL BLAKESTON; Proletarians of the Film, A. KRASZNA-KRAUSZ; Mickey's Rival,

H.C.; Sous les Toits de Paris, JEAN LENAUER; Review de Premier Semestre, CLIFFORD HOWARD; Interview with Douglas Fairbanks, R.H.; British Eye on Paris, C.E. STENHOUSE.

Vol. VII, no. 1, July 1930
As Is, KENNETH MACPHERSON; The Relativity of Transition, L. SAALSCHUTZ; Flesh, the All – Everything Scenario, HUGH CASTLE; The Revival of Naturalism, PAUL ROTHA; As Is in Paris, C.E. STENHOUSE; Telecinema, OSWELL BLAKESTON; Star, MICHAEL STUART; Shadow over Hollywood, CLIFFORD HOWARD; The Whiteman Front, ROBERT HERRING; Il Parle, la Belle Affair, FREDDY CHEVALLEY; The Michurinsky Nursery Garden, P.A.; Comment and Review.

Vol. VII, no. 2, August 1930
As Is, KENNETH MACPHERSON; But Something Quite Different Is Needed, ROBERT HERRING; Dirty Work, R. BOND; A New Belgian Film, A. CAUVIN; *Westfront 1918*, BRYHER; Playing with Sound, H.A. POTAMKIN; Movie: New York Notes, H.A. POTAMKIN; Dreams and Films, C.J. PENNETHORNE HUGHES; England's Strongest Suit, OSWELL BLAKESTON; This Thrilling Instalment, HUGH CASTLE; Eisenstein in Hollywood, CLIFFORD HOWARD; The Future of the Film (an interview with Eisenstein), MARK SEGAL.

Vol. VII, no. 3, September 1930
As Is, KENNETH MACPHERSON; Films and the Law, L.M. BANNER MENDUS; Kino Olympiad [*sic*], H.P.J. MARSHALL; Russian Notes, PERA ATTASHEVA; Attitude and Interlude, HUGH CASTLE; Check Up on Technique, OSWELL BLAKESTON; Continuous Performance – A Tear for Lycidas, DOROTHY RICHARDSON; Documentation: The Basis of Cinematography, JEAN DREVILLE; Action, CLIFFORD HOWARD; Avenue Pavilion (Third Edition), R. BOND.

Vol. VII, no. 4, October 1930
As Is, KENNETH MACPHERSON; Movie: New York Notes, H.A. POTAMKIN; The Cinema and the Censors, HERMAN G. WEINBERG; Motion Pictures in the Classroom, TRUDE WEISS; On Re-Reading Old Friends, OSWELL BLAKESTON; Blockheads, L.B. DUCKWORTH; Conrad Veidt, ROBERT HERRING; Dovjenko on the Sound Film, R. BOND; Sous les Toits de Paris, F. CHEVALLEY.

Vol. VII, no. 5, November 1930
As Is, KENNETH MACPHERSON; Danger in the Cinema, BRYHER; Three Funny Stories, ROBERT

Film School in Geneva; Book
Reviews.

Vol. X, no. 2, June 1933
An American Tragedy, S.M.
EISENSTEIN; 'Prague Castle' and
other Czech Stories, KAREL SANTAR;
Continuous Performance [Untitled],
DOROTHY M. RICHARDSON; Towards
a Co-Operative Cinema, E.
COXHEAD; The Nature of Film
Material, ROBERT A. FAIRTHORNE;
Something New in the Motion
Picture Theatre, FRANCES BLAKE;
Why War? Einstein and Freud,
International Institute of Intellectual
Co-Operation, H.A.M.; Teaching
Music by the Abstract Film, OSWELL
BLAKESTON; The Making of the
Russian 'Star', MARIE SETON; The
Foreign Language Film in the
United States, HERMAN G.

WEINBERG; The Travelling Circus,
ERNO METZNER; What Shall You Do
in the War?, BRYHER; Storm over
Hollywood, CLIFFORD HOWARD.

Vol. X, no. 3, September 1933
The Actor's work, V.I. PUDOVKIN;
Talkie Diseases of French Cinema, J.
LENAUER; Films and Values, O.B.;
Manifesto of 'Experimental Cinema',
[ANON]; Open Letter 'Thunder
over Mexico', A.B. MAUGARD; New
Films by Deslaw, J. BURFORD & O.
BLAKESTON ; Fiction or Nature,
MARIANNE MOORE; 'Lot in Sodom',
H.G. WEINBERG; Film Morals,
CLIFFORD HOWARD; Scottsboro,
NANCY CUNARD; Pseudomorphic
Film, O.B.; Comment and Review:
Sound City of Shepperton;
Filmwork in Vienna; Alibis; Book
Reviews.

Vol. X, no. 4, December 1933
Turkish Prelude, MARIE SETON; Lot
in Sodom; MARIANNE MOORE; Two
Documentaries, R. BOND; Manifesto
on the Documentary, O.B.; The
Primeval Age of Cinema, TRUDE
WEISS; The Pabst Arrival, FRANK
DAUGHERTY; Portugal, ALVES
COSTA; The Historical Conception of
Stage and Film, C.J. PENNETHORNE
HUGHES; Symphonic Symphony,
CLIFFORD HOWARD; The Emperor
Jones, HERMAN G. WEINBERG; Japan
as Seen in Films, YASUSHI OGINO;
Thunder over Mexico, UPTON
SINCLAIR; Comment and Review:
Close Up Contributors and a
Murder; A Cinema Arts Film Club;
Paris Margin Note; Regulations
Governing the Second International
Exhibition of Cinematography; The
New Belgian Weekly.

APPENDIX 2

Notes on the Contributors and Correspondents

The Contributors

Oswell Blakeston [Henry Joseph Hasslacher] (1907–85). Oswell Blakeston joined the staff of *Close Up* in August 1927, having previously worked as a cinema organist and studio clapperboy. He continued to work in a variety of capacities in the British film industry while writing for *Close Up* and was for a time an assistant cameraman at Gaumont Studios. While he was not listed as a 'correspondent', Blakeston contributed more frequently to *Close Up* than any other single writer – a total of 84 articles appearing in all but four of the journal's issues. Blakeston's articles were laced with anecdotes of British ineptitude in film production: he was generally derisive towards British studios, directors and cameramen, and dubious about the British film revival promised by the Quota Act. POOL published two books by Blakeston – *Through a Yellow Glass* (1928), a survey of lighting and camera terminology and styles of cinematography, and *Extra Passenger* (1929), an experimental novel about life in a film studio, with a cover designed by the American abstract photographer Francis Brugière. During his years of involvement with *Close Up*, Blakeston also produced several of his own film projects. These included *I Do Love To Be Beside the Seaside* (1929) (later described by Blakeston as 'a visual commentary on some of the absurd pretensions of high-brow film criticism of the time'), featuring H.D. and with a film score by Edmund Meisel, and (with Brugière) an abstract film called *Light Rhythms* (1930), first shown in London at the Shaftesbury Avenue Pavilion. After the demise of *Close Up*, Blakeston continued to work as a journalist and writer. Among his forty published titles were works of fiction (including detective novels), poetry and travel. In the 1960s he turned predominantly to drawing and painting, exhibiting his work widely. [AF/LM]

Bryher (1894–1983) was the *nom de plume* of Annie Winifred Ellerman, the first child of John Reeves Ellerman and Hannah Glover Ellerman. In 1920, Annie Winifred Ellerman legally took the name of Bryher – her favourite island in the Scillies, a group of islands 28 miles west-south-west of Land's End. Bryher's life was marked by her lifelong friendship/companionship with the American poet Hilda Doolittle (H.D.), whom she met in 1918. She was married briefly to Robert McAlmon (whom she met in 1921 and divorced in 1927) and then to Kenneth Macpherson (from 1927 to 1947).

Although Bryher became best known as a historical novelist, she did not write her first historical novel (*The Fourteenth of October*) until 1951, at the age of fifty-eight. Bryher divided her autobiography into two volumes: the first (*The Heart to Artemis*, 1962) provides a detailed account of her childhood, education and adult life until World War II; while the second (*Days of Mars*, 1972) is a brief memoir of London during the war. Bryher wrote a total of twenty-five books, including fifteen novels, the two volumes of autobiography, one book of verse (*Arrow Music*, 1922), two film books (*Film Problems of Soviet Russia*, 1929; *Cinema Survey*, 1937), one volume of criticism (*Amy Lowell: An Appreciation*, 1918), one translation from the Greek (*The Lament for Adonis*, 1918), one German-teaching text (*The Light-hearted Student*, 1930), one non-fiction book translated into French by Sylvia Beach and Adrienne Monnier (*Paris 1900*, 1938). Bryher spent the last years of her life living somewhat hermitically in Kenwin, the house facing Lake Geneva in Territet, Switzerland, that she and Kenneth Macpherson built in 1931.

Bryher's father, Sir John Reeves Ellerman (1862–1933), a shipping magnate and active financier, was made a baronet in 1905. When Sir John died in 1933 he was described as the wealthiest man in England – second only to the king. 'The Ellerman Group' – an alliance of prominent shipping lines – expanded rapidly after World War I as Britain consolidated its empire and Ellerman became a large stock- and shareholder in the other leading shipping companies, Cunard and P.&O. In addition, he had a large financial interest in newspapers, being a part shareholder in *The Times* and a principal shareholder in a group of illustrated weeklies known as the 'Big Six' of luxury journalism – *The Illustrated London News*, *Sphere*, *Tatler*, the *Sketch*, *Eve* and the *Illustrated Sporting and Dramatic News*. Sir John also had vast real estate holdings (his investments included 78 acres in Earl's Court that he bought in 1930 and sold in 1933, and 14 acres in Chelsea, purchased in 1929; in all he owned between five and six hundred houses with a street frontage of 2½ miles).

Sir John had no public life and was rarely photographed. When he died, his estate was estimated by *The Times* as £17 million. The *Times* obituary eulogized: 'He will be long remembered as one of the greatest forces behind British shipping that has ever been known.' (*The Daily Mail* estimate of his fortune was less conservative – £40 million – with a headline: 'Britain's Wealthiest Man Dead'.) *The Times*'s obituary failed to mention that Sir John had a daughter, referring only to his 'one son', John Jr, who would succeed to his title of second baronet (*The Times* (London), 18 July 1933, p. 9). [AF]

René Crevel (1900–35), the Surrealist poet and member of the *Littératur* group, published two pieces in *Close Up*, 'Les hommes aux milles visages', and 'Champ de bataille et lieux communs' in August and November 1927, respectively. [AF]

H.D. (1886–1960), American-born poet, Hilda Doolittle, first published under her initials, H.D. When her first poems were published in Harriet Monroe's *Poetry*, in January 1913, they were signed 'H.D., Imagiste'. Best known for her Imagist verse, her association with Pound and her brief analysis with Freud, H.D. was also fascinated by the cinema, an apparatus wrought with potential for metaphors of light, vision, projection and superimposition. As Susan Stanford Friedman argues: 'H.D., not Macpherson, was the driving creative force in her intimate circle, although

Bryher and Macpherson and a number of other friends were crucial to her work' (see Bonnie Kime Scott (ed.), *Gender of Modernism* (Bloomington: Indiana University Press, 1990, p. 89). In the algebra of their complicated domestic arrangements and sexual liaisons, H.D. was a sort of prime number. H.D. and Macpherson were both bisexual, and Bryher had been a devoted lover and companion to H.D. since 1919. When Macpherson was introduced to H.D. by her childhood friend Frances Gregg in 1926, he became a key component for her and Bryher in both their public and private lives. Bryher divorced Robert McAlmon in March 1927 and married Macpherson that September. For a more detailed account of the complicated domestic arrangements and sexual liaisons between H.D., Bryher and Macpherson, see Susan Stanford Friedman, *Penelope's Web: Gender, Modernity, H.D.'s Fiction* (New York: Cambridge University Press, 1990).

After 1928, H.D.'s writing in the journal diminished and a number of other contributors became more visibly identified with the publication. Yet her writing about cinema in the first year and a half of *Close Up*'s life and her work on the POOL films between 1927 and 1930 were direct manifestations of a keen enthusiasm for the cinema. H.D.'s interest in film occurred at the conclusion of a period of high literary productivity, and she never wrote directly about film again after 1929. H.D. was in analysis with Freud in 1933 and 1934 and wrote a memoir of it, entitled *Tribute to Freud*. [AF]

Robert Herring (1903–1975), a London-based writer, was the assistant editor of the *London Mercury* from 1925 to 1927 and was largely responsible for that journal's serious consideration of the cinema. A graduate of King's College, Cambridge, in English and History, Herring had the air and expertise of a well-educated member of the British *literati*. Herring published several of his own poems in *London Mercury*, plus reviews of dramatic literature, poetry, literary histories and books of criticism. In 1927, he published a book about cinema, *Films of the Year*. Herring joined *Close Up* as London correspondent in November 1927. Having just returned from Germany, he urged Bryher and Macpherson to go to Berlin. His writing for *Close Up* provides evidence of his literary training. In 1928, Herring wrote a

series of articles on what he called 'film imagery' in the films of Eisenstein, Pudovkin and Seastrom. In 1935, at Bryher's urging, Herring became editor (along with Petrie Townshend) of *Life and Letters To-day*. *Life and Letters To-day* had a large cinema section and continued to translate Eisenstein's work into English, in addition to publishing articles by Havelock Ellis, André Gide, Gertrude Stein, Osbert Sitwell, Lotte Reiniger and H.D. [AF]

Barbara Low (1877–1955) was a member of the British Psychoanalytic Society which had, by 1927, already gathered a number of distinguished women analysts – including Melanie Klein, Joan Riviere and Mellita Schmideberg (Melanie Klein's daughter by Walter Schmideberg, also an analyst and member of the British Psychoanalytic Society. H.D. saw Schmideberg for psychoanalytic sessions in 1936 and 1937). Low's book *Psychoanalysis: A Brief Account of Freudian Theory* was reviewed in the first volume of the *International Journal of Psychoanalysis* in 1921: 'There is not a word in it we could wish altered.' Low was clearly established within the sanctioned orthodoxy of the Freudian canon. A friend of Dorothy Richardson and Alan Odle, she was probably introduced to Bryher and the *Close Up* group through them. Thus in 1927 when *Close Up* commenced, Bryher had not yet met Hanns Sachs but she did know Barbara Low. Low's single contribution to *Close Up*, 'Mind-growth or Mind-mechanization? Cinema in Education', was published in September 1927. [AF]

Kenneth Macpherson (1903–71), Scottish artist, photographer, film-maker, novelist. Macpherson was introduced to H.D. by her childhood friend Frances Gregg in 1926; he became very close to both Bryher and H.D., marrying Bryher in 1927. In the same year, when he became the editor of *Close Up*, Macpherson also began making films – three shorts (*Wing Beat*, 1927; *Foothills*, 1929; *Monkey's Moon*, 1929) and one feature-length (*Borderline*, 1930). During the years of *Close Up*, his passionate ambitions were evident in the lively three-way correspondence conducted between Bryher, Macpherson and H.D.

Macpherson's life from 1933–43 bears few traces; he travelled with Norman Douglas in the 1930s and his correspondence to Bryher and H.D. tapered off. Sometime between

1941 and 1943 Macpherson moved to New York. A lurid description of his personal life during his New York years can be found in Peggy Guggenheim's confessional autobiography, *Out of This Century: Confessions of an Art Addict* (New York: Anchor Books, 1980). Macpherson, who had become a significant art collector – owning paintings by Tanguy, Picasso, Klee, Miro and Braque – first met Guggenheim when he came to buy some work by Max Ernst, whom she lived with. Two chapters of *Out of This Century* are devoted to the years that Macpherson and Guggenheim shared a duplex apartment together. While in New York, he wrote occasional pieces for Parker Tyler's *View*.

In 1947, after the war, Macpherson returned to Italy. When he and Bryher divorced in the same year, he bought a villa in Capri where he cared for Norman Douglas until his death in 1952. After Douglas's death, Macpherson became his literary executor. He lived in Rome from 1952 to 1965, and then he 'retired' to Tuscany to write a book on Douglas's Austrian doctor, Dotoressa Moor. Macpherson published his third novel, *Rome 12 Noon* (New York: Coward-McCann), in 1964. He died in Cetona, Italy, on 14 June 1971. [AF]

Dorothy Miller Richardson (1873–1957) was born in Berkshire, England, the third of four daughters, into a comfortable middle-class household. Her father, a businessman more interested in science and culture than commerce, became bankrupt in 1891, and Richardson left home to become a teacher, first in Germany and then in North London. In 1896, the year after her mother's death by suicide, Richardson became a secretary to a Harley Street dentist. She took lodgings in Bloomsbury, and became involved with a range of left-wing and free-thinking intellectual and political groups. Her first piece of journalism was published in 1902.

In 1896, Richardson had met H.G. Wells, with whom she maintained a lifelong, if intellectually and personally embattled, friendship. His ideas had a significant impact on Richardson's journalism and reviewing in the 1900s. In 1912, she began the book that was to become *Pointed Roofs*, the first volume of her thirteen-volume novel sequence *Pilgrimage*, her lifelong project. *Pilgrimage* is to a large extent an autobiographical work, covering the period in Richardson's life between

1891 and 1912 through the consciousness of her autobiographical/fictional persona, Miriam Henderson. Written primarily in the third person, though occasionally moving into first-person narration, it creates a literary space of its own that lies between the genres of the novel and autobiography. Although Richardson was herself wary of the comparison, the project of *Pilgrimage* was linked to that of Proust's monumental *A la recherche du temps perdu*.

Virginia Woolf, in her review of *Revolving Lights* (the seventh volume in the sequence), refers to Richardson's invention of 'a woman's sentence'. The issues of a gendered language and of the possibility of a 'female aesthetic' are central to the novel and to recent analyses of Richardson's work. Her experiments with form and narrative method have now ensured her a place as one of the most important literary modernists, although her work was neglected for many years. The fascination of Richardson's writing resides both in its formal experimentation and in its engagement with cultural forms and historical consciousness, including the cultural discourse of its times – Darwinism, Fabianism, feminism, aesthetics and cinematic perception.

In 1917, Richardson married the young artist Alan Odle; they lived, until Odle's death in 1948, in London and Cornwall. Richardson continued to work as a translator, journalist and essayist, always concerned that her writing for money was taking her energies away from *Pilgrimage*. Bryher, whom Richardson and Odle met in 1923, helped them financially for many years, and provided significant encouragement to Richardson as a writer.

The time spent by Richardson and Odle in Switzerland in 1923–4, facilitated by Bryher, was particularly significant for Richardson's subsequent contributions to *Close Up*. The trip in part inspired the writing of *Oberland* (which records Miriam's first trip to Switzerland): this, 'her most pictorial fiction', in

the words of Richardson's biographer Gloria Fromm, 'was almost pure illustration of the theoretical text she would publish later in *Close Up*'.

In addition to her translations, journalism (including her film articles for *Close Up*), autobiographical sketches, short stories, poems and, centrally, the novels that make up *Pilgrimage*, Richardson also wrote two books on the Quakers, the sect to which she felt most drawn. Dorothy Richardson died in a nursing home in 1957. [LM]

Hanns Sachs (1881–1947), Vienna-born, Berlin-based psychoanalyst and member of Freud's circle. Trained as a lawyer, Sachs began attending Freud's lectures in 1904. At the Weimar Congress in 1911, Freud announced that he, Rank and Sachs were to be founding editors of a new journal – *Imago* – devoted to the non-medical applications of psychoanalytic theory. Sachs was one of the first to receive Freud's signet ring and to be initiated into his secret 'circle of seven'. Of the seven (Jones, Ferenczi, Abraham, Rank, Eitingon, Sachs and Freud) only Rank and Sachs were not physicians. In 1919, Sachs moved to Berlin where the first psychoanalytic training institute had been established. Among Sachs's analysands in Berlin were Karen Horney, Erich Fromm, Gregory Zilboorg and Barbara Low. In 1932, Sachs left for the United States, where he founded *American Imago*. His tribute to Freud – *Freud: Master and Friend* (Cambridge, MA: Harvard University Press, 1944) – is evidence of his faithful discipleship. Concurrent with her editorial work at *Close Up*, from 1928 to 1932, Bryher was in a training analysis with Sachs in Berlin. As Paul Roazen writes in *Freud and His Followers* (New York: New American Library, 1971, p. 326): 'He was disappointed in his hopes of converting an English patient into a faithful disciple: a writer who calls herself Bryher, she preferred instead to retire to Switzerland.' [AF]

The Correspondents

The correspondents, added intermittently, were listed in the Table of Contents, but did not necessarily contribute to each issue.

Marc Allégret, the protégé and adopted son of André Gide and maker of the lyrical documentary, *Voyage au Congo*, became the Paris correspondent in August 1927.

Pera Attasheva, companion of Eisenstein, was added as the Moscow correspondent in April 1929.

Freddy Chevalley, a critic for *La Suisse*, became the Geneva correspondent in July 1928.

Simon Gould of the Film Arts Guild in New York was listed as 'New York editor' and was put in charge of American and Canadian correspondence for the journal.

Robert Herring, film reviewer from the *London Mercury*, began as the London correspondent in November 1927.

Clifford Howard, a Los Angeles-based journalist, was added as the Hollywood correspondent in March 1928.

Andor Kraszna-Krausz, editor of *Film für Alle* and *Film Technik*, was employed as the Berlin correspondent in September 1928.

Jean Lenauer joined as a second Paris correspondent in November 1928.

Harry Alan Potamkin, critic-at-large, began as New York correspondent in September 1929.

Trude Weiss became Vienna correspondent in May 1930, in addition to a stint from March until December 1928.

Publishing History

For the first issues of *Close Up*, Bryher chose the master printer Maurice Darantière of Dijon. Bryher knew of Darantière because he had managed the Herculean task of printing James Joyce's *Ulysses* for Sylvia Beach's 1922 edition and had been the printer for Robert McAlmon's Contact Editions, launched with Bryher's support in 1922. The publishing records from Darantière (which are in the Bryher papers at the Beinecke Library, Yale University) provide some insight into the publication. The production cost for 500 copies of *Close Up* was 1500 francs, making each individual copy 3 francs and the sale price 5 francs. The receipts from Darantière also indicate where the copies were sent: direct to bookshops in Paris (Gallimard, Flammarion, Shakespeare), Berlin, London, Geneva, New York and Los Angeles. Darantière printed *Close Up* for twelve issues from July 1927 until August 1928, when the contract was transferred to Mercury Press in London, Ilford and Chelmsford. The reason for the change is not apparent but proximity to London was probably a necessity. (London offices were announced on the back cover of the August 1928 journal but not included in the Table of Contents until November 1928.) Despite the switch of printers, any change in the magazine is barely noticeable. The colour of the covers is consistent, and the magazine's text appears almost identically typeset and printed. In addition, Darantière was also responsible for printing the first POOL books.

H.D. also printed a number of her limited-edition novels with Darantière (known now as the 'Dijon novels': *Kora and Ka*, *Mira Mare*, *Two Americans*, *The Usual Star* and *Nights*). In addition, Gertrude Stein also printed her *Plain Editions* with the firm.

Sylvia Beach was probably the first of the Parisian literati to use the firm of Darantière. Darantière agreed to print *Ulysses* on receipt of payment from the proper number of subscribers and to have all other bills paid on instalment. Subscriptions were sold at Sylvia Beach's bookshop, Shakespeare & Company, and at Adrienne Monnier's Les Amis des Livres. The most ardent salesperson was Robert McAlmon, who typed much of the draft of *Ulysses*. Darantière's experience printing the Joyce manuscript gives one some idea of how complicated the procedures for *Close Up* may have been. Darantière was a firm that specialized in hand-set type, in the Gutenberg manner, and the twenty-six typesetters who worked for him spoke no English. The printing of the 1921–2 edition of *Ulysses* is testimony to the printer's patience. The hand-setting and the language problem account for the great number of mistakes in the first edition of the work. Bryher had an unseen hand in the production of *Ulysses*: Robert McAlmon, who was married to Bryher in 1921, reportedly gave Joyce $150 a month while he was writing *Ulysses*.

McAlmon's relations with Darantière were less complex. In 1923, Sir John Ellerman gave McAlmon £14,000 for his publishing ventures. Darantière finished the first Contact Edition, McAlmon's *Hasty Bunch*, a month before *Ulysses* was completed. But when McAlmon took on the project of Gertrude Stein's thousand-page *Making of Americans* in 1925, he ran into some of the same problems that Sylvia Beach had faced with Joyce. An account of Stein and Toklas reading the Darantière proofs (taking lunches to the countryside outside Dijon and reading proofs until Alice's glasses broke and Gertrude had to continue on her own) is offered in James Mellow's *Charmed Circle* (New York: Avon Books, 1974, pp. 378–83).

POOL Books

The following books were published by POOL: in spring 1927, *Poolreflection*, a novel by Kenneth Macpherson and *Why Do They Like It?*, a reflection on British public school education by Bryher's younger brother (John Ellerman Jr) under the pseudonym E.L. Black (with a foreword by Dorothy Richardson); in autumn 1927, *Civilians*, an account of civilian sacrifice in World War I by Bryher, and *Gaunt Island*, Kenneth Macpherson's second novel; in 1928, Oswell Blakeston's 'complete guide to the cinema studio', *Through a Yellow Glass*, and Eric Elliott's technical history of cinematography, *Anatomy of a Motion Picture Art*; in 1929, Bryher's *Film Problems of Soviet Russia* and Oswell Blakeston's novel about British film studio life, *Extra Passenger*; in 1930, a pamphlet-length essay by Hanns Sachs, *Does Capital Punishment Exist?* and a German-teaching text by Bryher and Trude Weiss, *The Light-hearted Student*.

Anne Friedberg

A Chronology of *Close Up* in Context

1926

H.D. publishes *Palimpsest*
Pound publishes *Personae*
Kafka publishes *Das Schloss*
D.H. Lawrence publishes *The Plumed
    Serpent*
Freud publishes *The Question of Lay
    Analysis*
Karen Horney publishes *Flight from
    Womanhood*
Ratification of degree course 'Modern
    English' at Cambridge
Blaise Cendrars publishes *L'A.B.C. du
    cinéma*
Ricciotto Canudo publishes *L'Usine
    des images*

January
1   Moscow premiere of *Potemkin*,
    Bolshoi Theatre
Studio des Ursulines founded in
    Ursuline convent, Paris
27   Film Society of London, fourth
    programme (*Entr'Acte, The
    Marriage Circle* shown)

February
14   Film Society of London, fifth
    programme (*Nju, Krazy Kat*
    shown)
27   International Theatre
    Exhibition, New York, opens;
    designs by Frederick Kiesler

March
14   Film Society of London, sixth
    programme (*Ballet Mécanique,
    Cabinet of Dr Caligari* shown)
18   Cameo Theatre, Baltimore
    shows *Ballet Mécanique*
24   Berlin censors ban *Potemkin*
26   Siegfried Kracauer publishes
    'Kult der Zerstreuung' in
    Frankfurter Zeitung

April
Eiga Hyoran (Film Criticism) journal
    begins as monthly in Japan
29   Berlin premiere of *Potemkin*,
    ban lifted

May
3–12   General Strike in England
30   Film Society of London, eighth
    programme (*Menilmontant,
    Come to Kipho, Easy Street*
    shown)

June
Eiga Hyoran, special issue on
    L'Herbier

July
Berlin renews ban on *Potemkin*
Fairbanks and Pickford visit Moscow

October
24   Film Society of London begins
    second season, ninth
    programme (*Hands of Orlac,
    One AM* shown)

November
28   Film Society of London, tenth
    programme (*Dr Mabuse der
    Spieler* shown)

December
Rilke dies, aged fifty-one
New York premiere of *Potemkin*,
    Biltmore Theatre
Film Society of London, eleventh
    programme (*Greed* screened)

1927

Virginia Woolf publishes *To the
    Lighthouse*
H.D. publishes *Hippolytus Temporizes*
Kafka publishes *Amerika*
Freud publishes *The Future of an
    Illusion, Some Psychological
    Consequences of Anatomical
    Distinctions*
Eikhenbaum edits *Poetika Kino
    (Poetics of Cinema)*

January
27   Film Society of London,
    twelfth programme (*Emak
    Bakia, Joyless Street* shown)

February
13   Film Society of London,
    thirteenth programme
    (*L'Inhumaine*, extracts from
    Father Sergius shown)
Germaine Dulac publishes collection
    of film writing, *Schémas*
Macpherson films *Wing Beat* near
    Territet

March
13   Film Society of London,
    fourteenth programme (*Tillie's
    Punctured Romance* shown)
11–19 Siegfried Kracauer publishes
    'Die kleinen Ladenmädchen
    gehen ins Kino' as a series of
    articles in *Frankfurter Zeitung*

April
Walter Benjamin begins his massive
    Arcades Project in Paris

May
Bryher and Macpherson fly to Vienna
    and visit Freud

June
9   Siegfried Kracauer publishes
    'Das Ornament der Masse' in
    Frankfurter Zeitung

29   Macpherson writes to Gertrude
    Stein, sends her first edition of
    Close Up

July
Close Up, vol. 1, no. 1 issued

August
Close Up adds Marc Allégret as Paris
    correspondent
Freud writes a short paper on
    'Fetishism'

September
1   Bryher and Macpherson are
    married at Chelsea Register
    Office
7   London Television Society
    founded

October
5   *Jazz Singer* opens in New York
12   Eisenstein begins his notes for a
    film of *Capital*
Film Society of London,
    seventeenth programme; shows
    colour film demonstrations
28   Siegfried Kracauer publishes
    'Die Photographie' in
    Frankfurter Zeitung

November
Bryher and Macpherson in Berlin,
    where they meet Pabst; Bryher
    meets Hanns Sachs
Close Up adds Robert Herring as
    London correspondent
9   Eisenstein's 'Mass Movies'
    appears in *Nation*

December
Jeanne Ney premieres in Berlin
Cinematograph Films Bill ('The
    Quota Act') passed in British
    Parliament
Alfred Barr meets Tretyakov and
    Eisenstein in Moscow

1928

H.D. writes *Usual Star*
H.D. publishes *Hedylus*
D.H. Lawrence publishes *Lady
    Chatterley's Lover*
Virginia Woolf publishes *Orlando*
Representation of People Act ('The
    Flapper Vote') enfranchises
    women twenty-one to
    thirty-one, excluded from 1918
    Act in England
Ralph Bond founds Atlas Films to
    import and distribute Soviet
    films in England
POOL publishes Kenneth
    Macpherson's *Poolreflection*,
    Oswell Blakeston's *Through a*

Yellow Glass and Eric Elliott's *Anatomy of Motion Picture Art*

January
20   *October* released in Moscow

February
Studio 28 founded in Paris

March
4   Film Society of London, twenty-second programme (*Berlin, Symphony of a City* shown)
Foothills, a POOL film, shot in a studio in Clarens, Switzerland, between March and September
Close Up adds Clifford Howard as Hollywood correspondent

April
Eisenstein concludes his notes for *Capital*
Ciné-clubs de Genève begins

June
Avenue Pavilion opens in London, beginning a repertory programme
Bryher publishes three poems in *transition*

July
Close Up adds Freddy Chevalley as Geneva correspondent

August
5   'Soviet Sound Statement' appears in Leningrad magazine
Close Up changes printer from Darantière to Mercury Press, London

September
Close Up adds Andor Kraszna-Krausz as Berlin correspondent
Close Up publishes 'Russian issue'

October
Close Up publishes 'Soviet Sound Statement'
21   Film Society of London, twenty-fifth programme; shows *Mother*

November
Bryher in Berlin in analysis with Sachs
Sachs publishes first article in *Close Up*, 'Film Psychology'
Close Up adds Jean Lenauer as Second Paris correspondent

December
Jean-George Auriol launches *La Revue du cinéma*

1929

POOL publishes *Film Problems of Soviet Russia*
Kuleshov publishes *Iskusstvo Kino*
Freud publishes *Civilization and Its Discontents*
Museum of Modern Art founded in New York
Kodak develops 16mm colour film

January
Trotsky exiled

Man with a Movie Camera premieres in Kiev
Berlin premiere of *Storm over Asia*
Close Up publishes picture of Eisenstein dedicated to Macpherson, encloses Censorship Petition in back pages

February
Close Up's 'Censorship Number'
Die Büchse der Pandora released in Berlin

March
Close Up's 'British Number'

April
Close Up adds Pera Attasheva as Moscow correspondent
31   Film Society of London, thirty-first programme (*Bed and Sofa* shown)

May
18   Film and Foto show opens in Stuttgart
Eisenstein publishes 'New Language of Cinematography' in *Close Up*
Macpherson begins to plan *Borderline*

June
13–29 Film and Foto show, Film Programme: an international exhibit of photographs, films and typography in Stuttgart
Hitchcock's *Blackmail* released

July
Stills from *Foothills* and *Monkey's Moon* published in *Close Up*
Bryher, Macpherson and Herring take a trip to Iceland to shoot film

August
Close Up special issue on race

September
2–7   La Sarraz Congress: Ruttman, Balázs, Richter, Montagu, Cavalcanti, Eisenstein, Tisse, Alexandrov attend
Eisenstein's *Old and New* released in Moscow
Harry Alan Potamkin returns to United States from Europe
H.D. records: 'K works hard on sketches for proposed film, Borderline'
Close Up adds Potamkin as New York correspondent

October
24   Stock-market crash in United States

November
10   Film Society of London, thirty-third programme (*Potemkin* and *Drifters* shown; Eisenstein and Grierson present)
Federation of Workers' Film Societies launched in England

1930

T.S. Eliot publishes *Ash Wednesday*

Musil publishes *Der Mann ohne Eigenschaften*
Nancy Cunard publishes *Henry Music* by Henry Crowder

January
2   Eisenstein writes to Macpherson from Paris

February
Eisenstein lectures at the Sorbonne
Experimental Cinema no.1 issued

March
2   D.H. Lawrence dies
16   Film Society of London, thirty-eighth programme (all films shown by women directors – Lotte Reiniger, Dorothy Arzner, Germaine Dulac, Olga Preobrazhenskaia)
Eisenstein publishes 'Fourth Dimension in Kino' in *Close Up*
22–29 *Borderline* shot near Territet with Paul and Eslanda Robeson

April
Close Up switches office location to 26 Litchfield Street, above Zwemmer's Bookshop

May
4   Film Society of London, fortieth programme (*General Line* shown)
Close Up adds Weiss as Vienna correspondent

June
Experimental Cinema, issue no.2
Eisenstein arrives in California
Borderline completed

September
17   Eisenstein gives lecture 'The Dinamic Square' at Motion Picture Academy in Hollywod

October
13   *Borderline* screened in London

November
24   Eisenstein signs contract with Mexican Film Trust

December
Close Up announces switch to quarterly format

1931

Academy Cinema, London, opens repertory cinema

February
H.D. records: 'K seems moral and psychic wreck.'

March
Borderline shown at Neuchâtel ciné-club
Pudovkin in Hamburg preparing his sound film, *Deserter*

April
H.D. begins analysis with Mary Chadwick in London
Borderline screened in Berlin

July
Kenwin finished in Burier,
    Switzerland

August
Vertov's sound film, *Enthusiasm*, shows
    in Berlin

September
Eisenstein publishes 'Principles of
    Film Form' in *Close Up*

November
H.D. in Berlin in analysis with Sachs
15   Film Society of London,
        forty-ninth programme
        (*Enthusiasm* shown)

___

1932

Huxley publishes *Brave New World*
Freud publishes *New Introductory
    Lectures*
H.D. travels to Greece with her
    daughter, Perdita
FDR defeats Herbert Hoover

January
Berlin premiere of *Mahagonny*

March
31   Eisenstein returns from Mexico
        to New York

April
19   Eisenstein sails to Europe

May
Eisenstein back in Moscow

Soviet premiere of *Kühle Wampe*
30   *Kühle Wampe* opens in Berlin

June
Bryher leaves Berlin for Kenwin

July
Reichstag elections; Nazis win 38 per
    cent of seats

August
Freud writes 'On Femininity', which
    will be published in *New
    Introductory Lectures on
    Psychoanalysis*

September
'Surrealiste' issue of *This Quarter*

December
11   Film Society of London,
        fifty-ninth programme (*Bronx
        Morning*, *Kühle Wampe* shown)

___

1933

Freud publishes *New Introductory
    Lectures on Psychoanalysis*

January
30   Hitler becomes Chancellor

February
27   Reichstag fire
28   The Brechts leave for Prague

March
5   H.D. begins analysis with Freud
        in Vienna

13   Goebbels made Minister of
        Propaganda

April
1   Boycott of Jewish firms begins
        in Germany
10   Bauhaus, Berlin, is closed
26   Gestapo founded

May
Book-burning in Berlin ordered by
    Goebbels

June
Close Up begins policy of no further
    German captions
15   H.D. returns from Vienna to
        Kenwin

July
19   H.A. Potamkin dies; given 'Red
        Funeral' in New York

September
14   Jay Leyda arrives in Leningrad
        on way to Moscow Film
        Institute
Bryher sets up fund to assist the
    training of analysts in Vienna
    and to help finance Jewish
    emigration

December
Last issue of *Close Up* published
20   Freud writes to H.D.: 'very glad
        to hear you are reading in my
        new lectures'

Compiled by Anne Friedberg

NOTES

NOTES TO PREFACE

1. Vladimir Petric, 'The Soviet Revolution in America (1926 – 1935), Part 1: The Theoretical Impact', unpublished Ph.D. dissertation, New York University, 1973.
2. Details of the contents of all the issues of *Close Up* are given in Appendix 1.
   The articles by Eisenstein are :
   'The New Language of Cinematography', originally published as foreword to Guido Seeber's *Der Trickfilm* (Moscow, 1929); vol. IV, no. 5, May 1929.
   'The Fourth Dimension in the Kino, Part I', written in August 1929, translated by Winifred Ray from an original in *Kino*, a Moscow newspaper; vol. VI, no. 3, March 1930.
   'The Fourth Dimension in the Kino, Part II', written in autumn 1929, translated by Winifred Ray; vol. VI, no. 4, April 1930.
   'The Dinamic Square, Part I', based on a speech given by Eisenstein in Hollywood, 1930; vol. VIII, no. 1, March 1931.
   'The Dinamic Square, Part II'; vol. VIII, no. 2, June 1931.
   'The Principles of Film Form', translated by Ivor Montagu, dated Zurich 1929, possibly delivered at La Sarraz; vol. VIII, no. 3, September 1931.
   'Detective Work in the GIK', written for *Close Up*, dated Moscow, October 1932, translated by Winifred Ray; first of a series of three articles, vol. IX, no. 4, December 1932.
   'Cinematography with Tears', second of the above series, March 1933.
   'An American Tragedy', third of the above series; vol. X, no. 2, June 1933.
   'The Future of the Film' (vol. VII, no 2, August 1930) and 'Filmic Art and Training' (vol. VI, no. 3, March 1930) are both interviews with Eisenstein by Mark Segal, and Samuel

Brody's 'Paris Hears Eisenstein' (vol. VI, no. 4, April 1930) is a report on a lecture delivered at the Sorbonne on 17 February 1930.
3. See *Film Form: Essays in Film Theory*, edited and translated by Jay Leyda (New York: Harcourt Brace Jovanovich, 1949); *The Film Sense*, edited and translated by Jay Leyda (London: Faber, 1945); *Selected Writings, Volumes I–IV*, edited by Richard Taylor and Michael Glenny (London; BFI, 1988–96).
4. H.D., *Collected Poems*, edited by L.L. Martz (Manchester: Carcanet, 1984).
5. See, for example, Anne Friedberg, *Window Shopping: Cinema and the Postmodern* (Berkeley, Los Angeles, and London: University of California Press, 1992); Miriam Hansen, *Babel and Babylon: Spectatorship in American Silent Film* (Cambridge, MA: Harvard University Press, 1991); Leo Charney and Vanessa R. Schwartz (eds), *Cinema and the Invention of Modern Life* (Berkeley, Los Angeles and London: University of California Press, 1995).

NOTES TO INTRODUCTION

1. Jean Epstein, 'Grossisment' (first published 1921), translated by Stuart Liebman as 'Magnification', *October*, 3 (Spring 1977), p. 15.
2. Béla Balázs, 'The Close Up', in *Theory of Film: Character and Growth of a New Art* (New York: Dover Publications, 1970), p. 55.
3. Walter Benjamin, 'The Work of Art in the Age of Mechanical Reproduction', in *Illuminations*, edited by Hannah Arendt, translated by Harry Zohn (New York: Schocken Books, 1969), p. 236.
4. Sergei Eisenstein, 'A Close-up View' (written in 1945), in *Film Essays and a Lecture*, edited by Jay Leyda (Princeton: Princeton University Press, 1982), p. 152.
5. Béla Balázs, 'The Face of Man', in *Theory of Film*, p.65. See also Gertrud Koch, 'Béla Balázs: The Physiognomy of Things',

New German Critique, **40** (Winter 1987), p. 167–77.
6. Benjamin, 'The Work of Art', p. 236. Benjamin's phrase 'neue Strukturbildungen der Materie', translated as 'entirely new formations of the subject', refers to the material representation of the close-up and not to subjectivity.
7. Eisenstein, 'Close-up View', p. 154. Eisenstein's essay, written in 1945, was designed to be 'the fighting line of the newly re-born journal, *Iskusstvo Kino*'. How consciously, if at all, Eisenstein was recalling the writing in *Close Up* from the 1920s is unclear, but he was suggesting that *Iskusstvo Kino* adopt a certain style of writing as its editorial optic, writing that resembled the writing in *Close Up* .
8. Metz relied on Melanie Klein's description of the phantasy relation – an 'object relation' – between infant and mother when oral drives are split into loving and destructive ones; constituting a 'bad object' as a projection of hate and a 'good object' as a projection of love. In cinema writers, Metz maintained, there is 'an intention to establish, maintain or re-establish the cinema (or films) in the position of good object'. (See Christian Metz, 'The Imaginary Signifier', translated by Ben Brewster, *Screen*, 16 (2), p. 25. Republished in *The Imaginary Signifier: Psychoanalysis and the Cinema* (Bloomington: Indiana University Press, 1982), p. 9.) *Close Up* created its own canon of 'good objects' – the films of G.W. Pabst and Sergei Eisenstein – and maintained its 'bad objects' – Hollywood and British cinema – in an effort to transform the cinema itself into an aesthetic form that would live up to its potentials and become a 'good object'.
9. In a two-part article entitled 'The Hollywood Code', Bryher indicted Hollywood values and the 'code' of film-making which, by 1931, seemed apparent. See Bryher, 'The Hollywood Code

I', *Close Up*, vol. VIII, no. 3, September 1931; 'The Hollywood Code II', *Close Up*, vol. VIII, no. 4, December 1931.

10. Walter Benjamin described the method for his Arcades Project – also begun in 1927: 'Method of this work: *literary montage*. I need say nothing. Only show … to carry the montage principle into history.' See Walter Benjamin, 'N [Theoretics of Knowledge: Theory of Progress]', *Philosophical Forum* 15 (1–2) (Autumn–Winter 1983–4), pp. 5–6. Certainly, the journal reader receives information serially, without carefully wrought design or novelistic devices to orchestrate or structure the reader's response.

11. Advertisement in the back of *Close Up*, vol. IV, no. 5, May 1929.

12. 'If we are to approach (*aborder*) a text, it must have a*bord*, an edge,' writes Jacques Derrida in an essay to which he self-consciously appends a running strip of marginalia called 'Border Lines'. Derrida argues – in the full polysemy of ever-sliding signifiers – that a text is not simply a corpus enclosed in its own margins, but a *de-bordment*, overrunning its limits into some other network – an intertext, metatext, context. See Jacques Derrida, 'LIVING ON: Border Lines', in *Deconstruction and Criticism* (New York: Seabury Press, 1979), pp. 81, 83. The trope of 'borderline' was a central image for the *Close Up* editors, entitling, as they did, their one feature film *Borderline* (POOL films, 1930). See Part 5 of this volume.

13. The writing of Soviet film-makers formed an early canon of film theory. See Eisenstein's two volumes, *Film Form*, edited and translated by Jay Leyda (New York: Harcourt Brace and Company, 1949), and *Film Sense*, edited and translated by Jay Leyda (New York: Harcourt Brace and Company, 1942); *Kuleshov on Film: Writings by Lev Kuleshov*, translated and edited by Ronald Levaco (Berkeley: University of California Press, 1974); *Kino-Eye: The Writings of Dziga Vertov*, edited with an introduction by Annette Michelson, translated by Kevin O'Brien Levaco (Berkeley: University of California Press, 1984).

Since the mid-1980s, the work of Walter Benjamin, Siegfried Kracauer and others have been the topic of a plentitude of excellent essays in *New German Critique*. See, for example, the 'Special Issue on Weimar Film Theory', *New German Critique*, 40 (Winter 1987). More recently, Richard Abel has admirably collected and analysed French film writing in his two anthologies, *French Film Criticism and Theory 1907–1939, Volume 1: 1907–1929* (Princeton: Princeton University Press, 1988) and *French Film Criticism and Theory 1907–1939, Volume 2: 1929–1939* (Princeton: Princeton University Press, 1993). Abel's work establishes a rigorous model for the historiographic importance of re-examining film-writing as primary documents:

> [M]ay the method and format of this book offer a model for others doing research on related bodies of film theory and criticism. For here the writing of history is accompanied by the unearthing of something close to an archive, which – through further sifting, interrogation, and analysis – may well contain the seeds of that history's rewriting. (Abel, *French Film Criticism and Theory, Volume 1*, p. xix.)

14. See Siegfried Kracauer, *Das Ornament der Masse* (Frankfurt: Suhrkamp Verlag, 1963), translated and edited, with an introduction by Thomas Y. Levin as *The Mass Ornament: Weimar Essays* (Cambridge, MA: Harvard University Press, 1995); Walter Benjamin, *Passagen-Werk, Volume 1 and 2*, edited by Rolf Tiedemann (Frankfurt: Suhrkamp Verlag, 1983); and, as excellent concordance to the massive Arcades Project, Susan Buck-Morss, *The Dialectics of Seeing: Walter Benjamin and the Arcades Project* (Cambridge, MA: MIT Press, 1989).

15. Annette Michelson, 'Film and the Radical Aspiration', in P. Adams Sitney (ed.), *Film Culture Reader* (New York: Praeger, 1970), p. 407. Michelson describes the range of theoretical speculation about the cinema in the years preceding 1929, when a number of 'repressive factors', including

the transition to sound, caused a 'dissociation of sensibility' in both film-making and film theory.

16. Foucault's oft-cited dictum from *Archeology of Knowledge* has become a touchstone for much of the new film history: 'The document, then, is no longer for history an inert material through which it tries to reconstitute what men have done or said, the events of which only the trace remains; history is now trying to define within the documentary material itself, unities, totalities, series, relations' (Michel Foucault, *Archeology of Knowledge*, translated by A.M. Sheridan Smith (New York: Harper & Row, 1972), pp. 6–7).

17. Reflecting a more Foucauldian influence on film history and theory, the British film journal, *Framework*, edited by Donald Ranvaud, initiated a column entitled 'Towards an Archaeology of Film Theory' in 1980. By the late 1980s, a new generation of film historians began to rewrite cinema history with theoretically inflected agendas. See, for example, Thomas Elsaesser (ed.), *Early Cinema: Space, Frame, Narrative* (London: BFI, 1990); Miriam Hansen, *Babel and Babylon: Spectatorship in American Silent Film* (Cambridge, MA: Harvard University Press, 1991); Abel, *French Film Criticism and Theory*, vols 1 and 2.

18. Jay Leyda, *Kino: A History of the Russian and Soviet Film* (New York: George Allen & Unwin, 1960); Siegfried Kracauer, *From Caligari to Hitler* (Princeton: Princeton University Press, 1947).

19. Rachel Low, *History of British Film 1918–1929* (London: George Allen & Unwin, 1971), p. 22.

20. See 'Notes on the Contributors and Correspondents' in Appendix 2.

21. Low, *British Film*, p. 20.

22. Don Macpherson (ed.), *Traditions of Independence: British Cinema in the Thirties* (London: British Film Institute, 1980), p. 5.

23. Undoing all prior historical oversights, Dusinberre mentions the films produced in the *Close Up* 'milieu' and lists Oswell Blakeston, Kenneth Macpherson and H.D. in an Appendix, 'Provisional List of English Avant-Garde Film-

makers'. See Deke Dusinberre, 'The Avant-garde Attitude in the Thirties', in Macpherson (ed.), *Traditions of Independence*, pp. 34–50.

24. Macpherson and Bryher began their pleas against censorship restrictions from their first issues, but the journal's campaign did not gain strength or organization until late 1928. In the January 1929 issue, a formal petition with signature form was enclosed in the magazine's back pages. The form was to be signed and returned to the *Close Up* offices; signatures were to be added to a formal petition to be presented to Parliament.

The *Close Up* petition was not addressed to a revision of the 1909 Act but to the operation of the British Board of Film Censors, a trade body similar to the Hays Office of the MPPDA, which rated films U (Universal) or A (Adult). The petition requested broader categories, a reduction in customs duties on foreign films, and that the board of censors also include judges who were concerned with artistic merits of films, not just their commercial potential. For a more detailed discussion, see Part 7 of this volume.

25. Advertisement from *transition*, 1 (April 1927).

26. Before they formed their collaborative 'pool', H.D., Bryher and Macpherson had each used 'pool' as an operative poetic metaphor. In March 1915, H.D. had published a poem, 'The Pool', in Harriet Monroe's magazine, *Poetry*. Bryher also published a poem entitled 'The Pool' in a collection of her poetry, *Arrow Music* (London: J. & E. Bumpus, 1922). Macpherson's novel, *Poolreflection*, was the first POOL book advertised and published in 1927. Bryher remembers *Close Up*'s almost casual beginnings:

We lived at Territet and one day we were walking beside the lake and Kenneth compared the ripples drifting across the water with an effect that should be tried on the screen. I remembered my Paris training of the early twenties and said, 'If you're so interested, why don't you start a magazine.' *Close Up* was born on a capital of

sixty pounds. (Winifred Bryher, *The Heart to Artemis: A Writer's Memoirs* (New York: Harcourt Brace & World, 1962), p. 245).

27. See 'Notes on the Contributors and Correspondents' in Appendix 2.

28. See entry for H.D. in Appendix 2, 'Notes on the Contributors and Correspondents'.

29. For more details, see Part 5 of this volume.

30. See 'Publishing History' in Appendix 3.

31. Riant Chateau was a large balconied apartment house built in 1912, facing Lake Geneva. Even after Bryher built her own house on Lake Geneva in 1931, *Close Up* maintained its offices in Riant Chateau. Editorial offices in London (24 Devonshire Street) were added in August 1928 when the printing and editorial activity required a location in England. In April 1930, the *Close Up* offices were moved to 26 Litchfield Street at Charing Cross, above Zwemmer's bookshop and gallery. Zwemmer's advertised its books in *Close Up* and was known for its gallery shows of new photography from Germany. At the end of 1930, when *Close Up* switched to a quarterly format, the Riant Chateau address was finally dropped, and the Swiss address was changed to c/o F. Chevalley, the Swiss correspondent.

32. A few articles from French authors were published untranslated in French. For example, René Crevel, the Surrealist poet and member of the Littératur group, published two pieces in *Close Up* , 'Les Hommes aux milles visages' and 'Champ de bataille et lieux communs' in August and November 1927, respectively.

33. See 'Notes on the Contributors and Correspondents' in Appendix 2.

34. See Paul Fussell, *Abroad* (Oxford: Oxford University Press, 1980), p. 11.

35. Kenneth Macpherson wrote about the advantages of their Swiss location in his October 1927 editorial, 'As Is':
and in Switzerland we have this advantage. We see films as soon as they are released. Heavy advance booking is not made. And we read six months after we have seen

them of films just reaching London and New York. They come from Germany, France, Italy, Sweden, Russia, America and somewhat tardily from England, from everywhere uncensored, think of that! and all the better for it. (Kenneth Macpherson, 'As Is', *Close Up*, vol. I, no. 4, October 1927, p. 16).

36. In a finely detailed history and 'synoptic analysis' of French writing on cinema, Richard Abel analyses a spectrum of 'discourse modes' that waxed and waned in the discursive forum of French film culture. See Abel, *French Film Criticism and Theory*, vols 1 and 2.

In France, there was a great deal of discursive activity devoted to the cinema – from the journalistic coverage of films in daily and weekly newspapers to specialized publications devoted fully to the cinema like *Ciné-Journal* (1908–) and *Le Courrier cinématographique* (1911–14). Although these were ostensibly trade journals geared toward readers who considered the cinema as a business, they also contained occasional articles devoted to aesthetic questions.

The list of French film journals which set precedents for *Close Up* is daunting: in addition to *Le Film* (1914–19); Pierre Henri's *Ciné pour Tous* (1919–23); Adrien Maître and Jean Pascal's *Cinémagazine* (1921–); Delluc's *Cinéa* (1921–3), which in 1923 merged with *Ciné pour Tous* and became a bimonthly, *Cinéa-Ciné pour Tous*, edited by Jean Tedesco; Ricciotto Canudo's *Gazette des Septième Arts* (1923–).

37. Colette's reviews were written weekly between 28 May and 21 July 1917. See *Colette at the Movies*, edited by Alain and Odette Virmaux, translated by Sarah W.R. Smith (New York: Frederick Ungar, 1980).

38. Delluc went on to establish (and then leave) other film journals: *Le Journal du Ciné-Club* (begun in 1920, designed to offer listings of *ciné-club* programmes all over Paris) and *Cinéa* (begun in 1921). See Richard Abel, 'Louis Delluc: The Critic as Cinéaste', *Quarterly Review of Film Studies*, 1 (2) (May 1976), pp. 205–44. Macpherson attempted to emulate the authority of Delluc. Like

Delluc, Macpherson was a novelist-turned-critic, and a theorist-turned-film-maker; but unlike Delluc never became the effective leader of a group of film-makers.

39. See Richard Abel, 'The Contribution of the French Literary Avant-Garde to Film Theory and Criticism (1907–1924)', *Cinema Journal*, 14 (3) (Spring 1975), pp. 18–40.

40. Delluc's *ciné-club* began in 1920 in conjunction with his *Le Journal de Ciné-Club*; also established in 1920 was Ricciotto Canudo's Club des Amis du Septième Art; and in 1922, Le Club Francais du Cinema was formed by Leon Moussinac. The three separate clubs merged together after the deaths of Canudo (in 1923) and Delluc (in 1924) and became Le Ciné-Club de France.

41. Harry Alan Potamkin, 'The Cinema in Great Britain', *Cinema*, May 1930, pp. 24–5, 50. Reprinted in *The Compound Cinema: The Film Writings of Harry Alan Potamkin*, selected and arranged by Lewis Jacobs (New York: Teachers College Press, 1977), p. 318–24.

42. Hugh Castle, 'Some British Films', *Close Up*, vol. V, no. 1, July 1929, p. 4.

43. Robert Herring, 'London Letter', *Close Up*, vol. II, no. 5, May 1928, pp. 57–8.

44. With eight programmes in its first season (October 1925–May 1926) and eight programmes in its second season (October 1926–May 1927), the Film Society had shown a total of seventy-four films. Twenty of the films in the first season (thirteen French, six German, one Japanese) had not been seen in Britain before. In the second season, this fell to nine (four German, two French, two British, and one Russian). The Film Society's programme notes were reprinted in their entirety as *The Film Society Programmes: 1925–1939* (New York: Arno Press, 1972).

45. Editorial *London Mercury*, November 1925. As if in response to the *London Mercury*'s concern about there being no 'National Gallery' for classic films, in the 'Comment and Review' section of the first issue of *Close Up*, there was a proposal for a 'film library'('The public of the future should be able to buy or borrow films as it now buys or borrows books')

and for repeated viewing at a variety of film speeds ('it may be desirable to see over and over again at different speeds, some fragment of a work …'). 'Comment and Review', *Close Up*, vol. I, no. 1, July 1927, pp. 51–2.

46. The frontispiece of the August 1927 issue proclaimed: 'We beg to announce: Osbert Sitwell, Havelock Ellis, André Gide, Barbara Low, Oswell Blakeston.' Of these, Gide and Sitwell never contributed a piece; while Havelock Ellis only contributed a letter.

47. Woolf replied to the request to reprint her article, 'Movies and Reality', which had been published in the *Nation* in 1926. In a reply dated 10 July 1927, Woolf wrote: *Nation* does not want it reprinted in another English magazine. I was under the impression when I wrote that *Close Up* was foreign. It was very good of you to say that you would wait for me, but I am so busy during the next few months that I cannot undertake to write anything fresh. (Letter from Virginia Woolf to Kenneth Macpherson, 10 July 1927, Beinecke Rare Book and Manuscript Library, Yale University.)

48. Kenneth Macpherson, letter to Gertrude Stein, 24 June 1927. Published in *The Flowers of Friendship: Letters to Gertrude Stein*, edited by Donald Gallup (New York: Alfred A. Knopf, 1953), pp. 208–9.

49. Gertrude Stein, 'Mrs Emerson', *Close Up*, vol. I, no. 2, August 1927, p. 24.

50. William Hunter, 'The Art Form of Democracy?', *Scrutiny*, I (1) (May 1932), p. 61.

51. William Hunter, *Scrutiny of Cinema* (London: Wishart and Company, 1932), pp. 12–13.

52. *Ibid.*

53. Kenneth Macpherson, 'As Is', *Close Up*, vol. VIII, no. 2, June 1931, p. 72.

54. *Close Up*, vol. I, no. 1, July 1927, p. 5. Of course, fifty years previous – 1877 – marks the cinema's beginnings in what is now considered its pre-history.

55. In addition to his editorials, Macpherson published fifteen other articles during the course of the journal's six years.

56. 'One hundred pounds will make a film as noble as anything you can wish to see. Money is no excuse.' Kenneth Macpherson,

'As Is', *Close Up*, vol. I, no. 1, July 1927, p. 10.

57. 'I want to arrange that people making films, and experimenting in all sorts of ways shall be able to see what others are doing in the same way', *ibid.*, p. 15. This suggestion was taken up in more detail in the 'Comment and Review' section: 'Now why shouldn't all the big towns, Birmingham, Liverpool, etc. have their own film societies? … One often wants to see films one has missed. It is never possible. … If it could be felt that some organisation made it possible to be seen definitely in some definite place at some definite future date, one could arrange accordingly. Some theatre might develop this reputation with great advantage' (pp. 51–4).

58. 'When the film is not good enough to keep the brain working, the public sinks into a kind of hypnotic daze. The screen, with its changing forms becomes something in the nature of a crystal, and the public in the nature of a crystal gazer. Mind in some way neatly obliterates itself' (*Close Up*, vol. I, no. 4, October 1927, p. 14).

59. 'Translate such procedure into terms of any of the other arts and its monstrosity hits you between the eyes' (*ibid.*, no. 6, December 1927, p. 6).

60. 'The glorious Strength of the movies is just that they have no past, no history' (*ibid.*, no. 2, August 1927, p. 8).

61. *Ibid.*, no. 1, July 1927, p. 6.

62. In his July 1928 'As Is' editorial, Macpherson made the following assessment: 'In a word, *Close Up* was determined to … be a sort of battleground' (p. 7).

63. *Ibid.*, pp. 8–9.

64. *Close Up*, vol. IV, no. 3, March 1929, p. 9.

65. Bryher, 'Danger in the Cinema', *Close Up*, vol. VIII, no. 5, November 1930, pp. 303–5.

66. Bryher, 'Hollywood Code II', *Close Up*, vol. VIII, no. 4, p. 281.

67. Bryher, 'G.W. Pabst. A Survey', *Close Up*, vol. I, no. 6, December 1927, p. 58.

68. *Ibid.*

69. Jean Lenauer, 'Letter to an Unknown', *Close Up*, vol. IV, no. 6, June 1929, p. 65.

70. Bryher, letter to H.D., 28 October 1927. Beinecke Rare Book and Manuscript Library, Yale University.

71. Bryher, letter to H.D., 29 October 1927.

72. Kenneth Macpherson, 'As Is', *Close Up*, vol. II, no. 3, March 1928, pp. 7–8.

73. Lotte Eisner, *The Haunted Screen* (Berkeley: University of California Press, 1973), p. 296.

74. H.D., 'An Appreciation', *Close Up*, vol. IV, no. 3, March 1929, p. 62.

74. Kenneth Macpherson, letter to H.D., undated 1928/9. Beinecke Rare Book and Manuscript Library, Yale University.

75. Kenneth Macpherson, letter to H.D., undated 1928/9. Beinecke Rare Book and Manuscript Library, Yale University. Macpherson, Bryher and H.D. wrote to each other in a private vernacular, dependent on a set of idioms of cross-species identification. H.D. was 'Kat' or 'the Kitten', Bryher was 'small dog' and 'FIDO' and Macpherson was 'big dog' and 'ROVER'. Although their canine and feline identities rarely appeared in *Close Up*, occasionally references slip in. For example, in describing their excitement at German lighting in his first 'As Is', editorial, Macpherson writes: 'We said thank god when Germany pulled a wry mouth at all of it and blacked out seven eighths of the arc lamps. And so we looked to Germany with expectant eyes. And again our tails wagged' (*Close Up*, vol. I, no. 1, July 1927, pp. 6–7).

76. For a further discussion of the failed Pabst–Macpherson collaboration see Anne Friedberg, 'Gemeinsame Tagträume: Eine Psychoanalytische Film-Affäre – Pabst, Sachs und das Filmjournal Close Up', in Gottfried Schlemmer, Bernhard Riff and Georg Haberl (eds), *G.W. Pabst, Schriften der Gesellshaft für Filmtheorie* (Münster: MAkS Publication, 1990), pp. 36–62.

77. Bryher, letter to Macpherson, May 1931. Beinecke Rare Book and Manuscript Library, Yale University.

78. Bryher, letter to Macpherson, June 1932. Beinecke Rare Book and Manuscript Library, Yale University.

79. Bryher, letter to Macpherson, 15 August 1932. Beinecke Rare Book and Manuscript Library, Yale University.

80. Frank Daugherty, 'The Pabst Arrival', *Close Up*, vol. X, no. 4, December 1933, p. 334.

81. Kenneth Macpherson, 'As Is', *Close Up*, vol. IV, no. 1, January 1929, p. 9.

82. *Close Up*, vol. V, no. 6, December 1929, pp. 448, 454.

83. *Close Up*, vol. VII, no. 1, July 1930, p. 1.

84. See Part 5, '*Borderline* and the POOL Films'.

85. *Köpfe des Alltags (Unbekannte Mensch)*, eighty studies by Lerski (Berlin: Hermann Reckendorf Verlag, 1931). In the September 1931 issue, *Close Up* included three of the Helmar Lerski photographs. One of Macpherson's 'photo-montages' was made from stills from Joris Iven's 'Phillips Radio Film'. The other was of Kenwin – the house that Bryher and Macpherson built on Lake Geneva, in Burier, a few miles from Territet. The Corbusier-inspired Kenwin was designed by a German architect, Hermann Henselmann and finished in 1931. The house was designed to contain a film studio.

86. In March 1932, Macpherson wrote one last editorial deploring censorship as a 'sanitation anxiety ... a strange contemporary virus, that deodorizing neurosis, born in the States and already invading the four corners of the earth'. The censors were afflicted with a 'neurosis ...': 'The mind that wants cleanliness is the mind that believes in dirt.' Kenneth Macpherson, 'As Is', *Close Up*, vol. IX, no. 1, March 1932, p. 25.

87. Blakeston was by far the most prolific contributor to the magazine, writing a total of eighty-four articles during the six and a half years of publication; by contrast, Macpherson wrote sixty-one, Clifford Howard sixty-four, Robert Herring forty-three and Bryher twenty-five. Blakeston also published two books with POOL: a 'complete guide to the cinema studio', *Through a Yellow Glass* (Territet: POOL, 1928), and a novel about British film studio life, *Extra Passenger* (Territet: POOL, 1930).

88. Bryher, 'Films in Education', *Close Up*, vol. I, no. 2, August 1927, pp. 49–54; 'How I Would Start a Film Club', *Close Up*, vol. II, no. 6, June 1928, pp. 30–6; 'Films for Children',

Close Up, vol. III, no. 2, August 1928; 'How to Rent a Film', *Close Up*, vol. III, no. 6, December 1928.

89. Bryher, *Film Problems of Soviet Russia* (Territet, Switzerland: POOL, 1929). The book had more than seventy photographs; the stills that were published in this volume and in *Close Up* were the most visible conduit of Soviet film-making to film-goers in England.

90. Bryher, 'What Shall You Do in the War?', *Close Up*, vol. X, no. 2, June 1933, pp. 188–92.

91. Kenneth Macpherson, 'As Is', *Close Up*, vol. VII, no. 6, December 1930, p. 367.

92. 'ANNOUNCEMENT', *Experimental Cinema*, 3 (January 1931), last page, unnumbered.

93. Macpherson travelled extensively with Norman Douglas and became his literary executor. Bryher, who had first visited Freud in May 1927, described how, when she met Hanns Sachs at a party at Pabst's house in 1928, 'The films had brought us together but an inquiry into the secrets of the mind was nearer to me than the world of the studios.' See Bryher, *Heart to Artemis*, p. 251. From 1928 to 1932, Bryher spent several months of the year in Berlin seeing films and being analysed by Sachs. In April 1932, she met Anna Freud in Berlin and continued to attend psychoanalytic conferences in Lucerne (1934), Marienbad (1936) and Paris (1938); H.D. lived in Vienna to be in analysis with Freud in 1933 and 1934. See her own 'case study' of the analysis, written as *Tribute to Freud* (Boston: David R. Godine, 1974).

94. Kenneth Macpherson, 'As Is', *Close Up*, vol. VII, no. 6, December 1930, p. 367.

95. *Experimental Cinema* (1930–4) was edited by Seymour Stern and published in New York.

96. *Cinema Quarterly* (1932–5) was edited by Norman Wilson and published in Edinburgh. *Film* and the subsequent *Film Art* were edited by B. Vivian Braun. See Claire Johnston, 'Independence and the Thirties', in *Traditions of Independence*, Macpherson (ed.), pp. 9–23.

NOTES TO INTRODUCTION TO PART 1

1. Andrew Higson offers a balanced judgement on the role of *Close Up* in the formation of an intellectual film culture in Britain in his book *Waving the Flag: Constructing a National Cinema in Britain* (Oxford: Oxford University Press, 1995), pp. 13–15.
2. Bryher, 'The Hollywood Code I', *Close Up*, vol. VIII, no. 3, September 1931, pp. 237–8. The editors of *Experimental Cinema* liked the extended version of this passage so much that they quoted it in its entirety in their fourth issue.
3. Peter Wollen, 'The Two Avant Gardes', in *Readings and Writings* (London: Verso, 1982), p. 93.
4. See Part 7.
5. A useful summary can be found in Deke Dusinberre, 'The Other Avant-gardes', in *Film as Film: Formal Experiment in Film, 1910–1975* (London: Arts Council of Great Britain, 1979), pp. 53–80. Dusinberre here reports conversations with Oswell Blakeston about *Close Up* and POOL Productions. For relevant historical background, see also A.L. Rees's foreword to Hans Richter, *The Struggle for the Film* (Aldershot: Wildwood House, 1986).
6. Wollen, 'Two Avant Gardes', p. 94.
7. Reprinted in Part 6.
8. Kenneth Macpherson, 'An Introduction to "The Fourth Dimension in the Kino, Part I"', *Close Up*, vol. VI, no. 3, March 1930, pp. 183–4.
9. Paul Willemen, 'On Reading Epstein on *photogénie*', *Afterimage*, 10 (Autumn 1982), p. 42.
10. Christian Metz, 'The Imaginary Signifier', *Screen*, 16 (2) (Summer 1975).
11. A brief report for *Close Up*, by Jean Lenauer, is included in Part 7.
12. On the meetings of La Sarraz and Brussels, see Ian Christie, 'French Avant-garde Film in the Twenties: from "Specificity" to Surrealism', in *Film as Film*, and Rees's foreword to Richter, *Struggle for the Film*.
13. Kenneth Macpherson, 'As Is', *Close Up*, vol. V, no. 2, August 1929, p. 87.
14. *Ibid.*, pp. 87–8.
15. Thomas Cripps, *Slow Fade to Black: The Negro in American Film 1900 – 1942* (New York and Oxford: Oxford University Press, 1977), pp. 209–11.
16. Robert Herring, 'Black Shadows', *Close Up*, vol. V, no. 2, August 1929, p. 101.
17. Dorothy Richardson, 'Dialogue in Dixie', *ibid.*, no. 3, September 1929, p. 214.
18. Kenneth Macpherson, 'As Is', *Close Up*, vol. V, no. 2, August 1929, p. 90.
19. Kenneth Macpherson, 'A Negro Film Union – Why Not?', in Nancy Cunard (ed.), *Negro: An Anthology*, abridged edition, edited by H.D. Ford (New York: Ungar, 1974, originally published in 1934), p. 206.
20. *Ibid.*, pp. 206–7.

NOTES TO INTRODUCTION TO PART 2

1. Quoted in Alan Williams, 'Historical and Theoretical Issues in the Coming of Recorded Sound to the Cinema', in Rick Altman (ed.), *Sound Theory / Sound Practice* (London: Routledge, 1992), p. 131.
2. David Bordwell, Janet Staiger and Kristin Thompson, *The Classical Hollywood Cinema: Film Style and Mode of Production to 1960* (London: Routledge, 1985), p. 131.
3. Ian Christie, 'Introduction', in Richard Taylor and Ian Christie, *The Film Factory: Russian and Soviet Cinema in Documents* (Cambridge, MA: Harvard University Press, 1988), p. 6.
4. Kenneth Macpherson, 'As Is', *Close Up*, vol. III, no. 3, September 1928, p. 13.
5. *Close Up*, vol. V, no. 1, July 1929, pp. 7–8.
6. S.M. Eisenstein, W.I. Pudowkin [Pudovkin] and G.V. Alexandroff [Alexandrov], 'The Sound Film: A Statement From U.S.S.R.', *Close Up*, vol. III, no. 4, October 1928, p. 12.
7. In his *Theory of Film*, Siegfried Kracauer wryly noted that such predictions about the consequences of dialogue ignored the reality of mainstream Hollywood or English cinema which was so frequently and vigorously condemned by contributors to *Close Up*: 'The silent screen was crammed with "highly cultured dramas"' (Siegfried Kracauer, 'Dialogue and Sound', in Elisabeth Weis and John Belton (eds), *Film Sound: Theory and Practice* (New York: Columbia University Press, 1985), p.127).
8. See Taylor and Christie, *Film Factory*, p. 410.
9. Weis and Belton, *Film Sound*, p. 77.
10. Quoted in Douglas Kahn, 'Introduction', in Douglas Khan and Gregory Whitehead (eds), *Wireless Imagination: Sound, Radio and the Avant-Garde* (Cambridge, MA: MIT Press, 1992), pp. 12–13.
11. Quoted in Kahn and Whitehead, *Wireless Imagination*, p. 28.
12. Kenneth Macpherson, 'As Is', *Close Up*, vol. V, no. 4, October 1929, p. 262.
13. For an account of another film whose use of sound was praised in *Close Up*, Anthony Asquith's *A Cottage on Dartmoor* (1929), see Murray Smith, 'Technological Determination, Aesthetic Resistance; or, *A Cottage on Dartmoor*: Goatgland Talkie or Masterpiece?', *Wideangle*, 12 (3) (July 1990), pp. 80–97.
14. Macpherson, 'As Is', vol. V, no. 4, October 1929, p. 263.

NOTES TO INTRODUCTION TO PART 3

1. H.D., letter to Viola Jordan, 6 June 1927, Viola Jordan Papers, Beinecke Rare Book and Manuscript Library, Yale University. Quoted in Jayne E. Marek, *Women Editing Modernism: 'Little' Magazines and Literary History* (Lexington: University Press of Kentucky, 1995), p.129.
2. H.D. (attributed), *Borderline – A POOL Film with Paul Robeson* (London: Mercury Press, 1930). Reprinted as 'The *Borderline* pamphlet' in Bonnie Kime Scott (ed.), *The Gender of Modernism: A Critical Anthology* (Bloomington and Indianapolis: Indiana University Press, 1990), pp. 110–24.
3. H.D., 'Russian Films', *Close Up*, vol. III, no. 3, September 1928, p. 27.
4. Imagism was a short-lived but influential poetic movement in the 1910s; its main exponents included Ezra Pound, John Gould Fletcher, Richard Aldington (H.D.'s then husband), Amy Lowell and H.D. herself, 'named' by Pound as 'H.D. imagiste' when her first published poems appeared in *Poetry* in 1913. As defined by

Pound and by F.S. Flint, 'Imagism' entails a concrete, condensed, non-ornamental poetics, central to which is 'the direct presentation of the object', with, in Pound's description of H.D.'s poetry, 'no excessive use of adjectives, no metaphors that won't permit examination' ('To Harriet Monroe', October 1912, *The Letters of Ezra Pound: 1907–1941*, edited by D.D. Page (New York: Harcourt, 1950), p. 11). For discussion of the Imagist movement, see the introduction to Peter Jones (ed.), *Imagist Poetry* (Harmondsworth: Penguin, 1972), pp. 13–43. As has frequently been noted, Imagism became something of a straitjacket for H.D.; a number of her later writings refer to its limitations, and to her desire for 'suggestion' rather than 'direct presentation' in language and images.

In 1916, H.D. published her first book of poetry, *Sea Garden*. As Claire Buck notes, the extensive use of classical allusions, which marked H.D. out from the other Imagist poets, implies a coded significance: 'The elaborate repertoire of plants, flowers, gods and goddesses ... all signal hidden meaning and the need for interpretation' (Claire Buck, *H.D. and Freud: Bisexuality and a Feminine Discourse* (Hemel Hempstead: Harvester, 1991), pp. 32–3). H.D. continued to use classical culture as a 'symbolic topography' and to construct 'revisionary' poetic models of classical myth and legend throughout her writing career. Many of her lyric poems are refabrications of Sappho's fragments. See Rachel Blau Duplessis, *H.D. The Career of That Struggle* (Brighton: Harvester, 1986), especially pp. 1–30, for discussion of H.D.'s classicism.

5. H.D., 'Restraint', *Close Up*, vol. I, no. 2, August 1927, pp. 30–9.
6. H.D., 'Expiation', *Close Up*, vol. II, no. 5, May 1928, p. 44.
7. H.D., 'Joan of Arc', *Close Up*, vol. III, no. 1, July 1928, p. 15. The figure of Joan of Arc is also central to H.D.'s autobiographical novel *Asphodel* (Durham, NC: Duke University Press, 1992). 'They had trapped her, a girl who was a boy and they always do that' (p. 9).
8. *Ibid.*, p. 22.

9. H.D., 'Expiation', pp. 38–9.
10. H.D., 'The Usual Star' (Dijon: Darantière, 1934), p. 21. Other short stories/novellas of this period (all of them privately printed by Darantière) include 'Kora and Ka' and 'Mira Mare' (1934), 'Nights' (1935) and 'Two Americans' (published with 'The Usual Star'), which gives a fictionalized account of H.D.'s meeting with Paul Robeson. The representation of cinematic screening and projection, and of female beauty on the screen (the image of Garbo), is central to the novel *Bid Me to Live*, which H.D. began writing in 1918, rewrote in the 1930s and completed in the late 1940s. It appears that H.D.'s analysis with Freud incited her return to this work. The novel was finally published in 1960. The narrative re-presents the collapse of her marriage with Richard Aldington during World War I. H.D., *Bid Me to Live (A Madrigal)* (New York: Grove, 1960).
11. H.D., 'Russian Films', p. 28.
12. H.D., response to questionnaire (1929), reprinted in *Little Review Anthology*, edited by Margaret Andersen (New York: Hermitage, 1953), p. 364.
13. H.D., 'Restraint', p. 35.
14. 'the stage is set now/for his mighty rays;/light/light that batters gloom,/the Pythian/lifts up a fair head/in a lowly place,/he shows his splendour/in a little room;' *Projector (Close Up*, vol. I, no. 1, July 1927, p. 49). *Projector II (ibid.*, no. 4, October 1927, pp. 35–44) continues the theme: 'For such is his rare power;/he snares us in a net/of light/on woven/fair light;/so has the sun-god won us;/he knots the light to light,/he casts the thing afar,/he draws us to his altar;' (pp. 39–40). The poems are reprinted in H.D., *Collected Poems: 1912–1944*, edited by Louis Martz (New York: New Directions, 1986), pp. 349–59.
15. H.D., 'The *Borderline* Pamphlet', p.121.
16. Recent decades have seen the growth of a very extensive critical literature on H.D. Important studies include: Buck, *H.D. and Freud;* Dianne Chisholm, *H.D.'s Freudian Poetics: Psychoanalysis in Translation* (Ithaca, NY: Cornell University Press, 1992); Blau Duplessis, *H.D.: The Career of*

That Struggle; Susan Edmunds, *Out of Line: History, Psychoanalysis and Montage in H.D.'s Long Poems* (Stanford, CA: Stanford University Press, 1994); Susan Stanford Friedman, *Penelope's Web: Gender, Modernity, H.D.'s Fiction* (Cambridge: Cambridge University Press, 1990) and *Psyche Reborn: The Emergence of H.D.* (Bloomington: Indiana University Press, 1981); Susan Stanford Friedman and Rachel Blau Duplessis (eds), *Signets: Reading H.D.* (Madison: University of Wisconsin Press, 1990); Barbara Guest, *Herself Defined: The Poet H.D. and Her World* (Garden City, NY: Doubleday, 1984); Michael King (ed.), *H.D. Woman and Poet* (Orono, ME: National Poetry Foundation, 1986), a collection which contains important essays on H.D., film and photography by Charlotte Mandel, Diane Collecott and Anne Friedberg. For essays specifically on H.D. and cinema, see also Friedberg, 'On H.D.: Woman, History, Recognition', *Wide Angle: A Film Quarterly of Theory, Criticism and Practice*, 5 (1982), pp. 26–31; Charlotte Mandel, '"The Redirected Image": Cinematic Dynamics in the Style of H.D.', *Literature/Film Quarterly*, 11 (1) (1983), pp. 36–45; Adalaide Morris, 'The Concept of Projection: H.D.'s Visionary Powers', *Contemporary Literature*, 25 (4) (Winter 1984), pp. 411–36.
17. See, in addition to the *Close Up* articles on film censorship in this collection, Bryher's study, *Film Problems of Soviet Cinema* (Territet, Switzerland: POOL, 1929).
18. H.D., 'The *Borderline* Pamphlet', p. 114.
19. Quoted in Paul Virilio, *War and Cinema: The Logistics of Perception*, translated by Patrick Camiller (London and New York: Verso, 1989), p. 20.
20. Robert Herring, 'A New Cinema, Magic and the Avant Garde', *Close Up*, vol. IV, no. 4, April 1929, pp. 51–2.
21. Dorothy Richardson, 'Continuous Performance – Narcissus', *Close Up*, vol. VIII, no. 3, September 1931, p. 185.
22. The final section of *Trilogy* is indeed called 'The Flowering of the Rod'. The poem, written between 1942 and 1944, is included in *Collected Poems*.

23. H.D., 'Turksib', *Close Up*, vol. 5, no. 6, December 1929, p.491.

24. Walter Benjamin, 'The Work of Art in the Age of Mechanical Reproduction', translated by Harry Zohn, in *Illuminations* (New York: Harcourt, Brace and World, 1968), p. 234.

25. The term is used by Dianne Chisholm, in *H.D.'s Freudian Poetics*.

26. H.D., *Tribute to Freud* (Manchester: Carcanet, 1985), p. 21.

27. Ibid, pp. 44–56. At the close of this section, H.D. describes how Bryher carried on the 'reading' of the 'writing on the wall' when H.D. was no longer able to: 'as I relaxed, let go, from complete physical and mental exhaustion, she saw what I did not see. It was the last section of the series, or the last concluding symbol – perhaps that "determinative" that is used in the actual hieroglyph, the picture that contains the whole series of pictures in itself or helps clarify them. In any case, it is apparently a clear enough picture or symbol. She said it was a circle like the sun-disk and a figure within the disk; a man, she thought, was reaching out to draw the image of a woman (my Nike) into the sun beside him' (p. 56). See the discussion of hieroglyphics later in this section.

28. H.D., *The Gift* (London: Virago, 1984).

29. Chisholm, *H.D.'s Freudian Poetics*, p.93.

30. Bryher, *The Heart to Artemis: A Writer's Memoirs* (London: Collins, 1963), pp. 247–8. Although Bryher suggests that her interest in film came to an end with the demise of silent cinema and of *Close Up*, she in fact soon took on ownership of another journal which made a significant contribution to film culture. Bryher founded *Life and Letters To-Day* in 1935, making Robert Herring, one of the key *Close Up* contributors, its editor. In its earlier manifestation it was called *Life and Letters*, and was first edited by Desmond MacCarthy, a central figure in Bloomsbury culture. *Life and Letters* now appears belletrist, biographical-essayistic and somewhat 'Victorian' – on its takeover, it became culturally diverse and international. Herring also introduced a very extensive cinema section. The first issue

of *Life and Letters To-Day* included work by Havelock Ellis, Gide and Gertrude Stein – the 'star' writers also billed in the first issues of *Close Up*. Bryher continued to write about cinema, producing an essay on 'Film in Education' for the pamphlet *Cinema Survey*, which she co-edited with Robert Herring and Dallas Bower (London: Brendin Publishing Company, 1937). Yet the legend of *Close Up*, the 'first' of its kind, also demands that it have no successor.

31. H.D., 'The Mask and the Movietone' (The Cinema and the Classics III), *Close Up*, vol. 1, no. 5, November 1927, pp. 18–31.

32. H.D., 'Conrad Veidt: *The Student of Prague*', *ibid.*, no. 3, September 1927, p. 42.

33. The distinction between 'thing-presentation', which in Freud's account characterizes dream mentation and the unconscious, and 'word-presentation', which belongs to the system preconscious/conscious, runs throughout *The Interpretation of Dreams*. Freud also discussed the presentations of words and of things more fully in his paper on the 'Unconscious' (1915), Penguin Freud Library, volume 11, pp. 206–10, 221–2. The conceptual connection between dreams and films is forged in large part on the basis of their shared 'visual' thinking, but for both psychoanalysis and film theory the question of language, and of the linguistic dimensions of 'visual' imagery, is a complex and vexed one.

34. The concept of 'inner speech', defined by Peirce as an 'internal dialogue', has been central to linguistics. It enters debates in film theory primarily through writings by Eisenstein and by the Formalist thinker Boris Eikhenbaum, whose 'Problems of film stylistics', which addressed the ways in which filmic images can be understood, was published in 1927. Eikhenbaum argued that it is 'inner speech' which allows the spectator to make the connections between separate shots, verbal discourse being the ground upon which the filmic is figured. Other thinkers, including the linguist Lev Vygotsky, have emphasized the differentially discursive aspects of 'inner speech': 'Inner speech

is to a large extent thinking in pure meanings. It is a dynamic, shifting, unstable thing, fluttering between word and image' (Lev Vygotsky, *Thought and Language* [1936] (Cambridge, MA: MIT Press, 1962), p. 2). For discussions of 'inner speech' and cinema, see Paul Willeman, 'Cinematic Discourse: The Problem of Inner Speech', in *Looks and Frictions: Essays in Cultural Studies and Film Theory* (London: BFI, 1994), pp. 27–55; and Stephen Heath, 'Language, Sight and Sound', in *Questions of Cinema* (Bloomington: Indiana University Press, 1980), pp. 194–220.

35. H.D., 'Conrad Veidt', p. 4.

36. H.D., *Tribute to Freud*, p. 71.

37. The links were both personal and literary. Hilda Doolittle met Pound in Philadelphia when she was fifteen and he was a student at the University of Pennsylvania. In Barbara Guest's words, Pound 'forced an education on her ... [with which] Bryn Mawr [which H.D. attended for a time] with its slower and more realistic demands could not keep pace' (Guest, *Herself Defined*, p.4). H.D. and Pound became engaged, and in 1911 H.D. left Philadelphia to travel in Europe and to meet Pound in London, where he had begun to establish his literary reputation. He introduced her to other writers and editors at a time when poetic Imagism was being developed, and it was in this context that H.D.'s earliest work was published. In 1913, H.D. married the writer Richard Aldington. For an account of H.D.'s relationship with Pound, see her *End to Torment* (Manchester: Carcanet, 1980).

38. Peter Nicholls, *Modernisms: A Literary Guide* (Basingstoke: Macmillan, 1995), p. 175.

39. Sergei Eisenstein, 'The Cinematographic Principle and the Ideogram', in *Film Form: Essays in Film Theory* (New York: Harcourt Brace Jovanovitch, 1977), pp. 28–44. *Film Form* contains a number of further essays on Japanese culture, Kabuki theatre and montage theory. See also 'The Cinematographic Principle and Japanese Culture (with a digression on montage and the shot)', *transition*, **19–20** (Spring/Summer 1930),

pp. 90–103. As V.V. Ivanov has noted, Eisenstein's earlier study of oriental languages strongly influenced his theoretical investigation of the sign nature of film language and his experiments in constructing cinematic 'hieroglyphs' (V.V. Ivanov, 'Eisenstein's Montage of Hieroglyphic Signs', in Marshall Blonsky (ed.), *On Signs* (Baltimore: Johns Hopkins University Press, 1985), pp. 221–35).

40. Freud, *The Interpretation of Dreams*, Penguin Freud Library, volume 4 (Harmondsworth: Penguin, 1976), pp. 381–2.

41. Chisholm, *H.D.'s Freudian Poetics*, p. 98.

42. H.D., *Tribute to Freud*, p. 23.

43. In 1922–3, Bryher and H.D. (accompanied by H.D.'s mother) travelled in Italy, Greece, Constantinople and Egypt. In the spring of 1923, they visited the recently opened tomb of King Tutankhamun, an experience depicted by H.D. in the final part of her novel *Palimpsest*, 'Secret Name: Excavator's Egypt'. 'The Greeks came to Egypt to learn', H.D. writes, and, as Guest notes, the world of ancient Egypt (defined for her through mysticism, ritual, magic) became increasingly important for H.D.'s philosophy and poetics, forming an axis with classical Greece (Guest, *Herself Defined*, pp. 157–8).

44. John T. Irwin, *American Hieroglyphics: The Symbol of the Egyptian Hieroglyphics in the American Renaissance* (New Haven and London: Yale University Press, 1980). Chisholm usefully discusses this tradition in relation to H.D.'s work, focusing on the echoes of Emerson in her poetics. See *H.D.'s Freudian Poetics*, pp. 36–60. Susan Edmunds's *Out of Line* contains an excellent chapter on H.D.'s representations of Egypt in the 'montage poem' *Helen in Egypt* (1961) (Edmunds, *Out of Line*, pp. 95–148).

45. Vachel Lindsay, *The Art of the Moving Picture* (New York: Liveright, 1915).

46. Vachel Lindsay, *The Progress and Poetry of the Movies*, edited and with commentary by Myron Lounsbury (Lanham, MD: Scarecrow Press, 1995), p. 90.

47. Lindsay, *Moving Picture*, p. 173.

48. *Ibid.*, p. 259.

49. Nick Browne, 'American Film Theory in the Silent Period: Orientalism as an Ideological Form', *Wide Angle*, 11 (4) (1989), pp. 23–31. Browne, like Miriam Hansen, notes the complexity of the 'universal language' myth of cinema at a time of mass working-class immigration into the United States (and of a substantially immigrant and working-class audience for the cinema). He also discusses the relationship between the 'Orientalism' of film culture, with 'picture palaces' designed as Egyptian and Chinese temples, and the hostile attitudes towards Chinese and other immigrants in the early decades of the century.

50. At the heart of the theosophy of the Swedish scientist, philosopher and mystic Emanuel Swedenborg (1688 – 1772) is the image of Divine love as the life of the universe. From God emanates a divine sphere, which is manifested in the spiritual world as a sun – from this spiritual sun proceeds the sun of the natural world. Swedenborg also wrote *The Hieroglyphical Key to Natural and Spiritual Mysteries by Way of Representations or Correspondences* (1784), a work which had a significant influence on writers such as Emerson, who referred to Swedenborg as one of those for whom the world is 'a grammar of hieroglyphs' (quoted by Irwin in *American Hieroglyphics*, p.11), and Walt Whitman. Whitman was deeply interested in Swedenborg, and in the hieroglyphics and Egyptology. A Swedenborgian New Church became established in America in the early nineteenth century; Swedenborg's writings were collected and disseminated in the later nineteenth century, reawakening interest in his thought. H.D. (another 'hieroglyphic' thinker) had read Swedenborg with Ezra Pound, and reflects on Balzac's 'Swedenborgian' novel *Seraphitus* throughout *End to Torment*, focusing particularly on the figure of the androgyne, Seraphitus-Seraphita. Vachel Lindsay was strongly influenced by the Swedenborgian community in his hometown, Springfield, Illinois. He writes in 'Adventures Preaching Hieroglyphic Sermons', the Preface to his *Collected Poems*, linking Swedenborgian and 'movie' vision: 'What I want and pray for is a Springfield torn down and rebuilt from the very foundations, according to visions that might appear to an Egyptian or Shaw's Joan of Arc, or any one else whose secret movie-soul was part of the great spiritual movie' (*Collected Poems* (New York: Macmillan, 1949), p. xxv). It is also interesting to note that both H.D.'s and Lindsay's early poems were published by the poetry editor and publisher Harriet Monroe.

51. Miriam Hansen, *From Babel to Babylon: Spectatorship in American Silent Film* (Cambridge, MA: Harvard University Press, 1994), p. 16.

52. *Ibid.*, p. 195.

53. H.D., *Tribute to Freud*, p. 51.

54. *Ibid.*, p. 59. See Jan Montefiore, 'Three Women Poets Reading H.D.', *Agenda* (H.D. Special Issue), 25 (3–4) (Autumn/Winter, 1987/8), pp. 172–3, for an interesting discussion of this passage.

55. H.D., 'Russian Films', p. 20.

NOTES TO INTRODUCTION TO PART 4

1. Dorothy Richardson (hereafter D.R.), letter to Bryher, Spring 1927, in Gloria Fromm (ed.), *Windows on Modernism: Selected Letters of Dorothy Richardson* (Athens, GA: University of Georgia Press, 1995), p. 134.

2. D.R., letter to P. Beaumont Wadsworth, July 1927, in Fromm (ed.), *Windows on Modernism*, p. 139.

3. D.R. letter to Bryher, June 1927, in Fromm (ed.), *Windows on Modernism*, p. 135.

4. *Ibid.*, July 1927, in Fromm (ed.), *Windows on Modernism*, p. 138.

5. D.R. 'Continuous Performance [untitled]', *Close Up*, vol. X, no. 2, June 1933, pp. 131–2.

6. In this sense, Richardson's writing for *Close Up*, like Siegfried Kracauer's essays on cinema, could be said to mark a shift from 'film theory' to 'cinema theory', the latter, in Thomas Levin's words, 'understood as a practice that is both more historically reflexive and more sensitive to larger institutional factors'. See Levin's introduction to Siegfried Kracauer, *The Mass Ornament: Weimar Essays*

(Cambridge, MA: Harvard University Press, 1995), p. 25.

7. D.R. 'Continuous Performance [untitled]', *Close Up*, vol. 1, no. 1, July 1927, p. 35.

8. There are interesting echoes here of words written by Patrick Geddes, quoted by Huntly Carter in *The New Spirit of the Cinema*: 'When the famous Professor Patrick Geddes planned his new sociological world he said, "there shall be little chapels of meditation everywhere to which human beings may retire for rest and meditation and so escape for a time the hard realities of the material world and meditate upon the past, and so enter a world of phantasy to re-emerge with their ideas remodelled." Thus back, unconsciously it may be, to scratch, returning laden with the new phantasies or revitalised inner desires to be consciously projected in fresh symbols of a new form of human life' (Huntly Carter, *The New Spirit of the Cinema* (London: Harold Shaylor, 1930), p. xxx). Throughout *Pilgrimage*, as well as her film-writing, Richardson represents such 'retreats', many of them specifically female spheres – Lyons Corner Houses, rooms, cafes, churches, women's clubs. The cinema could indeed be the ideal space for which Richardson's heroine searches; one that crosses the private/public divide in enabling interiority, 'meditation', in a public arena.

9. Georg Simmel, 'The Metropolis and Mental Life', in Kurt H. Wolff (ed.), *The Sociology of Georg Simmel* (New York: Free Press, 1950).

10. D.R., 'Continuous Performance. XII – the Cinema in Arcady', *Close Up*, vol. III, no. 1, July 1928, p. 55.

11. D.R., 'Continuous Performance – This Spoon-fed Generation?', *Close Up*, vol. VIII, no. 4, December 1931, p. 306; 'Continuous Performance. VII – the Front Rows', *Close Up*, vol. II, no. 1, January 1928, p. 64; 'Continuous Performance. VI – the Increasing Congregation?', vol. I, no. 6, December 1927, p. 65.

12. The thirteen volumes of *Pilgrimage* have been reprinted in four volumes by Virago Press. Volume numbers in the notes refer to this edition.

13. Bryher, *The Heart to Artemis: A Writer's Memoirs* (London: Collins, 1962), p. 7.

14. *Ibid.*, p. 174.

15. By 1946, Richardson was seventy-three and had spent six years on the writing of what was to be the last volume of *Pilgrimage*, *March Moonlight*. Bryher and Robert Herring suggested that Richardson publish what she had written of the volume as 'Work in Progress' in *Life and Letters To-day*. The extracts appeared in the April, May and November 1946 issues of the journal.

16. D.R., 'This Spoon-fed Generation?', pp. 337–8.

17. D.R., letter to Bryher, 22 December 1931, in Fromm (ed.), *Windows on Modernism*, p. 231. There is now a growing critical literature on Richardson's film-writing, and on the impact of film on her fiction. In my thinking about Richardson I am particularly indebted to Carol Watts's excellent study *Dorothy Richardson* (Plymouth, Devon: Northcote House, 1995). See also Susan Gevirtz, *Narrative's Journey: The Fiction and Film Writing of Dorothy Richardson* (New York: Peter Lang, 1996); Paul Tiessen, 'A Comparative Approach to the Form and Function of Novel and Film: Dorothy Richardson's Theory of Art', *Literature / Film Quarterly*, 3 (1) (Winter 1975), pp. 83–90; Anne Friedberg, 'Because They Speak Separate Languages: Dorothy Richardson and the Film Gone Male', *Framework*, 20 (1983), pp. 6–8; Rebecca Egger, 'Deaf Ears and Dark Continents: Dorothy Richardson's Cinematic Epistemology', *Camera Obscura*, 30 (May 1992), pp. 5–33. General studies of Richardson include Stephen Heath's brilliant essay 'Writing for Silence: Dorothy Richardson and the Novel', in S. Kappeler and N. Bryson (eds), *Teaching the Text* (London: Routledge and Kegan Paul, 1983), pp. 126–47; Gillian Hanscombe, *The Art of Life: Dorothy Richardson and the Development of Feminist Consciousness* (London: Peter Owen, 1982); Jean Radford, *Dorothy Richardson* (Hemel Hempstead: Harvester Wheatsheaf, 1991). The fullest biography is Gloria Fromm's *Dorothy Richardson: A Biography*, new edn (Athens,

GA: University of Georgia Press, 1994), which also contains some excellent discussion of Richardson's film-writing and its relation to her fiction. See especially pp. 207–12.

18. D.R., *Pilgrimage*, Volume 2 (London: Virago, 1979), pp. 298–9. For further discussion of optical histories in *Pilgrimage*, see Watts, *Dorothy Richardson*, especially p. 60.

19. D.R., *Pilgrimage*, Volume 3 (London: Virago, 1979), pp. 85–6.

20. D.R., 'Continuous Performance [untitled]', *Close Up*, vol. X, no. 2, June 1933, p. 131.

21. D.R., *Pilgrimage*, Volume 4 (*Dawn's Left Hand*) (London: Virago, 1979), p. 168.

22. *Ibid.*, p. 141.

23. D.R., quoted in Stanley J. Kunitz and Howard Haycraft (eds), *Twentieth Century Authors* (New York: H.W. Wilson, 1942), p. 1169.

24. D.R., 'Continuous Performance – Pictures and Films', *Close Up*, vol. IV, no. 1, January 1929, p. 56.

25. D.R., 'The Garden', in *Journey to Paradise*, selected and introduced by Trudi Tate (London: Virago, 1989), p. 21. 'The Garden' was first published in *transatlantic review*, 2 (August 1924), pp. 141–3.

26. Virginia Woolf, 'The Cinema', in Rachel Bowlby (ed.), *The Crowded Dance of Modern Life* (Harmondsworth: Penguin, 1993), p. 54.

27. D.R., 'Films for Children', *Close Up*, vol. III, no. 2, August 1928, pp. 21–7.

28. D.R., 'Continuous Performance – Almost Persuaded', *Close Up*, vol. IV, no. 6, June 1929, pp. 34–5.

29. D.R., *Pilgrimage*, Volume 3, p. 134.

30. D.R., 'Continuous Performance. III – Captions', *Close Up*, vol. I, no. 3, September 1927, p. 55.

31. D.R., 'Continuous Performance – Dialogue in Dixie', *Close Up*, vol. V, no. 3, September 1929, p. 214.

32. D.R., 'Continuous Performance [untitled]', July 1927, p. 37.

33. D.R., 'Continuous Performance. II – Musical Accompaniment', *Close Up*, vol. I, no. 2, August 1927, p. 61.

34. D.R., 'Continuous Performance [untitled]', July 1927, p. 37.

35. Claudia Gorbman, *Unheard Melodies: Narrative Film Music* (London: BFI, 1987), p. 40.

36. See Hanns Eisler and Theodor Adorno, *Composing for the Films* (New York: Oxford University Press, 1947). Richardson's discussions of music in the cinema are predicated on live musical accompaniment rather than recorded sound.

37. D.R., 'Continuous Performance. VIII', *Close Up*, vol.II, no. 3, March 1928, pp. 51–2.

38. *Ibid.*, pp. 54–5.

39. Siegfried Kracauer, *Theory of Film: The Redemption of Physical Reality* (Oxford: Oxford University Press, 1960), p. 7.

40. D.R., 'Continuous Performance – The Film Gone Male', *Close Up*, vol.IX, no. 1, March 1932, pp. 37–8.

41. D.R., letter to Bryher, July 1927, in Fromm (ed.), *Windows on Modernism*, pp. 136–7. Later that year, Richardson wrote to E.B.C. Jones with the following request: 'I'm going to be an awful nuisance. I have no library & no books of reference of any kind & I want to know whether the woman satire of Juvenal [that] begins: *Animal impudens*, is as it were a survey of women thus summed up at the outset' (November 1927, in Fromm (ed.), *Windows on Modernism*, p. 141).

42. See, in particular, 'Women and the Future: A Trembling of the Veil before the Eternal Mystery of "La Gioconda"', *Vanity Fair*, 22 (April 1924), pp. 39–40, and 'Women in the Arts: Some Notes on the Eternally Conflicting Demands of Humanity and Art', *Vanity Fair*, 24 (May 1925), p. 47.

43. D.R., 'Continuous Performance – A Tear for Lycidas', *Close Up*, vol.VII, no. 3, September 1930, p. 197.

44. *Ibid.*, pp. 200–1.

45. For this argument, see Anne Friedberg, 'Because They Speak Separate Languages', pp. 6–8. Numerous passages in *Pilgrimage* articulate the belief that silence is 'female': see, for example, *Revolving Lights* (Volume 7 of *Pilgrimage*, published in 1923; reprinted in Volume 3 of the Virago edition). Richardson writes of Miriam:

> Suddenly it struck her that the life of men was pitiful. They hovered about the doors of freedom, returning sooner or later to the hearth, where even if they were autocrats they were not free; but passing guests, never fully initiated into the house-life, where the real active freedom of the women resided behind the noise and tumult of meetings. Man's life was bandied to and fro ... from *word* to *word*. Hemmed in by women, fearing their silence, unable to enter its freedom – being himself made of words – cursing the torrents of careless speech with which its portals were defended.
>
> (*Pilgrimage*, Volume 3, p. 278)

We might wish to read this with a degree of irony, given the volubility of Miriam (and, according to those who knew her, her creator) and the sheer weight of words that make up *Pilgrimage* itself, which Richardson never perceived as finally completed.

46. D.R., 'Cinema in Arcady', p. 57. Of a later article on this topic, Richardson wrote to Louise Morgan Theis: 'Reference to peasants must come out. Since wireless [sic] & cinema they are incredibly transformed' (14 October 1931, in Fromm (ed.), *Windows on Modernism*, p. 222).

47. D.R., 'Film Gone Male', p. 38.

NOTES TO INTRODUCTION TO PART 5

1. Of the four, *Borderline* is the only film that remains intact – *Foothills* and *Wing Beat* exist in fragmentary form, *Monkey's Moon* remains lost. The 'fragments' of *Foothills* and *Wing Beat* were reassembled by Anne Friedberg in 1979 after a box of nitrate film – in unknown condition – was discovered among H.D.'s papers at Yale. They are currently in the film collection of the Museum of Modern Art, New York.

2. The first issue of *Close Up* in the July 1927 issue contained two stills from the film, one of a starkly posed H.D. ('This is H.D.'s debut in films and her many admirers will welcome this opportunity to see her'), one of Macpherson with the caption: 'A film of telepathy. The feeling of "something is about to happen" pervades the whole, reaching the climax at the point from which this "still" is taken.' See pages 16 and 17.

3. H.D., 'Wing Beat', unpublished manuscript, Beinecke Rare Books and Manuscript Library, Yale University. The essay seemed to be intended for publication in *Close Up*, but was never published. In it, H.D. extols 'Mr Macpherson' as 'one of the young pioneers of the cinema as art' and credits Macpherson and Marc Allégret (see Appendix 2, Notes on the Contributors and Correspondents) as film-makers who 'won't accept the standardization for the film anymore than they have accepted the dead as dust standardization of the arts that the bird stuffers and the bird slayers have imposed on them'.

4. For a further discussion of editing in *Wing Beat* see Anne Friedberg, 'Writing about Cinema: *Close Up* 1927–1933' (unpublished Ph.D. dissertation, New York University, 1983), pp. 123–34. The metaphoric propensity of superimposition must have been attractive to H.D., a writer already drawn to the palimpsest. H.D.'s 1926 novel, *Palimpsest*, is structured in three different historical epochs, each designed to superimpose upon the other through the consciousness of the central character.

5. The *Borderline* pamphlet, p. 232 (this volume). The 39-page 'Borderline Pamphlet' was published by Mercury Press in London in 1930 and has been previously republished in *Sagetrieb*, 6 (Autumn 1987, pp. 29–50, and in Bonnie Kime Scott (ed.), *The Gender of Modernism: A Critical Anthology* (Bloomington: Indiana University Press, 1990, pp. 110–25.

6. Robert Herring, 'Synthetic Dawn', *Close Up*, vol. II, no. 3, March 1928, p. 44.

7. Kenneth Macpherson, 'Wie ein Meisterstuck enstand', *Film für Alle*, 12 (1929) [translation mine]. The amateur film-making journal, *Film für Alle*, was edited by Andor Kraszna-Krausz, who became the Berlin correspondent of *Close Up* in October 1928.

8. As Oswell Blakeston would write in 1931 '[Of the earlier POOL films] *Foothills* was, probably, the most notable. Although these films did not reach the general public they were eagerly viewed by sensitive critics, such as the famous G.W. Pabst, and deeply appreciated for their intense qualities'

(Oswell Blakeston, 'Foreign Notes: A New English Film', *Educational Screen*, January 1931).

9. 'Borderline Pamphlet', p. 236.

10. No trace of the film remains. Rachel Low mentions it in her *Films of Comment and Persuasion* (London: George Allen & Unwin, 1980), p. 108, but mistakenly calls it *Monkey's Man* and suggests that it was the only film Macpherson had made prior to *Borderline*. As Bryher describes in *The Heart to Artemis*: '[Macpherson's] first documentary, *Monkey's Moon*, starring his pet douracoulis (tiny owl-faced monkeys from South America) was shown a number of times and greeted with enthusiasm' (Bryher, *The Heart to Artemis: A Writer's Memoirs* (London: Collins, 1962), p. 261).

11. In the May 1930 issue, the cover and two inside stills were from *Borderline*. The June issue has six stills from the film, the July issue, which also used *Borderline* on the cover, had three stills, the August issue contained two, September one, October six more and in November the cover and five inside stills were devoted to the film. Of the twenty-eight stills from the film published in the journal, eleven were of Paul Robeson. Full-page advertisements for the film were included in the November and December issues; half-page advertisements for the film were included in the November and December issues; half-page ads in the March, June and September 1931 issues announced its length, its certification by the British Board of Censors and its availability for exhibition.

12. To make the film, Paul and his wife Eslanda spent ten days in Switzerland between the end of a busy concert touring schedule and the beginning of the Berlin run of *Emperor Jones*. Bryher and Kenneth's letters to 'Essie' Robeson indicate that Eslanda did most of the arranging.

Robeson's biographer Martin Duberman relies on Eslanda's diary for her account of the filming: 'Kenneth and H.D. used to make us so shriek with laughter with their naïve ideas of Negroes that Paul and I were often completely ruining our make-up with tears of laughter, had to make up all over again. We never once felt we were colored with them.' See

Martin Bauml Duberman, *Paul Robeson* (New York: Alfred A. Knopf, 1988), p. 131.

13. H.D. records that there were 910 shots or 'frames' in the finished scenario. In a film 5,700 feet long, this shot count indicates that the finished film was assertively edited. For further writing on *Borderline* see: Thomas Cripps, *Slow Fade to Black* (New York: Oxford, 1977), pp. 209–10; Richard Dyer, 'Paul Robeson: Crossing Over', in *Heavenly Bodies: Film Stars and Society* (New York: St Martin's, 1986), pp. 130–6; Duberman, *Paul Robeson*, pp. 130–2, 260, 609, n. 5, n. 10; Anne Friedberg, 'Approaching *Borderline*', *Millennium Film Journal*, 7/8/9 (Autumn/Winter 1980–1), pp. 130–9. Translated by Christine Noll Brinckman and reprinted in 'Psychoanalyse und Film' issue of *Frauen und Film*, 36 (February 1984), pp. 25–34; Anne Friedberg, 'Approaching *Borderline*' (revised and updated), in *H.D.: Woman & Poet*, edited by Michael King (Orono, ME: National Poetry Foundation, 1986), pp. 369–90; Anne Friedberg, '"And I Have Learned to Use the Small Projector": H.D., Woman, History, Recognition', *Wide Angle*, 5 (3) (1982), pp. 26–31. Reprinted in 'Literature, Cinema and the Image' issue of *Telescope*, 3 (3) (Autumn 1984), pp. 171–7; Anne Friedberg, 'Fragments de Films "POOL: 1927–1929"', *Travelling*, 56–7, Documents Cinémathèque Suisse (Spring 1980), pp. 60–2; Anne Friedberg, 'Writing about Cinema: *Close Up* 1927–1933', unpublished Ph.D. dissertation, New York University, 1983, pp. 141–72; Michael O'Pray, 'Borderline', *Art Monthly*, 116 (May 1988), pp. 36–7; Andrea Weiss, *Vampires and Violets: Lesbians in Film* (New York: Penguin, 1992), pp. 18–20; Jean Walton, 'Nightmare of the Uncoordinated White-folk: Race, Psychoanalysis and *Borderline*', *Discourse* (Autumn 1996); Jean Walton, 'White Neurotics, Black Primitives and the Queer Matrix of *Borderline*', in Ellis Hansen (ed.), *Out Takes* (Durham, NC: Duke University Press, 1996).

14. For a discussion of the visual coding of lesbians as an 'intermediate sex' and as a 'borderline' of sexual identity in

the film, see Weiss, *Vampires and Violets*, pp. 18–20.

15. *Borderline* programme note, Beinecke Rare Book and Manuscript Library, Yale University.

16. Jean Walton has provided the most extended analysis of the underlying racial and sexual dynamics in *Borderline*, forcefully arguing that the film's attempts to present anti-racist politics are crossed by the limitations of its (white) collaborators' model of modernity. See her two excellent essays: 'Nightmare of the Uncoordinated White-folk' and 'The Queer Matrix of *Borderline*'.

17. Kenneth Macpherson, 'As Is', *Close Up*, vol. VII, no. 5, November 1930, p. 294.

18. Hanns Sachs, 'Film Psychology', *Close Up*, vol. III, no. 5, November 1928, p. 8. Sachs writes: 'The film can be effective only in so far as it is able to make these psychological coherencies visible; in so far as it can externalise and make perceptible – if possible in movement – invisible inward events.' For a further discussion of Sachs's role in G.W. Pabst's *Secrets of a Soul*, see Anne Friedberg, 'An *unheimlich* Maneuver between Psychoanalysis and the Cinema: *Secrets of a Soul* (1926)', in Eric Rentschler (ed.), *The Films of G.W. Pabst: An Extraterritorial Cinema* (New Brunswick, NJ: Rutgers University Press, 1990), pp. 41–51.

19. Kenneth Macpherson, 'As Is', *Close Up*, vol. V, no. 6, December 1929, p. 451.

20. Kenneth Macpherson, 'As Is', *Close Up*, vol. VII, no. 5, November 1930, p. 293. Macpherson writes: '*Borderline* began to be composed about eighteen months ago.'

21. The 'task' of the 'new' cinematography was, according to Eisenstein, 'a transformation of generally accepted notions into the consciousness of the audience ... the new cinema *must include deep reflective processes ...*'. Sergei Eisenstein, 'The New Language of Cinematography', *Close Up*, vol. IV, no. 5, May 1929, pp. 10–13.

22. Sergei Eisenstein, 'The Fourth Dimension in the Kino, Part II', *Close Up*, vol. VI, no. 4, April 1930, p. 262. 'The Fourth Dimension in the Kino' was written in August 1929,

translated and published in two consecutive issues of *Close Up* in March and April 1930.

23. *Ibid.*, p. 268.

24. *Borderline* pamphlet, p. 230.

25. In 'A Dialectic Approach to Film Form', written in April 1929, Eisenstein describes the effect 'almost of double exposure' or 'clatter montage' when montage pieces of two frames are edited in sequence. See Sergei Eisenstein, 'A Dialectic Approach to Film Form', *Film Form*, translated by Jay Leyda (New York: Meridian Books, 1957), p. 55.

26. *Borderline* pamphlet. Although H.D. insists that Macpherson was solely responsible for the montage ('a meticulous and painstaking effort on the part of the director, who alone with the giants of German and Russian production is his own cutter and will not trust his "montage" to a mere technician however sympathetic'), she indicates, in her 'Autobiographical Notes', that both she and Bryher did some of the actual editing: 'When finished shooting, K develops a bad throat and Bryher and I work over the strips doing the montage as K indicates.' See H.D., 'Autobiographical Notes', Beinecke Rare Book and Manuscript Library, Yale University.

27. *Borderline* pamphlet, p. 235.

28. The critic for the *Observer* pointedly described it as 'an altogether warring picture in which fragments of every school, every thought, every symbolic language, strive and destroy one another ... the film is formless – urgent perhaps, but urgent in chaos, lacking that single broad stream of creation, whether of theme, or mood or simply rhythm ...' (C.A. Lejeune, 'The Critic as Creator', *Observer* (London), 19 October 1930).

29. Kenneth Macpherson, 'As Is', *Close Up*, vol. VII, no. 5, November 1930, p. 294.

30. *Ibid.*, p. 297.

NOTES TO INTRODUCTION TO PART 6

1. The literature on film and psychoanalysis is so extensive that I can only include a few indicative book-length works here. Relevant studies include: Christian Metz, *Psychoanalysis and Cinema: The Imaginary Signifier* (1977), translated by Celia Britton, Annwyl Williams, Ben Brewster and Alfred Guzzetti (London: Macmillan, 1982); Stephen Heath, *Questions of Cinema* (London: Macmillan, 1981); E. Ann Kaplan (ed.), *Psychoanalysis and Cinema* (London: Routledge, 1990); David Rodowick, *The Difficulty of Difference* (London: Routledge, 1991); Constance Penley, *The Future of an Illusion: Film, Feminism and Psychoanalysis* (London/New York: Routledge, 1989); Mary Anne Doane, *Femmes Fatales: Feminism, Theory, Psychoanalysis* (London: Routledge, 1991); Laura Mulvey, *Visual and Other Pleasures* (London: Macmillan, 1992); Harvey Roy Greenberg, *Screen Memories: Hollywood Cinema on the Psychoanalytic Couch* (New York: Columbia University Press, 1993); Vicky Lebeau, *Lost Angels: Psychoanalysis and Cinema* (London: Routledge, 1995); Elizabeth Cowie, *Representing the Woman: Cinema and Psychoanalysis* (London: Macmillan, 1997).

2. H.D. met Havelock Ellis in 1919, and wrote her *Notes on Thought and Vision* (1919), a meditation on creativity, femininity ('the womb-brain') and 'vision', with Ellis in mind. His negative response to the work bitterly disappointed her. As Susan Stanford Friedman observes, *Notes on Thought and Vision*, with its structure of 'fragmentary flashes and radical juxtapositions ... anticipated the moving images of light – cut, edited, and joined according to the principles of montage – that fascinated her in the silent film' (Susan Stanford Friedman, *Penelope's Web: Gender, Modernity, H.D.'s Fiction* (Cambridge: Cambridge University Press, 1990), p. 12). Ellis accompanied H.D. and Bryher on the first part of their trip to Greece in 1920, and the friendship remained a significant one. Ellis played a substantial role in introducing Bryher and H.D. to Freud's work and, subsequently, to Freud himself. As Bryher writes in her memoir: 'Ellis gave me the first paper by Freud that I ever read ... I started to read whatever was available of Freud in translation and became one of the first subscribers to the British *Journal of Psychoanalysis* and it was Ellis himself who gave me the introduction that enabled me to meet Freud himself in 1927' (Bryher, *The Heart to Artemis: A Writer's Memoirs* (London: Collins, 1962), p. 199). For an account of H.D.'s relationship with Ellis, see Phyllis Grosskurth, *Havelock Ellis: A Biography* (London: Quartet Books, 1980).

In 1931, H.D. started analysis with the British analyst Mary Chadwick. This was unsuccessful, and towards the end of the year H.D. began analysis with Dr Hanns Sachs, Bryher's analyst since 1928. The analysis was curtailed by Sachs's move to the United States, and in 1932 H.D. began extensive reading and preparation for the analysis with Freud that she undertook in 1933. (See Friedman, *Penelope's Web*, p. 286 ff.)

Bryher described her analysis with Sachs in *Heart to Artemis*, calling it 'the central point in my life' (p. 253). It was clearly envisaged as a training-analysis. She also contributed funds and practical support to the psychoanalytic community in the 1930s.

3. Kenneth Macpherson, *Gaunt Island* (Territet, Switzerland: POOL, 1927); *Poolreflection* (Territet, Switzerland: POOL, 1927).

4. See, in particular, H.D.'s novels *Palimpsest* (1926) (Carbondale: Southern Illinois University Press, 1968) and *Hedylus* (1928) (Manchester: Carcanet, 1980).

5. See, for example, Bryher's early work *Development: A Novel* (London: Constable, 1920).

6. Bryher, *Heart to Artemis*, p. 257.

7. *Ibid.*, p. 244. Bryher's exceptional study, *Film Problems of Soviet Russia* (Territet, Switzerland: POOL, 1929), opens with an account of a flight into Berlin for a season of Russian films. From the aerial view: 'Fields and tiny hills and woods mass themselves together like a crowd Eisenstein is directing ... Even the colors in a landscape become new and the earth is as flat as a screen upon which shadow and wind and the aeroplane itself project pictures.' Suddenly, however, the engine falters: 'I looked out – on a bank of trees. Immediately the shot of the aeroplane crashing in a swift slant through branches in René

Clair's *Prey of the Wind* came into my mind' (p. 9). Bryher's fascination with air travel is closely linked to her interest in cinema; she believed, as did other commentators of her time, that film was the only form capable of representing the speed and mobility of the modern world. She is also making the (slightly muddled) point in her introduction to *Film Problems in Soviet Russia* that, just as there was no acceptable response to the harrowing experience in the aeroplane, there seems to be no acceptable response in England to Soviet cinema. The 'engine problems' shatter the view seen whole and entire, as it is in an Eisenstein film; a distorted perspective, in which the traveller/spectator can only be quiescent in the state of emergency, takes its place. Soviet film is never seen as a separate question from Soviet politics, as Bryher believes it should be; she is particularly scathing about British censorship of Russian films.

8. *Ibid.*, p. 252.
9. Hilda C. Abraham and Ernst L. Freud (eds), *A Psychoanalytic Dialogue: The Letters of Sigmund Freud and Karl Abraham 1907– 1926* (New York: Basic Books, 1964), p. 80.
10. Hanns Sachs, *Psychoanalyse. Rätsel des Unbewussten* (Berlin: Lichtbilde- Bühne, 1926).
11. Kenneth Macpherson, 'As Is', *Close Up*, vol. VII, no. 5, November 1930, p. 294.
12. See Anne Friedberg, 'Introduction' to Part 5 of this volume, and 'An *unheimlich* Maneuver between Psychoanalysis and the Cinema: *Secrets of a Soul* (1926)', in Eric Rentschler (ed.), *The Films of G.W. Pabst: An Extraterritorial Cinema* (New Brunswick, NJ: Rutgers University Press, 1990), pp. 41–51.
13. Dr Hanns Sachs, 'Film Psychology', *Close Up*, vol. III, no. 5, November 1928, p. 10.
14. Sigmund Freud, *Fragment of an Analysis of a Case of Hysteria ('Dora')* (1905 [1901]), Penguin Freud Library, volume 8 (Harmondsworth: Penguin, 1977), p, 114.
15. Sachs, 'Film Psychology', p. 12.
16. Béla Balázs, *Theory of the Film: Character and Growth of a New Art* (London: Dennis Dobson, 1952), p. 55.
17. *Ibid.*, p. 112.

18. Béla Balázs, *Schriften zum Film II (1926–1931)*, edited by Wolfgang Gergsh (Berlin: Henschel, 1984), p. 60. Quoted by Gertrud Koch, 'Béla Balázs: The Physiognomy of Things', *New German Critique*, 40 (Winter 1987), Special Issue on Weimar Film Theory, p. 173. In this issue, see also Miriam Hansen's 'Benjamin, Cinema and Experience: "The Blue Flower in the Land of Technology"', pp. 179–224, and Heide Schlupmann's 'Phenomenology of Film: On Siegfried Kracauer's Writings of the 1920s', pp. 97–114.
19. See Koch, 'Béla Balázs', pp. 171–3. For a sceptical discussion of Benjamin's category of the 'optical unconscious', see Rosalind E. Krauss, *The Optical Unconscious* (Cambridge, MA: MIT Press, 1993), especially pp. 178–80. 'Can the optical field,' Krauss asks, 'the world of visual phenomena: clouds, sea, sky, forest – *have* an unconscious?' (p. 179).
20. Walter Benjamin, 'A Small History of Photography', in *One-Way Street and Other Writings*, translated by Edmund Jephcott and Kingsley Shorter (London: Verso, 1997), p. 243.
21. Walter Benjamin, 'The Work of Art in an Age of Mechanical Reproduction', translated by Harry Zohn, in *Illuminations* (New York: Harcourt, Brace and World, 1968), pp. 236–7.
22. Siegfried Kracauer, *Theory of Film: The Redemption of Physical Reality* (Oxford: Oxford University Press, 1960), p. 45.
23. *Ibid.*, p. 52.
24. *Ibid.*, p. 55.
25. *Ibid.*, p. 58.
26. Benjamin, 'Work of Art', p. 236.
27. Kracauer, 'Theory of Film', p. 48.
28. Freud refers to Nietzsche's phrase – 'an attack on Christianity' – a number of times in *The Interpretation of Dreams*. See, for example, his claim that 'a complete "transvaluation of all psychical values" takes place between the material of the dream-thoughts and the dream. A direct derivative of what occupies a dominating position in the dream-thoughts can often only be discovered precisely in some transitory element of the dream which is quite overshadowed by more powerful images' (Penguin

Freud Library, volume 4 (Harmondsworth: Penguin, 1976, p. 443).
29. This position is not universally held, or, at least, not held to be true of all films. Kracauer, for example, wrote in his essay 'Film 1928' of the ways in which, in films based on pre- existing scripts, whether novels, plays or historical events, details become robbed of their significance:
  'It is true that established film techniques make extensive use of cars, show the pistons of the express-train engine every time the hero goes on a trip, depict legs walking and car wheels rolling, and are not afraid to stage expensive catastrophes. But all these fragments are of only *ornamental* significance, and could easily be eliminated without in any way diminishing the film's intelligibility. This contrasts starkly with a real film, which becomes immediately unintelligible or at least suffers a noticeable loss in perfection when a single image-atom is removed.
  See Kracauer, 'Film 1928', in *The Mass Ornament: Weimar Essays*, translated and edited by Thomas Y. Levin (Cambridge, MA: Harvard University Press, 1995), pp. 313–14.
30. Freud, *Interpretation*, p. 417.
31. Sachs, 'Film Psychology', p. 15.
32. Antonin Artaud, 'Witchcraft and the Cinema', in Paul Hammond (ed.), *The Shadow and Its Shadow: Surrealist Writings on Cinema* (London: BFI, 1978), p.64.
33. H.D. (attributed), *Borderline – A Pool Film with Paul Robeson* (London: Mercury Press, 1930). Reprinted in Bonnie Kime Scott (ed.), *The Gender of Modernism: A Critical Anthology* (Bloomington and Indianapolis: Indiana University Press, 1990), pp. 110–24. Quotation p. 121.
34. See Hanns Sachs, 'Day-dreams in Common', *International Journal of Psychoanalysis*, 1 (1920), pp. 349–50 (a report of a paper read before the Sixth International Psychoanalytic Congress in The Hague, 1920).
35. Sigmund Freud, 'Creative Writers and Day-dreaming' (1908 [1907]), in Penguin Freud Library, volume 14, *Art and Literature*, p. 141.
36. Dr Hanns Sachs, 'Kitsch', *Close Up*, vol. IX, no. 3, September 1932, p. 202.

37. Siegfried Kracauer, 'The Little Shopgirls Go to the Movies', in *The Mass Ornament*, p. 292.
38. Barbara Low, *The Unconscious in Action: Its Influence upon Education* (London: University of London Press, 1928).
39. Bryher's article 'Films in Education: The Complex of the Machine' provides an interesting counter to Low's article: 'full development educationally', Bryher argues, 'is not possible until the ground is cleared of the old "complex of the machine"' (*Close Up*, vol. I, no. 2, August 1927, p.54).
40. Barbara Low, 'Mind-growth or Mind-mechanization? The Cinema in Education', *Close Up*, vol. I, no. 3, September 1927, p. 49.
41. The representation of film as a 'primitive' form occurs frequently in discussions from the early part of the twentieth century. See, for example, Virginia Woolf's essay 'The Cinema', which, despite its imaginative exploration of the possibilities of cinema, opens and closes with an account of 'the savages of the twentieth century watching the pictures'. See Virginia Woolf, 'The Cinema', first published in *Nation and Athenaeum*, 3 July 1926. Reprinted in Rachel Bowlby (ed.), *The Crowded Dance of Modern Life* (Harmondsworth: Penguin, 1993), pp. 54–8.
On a different note, it is significant that Freud's account of dreams as visual representations entails an understanding of a 'regression' to the visual stage, belonging to an earlier stage of development in the individual and in the species. In this sense, visual and pictorial thinking are seen as more 'primitive' forms of mentation. (See Freud, *Interpretation of Dreams*, especially Chapter VII, B, on 'Regression'.)
42. Throughout the literature on dreams and dreaming, there is in fact an emphasis on 'controlled' or, in Sandor Ferenczi's phrase, 'dirigible' dreams, which increased as the 'scientific' study of dreams turned dreaming into auto-experimentation.

NOTES TO INTRODUCTION TO PART 7

1. Kenneth Macpherson, 'As Is', *Close Up*, vol. IV, no. 3, February 1929, p. 8.
2. *Daily Express*, 15 January 1929, quoted in *Close Up*, vol. IV, no. 2, February 1929, p. 92.
3. Dorothy Richardson, 'The Censorship Petition', *Close Up*, vol. VI, no. 1, January 1930, p. 8.
4. *Ibid.*, p.10.

INDEX